Lecture Notes in Computer Science   14501

Founding Editors

Gerhard Goos
Juris Hartmanis

Editorial Board Members

Elisa Bertino, *Purdue University, West Lafayette, IN, USA*
Wen Gao, *Peking University, Beijing, China*
Bernhard Steffen, *TU Dortmund University, Dortmund, Germany*
Moti Yung, *Columbia University, New York, NY, USA*

The series Lecture Notes in Computer Science (LNCS), including its subseries Lecture Notes in Artificial Intelligence (LNAI) and Lecture Notes in Bioinformatics (LNBI), has established itself as a medium for the publication of new developments in computer science and information technology research, teaching, and education.

LNCS enjoys close cooperation with the computer science R & D community, the series counts many renowned academics among its volume editors and paper authors, and collaborates with prestigious societies. Its mission is to serve this international community by providing an invaluable service, mainly focused on the publication of conference and workshop proceedings and postproceedings. LNCS commenced publication in 1973.

Stéphane Devismes · Partha Sarathi Mandal ·
V. Vijaya Saradhi · Bhanu Prasad ·
Anisur Rahaman Molla · Gokarna Sharma
Editors

Distributed Computing and Intelligent Technology

20th International Conference, ICDCIT 2024
Bhubaneswar, India, January 17–20, 2024
Proceedings

 Springer

Editors
Stéphane Devismes 🆔
University of Picardie Jules Verne
Amiens, France

V. Vijaya Saradhi
Indian Institute of Technology Guwahati
Guwahati, India

Anisur Rahaman Molla 🆔
Indian Statistical Institute
Kolkata, India

Partha Sarathi Mandal 🆔
Indian Institute of Technology Guwahati
Guwahati, India

Bhanu Prasad
Florida Agricultural and Mechanical
University
Tallahassee, FL, USA

Gokarna Sharma 🆔
Kent State University
Kent, OH, USA

ISSN 0302-9743   ISSN 1611-3349 (electronic)
Lecture Notes in Computer Science
ISBN 978-3-031-50582-9   ISBN 978-3-031-50583-6 (eBook)
https://doi.org/10.1007/978-3-031-50583-6

Preface

This volume contains the papers selected for presentation at the 20th International Conference on Distributed Computing and Intelligent Technology (ICDCIT 2024), held during January 17–20, 2024, at Kalinga Institute of Industrial Technology (KIIT), Bhubaneswar, India.

Starting from its first edition in 2004, the ICDCIT conference series has grown to an annual conference of international repute and has become a global platform for computer science researchers to exchange research results and ideas on the foundations and applications of distributed computing and intelligent technology. ICDCIT 2024 was the 20th meeting in the series. ICDCIT strives to provide an opportunity for students and young researchers to get exposed to topical research directions in distributed computing and intelligent technology.

ICDCIT is generally organized into two tracks: Distributed Computing (DC) and Intelligent Technology (IT). The DC track solicits original research papers contributing to the foundations and applications of distributed computing, whereas the IT track solicits original research papers contributing to the foundations and applications of Intelligent Technology. Each track has a separate program committee (PC) including PC chairs, who evaluate the papers submitted to that track.

This year we received 116 full paper submissions – 31 papers in the DC track and 85 papers in the IT track. Each submission considered for publication was reviewed by at least three PC members, with the help of reviewers outside of the PC. Based on the reviews, the PC decided to accept 24 papers for presentation at the conference, with an acceptance rate of 21%. The DC track PC accepted 9 papers, with an acceptance rate of 29%. The IT track PC accepted 15 papers, with an acceptance rate of 18%. ICDCIT 2024 adopted a double-blind review process to help PC members and external reviewers come to a judgment about each submitted paper without possible bias. Additionally, each paper that was in conflict with a chair/PC member was handled/reviewed by another chair/PC member who had no conflict with the paper.

We would like to express our gratitude to all the researchers who submitted their work to the conference. Our special thanks go to all colleagues who served on the PC, as well as the external reviewers, who generously offered their expertise and time which helped us select the papers and prepare the strong conference program.

This year, we were able to award best paper as well as best student paper awards in both DC and IT tracks. The awards were announced during the conference. Notice that the best paper awardee in each track received 50,000 Indian Rupees in total and the best student paper awardee in each track received 25,000 Indian Rupees in total. We congratulate the authors of the selected papers for their outstanding research.

We were fortunate to have seven distinguished invited speakers – Nicola Santoro (Carleton University, Canada), C. Pandurangan (Indian Institute of Science, India), Bud Mishra (New York University, USA), Krishna Kummamuru (Accenture, India), Janardhan Rao Doppa (Washington State University, USA), Sivaramakrishnan R.

Guruvayur (Aaquarians.ai, UAE), and Atul Kumar (IBM Research, India). Their talks provided us with the unique opportunity to hear about research advances in various fields of DC and IT from the leaders in those respective fields. The abstracts of the invited talks are included in this volume.

We wish to express our thanks to the local organizing committee who worked hard to make this conference a success, especially our organizing chair Hrudaya Kumar Tripathy. We also wish to thank the organizers of the satellite events as well as the many student volunteers. The School of Computer Engineering of KIIT, the host of the conference, provided excellent support and facilities for organizing the conference and its associated events.

Finally, we enjoyed institutional and financial support from KIIT, for which we are indebted. We express our appreciation to all theSteering/Advisory Committee members, and in particular Sathya Peri, Sandeep Kulkarni, and Samaresh Mishra, whose counsel we frequently relied on. Thanks are also due to the faculty members and staff of the School of Computer Engineering of KIIT for their timely support.

January 2024

Stéphane Devismes
Partha Sarathi Mandal
Vijaya Saradhi
Bhanu Prasad
Anisur Rahaman Molla
Gokarna Sharma

Organization

Chief Patron

Achyuta Samanta   KIIT & KISS, India

General Chairs

Anisur Rahaman Molla   ISI Kolkata, India
Gokarna Sharma   Kent State University, USA

Program Committee Chairs

Stéphane Devismes (DC Track)   Université de Picardie Jules Verne, France
Partha Sarathi Mandal (DC Track)   IIT Guwahati, India
Vijaya Saradhi (IT Track)   IIT Guwahati, India
Bhanu Prasad (IT Track)   Florida A&M University, USA

Conference Management Chair

Krishna Chakravarty   KIIT, India

Organizing Chair

Hrudaya Kumar Tripathy   KIIT, India

Finance Chairs

Santosh Kumar Baliarsingh   KIIT, India
Ramakanta Parida   KIIT, India

Publicity Chairs

Bindu Agarwalla   KIIT, India

Registration Chairs

Harish Kumar Patnaik   KIIT, India
Pratyusa Mukherjee   KIIT, India

Session Management Chairs

Kunal Anand   KIIT, India
Roshni Pradhan   KIIT, India

Publications Chairs

Mainak Bandyopadhyay   KIIT, India
Junali Jasmine Jena   KIIT, India

Student Symposium Chairs

Sushruta Mishra   KIIT, India
Subhasis Dash   KIIT, India

Industry Symposium Chair

Prachet Bhuyan   KIIT, India

Project Innovation Chairs

Satya Ranjan Dash   KIIT, India
Jagannath Singh   KIIT, India
Saurabh Bilgaiyan   KIIT, India

Workshop Chairs

Rajat Kumar Behera	KIIT, India
Manas Ranjan Lenka	KIIT, India

Ph.D. Symposium Chairs

Himansu Das	KIIT, India
Arup Abhina Acharya	KIIT, India

Hackathon Chairs

Chittaranjan Pradhan	KIIT, India
Abhaya Kumar Sahoo	KIIT, India
Namita Panda	KIIT, India
Bhaswati Sahoo	KIIT, India

Advisory Committee

Saranjit Singh	KIIT, India
Sathya Peri	IIT Hyderabad, India
Sandeep Kulkarni	Michigan State University, USA

Steering Committee

Raj Bhatnagar	University of Cincinnati, USA
Rajkumar Buyya	University of Melbourne, Australia
Diganta Goswami	IIT Guwahati, India
Samaresh Mishra	KIIT, India

Program Committee

Distributed Computing Track

Giuseppe Antonio Di Luna	Sapienza University of Rome, Italy
Kaustav Bose	Jadavpur University, India

Romaric Duvignau	Chalmers University of Technology, Sweden
Volker Turau	Hamburg University of Technology, Germany
Srabani Mukhopadhyaya	BIT, Mesra, India
Subhash Bhagat	Indian Institute of Technology Jodhpur, India
Kaushik Mondal	Indian Institute of Technology Ropar, India
Debasish Pattanayak	LUISS Guido Carli, Italy
Yuichi Sudo	Hosei University, Japan
Barun Gorain	Indian Institute of Technology Bhilai, India
Anaïs Durand	LIMOS, Université Clermont Auvergne, France
Nabanita Das	Indian Statistical Institute, India
Andrew Berns	University of Northern Iowa, USA
Sayaka Kamei	Hiroshima University, Japan
Sushanta Karmakar	Indian Institute of Technology Guwahati, India
Krishnendu Mukhopadhyaya	Indian Statistical Institute, India
Doina Bein	California State University, Fullerton, USA
Quentin Bramas	ICUBE, Université de Strasbourg, France
Sruti Gan Chaudhuri	Jadavpur University, India
Anissa Lamani	ICUBE, Université de Strasbourg, France

Intelligent Technology Track

Amit Awekar	IIT Guwahati, India
Rashmi Dutta Baruah	IIT Guwahati, India
Jhansi Rani	CMR Institute of Technology, India
Puneet Gupta	IIT Indore, India
Arul Valan	National Institute of Technology, Nagaland, India
Achyut Mani Tripathi	IIT Guwahati, India
Gayathri Ananthanarayanan	IIT Dharwad, India
Kaustuv Nag	Indian Institute of Technology Guwahati, India
Anshul Agarwal	Visvesvaraya National Institute of Technology, Nagpur, India
Ashish Kumar	National Institute of Technology, Jamshedpur, India
Ramachandra Reddy	National Institute of Technology, Jamshedpur, India
Karthik Kannan	Indian Institute of Technology Guwahati, India
Amit Majumder	National Institute of Technology, Jamshedpur, India
Yadunath Pathak	Visvesvaraya National Institute of Technology, Nagpur, India
Nidhi Lal	Visvesvaraya National Institute of Technology, Nagpur, India

Shoubhik Chakraborty	Indian Institute of Technology Guwahati, India
Hrudaya Kumar Tripathy	Kalinga Institute of Industrial Technology, India
Ashish Anand	Indian Institute of Technology Guwahati, India
Vibhav Prakash Singh	Motilal Nehru National Institute of Technology Allahabad, India
Om Jee Pandey	Indian Institute of Technology (BHU) Varanasi, India
Shafiz Yusof	Ajman University, UAE
Ramanajum E.	National Institute of Technology, Silchar, India
Suganya Devi	National Institute of Technology, Silchar, India
Priyanka Kumar	University of Texas at San Antonio, Texas
Gopal Krishna	REVA University, India
Deepak Gupta	National Institute of Technology, Arunachal Pradesh, India
Radhakrishna Bhat	Manipal Institute of Technology, India

Additional Reviewers

Debaditya Barman
Subhasis Bhattacharjee
Parama Bhaumik
Abhinav Chakraborty
Bibhuti Das
Prasenjit Dey
Bibhas Chandra Dhara
Rathindra Nath Dutta
Mathew Francis
Bishakh Chandra Ghosh

Rui Gong
Frédéric Hayek
Krishnandu Hazra
Saswata Jana
Dipankar Kundu
Partha Sarathi Paul
Maxime Puys
Sujoy Saha
Laltu Sardar

Invited Talks

Exploiting Synergies Between AI and Computing Systems for Sustainable Computing

Janardhan Rao Doppa

School of EECS, Washington State University, USA
jana.doppa@wsu.edu

Abstract. Advanced computing systems have long been enablers for breakthroughs in science and engineering applications including Artificial Intelligence (AI) either through sheer computational power or form-factor miniaturization. However, as algorithms become more complex and the size of datasets increase, existing computing platforms are no longer sufficient to bridge the gap between algorithmic innovation and hardware design. To address the computing needs of emerging applications from the edge to the cloud, we need high-performance, energy-efficient, and reliable computing systems targeted for these applications. Developing these application-specific hardware must become easy, inexpensive, and as seamless as developing application software.

In this talk, I will argue that synergistically combining the domain knowledge from hardware designers and AI algorithms will allow us to make faster progress towards this overarching goal. The key driving principle will be to learn appropriate models for performing intelligent design space exploration to significantly reduce the overall engineering cost and design time of application-specific hardware. I will also discuss how designing AI algorithms with the knowledge of underlying hardware will allow us to perform resource-efficient computing. I will conclude the talk with some open challenges in the quest for sustainable computing.

Building Gen AI Systems

Kummamuru Krishna

AI Innovations & Products, Accenture
Operations at Accenture Bengaluru, Karnataka, India
`krishna.kummamuru@accenture.com`

Abstract. Generative AI (Gen AI) is a rapidly developing field of artificial intelligence that has the potential to revolutionize many aspects of our lives. Gen AI systems are able to generate new and creative content, such as text, images, music, and code, based on their understanding of existing data.

Building Gen AI systems is a complex and challenging task, but it is one that is becoming increasingly feasible thanks to advances in machine learning and artificial intelligence. This talk will discuss the key challenges and opportunities involved in building Gen AI systems, and will provide an overview of some of the latest research in this area.

Modality Games with Distributed Fictitious Plays using Evolving Kripke Machines

Bhubaneswar (Bud) Mishra[1,2], Jointly with Foy Savas[1], Surya Dheeshjith[1, 2], Sophia Chou[1], Pradeep Mouli[1], Claudia Pecorella[1], Jean Post[1], and Shibo Xu[1]

[1] dotcontract.org
[2] Courant Inst, NYU

Graphical Abstract

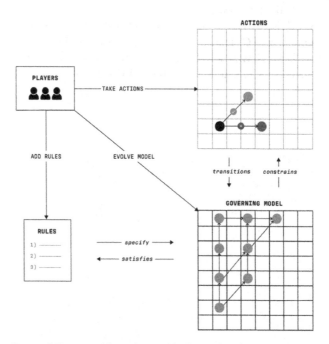

Fig. 1. Players in a modality game take actions, add rules, and evolve a governing model. Modality is a formal language for such games with evolving rules [1]. The interplay between actions, rules (e.g., for "guard rails") and a governing model enables mechanism design.

Abstract. Modality is a formal language for games with evolving rules [1]. It is reasonably expressive for a wide range of practical use cases and able to be embedded within governance or control systems [2]. Players specify rules as an evolving set of rights and obligations in temporal modal logic. For a new rule to be added, a player must provide a governing model where all rules remain satisfied. Players are free to strategically reinterpret the rules by replacing the governing model as allowed.

This approach allows Modality to formally verify and preserve specified properties across both use and revision [3], while leaving room for ambiguity and information-asymmetry about the unspecified properties of models. As a multi-agent system, Modality can enable iterative decision coordination through the establishment of evolutionary stable social conventions over time. A prototype embodiment of Modality has been implemented and exemplified by an efficient, non-trivial use-case of repositories for digital agreements.

References

1. DotContract | digital contract platform and standard — dotcontract.org. https://www.dotcontract.org/ (2023), Accessed 29 Aug 2023
2. Antoniotti, M., Mishra, B., et al.: Np-completeness of the supervisor synthesis problem for unrestricted CTL specifications. In: WODES (1996)
3. 3. Mishra, B., Clarke, E.M.: Hierarchical verification of asynchronous circuits using temporal logic. Theor. Comput. Sci. **38**, 269–291 (1985)

Genesis, Growth, and Future of Blockchains via Trilemmas

C. Pandurangan

Kotak Mahindra Visiting Chair Professor, IISc, Bangalore 560012, India
rpandu@iisc.ac.in

Abstract. Informally, a trilemma is a situation where you want three things, all the time and all together, but you cannot have more than two of them at any time! Thus, you compromise a bit and manage to get as many as you can When we started with these kinds of choices in the context of a decentralized computation, Blockchain technology is born. Blockchain technology continued to thrive on other solutions and innovations on dealing with other trilemmas. From genesis to growth to research trends, trilemmas are guiding force behind every innovation in the blockchain technology. I attempt to present the foundation aspects of these trilemmas in a simpler way.

Computing in Highly Dynamic Distributed Systems

Nicola Santoro

School of Computer Science, Carleton University, Ottawa, Canada
santoro@scs.carleton.ca

Abstract. The advent of highly dynamic distributed systems (e.g., ad-hoc wireless mobile networks, robotic swarms, vehicular networks, social networks), where changes in the interconnection structure are continuously occurring normal events, has motivated, in the field distributed computing, extensive investigations on the computational and complexity issues arising in such systems. In spite of the wide diversity of these systems, most investigations use a common representation to model the temporal dynamics of the topological changes. A wide variety of factors influence computability and complexity in these systems; a crucial one is the (amount and type of) a-priori knowledge that the system entities have about the dynamics of the changes. This lecture will focus on the basics of computing in such systems, starting from the representation of the temporal dynamics of the topological changes, to the discussion of some problems recently examined in the literature (e.g., exploration, search). Through these problems, I will describe some solution techniques as well as methodological insights, and highlight the factors that have an impact on computability and complexity.

Key Considerations in Implementing Ethical & Responsible AI with Generative AI Usecases

Sivaramakrishnan R. Guruvayur

aaquarians.ai
Dubai, UAE
gr_shibu@hotmail.com

Abstract. Artificial Intelligence (AI) is advancing at an unprecedented pace, and generative AI, in particular, is revolutionizing various domains such as Banking, Health, Retail, Education, Fine arts, Smart Cities and so on. However, with this technological prowess comes a myriad of ethical and responsible concerns that are now being addressed through a global wave of AI governance regulations. This keynote presentation delves into the intricate technical aspects of ethical and responsible AI, with a specific focus on generative AI use cases, and how these considerations should align with AI Regulatory compliance landscape. The Key note discussions would revolve around the following key themes: 1) Ethical Frameworks and AI Regulations: 2) Bias and Fairness; 3) Data Privacy and Security; 4) AI Governance and Regulation compliance; 5) Explainability, Transparency and Interpretability; 6) Case Studies and Real-World Applications; 7) Global AI Regulatory Landscape; The presentation will explore the ethical challenges and opportunities inherent to generative AI applications, including natural language processing, image generation, and creative content production. It will emphasize the importance of aligning AI development with ethical values, human rights, and societal norms, while addressing the potential biases, discrimination, and privacy concerns that may arise.

An attempt would be made to provide a detailed walkthrough of the technical nuances of ethical and responsible AI, with a specific focus on generative AI applications. Participants would gain technical insights into the evolving regulatory landscape, ethical imperatives, and the pivotal role of governance in shaping the future of AI. This key note would also provide a discussion on multiple global AI governance landscape such as EU AI Act, UNESCO AI guidelines & other AI governance & laws emerging from countries such as India, USA, China & others.

We will discuss the role of governance structures, best practices, and the need for collaborative efforts among governments, industry, and academia to develop responsible AI guidelines and policies. We will also discuss the technical requirements and compliance measures stipulated by AI regulations, highlighting their impact on the design and implementation of generative AI systems.

Attendees will gain insights into practical strategies for developing ethical AI systems and managing the risks associated with Generative AI deployment. This keynote presentation is designed to empower AI professionals, policymakers, and stakeholders to make informed decisions about generative AI technologies and drive the evolution of responsible AI governance. It will inspire attendees to shape a future where AI enhances human potential and ensures equitable, just, and transparent AI innovation in generative use cases.

Shaping the Future of Enterprise Computing: Confluence of AI, Hybrid Cloud, and Quantum Technologies

Atul Kumar

Senior Research Scientist and Manager, IBM Research,
Bengaluru, Karnataka, India
atulkumar@gmail.com

Abstract. Recent advances in AI, particularly the generative AI, large language models (LLMs) and foundation models have democratized the use of cutting edge AI systems. Rapid adoption of some of these technologies in enterprise software systems is taking place at a pace greater than ever. In this talk we will touch on some of the intelligent tools and services relevant to enterprises such as code generation, translation, AI testing, etc.

Some of the recent advances in hybrid cloud technologies have changed the software development lifecycle drastically. Container based software development and deployment tools allowing seamless orchestration and management have made it possible to rapidly develop, test and deploy enterprise grade software at a very fast pace. We will also discuss some of the recent advances in Quantum Computing and how it can transform the computing landscape not just for the scientific community and labs but for the common users and enterprises. Moreover, some of the guarantees such as strong encryption now require serious rethinking and redesign when quantum computing covers more and more application areas.

Contents

Intelligent Technology

Distributed Computing

Utility-Driven Joint Time-and-Power Allocation in Energy-Harvesting Cognitive Radio Relay Networks

Meenakshi Sharma$^{(\boxtimes)}$ and Nityananda Sarma

Tezpur University, Tezpur 784028, Assam, India
amee2187@gmail.com, nitya@tezu.ernet.in

Abstract. The increasing number of wireless devices has raised significant global concerns regarding energy efficiency and spectrum scarcity. To address this, wireless energy harvesting technology has emerged as a potential solution. By utilizing conventional radio frequency transmissions, this technology can extend the battery life of mobile devices and improve the operational period of energy-constrained wireless networks. This study focuses on a wireless energy harvesting and information transfer protocol within cognitive radio relay networks. In this setup, an energy-constrained secondary user shares the spectrum and simultaneously harvests energy while assisting with the primary transmission. To optimize the allocation of transmission time and harvested power, a challenging computational problem is formulated. The goal is to enhance the utility of the secondary user. To tackle this computationally hard problem, a heuristic solution based on a joint time-and-power allocation strategy is proposed. This approach achieves an impressive 98.5% accuracy while comparing the utility of the secondary users to the optimal benchmark results.

Keywords: Primary users · Secondary users · Energy Harvesting · Optimal Allocation · Utility

1 Introduction

Due to growing environmental concerns and the rising demand for wireless services, energy efficiency and spectral efficiency are two crucial design criteria in wireless communications [11]. Energy harvesting (EH) has recently gained popularity as a way to extend the lifespan of wireless networks with limited energy source. When compared to conventional energy sources like batteries, which have limited operating times, energy harvesting from the environment could offer wireless networks an endless source of power [20]. Radio frequency (RF) signals hold a promising future for wireless energy harvesting (WEH) in addition to other widely used energy sources like solar and wind, because it can also be used to simultaneously transmit wireless information. Recently, it is shown that

S. Devismes et al. (Eds.): ICDCIT 2024, LNCS 14501, pp. 3–17, 2024.
https://doi.org/10.1007/978-3-031-50583-6_1

simultaneous wireless information and power transfer (SWIPT) becomes appealing since it realizes both useful utilization of RF signals at the same time, and thus potentially offers great convenience to mobile users [12,21]. On the other hand, cognitive radio (CR) is a promising solution concept to improve spectrum utilization by allowing spectrum sharing, where unlicensed or secondary users (SUs) can use the unused portion of licensed spectrum resources of licensed or primary users (PUs) [1,2]. Thus, merging of CR technology with energy harvesting provides an efficient way of utilizing both spectrum and energy to prolong the operational time of SUs.

Many of the recent works have studied energy efficient communication in Cognitive Radio Network (CRN) using either the popular Time Switching (TS) based or Power Splitting (PS) based SWIPT technology. In [21], TS as well as PS based SWIPT techniques were separately applied on SU receiver side, and the rate-energy trade-off analysis in both techniques was investigated. Another work based on PS and TS receiver architectures at the relay node was studied in [19], and proposed a PS-based relaying protocol and a TS-based relaying protocol separately to enable wireless information transferring and EH at the battery-free relay node. Here, the end-to-end error performance and throughput of the proposed protocol during secondary transmission were investigated. In [18], an optimal power allocation problem using a PS-based approach within an energy-constrained CRN was proposed. This investigation encompassed several key aspects, including assessing outage probabilities for both PUs and SUs, evaluating system energy efficiency, and examining the trade-off between data rate and energy consumption. Another work addressed in [9], a PS-based SWIPT technology was implemented within a cooperative CRN. In this scenario, energy-constrained SUs harnessed energy not only from the primary transmitter's (PT) received signal but also from interfering sources. The research delved into the performance of two relay cooperation schemes, examining the tradeoff between the PU's and SU's performance, particularly concerning outage probabilities. In [17], author addressed an optimization problem involving transmitting time and transmission power of SU within an underlay RF energy-harvesting CRN. Their objective was to maximize the energy efficiency of the secondary network by enabling the SUs to reserve the residual energy after previous slots for upcoming transmissions. A rapid iterative algorithm based on Dinkelbach's method was proposed to achieve optimal resource allocation as well the QoS of SUs. In [6], a hybrid TS-PS model was established for EH in a bidirectional relay assisted communication and explored an end-to-end outage probability of the network. Primarily, this work solved an optimization problem of outage probability with respect to relay placement and time allocation factor. Another work [8] explored techniques for simultaneous EH and information transfer within an EH-based CRN model. This approach combined both TS and PS receiver architectures to derived and analyzed optimal expressions for transmission power and energy harvesting power to attain maximum energy efficiency within the secondary network. Finally, in the work [14], a radio-frequency (RF) energy harvesting enabled CRN adopts a PS-based SWIPT architecture. The study addresses two significant challenges: prolonging network lifetime and enhancing link reliability by accounting for transceiver hardware impairments.

The majority of the works cited above focus on either TS or PS SWIPT technology separately during the optimization of harvested energy and primary information decoding rates at SU. To the best of our knowledge, there is limited research, such as [6] and [8], where integration of TS and PS techniques is used in the CRN framework to harvest energy from RF signal. However, these studies do not tackle the vital issue of optimizing the utility and operational duration of energy-constrained SUs. By simultaneously employing both of these techniques during energy harvesting phase, SUs can accumulate a greater amount of energy compared to their separate uses, which in turn contributes to extending the lifespan of the secondary network. Therefore, this research introduces a unified model that integrates TS and PS SWIPT technology for EH in energy-constrained SUs within a cognitive radio relay network. Subsequently, it optimizes the allocation of harvested power to enhance the effectiveness of the secondary network. Each SU harvests maximum energy from the received primary signal and successfully forwards primary and secondary information to the intended receivers. Accordingly, we formulate an optimization problem to achieve the optimal allocation of TS-PS factors and harvested power. Heuristic approach is applied to obtain a near-optimal solution for this problem. Simulation-based results demonstrate that the heuristic solution succeeds in attaining the maximum possible utility for both the energy-constrained SUs and PUs.

The rest of the paper is organized as follows. Section 2 outlines the system model and the formulated optimization problem. The solution concept for the proposed optimization problem is discussed in Sect. 3. In Sect. 4, numerical results are analyzed, and finally, the paper is concluded in Sect. 5.

2   System Model and Assumptions

We consider a cognitive radio network framework with a set of M PU transceiver pairs, denoted as $\mathcal{M} = \{(PT_1, PR_1), .., (PT_i, PR_i), .., (PT_M, PR_M)\}$ and a set of N SU transceiver pairs, denoted as $\mathcal{N} = \{(ST_1, SR_1), .., (ST_j, SR_j), .., (ST_N, SR_N)\}$. The assumption is that the physical distance between PT (transmitter) and PR (receiver) exceeds the effective transmission range. Consequently, a relay node (ST) is needed to forward primary information to PR in order to attain at least the target rate R_{pt}^{tar}. At the same time, ST accepts the offer from the PU, exchanging the rendered relay service for a spectrum opportunity to enable secondary communication towards SR. It is important to note that STs are energy-constrained nodes, operating in an energy-harvesting data-transmission mode with a minimum target rate requirement of R_{st}^{tar}. Moreover, STs are equipped with rechargeable batteries and feature a non-linear energy harvester [4,7,14], which allows them to harvest energy from the received primary signal. In this paper, the terms SU and ST, and PU and PT, are used interchangeably.

The proposed work considers information transmission between PT and PR as illustrated in Fig. 1. In this scenario, a single PU transmits primary information to PR with the assistance of a suitable ST acting as a relay node. The entire

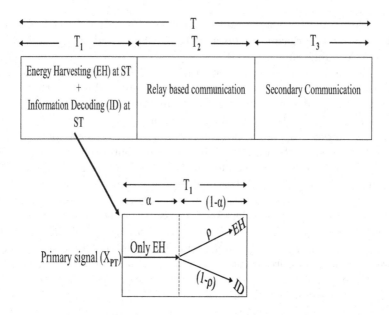

Fig. 1. Time-slot division of a PU band for EH and ID

time duration T of the PU band is subdivided into three sub-slots: T_1, T_2, and T_3. In the T_1 sub-slot (referred to as Phase 1), PT transmits its information towards the appropriate ST.Upon receiving the primary signal, ST harvests energy from it while simultaneously decoding it for further processing. During the T_2 time (termed as Phase 2), ST uses a portion of its harvested energy to forward the primary signal to PR through the Decode and Forward (DF) relaying technique. Finally, in the T_3 time (termed as Phase 3), ST performs secondary transmission using the remaining harvested energy.

Drawing on the principles of SWIPT and Dynamic Power Splitting (DPS) technology [13,21] a joint TS-PS technique is applied during the T_1 time slot, as depicted in Fig. 1. The T_1 time is further subdivided into two parts to serve the purposes of energy harvesting and information decoding. The time-switching factor α $(0 < \alpha < 1)$ determines the duration αT_1 allocated for energy harvesting, during which ST utilizes the entire signal power solely for this purpose. The remaining time $(1-\alpha)T_1$, is divided into two power streams with a power ratio of $\rho : (1-\rho)$. Here, ρ $(0 < \rho < 1)$ is used for energy harvesting, and $(1-\rho)$ is used to decode the primary information at ST. Therefore, in the proposed technique, ST can harvest energy during both αT_1 and $(1-\alpha)T_1$ time fractions, utilizing two different power values. However, information can only be decoded during the $(1-\alpha)T_1$ time fraction.

2.1   Utility of PUs and SUs

During the T_1 time, when PT transmits its information to ST, the received signal at ST, denoted as $Y^I_{pt,st}$, can be expressed as shown in Eq. (1) [17].

$$Y^I_{pt,st} = \sqrt{P_{pt}}h_{pt,st}X^I_{pt} + n_a + n_{cov} \tag{1}$$

Here, P_{pt} represents the transmit power of PT, and $h_{pt,st}$ is the channel gain between PT and ST. The channel gain is calculated as $h_{pt,st} = |d_{pt,st}|^{-2}$, where 2 corresponds to the pathloss index [15]. Additionally, X^I_{pt} represents the transmitted signal from PT intended for PR. The term $n_a \sim \mathcal{CN}(0, \sigma^2_1)$ denotes the narrowband Gaussian noise introduced by the antenna at ST, while $n_{cov} \sim \mathcal{CN}(0, \sigma^2_{\text{cov}})$ refers to the RF band to baseband signal conversion noise at ST. Taking inspiration from [21] and [18], we model the maximum possible harvested energy (EH^{max}_{st}) at ST (in Joule) and the maximum achievable instantaneous decoding rate ($R^{max}_{T_1}$) at ST (in bps) during the T_1 time using Eqs. (2) and (3).

$$EH^{max}_{st} = T_1\eta P_{pt} |h_{pt,st}|^2 \tag{2}$$

where η is the energy conversion efficiency ($0 < \eta < 1$) at ST.

$$\begin{aligned} R^{max}_{T_1} &= B * T_1 * \log_2(1 + SNR_{pt,st}) \\ &= B * T_1 * \log_2(1 + \frac{P_{pt} |h_{pt,st}|^2}{n^2_a + n^2_{cov}}) \end{aligned} \tag{3}$$

where B is the available bandwidth in PU band.

Now, building upon the proposed joint TS-PS technique shown in Fig. 1, the harvested energy at ST (Eq. (2)) can be reformulated for this work as given in Eq. (4) below.

$$\begin{aligned} EH^{prop}_{st} &= \alpha T_1\eta P_{pt} |h_{pt,st}|^2 + (1 - \alpha)T_1\eta\rho P_{pu} |h_{pt,st}|^2 \\ &= (\alpha + (1 - \alpha)\rho)T_1\eta P_{pt} |h_{pt,st}|^2 \end{aligned} \tag{4}$$

Likewise, the information decoding rate at ST (Eq. (3)) can be reformulated for this work as given in Eq. (5) below.

$$\begin{aligned} R^{prop}_{T_1} &= B * T_1 * \log_2(1 + SNR_{pt,st}) \\ &= B * (1 - \alpha)T_1 * \log_2(1 + \frac{(1 - \rho)P_{pt} |h_{pt,st}|^2}{(1 - \rho)n^2_a + n^2_{cov}}) \end{aligned} \tag{5}$$

Drawing inspiration from [14] and [4], the harvested power at ST (HP^{prop}_{st}) can be derived from the harvested energy, as expressed in Eq. 4. This harvested power is then utilized by ST for relaying primary information and transmitting secondary information.

During the T_2 time, ST forwards $(1 - \rho)Y^I_{pt,st}$ towards PR using a portion of the harvested power, specifically $x.HP^{prop}_{st}$, and reserves $y.HP^{prop}_{st}$ power for secondary transmission during Phase 3. Here, $0 < x, y < 1$. Consequently, the received signal-to-noise ratio (SNR) at PR can be modeled as given in Eq. (6) below.

$$\text{SNR}_{st,pr} = \frac{x.HP_{st}^{prop} |h_{st,pr}|^2}{x.n_a^2 + n_{cov}^2} \tag{6}$$

Likewise, the instantaneous achievable rate at PR for the proposed work during T_2 time $(R_{T_2}^{prop})$ can be formulated as given in Eq. (7).

$$R_{T_2}^{prop} = B * T_2 * \log_2(1 + \text{SNR}_{st,pr}) \tag{7}$$

At this juncture, we can analyze the cooperative capacity (C_{pu}^{coop}) achieved by PT through DF relaying assistance from ST over the duration of $T_1 + T_2$. Building on insights from [16], the attained cooperative capacity (C_{pu}^{coop}) over bandwidth B and the time duration of T_1+T_2 can be modeled using the Shannon-Hartley theorem [10,13] as shown in Eq. (8).

$$C_{pu}^{coop} = B * (T_1 + T_2) * log\,(1 + \text{SNR}_{pt,st} + \text{SNR}_{st,pr}) \tag{8}$$

Therefore, the utility of PU (U_{pu} in bps/Joule) can be represented as a fraction of the achieved C_{pu}^{coop}, relative to the energy consumption of PU during T_1 time, as defined in Eq. (9) below.

$$U_{pu} = \frac{C_{pu}^{coop} * a}{EC_{pu_{T1}}} \tag{9}$$

where a is the gain per unit of cooperative capacity achieved at the Maximal Ratio Combining output.

Lastly, in the duration of T_3 time, ST engages in secondary communication by transmitting its signal towards SR with a power of $y.HP_{st}^{prop}$. Consequently, the received SNR at SR is formulated as presented in Eq. (10) below.

$$\text{SNR}_{st,sr} = \frac{y.HP_{st}^{prop} |h_{st,sr}|^2}{x.n_a^2 + n_{cov}^2} \tag{10}$$

Likewise, the instantaneous achievable rate at SR for the proposed work during T_3 time $(R_{T_3}^{prop})$ can be formulated as shown in Eq. (11).

$$R_{T_3}^{prop} = B * T_3 * \log_2(1 + \text{SNR}_{st,sr}) \tag{11}$$

The utility of SU (U_{su} in bps/Joule) is now expressed as a fraction of the achieved instantaneous achievable rate of ST during Phase 3, relative to the total energy consumption (EC) of ST throughout T_2 and T_3 time. This model is formulated as shown in Eq. (12) below.

$$U_{su} = \frac{R_{T_3}^{prop}}{\underbrace{x.HP_{st}^{prop}}_{\text{EC during } T_2} + \underbrace{y.HP_{st}^{prop}}_{\text{EC during } T_3}} \tag{12}$$

2.2   Formulation of Optimization Problem

In this context, we present the optimization problem aimed at optimizing the allocation of transmission time and harvested power to enhance the utility of the secondary user. The objective of this optimization is to maximize U_{su}, achieved by maximizing $R_{T_3}^{prop}$, while minimizing the total energy consumption by ST. This optimal allocation is determined by the decision variables α, ρ, x, and y.

The key to achieving the maximum $R_{T_3}^{prop}$ lies in increasing $\text{SNR}_{st,sr}$ (as shown in Eq. (11)), which can be attained through three primary factors: (i) increasing HP_{st}^{prop}, (ii) optimizing $|h_{st,pr}|$, and (iii) finding the optimal allocation for power allocation factors x and y. By effectively managing these variables, we can significantly enhance the utility of the secondary user and optimize the resource consumption by ST. To achieve factor (i), we can maximize EH_{st}^{prop} at ST by allocating larger values of α and ρ as given in Eq. (4). However, while maximizing EH_{st}^{prop}, ST must simultaneously monitor the obtained $R_{T_1}^{prop}$ to meet R_{pt}^{tar}. Hence, optimal allocation of α and ρ is crucial at this stage. In contrast, factor (ii) depends solely on the distance between PT and ST and remains independent of any decision variables discussed in this paper. For factor (iii), ST naturally prefers to allocate the maximum possible y during T_3 time by assigning the minimum possible x for T_2 time. However, in the process of reducing x, ST must be attentive to the gradual reduction of $R_{T_2}^{prop}$ (Eq. (7)) while ensuring it satisfies R_{pt}^{tar}. Additionally, allocating a larger y increases the energy consumption of ST during T_3 time, which consequently reduces U_{su} (Eq. (12)). As a result, trade-offs arise that necessitate the optimal allocation of decision variables α, ρ, x, and y, satisfying PU constraints while maximizing U_{su}. Hence, we formulate the optimization problem for the same, as depicted in Eq. (13) below.

$$\textbf{OP:} \quad \max_{\alpha, \rho, x, y} \quad U_{su}$$

$$\text{s.t.} \quad (a)\, 0 < \alpha, \rho\ < 1$$
$$(b)\, 0 < x, y < 1$$
$$(c)\, (1 - (x + y)).HP_{st}^{prop} \leq P_{st}^{min} \tag{13}$$
$$(d)\, R_{pt}^{tar} \leq R_{T_1}^{prop}$$
$$(e)\, R_{pt}^{tar} \leq R_{T_2}^{prop}$$
$$(f)\, R_{st}^{tar} < R_{T_3}^{prop}$$

where P_{st}^{min} represents the minimum required power for an ST to remain active in the network.

However, it should be noted that the proposed optimization problem (Eq. (13)), exhibits a non-linear nature, and solving nonlinear systems is well-known to be an NP-hard problem [3]. In a related study [5], Gaganov demonstrated that nonlinear systems with polynomial equations having rational coefficients also fall under the NP-hard category. The proposed objective function (Eq. (13)) has polynomial equations, and the decision variables, viz. α, ρ, x, and y all act as coefficients with rational boundaries (each of them within the range (0, 1)). Therefore, inspired by [3,5] it can be stated that the proposed problem is also a hard problem that is intractable and difficult to solve in polynomial time. Such a non-linear and NP-hard nature of the optimization problem calls for advanced optimization techniques to find approximate or optimal solutions efficiently. Heuristic approaches are found widely used to address such problems. Therefore, a numerical analysis-based quick iterative heuristic approach can be applied to decide the near optimal solution of α, ρ, x and y with the aim of maximizing U_{su} as well as U_{pu} in polynomial time.

3   Proposed Heuristic Solutions

To tackle the formulated optimization problem involving decision variables α, ρ, x, and y, we propose two iterative heuristic solutions based on conventional numerical methods. These solutions aim to achieve near-optimal resource allocation points α^*, ρ^*, followed by x^* and y^*. For simplicity, we divide the entire optimization problem into two phases. In the first phase, we focus on analyzing the maximum harvested energy at ST by optimally allocating α and ρ values based on Eq. (4) and (5). Subsequently, in the second phase, we achieve optimal allocation of x and y, effectively utilizing the harvested energy to maximize U_{su} while adhering to all the associated constraints given in Eq. (13). The basic steps involved in both heuristic solutions are illustrated through flowcharts, as provided in Subsects. 3.1 and 3.2. These heuristic approaches offer quick iterative solutions to efficiently tackle the optimization problem, providing practical, near-optimal solutions for the resource allocation variables.

3.1   Flowchart for Allocation of α^* and ρ^*

The range of α and ρ is confined within the interval $(0, 1)$. The underlying principle of the proposed strategy revolves around iteratively narrowing down this $(0, 1)$ range towards the optimal α^* and ρ^* points, where the maximum EH_{st}^{prop} can be attained. The step-wise flow of the proposed allocation scheme for α^* and ρ^* is presented as shown in Fig. 2.

3.2   Flowchart for Allocation of x^* and y^*

The ranges of both x and y are constrained within $(0, 1)$. The fundamental concept behind the proposed strategy entails partitioning the given $(0, 1)$ range into two sub-ranges for x and y dynamically. As the sub-range of x narrows towards the left (i.e., towards 0) in the quest for x^*, the sub-range of y simultaneously expands in search of y^* that maximizes U_{su}. The step-wise flow of the proposed allocation scheme for x^* and y^* is presented as shown in Fig. 3.

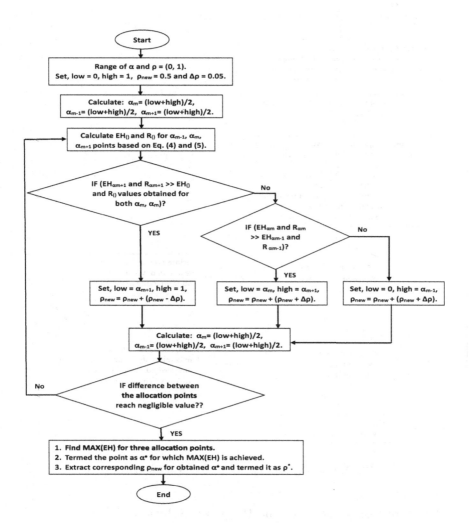

Fig. 2. Flowchart for the allocation of α^* and ρ^*

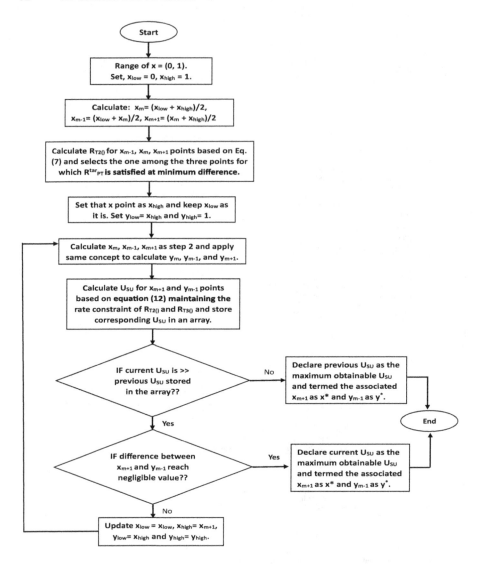

Fig. 3. Flowchart for the allocation of x^* and y^*

3.3 Proof of Convergence of the Proposed Solutions

In the formulated optimization problem, all decision variables are confined within the range $(0, 1)$. The proposed heuristic solutions aim to determine optimal points for each decision variable within this range. In the first solution, the search for α^* and ρ^* is designed such that as the number of iterations increases, the range $(0, 1)$ progressively narrows towards the optimal α and ρ values. These values enable ST to achieve maximum EH_{st}^{prop}.

In the second solution, the ranges of x and y are managed within a single $(0,1)$ range. As the number of iterations increases, the new range of $x \in (0,1)$ starts to contract in search of x^*, while the new range of $y \in (0,1)$ begins to expand in pursuit of the optimal y^* point. This iterative process continues until the x and y values of the current iteration yield a higher U_{su} than the values obtained in the previous iteration. This approach allows the solution to converge towards the optimal allocation of x and y that maximizes the utility U_{su} within the given range constraints.

At each iteration, ST calculates EH_{st}^{prop} and U_{su} for the corresponding allocation points α_{m-1}, α_m, α_{m+1}, x_{m+1}, and y_{m-1}. It then verifies their intervals on a per iteration basis. The process continues until the difference between the allocation points reaches a negligible value, approaching zero. As the proposed solutions reach this negligible difference, they terminate, yielding the maximum achievable EH_{st}^{prop} and U_{su} for their respective allocation points. Thus, we can conclude that the proposed heuristic solutions terminate when the difference between α_{m-1}, α_m, α_{m+1}, and x_{m+1}, y_{m-1} approaches almost zero or becomes zero.

4   Simulation Results and Comparison Analysis

The proposed solutions are evaluated through a simulation study conducted using MATLAB 7 (R2017a) on a 64-bit PC powered by a core i5 processor and 8 GB of RAM. The simulation is based on a Cognitive Radio (CR) network comprising M PUs and N SUs. Both the PUs and SUs are randomly distributed in a square area measuring 1000×1000 m^2. In the simulation setup, the transmission power of PT is fixed at 1 W, and each time slot's duration is set to $T_1 = T_2 = T_3 = 10$ s. Also the PU band's bandwidth is maintained at 1 MHz [16]. Moreover, the PU transceiver pairs are set at an average distance of approximately 30 m, while the SU transceiver pairs are spaced at an average distance of about 20 m. Furthermore, PU channels are modeled as Additive White Gaussian Noise (AWGN) channels, with the noise variance set to 1 mW. These parameters and settings provide the basis for the comprehensive evaluation of the proposed solutions in the context of the CR network under study..

The proposed solution technique, as discussed in Subsect. 3.1, is employed to obtain the graph for maximum energy harvesting at ST through appropriate allocation of α^* and ρ^*. The corresponding results are presented in Fig. 4, achieving an accuracy of 97.7% compared to the optimal (benchmark) result. Furthermore, when considering the individual values of α^* and ρ^*, the proposed solution demonstrates 96% and 95% correctness, respectively, in comparison to the benchmark α^* and ρ^*. These findings highlight the effectiveness and reliability of the proposed solution technique in obtaining near-optimal allocation points for α and ρ, thus leading to significant improvements in the energy harvesting at ST.

Once more, the graph depicting the maximum U_{su}, attained by suitably allocating x^* and y^* utilizing the solution technique discussed in Subsect. 3.2,

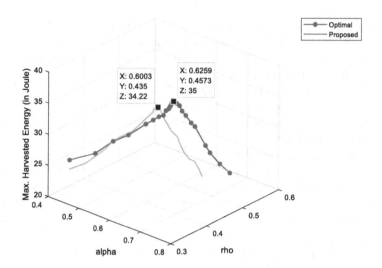

Fig. 4. Max. Harvested Energy vs. optimal allocation of α^* and ρ^* with $\eta = 1$

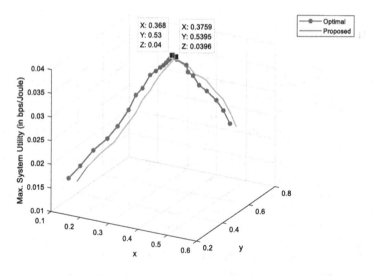

Fig. 5. Max. Utility of SU vs. optimal allocation of x^* and y^*

is presented in Fig. 5. This approach achieved a high accuracy of 98.5% when compared to the optimal result. Furthermore, in the case of x^* and y^* allocation, the proposed technique demonstrated 97.8% and 98% correctness, respectively, when compared to the optimal x and y. These results affirm the efficacy of the proposed solution technique, showcasing its ability to efficiently allocate near-optimal points for x and y, thereby significantly enhancing the U_{su} performance.

Finally, we analyze the impact of the distance between PT and ST on the allocation of x^* and y^* to achieve U_{su} and U_{pu}, as illustrated in Fig. 6. The figure

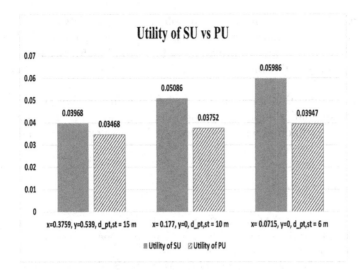

Fig. 6. Utility of SU vs. Utility of PU at obtained x^* and y^* for different distances between PT and ST

reveals that when the distance between PT and ST is very small (say 6 m in the figure) or when ST is in close proximity to PT, the $h_{pt,st}$ value is significantly favorable. Consequently, allocating a small fraction of total power ($x = 0.0715$) during T_2 time allows R_{pt}^{prop} to be easily satisfied in this phase. As a result, ST can allocate a large fraction of total power ($y = 0.53$) during Phase 3, achieving the maximum possible $Usu = 0.05986$.

On the other hand, as the distance between ST and PT gradually increases (say 15 m in the figure), the quality of $h_{st,pr}$ begins to deteriorate. Consequently, ST needs to invest more power during T_2 time by increasing the value of x, as depicted in Fig. 6, to meet R_{pt}^{tar}. However, this increase in x leads to higher energy consumption by ST during T_2 time, consequently reducing the achievable Usu.

Similarly, the gradual decrease in distance between PT and ST results in a gradual increment of U_{pu}. However, the rate of increment in U_{pu} is found to be less than that of U_{su}. This is due to the smart strategy adopted by ST, which allocates the minimum required fraction (x) of total power during T_2 only to meet R_{pt}^{tar}. This strategic approach ensures efficient power utilization by ST while optimizing the performance of both U_{su} and U_{pu}.

5   Conclusion

This paper presents an energy harvesting technique for energy-constrained Cognitive Radio Relay Networks, aimed at improving the utility of SUs. The study formulates an optimization problem to maximize the achieved utility of SUs through optimal allocation of time-switching and power-splitting factors. Given the computationally challenging nature of the problem, a heuristic approach is proposed, which provides a near-optimal solution by optimally allocating all the decision variables. Simulation results demonstrate that the proposed solution achieves high accuracy, with approximately 97.7% and 98.5% accuracy in terms of harvested energy and utility of SUs, respectively, compared to the benchmark result.

Additional simulation research, taking into account various parameter configurations to simulate different real-world deployment scenarios, is planned for future work. These findings will be incorporated into an expanded version of this study.

References

1. Ahmed, E., Gani, A., Abolfazli, S., Yao, L.J., Khan, S.U.: Channel assignment algorithms in cognitive radio networks: taxonomy, open issues, and challenges. IEEE Commun. Surv. Tutor. **18**(1), 795–823 (2016)
2. Akyildiz, I.F., Lee, W.Y., Vuran, M.C., Mohanty, S.: Next generation/dynamic spectrum access/cognitive radio wireless networks: a survey. Comput. Netw. J. **60**(13), 2127–2159 (2006)
3. Christian, J.: An np-hardness result for nonlinear systems. Reliable Comput. **4**, 345–350 (1998). https://doi.org/10.1023/A:1024463631728
4. Dong, Y., Hossain, M.J., Cheng, J.: Performance of wireless powered amplify and forward relaying over Nakagami-m fading channels with nonlinear energy harvester. IEEE Commun. Lett. **20**(4), 672–675 (2016). https://doi.org/10.1109/LCOMM. 2016.2528260
5. Gaganov, A.A.: Computation complexity of the range of a polynomial in several variables. Cybernetics **21**, 418–421 (1985). https://doi.org/10.1007/BF01070595
6. Ghosh, S., Acharya, T., Maity, S.P.: On outage minimization in RF energy harvesting relay assisted bidirectional communication. Wireless Netw. **25**, 3867–3881 (2019)
7. Gu, Y., Aïssa, S.: RF-based energy harvesting in decode-and-forward relaying systems: ergodic and outage capacities. IEEE Trans. Wireless Commun. **14**(11), 6425–6434 (2015). https://doi.org/10.1109/TWC.2015.2453418
8. Hasan, M.K., Chowdhury, M.M.J., Ahmed, S., Sabuj, S.R., Nibhen, J., Bakar, K.A.A.: Optimum energy harvesting model for bidirectional cognitive radio networks. EURASIP J. Wirel. Commun. Netw. **2021**(1), 1–23 (2021). https://doi.org/10.1186/s13638-021-02064-5
9. He, J., Guo, S., Pan, G., Yang, Y., Liu, D.: Relay cooperation and outage analysis in cognitive radio networks with energy harvesting. IEEE Syst. J. **12**(3), 2129–2140 (2018). https://doi.org/10.1109/JSYST.2016.2628862
10. Laneman, J.N., Tse, D.N.C., Wornell, G.W.: Cooperative diversity in wireless networks: efficient protocols and outage behavior. IEEE Trans. Inf. Theory **50**(12), 3062–3080 (1992)
11. Khan, A.A., Rehmani, M.H., Rachedi, A.: Cognitive-radio-based internet of things: applications, architectures, spectrum related functionalities, and future research directions. IEEE Wirel. Commun. **24**(3), 17–25 (2017). https://doi.org/10.1109/MWC.2017.1600404
12. Krikidis, I., Timotheou, S., Nikolaou, S., Zheng, G., Ng, D.W.K., Schober, R.: Simultaneous wireless information and power transfer in modern communication

systems. IEEE Commun. Mag. **52**(11), 104–110 (2014). https://doi.org/10.1109/MCOM.2014.6957150

13. Liu, H., Hua, S., Zhuo, X., Chen, D., Cheng, X.: Cooperative spectrum sharing of multiple primary users and multiple secondary users. Digit. Commun. Netw. **2**(4), 191–195 (2016)

14. Prathima, A., Gurjar, D.S., Jiang, Y., Yadav, S.: Wireless powered cognitive radio networks with multiple antenna sources and hardware impairments. Phys. Commun. **55**, 1–38 (2022). https://doi.org/10.1016/j.phycom.2022.101859

15. Sharma, S., Shi, Y., Hou, Y.T., Kompella, S.: An optimal algorithm for relay node assignment in cooperative ad hoc networks. IEEE/ACM Trans. Netw. **19**(3), 879–892 (2011). https://doi.org/10.1109/TNET.2010.2091148

16. Su, W., Matyjas, J.D., Batalama, S.: Active cooperation between primary users and cognitive radio users in heterogeneous ad-hoc networks. IEEE Trans. Signal Process. **60**(4), 1796–1805 (2012)

17. Tian, J., Xiao, H., Sun, Y., Hou, D., Li, X.: Energy efficiency optimization-based resource allocation for underlay RF-CRN with residual energy and QoS guarantee. EURASIP J. Wirel. Commun. Netw. **2020**(2), 1–18 (2020)

18. Wang, Z., Chen, Z., Xia, B., Luo, L., Zhou, J.: Cognitive relay networks with energy harvesting and information transfer: design, analysis, and optimization. IEEE Trans. Wireless Commun. **15**(4), 2562–2576 (2016). https://doi.org/10.1109/TWC.2015.2504581

19. Xu, W., Yang, Z., Ding, Z., Wang, L., Fan, P.: Wireless information and power transfer in two-way relaying network with non-coherent differential modulation. EURASIP J. Wirel. Commun. Netw. **2015**(1), 1–10 (2015). https://doi.org/10.1186/s13638-015-0368-4

20. Zhang, R., Ho, C.K.: MIMO broadcasting for simultaneous wireless information and power transfer. IEEE Trans. Wireless Commun. **12**(5), 1989–2001 (2013). https://doi.org/10.1109/TWC.2013.031813.120224

21. Zhou, X., Zhang, R., Ho, C.K.: Wireless information and power transfer: architecture design and rate-energy tradeoff. IEEE Trans. Commun. **61**(11), 4754–4767 (2013). https://doi.org/10.1109/TCOMM.2013.13.120855

An Improved and Efficient Distributed Computing Framework with Intelligent Task Scheduling

Pruthvi Raj Venkatesh[ID] and P. Radha Krishna[✉][ID]

Department of Computer Science and Engineering, National Institute of Technology, Warangal,
Telangana, India
pv712133@student.nitw.ac.in, prkrishna@nitw.ac.in

Abstract. Distributed Computing platforms involve multiple processing systems connected through a network and support the parallel execution of applications. They enable huge computational power and data processing with a quick response time. Examples of use cases requiring distributed computing are stream processing, batch processing, and client-server models. Most of these use cases involve tasks executed in a sequence on different computers to arrive at the results. Numerous distributed computing algorithms have been suggested in the literature, focusing on efficiently utilizing compute nodes to handle tasks within a workflow on on-premises setups. Industries that previously relied on on-premises setups for big data processing are shifting to cloud environments offered by providers such as Azure, Amazon, and Google. This transition is driven by the convenience of Platform-as-a-Service offerings scuh as Batch Services, Hadoop, and Spark. These PaaS services, coupled with auto-provisioning and auto-scaling, reduce costs through a Pay-As-You-Go model. However, a significant challenge with cloud services is configuring them with only a single type of machine for performing all the tasks in the distributed workflow, although each task has diverse compute node requirements. To address this issue in this paper, we propose an *Intelligent task scheduling* framework that uses a classifier-based dynamic task scheduling approach to determine the best available node for each task. The proposed framework improves the overall performance of the distributed computing workflow by optimizing task allocation and utilization of resources. Although Azure Batch Service is used in this paper to illustrate the proposed framework, our approach can also be implemented on other PaaS distributed computing platforms.

Keywords: Distributed Computing · Azure Batch · Decision Tree · PaaS · CSP

1 Introduction

Cloud transformation and distributed computing are two major fields that organizations presently emphasize to attain high efficiency in processing large amounts of data. The use of cloud resources and distributed computing as a PaaS (Platform as a Service) service has significantly reduced the implementation cost because of the pay-as-you-go

S. Devismes et al. (Eds.): ICDCIT 2024, LNCS 14501, pp. 18–33, 2024.
https://doi.org/10.1007/978-3-031-50583-6_2

model and techniques such as auto-scaling to optimize resource utilization. While these techniques are useful in reducing costs, there is a necessity for job scheduling algorithms that are efficient and adaptable to mitigate the following challenges:

1. **Diverse Computing Resource Demands:** Distributed computing (DC) jobs involve various tasks such as data ingestion, processing, and computation, each with different resource needs. While some tasks can work well on low-resource machines, others require high-memory, multi-core nodes. Distributed computing PaaS services lack flexibility in dynamically selecting compute nodes based on task type. These services only allow node initialization at job creation, thus limiting node type diversity. This restriction means tasks must use the same node type, irrespective of their resource requirements. This inability to dynamically change node type forces platform administrators to use the most optimal node for all tasks thus increasing costs. Figure 1 shows that only one option can be selected in the "VM Size" dropdown.
2. **Inflexible Autoscaling Parameters:** Although autoscaling is a useful method for managing sudden increases in workload, it cannot be handled at the task level. Certain tasks may require a greater number of nodes, while others may require fewer nodes. Figure 1 shows an example of Azure Batch where the only option available for autoscaling during pool creation is to select the total number of nodes using the "Target Dedicated Nodes" field. The value can be static or dynamically changed (auto-scaling) based on the number of tasks in the job, processor, or memory.

Below are some of the impacts due to the above limitations:

1. **High Execution Cost:** High costs arise in distributed job execution when low-compute tasks are assigned to high-compute machines. For instance, a web service call that consumes time can be executed on a low-compute machine. However, if this call is allocated to a high-compute VM, the cost of execution increases.
2. **High Execution Time:** To achieve cost optimization, the development team would prefer the most optimal compute node or Virtual Machine (VM) to perform all the tasks in the job pool. This cost optimization may lead to high execution time as high compute requirements tasks are executed on low-compute machines.

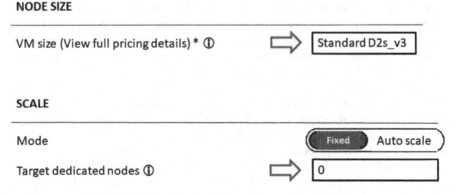

Fig. 1. Configuration screen for adding pool in Azure Batch

The Intelligent Task Scheduling (ITS) framework addresses the outlined constraints by using a decision tree classifier to determine the optimal compute node for a specific task and its corresponding job pool. For data transfer between tasks, the framework leverages Message Queue [1] for smaller data blocks, such as text messages and JSON objects, while the Blob service [1] is employed for larger blob objects, such as files, images, and videos.

The main contributions of the paper are as follows:

1. Proposed a novel framework for dynamically allocating compute resources to the DC tasks called ITS
2. Provided a decision tree classifier to determine the node type of a task. This approach is extensible as more parameters can be added to the model depending on the task requirement or through incremental learning.
3. Developed a task-driven node pool to streamline the restricted autoscaling setup. The auto-scaling configuration at the pool level is utilized to flexibly adjust node quantities, enabling dynamic expansion or reduction.

The rest of the paper is organized as follows. The related work is described in Sect. 2. Section 3 discusses the basic components of the PaaS batch service. Section 4 presents the proposed approach. In Sect. 5, we present the implementation approach in the cloud. Section 5 discusses the experimental results. Section 6 concludes the paper.

2 Related Work

Researchers have done considerable work in algorithms that optimize the compute resource utilization time in a distributed computing platform. However, little work has been done on optimizing resource utilization in a PaaS environment.

Chen et al. [2] proposed an autoencoder-based distributed clustering algorithm that helped cluster data from multiple datasets and combined the clustered data into a global representation. The approach highlights the challenges of handling huge and multiple datasets from different computing environments. Daniel et al. [3] proposed different distributed computing cloud services that can be used for machine learning in big data scenarios. Nadeem et al. [4] proposed a machine-learning ensemble method to predict execution time in distributed systems. The model takes various parameters, such as input and distributed system sizes, to predict workflow execution time. Sarnovsky and Olejnik [5] proposed an algorithm for improving the efficiency of text classification in a distributed environment. Ranjan [6] provided an in-depth analysis of cloud technologies focusing on streaming big data processing in data center clouds.

Al-Kahani and Karim [7] provided an efficient distributed data analysis framework for big data that includes data processing at the data collecting nodes and the central server, in contrast to the common paradigm that provides for data processing only at the central server. This process was very efficient for handling stream data from diverse sources. Nirmeen et al. [8] proposed a new task scheduling algorithm called Sorted Nodes in Leveled DAG Division (SNLDD), which represents the tasks executing in a distributed platform in the form of Directed Acyclic Graph (DAG). Their approach divides DAG into levels and sorts the tasks in each level according to their computation size in descending order for allocating tasks to the available processors. Jahanshahi et al. [9] presented an algorithm based on learning automata as local search in the memetic algorithm for minimizing Makespan and communication costs while maximizing CPU utilization. Sriraman et al. [10] proposed an approach called SoftSKU that enables limited server CPU architectures to provide performance and energy efficiency over diverse microservices and avoid customizing a CPU SKU for each microservice. Pandey and Silakari [11] proposed different platforms, approaches, problems, datasets, and optimization approaches in distributed systems.

The approaches in the literature primarily focus on a) optimizing source data organization for efficient processing, b) task allocation based on execution order to available resources, and c) utilizing cloud services for distributed computing. However, these methods do not address the limitations of PaaS DC services. Our proposed framework tackles the deficiencies of PaaS DC services and offers strategies for enhanced processor utilization.

3   Batch Basic Concepts

This section introduces the core batch service concepts provided by various cloud providers. Figure 2 illustrates the components of the batch service.

1. **Batch Orchestration:** Batch Service provides a comprehensive set of APIs for developers to efficiently create, manage, and control batch services. This API empowers developers to handle every aspect of a batch, encompassing pool creation, task allocation, task execution, and robust error handling.
2. **Task:** A task is a self-contained computing unit that takes input, executes operations and generates subsequent task results. Configured during batch service creation, tasks run scripts or executables, forming the core of a DC job which is a sequence of tasks working toward specific goals. Batch facilitates parallel execution of tasks via its service APIs.
3. **Job Pool:** A job pool is a collection of tasks. Any task that must be executed must be added to the job pool. The batch service orchestrates the execution of this task on any of the compute nodes available in the node pool.
4. **Node Pool:** VMs or compute nodes in the job pool are managed by the batch service, overseeing their creation, task tracking, and provisioning. It offers both fixed VM numbers and dynamic auto-scaling based on criteria. In batch service, VMs are also known as compute nodes.
5. **Batch Storage:** Blob storage is created by the batch service to manage the internal working of the service. Batch storage is used for storing task execution logs and binaries. The batch service orchestrates the installation of these binaries on all the VMs in the node pool.
6. **Start-Up Task:** The Start-Up task is the first task executed on the VM provisioned in the Node Pool. It contains the command to download binaries from batch storage and install them on the provisioned VM.
7. **Cloud Services:** The VMs in the node pool have access to all the services provided by the CSP. The VM commonly accesses services such as blob storage or message queue as a common store to persist and retrieve sharable data among the various tasks executed in parallel.

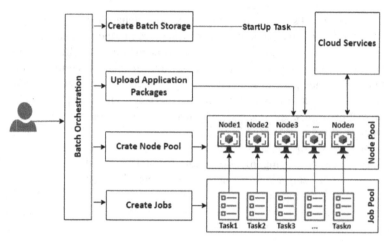

Fig. 2. Components of Batch Service

4 Proposed Approach

In this section, we describe the proposed approach that is used for scheduling tasks in a PaaS distributed computing environment. We use an example of document processing from an external source to explain the proposed approach. Document processing involves document download (Task t_0), text extraction (Task t_1), image extraction and optical character recognition (OCR)[12] (Task t_2) for images present in the document, entity extraction [13] from OCR output (Task t_3), text summarization of the text extracted (Task t_4), and updating extracted information to the database (Task t_5).

4.1 Initialization

The first step in the proposed approach is to identify the different tasks involved. All the tasks follow a specific sequence of execution called workflow to arrive at the results. These workflows can be represented as a directed acyclic graph (DAG) [14]. The graph nodes represent the tasks $t \in T$ where T is a set of n tasks in the workflow. The edge between the nodes e $\in$ E represents the tasks' execution or the message flow between the tasks. Figure 3 shows the DAG containing 6 tasks and 6 edges. The individual tasks are represented as $t_i \in T$, and the edge between task t_i and t_j is represented as $(t_i, t_j) \in$ E, which indicates that the t_j can be started after t_i is completed. It also indicates that t_i sends a message to t_j. The first task (t_0) with no incoming edge is the *starting task*, and a task (t_5) with no outgoing edge is called an *exit task*. It can be noted from Fig. 3 that document download is the first task in the workflow. The downloaded file is sent simultaneously to text extraction and image extraction. The output of text extraction is sent for text summarization and the text output of image extraction and OCR is sent to entity extraction. Once both activities are completed the last task would be to store the extracted summarized text and the entities extracted into a single record in the database.

A message $m_{i,j} \in M$ is sent between node t_i and t_j and it is associated with each edge (t_i, t_j). Here M is the set of all the messages exchanged between the nodes in the workflow. $m_{i,j}$ contains a set of attributes created by the task t_i and sent to t_j for further processing. A message $m_{i,j}$ comprises of $\{m_{index}, t_i, md_0, md_1, md_2, ..., md_n\}$ where m_{index} is a unique value created by the starting task to uniquely identify all the tasks in the complete workflow, t_i is the reference to the source task and $md_{(0\ to\ n)}$ include all message data attributes required to execute the task t_j. Each task t_j is associated with the PaaS queue service q_j, created to store the message $m_{i,j}$, which comes from the task t_i. Each task is associated with a compute node attribute set $a_i = \{ a_{i1}, a_{i2}, a_{i3}, ..., a_{in}\}$ where a_{ij} represents the compute node properties required to execute task t_i. Table 1 shows task attributes and their values for the tasks shown in Fig. 3. The attributes include.

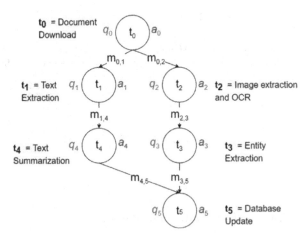

Fig. 3. DAG Task Processing Order

Table 1. Task Attributes

Task Name	Avg Exec Time(s)	Avg Exec Time Bucket	Processor Requirement	Memory Requirement	External Dependency	Operating System
Task t_0	23	(0–25)	Low	Low	Yes	Windows
Task t_1	12	(0–25)	Low	Low	No	Windows
Task t_2	200	(>50)	High	High	No	Linux
Task t_3	50	(25–50)	Medium	High	No	Windows
Task t_4	123	(>50)	High	High	No	Linux
Task t_5	35	(25–50)	Medium	High	No	Windows

1. **Avg Execution Time:** Average time required to execute the task
2. **Processor Requirement:** The possible values are High, Medium, and Low
3. **Memory Requirement:** The possible values are High, Medium, and Low

4. **External Dependency:** Jobs that wait for external dependencies like web requests or API calls.
5. **Operating System:** The host operating system is required to perform the task.

These attribute sets are gathered during the development phase of the project. It can be noted from Table 1 that tasks t_2 (Image extraction and OCR) and t_4 (Text summarization) require high memory, processor, and Linux systems, whereas the rest of the tasks can be executed on Windows machines. All the distinct attribute set a_i are consolidated into an attribute set $A = \{a_1, a_2, a_3, \ldots, a_n\}$, used for classifier training. Table 2 shows the distinct attribute set obtained from Table 1.

Table 2. Distinct Attribute Set

Avg Exec Time Bucket	Processor Requirement	Memory Requirement	External Dependency	Operating System
(0–25)	Low	Low	Yes	Windows
(0–25)	Low	Low	No	Windows
(25–50)	Medium	High	No	Windows
(>50)	High	High	No	Linux

4.2 Classifier Training and Compute Node Mapping

In the second step, a decision tree classifier is trained by taking the distinct compute node attribute set A and mapping them to a compute node type $c_i \in C$, where $C = \{c_1, c_2, c_3, \ldots, c_n\}$ is a set of all the compute node types provided by the CSP. Table 3 shows the mapping between the attribute set and the compute node types.

The decision tree classifier model takes task attributes A and generates the predictions C represented as $P(A) = C$. After the training, the model is used to create tuples (T, C). The tuple contains the elements (t_i, c_i), which indicates that task $t_i \in T$ requires predicted compute node $c_i \in C$ to execute. Table 3 shows the example of the task and compute node mapping generated from the model.

4.3 ITS Framework

The source documents are represented by the set $X = \{1, 2, 3, \ldots n\}$, where n is the total number of items in the source dataset. The ITS framework contains three separate flows that execute in parallel. Figure 4 shows the working of the ITS for the tasks shown in Fig. 3.

1. **Job Initializer:** Responsible for initiating the workflow's first task by processing input data. Pseudocode 1 outlines the job initializer steps. It reads and extracts necessary details from the source data, creating messages in q_0 for each item. In the example of Fig. 4, the Job Initializer processes files $f0$ to fn in the source data repository,

Table 3. Task Compute Node Mapping

Task Name	Compute Node Type
Task t_0 Document Download	Compute node Type 1
Task t_1 Text Extraction	Compute node Type 1
Task t_2 Image Extraction and OCR	Compute node Type 2
Task t_3 Entity Extraction	Compute node Type 3
Task t_4 Text Summarization	Compute node Type 2
Task t_5 Database Update	Compute node Type 3

generating messages in queue q_0 containing the location details of the file. The first message for file $f0$ in queue q_0 is represented using $m_{(0)0}$ where (0) in parenthesis represents the file number similarly for file $f1$ it is $m_{(1)0}$.

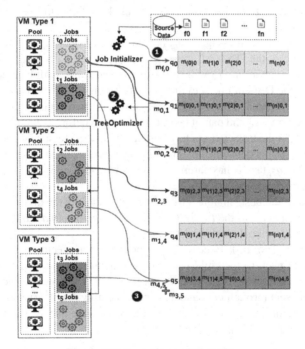

Fig. 4. ITS Execution and Data Flow

Pseudocode 1. Job Initializer Procedural Flow

Input: Input data that need to be processed.
Output: Populate input queue q_0 with $m_{(i)0}$ messages.
1. **Begin**
2.   **for all** $x_i \in X$ **do**
3.   Add message m_{i0} to the queue q_0
4.   **end for**
5. **End**

---

2. **ITS:** Responsible for scheduling the tasks in multiple job pools to ensure optimal utilization of resources at the task level. The ITS looks for messages in all the queues and schedules the tasks in the predicted job pool. Pseudocode 2 captures the steps in the ITS, which are explained below:

   a. ITS keeps monitoring the queues for any messages. In Fig 4 the ITS is monitoring q_0 to q_5.

   b. For the first task in the workflow, messages $m_{(f)0}$ are read from the queue q_0 after it is populated from the Job Initializer. In Fig. 4 the ITS will read messages $m_{(0)0}$ to $m_{(n)0}$ from q_0.

   c. For subsequent tasks message $m_{(f)i,j}$ is read from the queue q_j populated from the task t_i. In Fig. 4, the ITS reads messages $m_{(0)0,1}$ to $m_{(n)0,1}$ from q_1 similarly from other queues such as $m_{(0)1,2}$ will read from q_2 and $m_{(0)2,3}$ will be read from q_3.

   d. ITS checks the DAG in Fig. 3 to find parents for tasks t_j. If multiple parents exist, the queue q_j is searched for message $m_{(f)ij}$ for all the parent task t_i using the unique task identifier m_{index}, and parent tasks t_i and merged before executing the task t_j. In example Fig. 4 the tasks t_0 to t_4 have single parents so message $m_{(f)0}$ is consumed by task t_0, $m_{(f)0,1}$ is consumed by task t_1, $m_{(f)2,3}$ is consumed by task t_3, and so on. In the case of q_5, task t_5 has parent t_4 and t_3 so the messages $m_{(f)4,5}$ and $m_{(f)3,5}$ are merged before executing t_5.

   e. ITS identifies the best suitable VM Type required to run the task t_j.

   f. ITS creates the task in the t_j job pool. The message data(md) in the message are passed as parameters to task t_j.

3. **Task Executor:** The Task Executor is responsible for executing and writing the output message back to the child task message queue for the next task execution. Pseudocode 3 captures the steps in the Task Executor. The flow involves consuming the parameters sent through message data md, executing the binaries associated with the task, and writing the results to the child task message queue. The following are the task executions that happen (see Fig. 4):

Pseudocode 2. Tree Optimizer Flow

Input: Messages read from all the queues associated with the tasks.
Output: Create a task in the job pool to process the message read.

1. **Begin**
2.   **for all** $q_i \in Q$ **do**
3.   Read message m
4.   Read m_{index}
5. c_i = Find compute node for t_i in tuple (T,C)
6.   P = Get list of all the parents for task t_i
7. t_P = Get the source task from where m is recieved
8.   If length(P) == 1 **then**
9.   Add the task t_i to the pool c_i with message contents m
10.   Remove the message m from q_i
11.   **else**
12.   **for all** $p_z \in P$ **do** /* if a task has multiple parents look for message from all the parents, consolidate and send to the task */
13.   If p_z != t_P **then** /* Ignore the message currently read */
14. m_{zi} = read message with m_{index} and parent p_z
15.   m = merge the message data md from m_{zi} to the message m /*this will combine all the messages from the parent into a single message*/
16.   Remove the message m_{zi} from q_i
17.   messagesFound++
18.   **endIf**
19.   **endfor**
20.   If length(P) == messagesFound **then** /* Add task only if all the parent message are found*/
21.   Add the task t_i to the pool c_i with message contents m
22.   **endIf**
23.   **endIf**
24.   **endfor**
25. **End**

Pseudocode 3. Task Execution Flow

Input: Messages read from all the queues associated with the tasks.
Output: Create a task in the job pool to process the message read.
1. **Begin**
2.   Read message data md from the task properties
3.   Perform the task t_i
4.   Generate the results of task t_i
5.   j = Find the next task of t_i for DAG
6. $m_{i,j}$ = Create a message from the results of task t_i
7.   Add the message $m_{i,j}$ to the queue q_j
8. **End**

---

a. $t0$ (Document Download) downloads the file after reading the external file location in the message queue $q0$. The task stores the file in a common location in the local store and populates the message $m0,1$ in $q1$ and $m0,2$ in $q2$ with the location of the local store in the message.

b. $t1$ (Text Extraction) extracts the text from the document by reading the local file store location and populates the message $q4$ with the contents of the extracted text.

c. $t2$ (Image Extraction and OCR) extracts all the images from the document performs an OCR to extract the text and populates the message $q3$ with the contents of the extracted text.

d. $t3$ (Entity Extraction) extracts entities from the message received from $t2$ containing OCR text output and populates the message in $q5$ with the entities extracted.

e. t_4 (Text Summarization) summarizes the text output obtained from t_1 and populates the message in q_5 with the summarized text.

f. ITS merges the message data from t_2 containing entities extracted and t_4 containing the summarized text and triggers t_5.

g. t_5 (Database Update) updates the extracted information into the database.

5 Experimental Results

5.1 Dataset Details

We illustrate our approach for the Oil Industry domain to extract structured and unstructured data from images. The dataset was sourced from the BSEE website [15], an open repository of oil and gas industry data. The goal was to make images searchable based on text content and *well*-data attributes. The experiment involved processing 1000 images in Azure, involving tasks such as image download, classification, attribute extraction, OCR, NLP, and search index update. Figure 5 shows the image categories in the dataset.

5.2 Azure Setup for the Experiment

Figure 6 shows the experimental setup in Azure [1].

| Well Bore Sketch | Sun Dry Notice | Completion Report | Well Reports |

Fig. 5. Image Categories of Test Data Set

1. **Azure Storage:** Azure blobs are used to store the images.
2. **Processing Layer:** Consists of Azure Batch and Scheduled Jobs. Azure Batch is a distributed computing PaaS platform provided by Azure and Schedule Jobs are services that run scripts on a schedule. They are configured to execute Job Initialization and ITS.
3. **Search Layer:** Consists of Azure cognitive search service that provides metadata and free text search from the extracted content.
4. **ML Studio:** Hosts the classification model that derives the VM size required for the task.
5. **Forms Service:** Used to extract structured data(attributes) from images. Figure 7 shows attributes such as *well* name, and *lease* name extracted from the *forms services.*
6. **Custom Vision:** Used for categorizing the images present in the source dataset, as shown in Fig. 5.
7. **Storage Table:** Used to store the log table containing the task compute node requirement.

5.3 Experiment Steps

The execution steps are:

1. **Classifier Training:** This step involved training the classifier model with training data containing the task resource requirements. Table 4 contains the training data with a compute node requirement column containing the Azure VM [1] size most suitable for running the task.
2. **Task Attribute Update:** This step involved adding task attributes along with execution times into the storage table. Table 5 shows the entries in the Storage Table.
3. **Compute Node Prediction:** Run the classification model against the entries in the table storage (Table 5) to determine the VM size required for running the tasks. Table 6 contains the compute node mapping obtained for each task in the Job. The entries in Table 6 are updated to the Storage Table for scheduling the tasks.
4. **Run distributed Job using Azure Batch:** The experiment involved creating two pools, Low-Cost Pool containing Standard_A4_v2 [16] (4 core, 8 GB RAM) VM and High-Cost Pool containing Standard_A8_v2 [16] (8 core, 16 GB RAM) VM. The

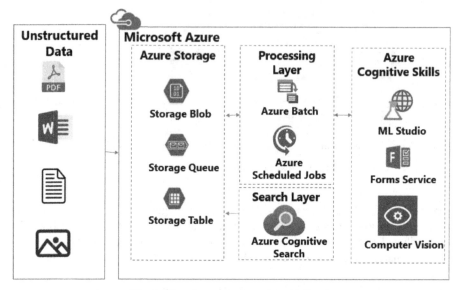

Fig. 6. Experimental setup of Azure Batch

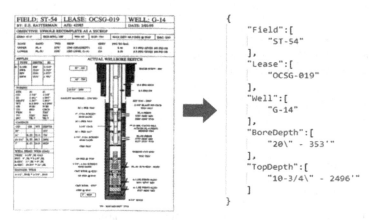

Fig. 7. Structured Data Extraction

number of machines used in the experiment was limited, considering the execution cost involved. The experiment involved three execution modes.

a) **Low Cost – High Execution Time Approach:** In this mode, we allocated three Standard_A4_v2 VMs in the Low Compute Pool and allocated the task of extracting data from 1000 images.

b) **High Cost – Low Execution Time Approach:** In this mode, we allocated three Standard_A8_v2 VMs in the High Compute Pool and allocated the task of extracting data from 1000 images.

c) **ITS Approach:** In this mode, we allocated two Standard_A1_v2 VMs in the Low Compute Pool and a single Standard_A8_v2 VM in the High Compute VM pool.

Table 4. Classifier Training Data

Avg Exec Time Bucket	Processor Requirement	Memory Requirement	External Dependency	Operating System	Compute Node Requirement
(0–10)	Low	Low	Yes	Windows	Standard_A4_v2
(0–10)	Low	Low	No	Windows	Standard_A4_v2
(10–50)	High	High	No	Windows	Standard_A8_v2

Table 5. Task Attributes

Task Name	Avg Exec Time(s)	Avg Exec Time Bucket	Processor Requirement	Memory Requirement	External Dependency	Operating System
Classify Image	1.23	(0–10)	Low	Low	No	Windows
Extract Fields	7.11	(0–10)	Low	Low	No	Windows
OCR Text	16.13	(10–50)	High	High	No	Windows
Search Service Update	0.19	(0–10)	Low	Low	No	Windows

Table 6. Task Compute Node Mapping

Task Name	Compute Node Requirement
Load	Standard_A4_v2
Classify Image	Standard_A4_v2
Extract Fields	Standard_A4_v2
OCR Text	Standard_A8_v2
Search Service Update	Standard_A4_v2

We used the classification model to predict the task job pool. The allocation of tasks to the pool depended on the output of the prediction model and the number of jobs in the pool. If the job pool length is less than the threshold set to 10 tasks, any job will be allocated to the respective pool. The OCR extraction task was primarily allocated to the high compute pool, whereas all the other tasks were allocated to the low compute pool. This allocation procedure ensures that no processor is idle during the data extraction.

Table 7 shows the execution time in all three modes. There is an 8% decrease in execution time of the ITS Approach compared to the Low Cost- High Execution Time Approach and a total reduction of 68% in cost when the ITS Approach is compared with the High Cost – Low Execution Time Approach. The percentage reduction in time is calculated using the total execution time captured in Table 7. The total reduction in cost is obtained by multiplying the execution time with the unit price for VM usage from the Azure VM price sheet [16]. A similar experimental setup can be done on batch services provided by other CSPs such as AWS [17] and Google [18].

Table 7. Batch Execution Results

Activity (in secs)	Low Cost – High Execution Time Approach			High Cost – Low Execution Time Approach			ITS Approach		
	Low Compute VM	Low Compute VM	Low Compute VM	High Compute VM	High Compute VM	High Compute VM	Low Compute VM	Low Compute VM	High Compute VM
Classify Image	9.76	9.01	9.95	9.20	8.87	9.89	13.25	13.56	1.10
Form Data Extraction	42.17	43.7	43.0	42.03	43.87	42.87	60.52	61.1	5.04
OCR	131.3	132.4	130	93.85	94.61	94.21	86.72	85.92	157.67
Search Service Update	1.58	1.34	1.44	1.18	1.45	1.37	1.70	1.56	0.14
Total Execution (min)	9.28			7.39			8.14		

6 Conclusion

Distributed systems are computing platforms that can be used to handle large amounts of data processing. However, they can be costly depending on the time it takes to complete a job. This paper introduces a new framework that optimizes both the execution time and cost associated with running data processing tasks on a massive scale. The suggested technique includes the dynamic identification of the compute nodes to execute the task based on the classification model's output. This model can be trained to optimize execution cost and execution time or additionally, it can be easily retrained with new parameters to enhance the system's flexibility in accommodating new rules.

References

1. Directory of Azure Cloud Services | Microsoft Azure. https://azure.microsoft.com/en-in/pro ducts/

2. Chen, C.-Y., Huang, J.-J.: Double deep autoencoder for heterogeneous distributed clustering. Information **10**(4), 144 (2019). https://doi.org/10.3390/info10040144
3. Pop, D., Iuhasz, G., Petcu, D.: Distributed platforms and cloud services: enabling machine learning for big data. In: Mahmood, Z. (ed.) Data Science and Big Data Computing, pp. 139–159. Springer, Cham (2016). https://doi.org/10.1007/978-3-319-31861-5_7
4. Nadeem, F., Alghazzawi, D., Mashat, A., Faqeeh, K., Almalaise, A.: Using machine learning ensemble methods to predict execution time of e-science workflows in heterogeneous distributed systems. IEEE Access **7**, 25138–25149 (2019). https://doi.org/10.1109/ACCESS.2019.2899985
5. Sarnovsky, M., Olejnik, M.: Improvement in the efficiency of a distributed multi-label text classification algorithm using infrastructure and task-related data. Informatics **6**(12), 1–15 (2019). https://doi.org/10.3390/informatics6010012
6. Ranjan, R.: Streaming big data processing in datacenter clouds, pp-78–83. IEEE Computer Society (2014)
7. Al-kahtani, M.S., Karim, L.: An efficient distributed algorithm for big data processing. Arab. J. Sci. Eng. **42**(8), 3149–3157 (2017). https://doi.org/10.1007/s13369-016-2405-y
8. Bahnasawy, N.A., Omara, F., Koutb, M.A., Mosa, M.: Optimization procedure for algorithms of task scheduling in high performance heterogeneous distributed computing systems. Egypt. Inform. J. **12**(3), 219–229 (2011). https://doi.org/10.1016/j.eij.2011.10.001. ISSN 1110-8665
9. Jahanshahi, M., Meybodi, M.R., Dehghan, M.: A new approach for task scheduling in distributed systems using learning automata. In: 2009 IEEE International Conference on Automation and Logistics, pp. 62–67 (2009). https://doi.org/10.1109/ICAL.2009.5262978
10. Sriraman, A., Dhanotia, A., Wenisch, T.F.: SoftSKU: optimizing server architectures for microservice diversity @scale. In: 2019 ACM/IEEE 46th Annual International Symposium on Computer Architecture (ISCA), pp. 513–526 (2019)
11. Pandey, R., Silakari, S.: Investigations on optimizing performance of the distributed computing in heterogeneous environment using machine learning technique for large scale data set. Mater. Today: Proc. (2021). https://doi.org/10.1016/j.matpr.2021.07.089. ISSN 2214-7853
12. Optical character recognition. https://en.wikipedia.org/wiki/Optical_character_recognition
13. Entity Extraction. https://en.wikipedia.org/wiki/Named-entity_recognition
14. Directed acyclic graph – Wikipedia. https://en.wikipedia.org/wiki/Directed_acyclic_graph
15. Scanned Well Files Query. https://www.data.bsee.gov/Other/DiscMediaStore/ScanWellFiles.aspx
16. Pricing - Windows Virtual Machines | Microsoft Azure. https://azure.microsoft.com/en-in/pricing/details/virtual-machines/windows/
17. Getting Started with AWS Batch - AWS Batch. https://docs.aws.amazon.com/batch/latest/userguide/Batch_GetStarted.html#first-run-step-2
18. Batch service on Google Cloud. https://cloud.google.com/blog/products/compute/new-batch-service-processes-batch-jobs-on-google-cloud

Scheduling of Containerized Resources for Microservices in Cloud

Kamalesh Karmakar[1,2]($\boxtimes$) (iD), Shramana Dey[2], Rajib K. Das[2],
and Sunirmal Khatua[2] (iD)

[1] Future Institute of Technology, Kolkata, WB, India
k.karmakar.ju@gmail.com
[2] University of Calcutta, Kolkata, WB, India

Abstract. Most developers consider that microservice-based application design and development can improve scalability and maintainability. The microservices are developed as small independent modules and
deployed in containers. The containers are deployed in virtual machines
(VMs), which in turn run in hosts. Effective consolidation of the service
requests to the containers may reduce the number of active hosts in a
cloud environment, resulting in lesser power consumption of the cloud
data centers. This research aims to maximize the resource utilization of
the hosts by effectively allocating the containers to the VMs and VMs
to the hosts. In this scheduling, a few additional containers and VMs are
kept in the available resource pool so that during peak demand for services, the users get their service at the earliest (preferably without any
delay). This paper presents a heuristic algorithm for microservice allocation in a containerized cloud environment to achieve these objectives.
The performance of the proposed algorithm is validated and justified
through the extensive experimental results. We have compared the performance of the proposed technique with the existing state-of-the-art.
The number of container deployments in the proposed policy is reduced
by 12.2–17.36% compared to the Spread policy and 6.13–10.57% compared to First-Fit and Best-Fit policies.

Keywords: Microservices · Cloud Computing · Container ·
Scheduling Technique · Resource Allocation

1 Introduction

With the fundamental shift in software development, service-oriented computing has become an attractive choice among software developers for its agility
and efficiency. In a service-oriented architecture (SOA) [5,16], web services are
small independent computing tasks (loosely coupled [16,20,23]) published as a
service over the Internet. Web services make the business functionalities of one
application accessible to other applications through web interfaces. These services can easily be integrated into client applications for low-cost development
and deployment.

S. Devismes et al. (Eds.): ICDCIT 2024, LNCS 14501, pp. 34–49, 2024.
https://doi.org/10.1007/978-3-031-50583-6_3

In a microservice architecture, an enterprise application is split into small self-contained modules, where a microservice is designated to perform a specific task. These microservices communicate among themselves using the *Simple Object Access Protocol (SOAP)*. Hence, instead of working on the shared codebase, the developers can be divided into many smaller groups who can work on developing business functions in different modules independently. It gives benefits for improving code re-usability and maintainability. More importantly, microservice-based applications should be scalable because of the highly fluctuating nature of demands.

The distributed deployment and fluctuating demand of the microservices require scalable resource provisioning for cost-effective deployment and execution. In this regard, cloud computing deals with the scenario by providing the backbone infrastructure as pay-per-use on-demand services. Furthermore, the Cloud Service Providers (CSPs) offer different pricing models for the end-users, depending on shared or dedicated resources. Hence, policy designing for resource allocation becomes a challenging task. Moreover, the cloud service providers want to reduce the energy consumption of the data centers and are facing challenges for dynamic resource provisioning of multiple clients within minimum infrastructural resources [11–14]. At the same time, service providers should ensure maintenance of the service level agreement of the users, like deadlines and quality of services [3, 3, 28]. This paper focuses on microservice deployment in Docker containers in Amazon EC2 on-demand instances to achieve these objectives.

Thus, this paper proposes a model for microservice-based task deployment and a heuristic algorithm for performance improvement. In this algorithm design, we try to minimize end-to-end delay for improved quality of services (QoS). Moreover, we ensure that the tasks are completed within their deadlines while keeping the monetary cost of task deployment low. Hence, the main contributions of this work are as follows:

- A microservice-based task deployment model.
- A heuristic algorithm to schedule the services to the containers.
- Extensive experimental results to analyze the performance of the proposed algorithm with existing techniques using benchmark data.

The rest of this paper is organized as follows. Section 2 illustrates a microservice architecture in a cloud environment. Later, we discuss the system model and formulate the problem in Sect. 3. Section 4 illustrates the proposed policy for task deployment. Section 5 presents and analyzes the experimental results. Finally, Sect. 6 concludes the paper with some future direction of research in this domain.

2 Literature Review

With the emergence of architectural patterns, microservice architecture has become necessary for achieving high flexibility in designing and implementing modern applications. Hence, in the recent past, various microservice architectures have evolved and are standardized.

In [1], authors provide a benchmark analysis for master-slave and nested-container-based microservice architecture. They analyze the performance of the models in terms of CPU resource usage and network communication. In a keynote speech [8], Wilhelm Hasselbring discussed the importance of microservices over monolithic architecture. Several studies have shown that microservice architecture improves performance and DevOps development cycle over monolithic architecture [18,35].

However, SOA faces challenges using existing communication mechanisms with very high workload scenarios [2,9]. To overcome this challenge, a new technology, *Enterprise Service Bus* (ESB), was introduced [19,25]. It can achieve low latency and high scalability of the application. However, ESB is unsuitable for a cloud environment as virtual machine deployment is elastic, i.e., the number of virtual machines may vary based on service demand. Hence, to avoid this problem in SOA, a microservice architecture pattern has emerged that helps in developing lightweight services [4,21].

Furthermore, in recent days, microservice deployments in the cloud environment have gained attention to achieve the benefits of acquiring inherently scalable cloud resources whose billing is dependent on resource usage. High adaptation of cloud services is possible by deploying microservices in a VM instance, which can scale as per the user's demand. However, in recent days, containers have been preferred instead of VM instances as containers are lightweight, quickly migratable, and scalable. These containers, in turn, are deployed in VM instances. Microservices use container technology, which provides operating system-level virtualization [10,17,22]. One such container technology is Docker [6], developed as a lightweight virtualization platform [22,27].

In the SOA aspect, container-based application deployment has received considerable attention, and different companies have taken the initiative. *CoreOS* defined Application Container (*appc*)[1] specification by the image format, the runtime environment, and discovery protocol. Another notable runtime container engine project is *runC*[2], started by Docker. In 2015, Docker, Google, IBM, Microsoft, Red Hat, and many other partners formed *Open Container Initiative (OCI)*[3] for further enhancement and standardized container specification. OCI consists of two specifications, namely Runtime Specification (*runtime-spec*) and Image Specification (*image-spec*). In brief, an OCI image is downloaded and unpacked into an OCI runtime environment to create a container service. The Cloud Native Computing Foundation[4] designed an open-source software stack that allows the deployment of applications as microservices packed into containers. Furthermore, this software stack performs dynamic orchestration of the containers for optimizing resource utilization.

---

[1] https://coreos.com/rkt/docs/latest/app-container.html.
[2] https://blog.docker.com/2015/06/runc/.
[3] https://www.opencontainers.org/.
[4] https://www.cncf.io/.

In container-based microservices, each microservice, along with the required libraries and databases is packaged in a container deployed on a platform that supports container technology. Containerized microservices are isolated execution environments and can be instantiated at runtime based on service demand. These containers may run in one or more virtual machine(s) depending on the resource demand, virtual machine configuration, and availability of resources. Deployment of different containers on different virtual machines may improve performance when the resource demand is high. However, this incorporates more communication delay, as the virtual machines can be scattered within the data center or across data centers placed in different geographical areas.

2.1   Standard Data Formats, APIs and Protocols

Deployment of microservices in different containers, running in the same or different virtual machines, requires information exchange among the containers. Information exchange requires standard data representation and standard protocols. However, XML is a well-known and widely used data format for message exchange, JSON becomes more popular in recent days. *Data Format Description Language* (DFDL) supports a variety of data input, output formats and is used in both open source and proprietary tools [7,34]. Besides these, the Open API Initiative standardized RESTful API Markup Language (RAML), which can be used for a variety of data formats [30,31].

The microservice architecture uses standard HTTP and HTTPS protocols for information exchange. Along with standard TCP and UDP protocols, Stream Control Transmission Protocol (SCTP) is used for streaming services [24,26]. In the context of the machine to machine communication, the Organization for Advanced Structured Information Systems (OASIS)[5] standardized the Message Queuing Telemetry Transport (MQTT) protocol for publishing and subscribing messages at high speed [29,32].

3   System Model and Problem Formulation

Most software applications use microservices to deliver diverse functionalities to the end users. Hence, microservices are to be deployed in heterogeneous containers. Furthermore, the heterogeneity of underlying cloud data center resources and pricing models makes microservice allocation much harder. In this regard, the system is modeled based on the following assumptions:

- the containers can migrate to other VMs for consolidating them in a minimum number of VMs
- the VMs do not migrate as the time and monetary cost involved in VM migration is very high.

However, if the utilization of a container is too low and the environment is underutilized, newly arrived microservice requests are not allocated to it, which results in the termination of the container without any running service migration.

---

[5] https://www.oasis-open.org/.

3.1   System Model

Let us consider a set of microservice requests $S = \{s_1, s_2, s_3, \ldots, s_m\}$, where each request is associated with a deadline, are to be deployed in a containerized cloud environment. We consider a set of container images $CI = \{ci_1, ci_2, \ldots, ci_x\}$, where each container is configured for a specific type of microservice. The microservice containers $C = \{c_1, c_2, \ldots, c_n\}$ are instantiated using the container images. The containers are deployed into the VMs, $V = \{v_1, v_2, \ldots v_q\}$, which in turn are deployed into physical machines/hosts, $P = \{p_1, p_2, \ldots, p_r\}$.

The service requests are routed to the containers, where the corresponding microservice runs. An increase or decrease in the number of microservice requests causes the creation of new instances of containers or the termination of existing containers while keeping the resource utilization of containers within a desired range. The decision to scale the containers depends on the demand for container resources and the current utilization of the containers. Similarly, the VMs, that deploy the containers, are also scaled as per the current utilization of the running VMs. However, a container or VM is not shut down/stopped as soon as utilization becomes low. The scale-down occurs only if the containers or VMs are under-utilized for a certain period. The resource utilization of the containers and VMs is calculated as follows:

Resource Utilization of a Container. Let us represent service request allocation in a container using matrix $X_{i,j,t}$ where a request s_i is allocated to a container c_j at clock t. The utilization of the container c_j at time t is calculated as

$$u_{j,t}^c = \frac{\sum_{i=1}^{m}(mips_{s_i} \cdot X_{i,j,t})}{mips_{c_j}} \tag{1}$$

where $X_{i,j,t}$ is defined as

$$X_{i,j,t} = \begin{cases} 1, \text{ if } s_i \text{ is allocated to } container \ c_j \text{ at time } t \\ 0, \text{ otherwise} \end{cases}$$

and $mips_{s_i}$ is the MIPS (million instructions per second) needed by the service request s_i, $mips_{c_j}$ is the capacity of the container in MIPS.

Resource Utilization of Virtual Machine. Similarly, we represent the container allocation to VMs using matrix $Y_{j,k,t}$, considering the container c_j is allocated to the VM v_k at time t. Thus, the utilization of a VM v_k at time t is measured as

$$u_{k,t}^v = \frac{\sum_{j=1}^{n}(mips_{c_j} \cdot u_{j,t}^c \cdot Y_{j,k,t})}{mips_{v_k}} \tag{2}$$

where $Y_{j,k,t}$ is defined as

$$Y_{j,k,t} = \begin{cases} 1, \text{ if } c_j \text{ is allocated to } VM \ v_k \text{ at time } t \\ 0, \text{ otherwise} \end{cases}$$

and $mips_{v_k}$ is capacity of the VM v_k in terms of million instructions per second. The service requests allocated to a container are kept in the reservation table of the container.

Resource Utilization of Host. The VMs are deployed in hosts of a cloud data center. $Z_{k,l,t}$ represents the allocation of v_k in p_l at time t. That is,

$$Z_{k,l,t} = \begin{cases} 1, & \text{if } v_k \text{ is allocated to } host \; p_l \text{ at time } t \\ 0, & \text{otherwise} \end{cases}$$

Hence, utilization of a host p_l at time t is measured as

$$u^p_{l,t} = \frac{\sum_{k=1}^{q}(mips_{v_k} \cdot u^v_{k,t} \cdot Z_{k,l,t})}{mips_{p_l}} \tag{3}$$

where q is number of VM instances, $mips_{v_k}$ and $mips_{p_l}$ are capacity of VM v_k and host p_l in terms of MIPS.

Energy Model of Host. The power consumption of a host is dependent on its utilization. This literature considers a linear power model shown below. The power consumption of a host p_l is calculated as:

$$En_{l,t} = \begin{cases} En_{l,t}^{idle} + (En_{l,t}^{busy} - En_{l,t}^{idle}) \cdot u^p_{l,t}, & \text{if } u^p_{l,t} \geq 0 \\ En_{l,t}^{off}, & \text{if host is shut down} \end{cases} \tag{4}$$

where $En_{l,t}^{idle}$ is the power consumption of an idle host and $En_{l,t}^{busy}$ is the power consumption of a fully utilized host.

3.2 Pricing Models of Different Platforms

Amazon AWS offers infrastructure services at different pricing schemes like *(i) reserved, (ii) on-demand, and (iii) spot instance* for the same instance type. The CSUs (cloud service users) can avail of on-demand instances at a fixed hourly rate with a guarantee of uninterrupted service. On the other hand, the price of spot instances varies with time, and availability depends on the bid price and overall demand for resources. The CSP can reclaim the spot instance whenever the price exceeds the bid. Nowadays, Amazon has changed its policy regarding the bid where the default bid is the on-demand price, and whenever the spot price is about to exceed the on-demand price, it issues a warning and revokes the spot instance after a short period (a few minutes). Thus, spot instances are generally cheaper than on-demand but come with a risk of revocation by CSPs (cloud service providers). We choose spot instances for microservice deployment as it is cost-effective and describe in Sect. 4 the techniques used to handle the problems arising out of revocation by CSPs.

3.3   Problem Formulation

Given a set of microservice requests $S = \{s_1, s_2, \ldots, s_m\}$, a set of container images $CI = \{ci_1, ci_2, \ldots, ci_x\}$, a set of virtual machines $V = \{v_1, v_2, \ldots v_q\}$ and a set of physical machines/hosts, $P = \{p_1, p_2, \ldots, p_r\}$, determine a schedule $f : s_i \rightarrow c_j$ where service request s_i is being allocated to container c_j, which are deployed in VMs $g : c_j \rightarrow v_k$, which in turn are deployed in physical hosts $h : v_k \rightarrow p_l$ in such a way that satisfies deadlines, minimizes the resource renting cost of the VMs, and achieves energy efficiency by minimizing the number of active hosts.

Algorithm 1: Service Allocation to Microservice Container

---

    input : $S = \{s_1, s_2, s_3, \ldots, s_m\}$; $CI = \{ci_1, ci_2, ci_3, \ldots, ci_x\}$;
              $C = \{c_1, c_2, c_3, \ldots, c_n\}$; $V = \{v_1, v_2, v_3, \ldots, v_q\}$
    output: Service request allocation to the Containers

1   keep un-allocated services of previous clock at the beginning of S.
2   **foreach** $s_i \in S$ **do**
3   determine image type ci_g for service request s_i
4   determine containers C_a which can serve service request s_i
5   sort C_a in descending order of $u^c_{j,t} \cdot u^v_{k,t}$, where $u^c_{j,t}$ $u^v_{k,t}$ are obtained from Eq. 1 and 2
6   set flag $isServiceDeployed \leftarrow false$
7   **foreach** $c_j \in C_a$ **do**
8   status $\leftarrow isDeployableContainer(s_i, c_j)$
9   **if** $status = true$ **then**
10   update reservation table of c_j; $isServiceDeployed \leftarrow true$
11   break;

12   **if** $isServiceDeployed = false$ **then**
13   rearrange the VMs V in descending order of resource utilization
14   select a container configuration c for s_i based on ci_a;
15   set flag $isContainerDeployed \leftarrow false$
16   **foreach** $v_k \in V$ **do**
17   **if** $isDeployableVM(c, v_k)$ **then**
18   instantiate container c in v_k based on container image ci_a
19   update $C \leftarrow C \cup c$; $isContainerDeployed \leftarrow true$

20   **if** $isContainerDeployed = false$ **then**
21   instantiate a new VM v
22   instantiate container c in v based on container image ci_a
23   update $V \leftarrow V \cup v$; $C \leftarrow C \cup c$

24 call Algorithm 2 to manage pool of containers and VMs.

Algorithm 2: Resource Pooling of Containers and VMs

    input : service request, s_i; deadline of service request, dl_{s_i}; container, c_j;
             reservation table, rt_{c_j}
    output: allocation status

1 rearrange the VMs V in descending order of resource utilization
2 **for** $a = 1$ *to* x **do**
3   select the containers C_a intantiated using container image ci_a
4   rearrange C_a in descending order of utilization
5   calculate utilization of microservice containers $u_{a,t}^{ci}$ using Eq. 8
6   **if** $\overline{u_{a,t}^{ci}} > \mu^{ch}$ **then**
7   add $\lceil (\overline{u_a^{ci}} - \mu^{ch}) * |C_a| \rceil$ number of containers, say C_a', are to be deployed
8   **foreach** $c_j \in C_a'$ **do**
9   set $flag \leftarrow false$
10   for $v \in V$ **do**
11   **if** $u_{k,t}^v + mips_{c_j}/mips_{v_k} < \mu^{vh}$ *as per Eq. 9* **then**
12   instantiate c_j in v_k; update $flag \leftarrow true$
13   **if** $flag = false$ **then**
14   instantiate a new VM v and add it to V
15   **else if** $u_{a,t}^{ci} < \mu^{cl}$ **then**
16   **while** $u_{a,t}^{ci} < \mu^{cl}$ **do**
17   remove the containers from C_a in which service is not allocated and the container is running in a most underutilized VM

---

4 Proposed Algorithm

The proposed algorithm deals with independent microservice requests for allocation in a set of containers C to run on a set of virtual machines V. A container, by design, can run only a specific type of microservice. Hence, the service requests S can be classified based on their attributes and mapped to the respective containers. Based on users' service demand, multiple containers instantiated from the same container image may provide the same microservice. On the other hand, we must instantiate at least one container for each type of microservice. These containers and VMs are to be scaled to reduce monetary costs. Thus, the proposed policy has two phases: *(i) Service request allocation, (ii) Containers and VMs Pool management*, as presented below.

4.1 Service Request Allocation

In a scheduling clock, the resource provisioner receives a set of service requests S and routes the requests to the containers. Before allocating any service request, the containers are to be rearranged in descending order of resource utilizations so that the resource provisioner allocates service requests to maximally utilized but not overloaded containers. If we combine with this, the policy of freeing underutilized containers when demand for services reduces, we can decrease the number of container deployments. However, the monetary cost is not associated with the number of container deployments but with the number of VM deployments. Also, the resource utilization of the VMs impacts the energy consumption of the data center. Hence, to ensure the concentration of the containers in a lower number of VMs, the containers are sorted in descending order of the product of container and VM utilization ($u_{j,t}^c \cdot u_{k,t}^v$) as shown in line no. 4 of Algorithm 1. Here, $u^c j, t$ and $u_{k,t}^v$ are computed by Eqs. 1 and 2. Using line no 7–11, a container is selected for the service request s_i if $u_{j,t}^c$ is less than the upper threshold of container utilization μ^{ch} and if s_i is deployable in the container c_j, i.e., $mips_{s_i} + u_{c_j} \cdot mips_{c_j} \leq mips_{c_j}$. If the service request is not deployable in any existing container, a container must be instantiated using the container image ci_a on a suitable VM. A container is deployable in a VM if it has enough resources available. The resource availability of a VM v_k at time t is given by:

$$R_{k,t}^v = mips_{v_k} \cdot \mu^{vh} - \sum_j u_{j,t}^c .mips_{c_j} .X_{j,k,t} \qquad (5)$$

where μ^{vh} is upper threshold of VM utilization.

To avoid resource contention among the containers, we assume that resources are fully reserved for a container irrespective of its utilization. Thus, the resource availability of v_k is redefined by substituting 1 for $u_{j,t}^c$ as

$$R_{k,t}^v = mips_{v_k} \cdot \mu^{vh} - \sum_j mips_{c_j} .X_{j,k,t}. \qquad (6)$$

The function $isDeployableVM(c_j, v_k)$ returns true if the VM v_k can satisfy the resource requirement of the new container, i.e. $mips_{c_j} \leq R_{k,t}^v$.

Each container maintains a reservation table for the service requests. The reservation table of container c_j at time t (rt_{c_j}) has the tuples $<s_i, st_{s_i} l_{s_i}, at_{s_i}> |\ \forall\ X_{i,j,t} = 1$. Here, st_{s_i} is the start time, l_{s_i} is the service execution time, and at_{s_i} is the arrival time. In every scheduling clock, the reservation table is updated according to the arrival of new service requests and completion of existing service requests.

4.2 Resource Pooling of Containers and VMs

At the end of each scheduling clock, the algorithm investigates the health of container instances of each service type (container image type) and analyzes resource utilization to make scaling decisions.

The utilization of the containers $u_{a,t}^{ci}$ of container image type ci_a at time t is calculated as

$$u_{a,t}^{ci} = \frac{\sum_j u_{j,t}^c .mips_{c_j}}{\sum_j mips_{c_j}} \quad \forall c_j \in C_a \qquad (7)$$

where $u_{j,t}^c$ is utilization of container c_j and C_a is the set of containers instantiated from container image ci_a. If the average utilization for a certain period t' to t is higher than the upper threshold μ^{ch}, we should increase the size of C_a (a scale-up). The average utilization for a certain period is calculated as

$$\overline{u_{a,t}^{ci}} = \frac{1}{t - t'} \int_{t'}^{t} u_{a,t}^{ci} \delta t \qquad (8)$$

If the average utilization $\overline{u_{a,t}^{ci}}$ is greater than μ^{ch}, $\lceil (\overline{u_{a,t}^{ci}} - \mu^{ch}) * |C_a| \rceil$ number of containers are to be instantiated. While instantiating a container in an existing VM v_k, we must check that its new utilization does not exceed utilization threshold μ^{vh} as per the following equation:

$$u_{k,t}^v + \frac{mips_{c_j}}{mips_{v_k}} < \mu^{vh} \qquad (9)$$

Other resource constraints such as memory etc., are also considered while deploying a container in v_k. If the container does not fit in any existing VM, we must instantiate a new VM to allocate the container. As the VM instantiation takes 1–2 min, to avoid any delay in launching the container, at the end of every scheduling clock, VMs are also scaled up to keep them in a reserved pool to allow immediate deployment of containers in them.

The containers are scaled down if the average utilization of the containers $\overline{u_{a,t}^{ci}}$ is less than the lower threshold μ^{cl}. The idle containers (maximum $\mu^{cl} - \overline{u_{a,t}^{ci}}.|C_a|$ of them are selected for shutting down). Similarly, the VMs are scaled down if resource average utilization $\overline{u_t^v}$ is less than the lower threshold μ^{vl}. The VMs without any allocated containers are selected for shutting down (maximum $\mu^{vl} - \overline{u_t^v}.|V|$ number of VMs).

The VMs are deployed in hosts using a polynomial-time heuristic technique, Resource Affinity-based VM Placement (RAbVMP), aiming for a reduction of active hosts (presented in [15]).

The rearrangement of containers and VMs according to the descending order of resource utilization ensures that during scale-up, allocation of microservices to the containers is such that utilization of the containers is highest at the front of the list and least at the tail. This approach ensures that the VMs at the tail of the list become idle. Similarly, the containers at the tail of the list, if idle, can be considered for shutting down. A priority queue based implementation for the lists of VMs and containers minimizes computational time.

5   Experimental Results and Discussion

In our experiment, we simulated the microservice deployment environment as presented in this article and obtained the results. In the simulation, different parameters act as input to the algorithms. The simulation environment assumes the continuous arrival of microservice requests from multiple users at runtime. Thus, the algorithm works as an online algorithm to manage dynamic arrivals of microservice requests.

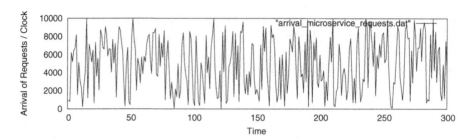

Fig. 1. Arrival of Microservice Requests in a Simulation, where the average arrival rate of microservices is 5000 per scheduling clock.

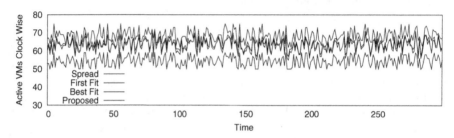

Fig. 2. Number of active VMs clock-wise, during a simulation where the arrival rate of microservice requests is 25000 in a minute.

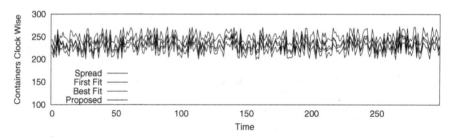

Fig. 3. Number of running Containers clockwise during a simulation where the arrival rate of microservice requests is 25000 in a minute.

5.1 Simulation Environment Setup

The simulation environment is designed based on the Fat-Tree data center network topology that uses 8-ary switches. The environment consists of 128 physical machines (hosts), where each host can accommodate 8 medium-sized VMs. The average number of container deployments in a VM is 4; this number may vary based on the resource availability of the VMs. Hence, the environment consists of approximately 1024 VMs in which nearly 4096 containers may run simultaneously.

In this simulation, the containers are deployed on c7g.xlarge (a compute-intensive VM type) with 4 vCPU and 8 GiB memory that supports up to 12.5

Gbps network bandwidth. As per the Microsoft Azure reference manual, one vCPU supports nearly 150 MIPS[6]. We consider that a container provides support upto 120 MIPS. Thus a VM may contain 4 containers at a time if the containers run at their maximum capacity because a VM is permitted to run at a maximum 85% utilization. If the containers are tuned to a lower MIPS, a VM can deploy more of them.

Furthermore, we consider that the average execution time of a microservice request in a container (running in maximum capacity) is 490 ms where microservice execution time varies within the range of 0.05 s to 2.0 s. Thus, every minute, an average of 122 microservices can be executed. Then, on average, a VM can complete $122 \times 4 = 488$ microservice requests per minute. In our simulation, we vary the number of microservice requests from 5000 to 25000 per minute.

For evaluating the performance of the proposed scheduling policy, we compared with the well-known common industrial strategies –Spread, BinPack, Random[7,8], and some state-of-the-art strategies– First-Fit and Best-Fit [33].

5.2   Result Analysis

In this simulation, the average arrival rate of microservice requests varies between 5000 and 25000 per minute. The arrival of the microservice requests is dynamic and follows the Poisson distribution. In this regard, Fig. 1 depicts the arrivals of microservice requests for a 300-min period where the arrival rate of requests is 5000. Figure 2 shows the number of active VMs using the proposed algorithm in a simulation where the arrival rate of the microservices is 25000. Figure 3 depicts the number of containers running in the VMs during a simulation period using the proposed algorithmic policy.

The results, shown in Fig. 4a, depict that the proposed policy significantly reduces the number of containers. The number of containers required for the execution of the microservices is a little high in the Spread policy, and the performances of the First-Fit/Best-Fit policies are close. The number of container deployments in the proposed method is lower than that for the Spread policy by 12.2–17.36%, and that for First-Fit/Best Fit policies by 6.13–10.57%.

Figure 4b shows the number of active VMs, and we observe that a decrease in the number of containers deployed results in fewer active VMs. The proposed policy reduces the number of active VMs by 11.23–15.42% compared to the Spread policy and 6.43–8.76% compared to First-Fit and Best-Fit policies. Reduction in the number of active VMs results in significant improvement in monetary cost, shown in Fig. 4c. This lower cost results from very high VM utilization caused by efficient consolidation of the containers. In this simulation, the upper threshold of VM utilization is 85% with a relaxation of 5%.

---

[6] https://docs.microsoft.com/en-us/azure/virtual-machines/workloads/mainframe-rehosting/concepts/mainframe-compute-azure.

[7] https://docs.docker.com/engine/swarm/.

[8] https://github.com/docker-archive/classicswarm/tree/master/scheduler/strategy.

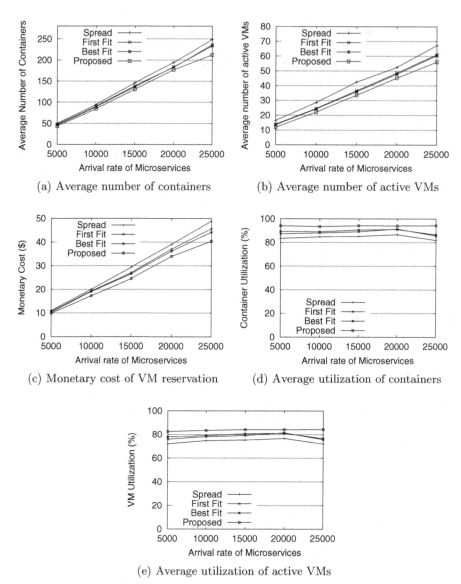

(a) Average number of containers

(b) Average number of active VMs

(c) Monetary cost of VM reservation

(d) Average utilization of containers

(e) Average utilization of active VMs

Fig. 4. Results of microservice deployment in containers with varying arrival rate of microservice requests.

6 Conclusion and Future Scope

This paper presented a policy for allocating the microservice requests to the containerized cloud environment and auto-scaling the containers and underlying VMs. The objective is to reduce the monetary cost of task execution and minimize resource usage by maximizing resource utilization of the active VMs. More specifically, the microservice requests are categorized based on their types and consolidated in a minimum number of containers that are deployed in a minimum number of VMs. We compared the performances of the proposed algorithm with Spread, First-Fit, and Best-Fit policies. The results of extensive experiments show that the proposed method significantly reduces the number of containers and active VMs.

Though the proposed policy improves the utilization of the resources in cloud infrastructure, there is a scope for further improvement in microservice deployment. Moreover, we plan to analyze workflow-based microservice deployment considering communication overhead among the containers. Furthermore, there is a need to develop a policy that allocates dependent microservices at proximity to improve performance.

References

1. Amaral, M., Polo, J., Carrera, D., Mohomed, I., Unuvar, M., Steinder, M.: Performance evaluation of microservices architectures using containers. In: 2015 IEEE 14th International Symposium on Network Computing and Applications, pp. 27–34. IEEE (2015)
2. Becker, A., Buxmann, P., Widjaja, T., et al.: Value potential and challenges of service-oriented architectures-a user and vendor perspective. In: ECIS, pp. 2085–2096 (2009)
3. Tarafdar, A., Karmakar, K., Khatua, S., Das, R.K.: Energy-efficient scheduling of deadline-sensitive and budget-constrained workflows in the cloud. In: Goswami, D., Hoang, T.A. (eds.) ICDCIT 2021. LNCS, vol. 12582, pp. 65–80. Springer, Cham (2021). https://doi.org/10.1007/978-3-030-65621-8_4
4. Dragoni, N., et al.: Microservices: yesterday, today, and tomorrow. In: Mazzara, M., Meyer, B. (eds.) Present and Ulterior Software Engineering, pp. 195–216. Springer, Cham (2017). https://doi.org/10.1007/978-3-319-67425-4_12
5. Erl, T.: Service-Oriented Architecture: Concepts, Technology, and Design. Pearson Education India (1900)
6. Felter, W., Ferreira, A., Rajamony, R., Rubio, J.: An updated performance comparison of virtual machines and Linux containers. In: 2015 IEEE International Symposium on Performance Analysis of Systems and Software (ISPASS), pp. 171–172. IEEE (2015)
7. Gao, T.T., Huang, F.W., Zhai, X.D., Zhu, P.: Generating data format description language schema. US Patent App. 14/724,851 (2015)
8. Hasselbring, W.: Microservices for scalability: keynote talk abstract. In: Proceedings of the 7th ACM/SPEC on International Conference on Performance Engineering, pp. 133–134 (2016)
9. Hutchinson, J., Kotonya, G., Walkerdine, J., Sawyer, P., Dobson, G., Onditi, V.: Evolving existing systems to service-oriented architectures: Perspective and challenges. In: IEEE International Conference on Web Services (ICWS 2007), pp. 896–903. IEEE (2007)
10. Kang, H., Le, M., Tao, S.: Container and microservice driven design for cloud infrastructure devops. In: 2016 IEEE International Conference on Cloud Engineering (IC2E), pp. 202–211. IEEE (2016)

11. Karmakar, K., Banerjee, S., Das, R.K., Khatua, S.: Utilization aware and network I/O intensive virtual machine placement policies for cloud data center. J. Netw. Comput. Appl. **205**, 103442 (2022)
12. Karmakar, K., Das, R.K., Khatua, S.: Minimizing communication cost for virtual machine placement in cloud data center. In: TENCON 2019–2019 IEEE Region 10 Conference (TENCON), pp. 1553–1558. IEEE (2019)
13. Karmakar, K., Das, R.K., Khatua, S.: Balanced graph partitioning based I/O intensive virtual cluster placement in cloud data center. In: 2021 12th International Conference on Computing Communication and Networking Technologies (ICCCNT), pp. 01–06. IEEE (2021)
14. Karmakar, K., Das, R.K., Khatua, S.: An ACO-based multi-objective optimization for cooperating VM placement in cloud data center. J. Supercomput. 1–29 (2022)
15. Karmakar, K., Khatua, S., Das, R.K.: Efficient virtual machine placement in cloud environment. In: 2017 International Conference on Advances in Computing, Communications and Informatics (ICACCI), pp. 1004–1009. IEEE (2017)
16. Krafzig, D., Banke, K., Slama, D.: Enterprise SOA: Service-oriented Architecture Best Practices. Prentice Hall Professional (2005)
17. Kratzke, N.: About microservices, containers and their underestimated impact on network performance. arXiv preprint arXiv:1710.04049 (2017)
18. Lloyd, W., Ramesh, S., Chinthalapati, S., Ly, L., Pallickara, S.: Serverless computing: an investigation of factors influencing microservice performance. In: 2018 IEEE International Conference on Cloud Engineering (IC2E), pp. 159–169. IEEE (2018)
19. Luo, M., Goldshlager, B., Zhang, L.J.: Designing and implementing enterprise service bus (ESB) and SOA solutions. In: 2005 IEEE International Conference on Services Computing (SCC 2005), vol. 1, 2, p. xiv-vol. IEEE (2005)
20. McGovern, J., Sims, O., Jain, A., Little, M.: Enterprise Service Oriented Architectures: Concepts, Challenges, Recommendations. Springer, Dordrecht (2006). https://doi.org/10.1007/1-4020-3705-8
21. Nadareishvili, I., Mitra, R., McLarty, M., Amundsen, M.: Microservice Architecture: Aligning Principles, Practices, and Culture. O'Reilly Media, Inc. (2016)
22. Pahl, C., Jamshidi, P.: Microservices: a systematic mapping study. In: CLOSER (1), pp. 137–146 (2016)
23. Papazoglou, M.P., Georgakopoulos, D.: Service-oriented computing. Commun. ACM **46**(10), 25–28 (2003)
24. Schlechtendahl, J., Kretschmer, F., Lechler, A., Verl, A.: Communication mechanisms for cloud based machine controls. Procedia CiRp **17**, 830–834 (2014)
25. Schmidt, M.T., Hutchison, B., Lambros, P., Phippen, R.: The enterprise service bus: making service-oriented architecture real. IBM Syst. J. **44**(4), 781–797 (2005)
26. Sill, A.: Standards at the edge of the cloud. IEEE Cloud Comput. **4**(2), 63–67 (2017)
27. Stubbs, J., Moreira, W., Dooley, R.: Distributed systems of microservices using docker and serfnode. In: 2015 7th International Workshop on Science Gateways, pp. 34–39. IEEE (2015)
28. Tarafdar, A., Karmakar, K., Das, R.K., Khatua, S.: Multi-criteria scheduling of scientific workflows in the workflow as a service platform. Comput. Electr. Eng. **105**, 108458 (2023)
29. Thangavel, D., Ma, X., Valera, A., Tan, H.X., Tan, C.K.Y.: Performance evaluation of MQTT and CoAP via a common middleware. In: 2014 IEEE Ninth International Conference on Intelligent Sensors, Sensor Networks and Information Processing (ISSNIP), pp. 1–6. IEEE (2014)

30. Verborgh, R., et al.: Survey of semantic description of REST APIs. In: Pautasso, C., Wilde, E., Alarcon, R. (eds.) REST: Advanced Research Topics and Practical Applications, pp. 69–89. Springer, New York (2014). https://doi.org/10.1007/978-1-4614-9299-3_5
31. Wilde, E., Pautasso, C.: REST: From Research to Practice. Springer, New York (2011). https://doi.org/10.1007/978-1-4419-8303-9
32. Xu, Y., Mahendran, V., Radhakrishnan, S.: Towards SDN-based fog computing: MQTT broker virtualization for effective and reliable delivery. In: 2016 8th International Conference on Communication Systems and Networks (COMSNETS), pp. 1–6. IEEE (2016)
33. Zhang, R., Zhong, A., Dong, B., Tian, F., Li, R.: Container-VM-PM architecture: a novel architecture for docker container placement. In: Luo, M., Zhang, L.-J. (eds.) CLOUD 2018. LNCS, vol. 10967, pp. 128–140. Springer, Cham (2018). https://doi.org/10.1007/978-3-319-94295-7_9
34. Zhao, Y., Dobson, J., Foster, I., Moreau, L., Wilde, M.: A notation and system for expressing and executing cleanly typed workflows on messy scientific data. ACM SIGMOD Rec. **34**(3), 37–43 (2005)
35. Zhou, X., et al.: Poster: benchmarking microservice systems for software engineering research. In: 2018 IEEE/ACM 40th International Conference on Software Engineering: Companion (ICSE-Companion), pp. 323–324. IEEE (2018)

ELITE: Energy and Latency-Optimized Task Offloading for DVFS-Enabled Resource-Constrained Devices in MEC

Akhirul Islam$^{(\boxtimes)}$ and Manojit Ghose

IIIT Guwahati, Guwahati, India
`akhirul.islam@iiitg.ac.in`

Abstract. Multi-access Edge Computing (MEC) technology offers promising support for modern, computation-intensive, and time-sensitive applications. Many of these applications are generated by resource-constrained handheld or mobile UE. Due to limited resources, offloading certain parts of these applications (tasks) to connected MEC servers becomes essential. However, MEC servers also have limited resources compared to cloud servers, highlighting the need for efficient task offloading policies for UE devices and optimal resource allocation policies for MEC servers. This paper introduces ELITE (Energy and Latency-optimized Task Offloading and Resource Allocation for DVFS-Enabled devices), a novel solution to the energy and latency minimization problem in a cooperative heterogeneous MEC architecture. The proposed policy aims to minimize the energy consumption of the UE devices and the latency of the applications while satisfying application deadlines and dependency constraints. Furthermore, we consider the UEs to be enabled by dynamic voltage and frequency scaling (DVFS). Through extensive simulations using a real dataset, we demonstrate that our proposed strategy surpasses the state-of-the-art policy, achieving a remarkable 10% reduction in latency and an impressive 2× reduction in energy consumption of UE devices.

Keywords: Multi-access Edge Computing (MEC) · DVFS · cooperative MEC system · Mobile Edge Computing (MEC) · energy and latency

1 Introduction

With the rise of compute-intensive and latency-sensitive applications like real-time online games, virtual reality (VR), image processing, and IoT applications, there is a growing need for a new network and computing paradigm to cater to these demands. Mobile Cloud Computing (MCC) has been a popular solution, forwarding resource-intensive tasks to powerful cloud servers [20]. However, the geographical distance between UE and cloud servers introduces significant delays. To address this latency issue, the Multi-access Edge Computing (MEC) framework has emerged as a promising approach, offering cloud computing capabilities at the edge of the network [14, 29]. This enables the execution of resource-intensive, latency-sensitive applications, leading to improved performance and reduced delays [23].

With MEC servers possessing limited computing resources unlike central cloud, efficient resource management becomes crucial to maximize the benefits of the MEC framework. Addressing three key challenges [1] is essential: 1) Offloading, which determines whether an application should be executed locally or remotely (MEC or cloud); 2) Resource allocation, responsible for efficiently allocating computing resources to applications; and 3) Task scheduling, deciding the order of processing applications or tasks while meeting constraints like deadlines.

Various researchers have explored different system models in the existing literature. For example, two-tier models have been studied in [6], three-tier models in [27, 30], and four-tier models in [2, 5]. Some authors have also explored SDN-based models in [1]. However, most of these models focus either on the MEC server alone (two-tier) or on the cooperation between the MEC server and the cloud server (three-tier). The existing literature has not considered cooperation among neighbouring MEC servers regarding task offloading, even though coordination and cooperation among MEC servers are considered in the context of caching [7]. In our research, we propose a cooperative MEC server architecture in conjunction with the cloud, where MECs hosted in different base stations cooperate with each other. This approach is essential for two reasons: i) It facilitates efficient resource management for MEC servers, which are typically resource-constrained compared to the cloud, and ii) It helps reduce task latency by executing a larger number of tasks in neighbouring base stations instead of forwarding them to the cloud. In addition to the cooperative MEC system, we have also considered the heterogeneity of MEC servers in terms of CPU capacity (in MIPS), memory size, and storage size [9].

The existing literature on task offloading in MEC has focused on various objectives, including energy optimization, latency optimization, or both, with many works adopting independent task offloading strategies to minimize UE energy consumption and application latency. Very recently, in [4], the authors utilize dependent task modeling to optimize energy consumption and task latency, but they do not account for the latency deadline in their approach. Additionally, the consideration of DVFS-enabled UE devices has been largely overlooked in the literature, despite its potential to significantly reduce energy consumption by adjusting the CPU frequency, which is particularly beneficial for energy-constrained devices like battery-powered devices [22].

In this study, we embrace a comprehensive approach to executing applications within the cooperative heterogeneous MEC framework, aiming to minimize both the energy consumption of UEs and the overall latency. This is achieved by considering dependent task modeling. We summarize the contribution of this paper below.

1. We consider DVFS-enabled UE devices in our cooperative heterogeneous system model.
2. We put forth a series of strategies to efficiently execute applications within an MEC framework, optimizing both the energy consumption of the UE devices and the latency of the applications while considering deadline-aware dependent task models.
3. Extensive simulations based on real-world datasets were conducted using a standard simulator.

The paper is structured as follows: Sect. 2 presents the literature review. In Sect. 3, we introduce the cooperative heterogeneous system model considered in this work. The application model, energy consumption model of UEs, communication model, and computation model are presented in Sect. 4, 5, 6, and 7 respectively. Section 8 provides a detailed problem formulation. Our solution for the latency and energy optimization problem is described in Sect. 9. The simulation and evaluation of our proposed strategy are presented in Sect. 10, and finally, we conclude the paper in Sect. 11.

2   Literature Review

In recent years, computation offloading in Mobile Edge Computing (MEC) has attracted significant attention from researchers, leading to the proposal of various task offloading schemes. Among the crucial objectives of these schemes is the energy-latency tradeoff in MEC server tasks. Different authors have approached the task offloading problem, formulating it as energy optimization [12,27,30], latency optimization [19,25,28], or jointly optimizing both energy and latency [2, 8,26].

Various authors have explored diverse system models as part of their task-offloading schemes. Based on existing literature, we can broadly categorize these models into different architectures: two-tier [6,15,26], three-tier [17,27,30], four-tier [2,5], and SDN-based [1] architectures. In the two-tier architecture, UE is at the first layer, MEC servers attached to a Base Station (BS) are at the second layer, and the remote cloud is absent. In the three-tier architecture, the remote cloud forms the third layer. The four-tier architecture includes an additional layer, where UEs communicate with the MEC server via an access point or an edge controller. In the SDN-based architecture, a centralized control plane acts as the backbone of the entire network.

In task offloading schemes, tasks can possess various properties and may be offloaded wholly or partially. While some existing works primarily consider input data size and CPU cycle requirements for task formulation [12,26], others also take into account task latency deadline and output size [27]. The literature often aims to optimize either energy consumption or latency, leading to the use of binary or partial offloading schemes. Some works focus on optimizing both energy and latency but still adopt a binary offloading model. When representing subtasks for partial offloading, most authors employ Directed Acyclic Graphs, while others divide tasks into multiple fractions.

Various authors have employed diverse methodologies to formulate and tackle the task offloading problem. Many of them have expressed the task offloading scheme as a mixed-integer program problem and demonstrated its NP-hardness. To solve the optimization problem, a significant number of authors have transformed the nonconvex nature of the problem into a convex one, achieved either by decomposing the original problem or without decomposing it. For solving the convex problem, different approaches have been utilized, such as Karush-Kuhn-Tucker (KKT) conditions, 0–1 integer programming problem, Lagrange dual decomposition, and the subgradient method. Additionally, several alternative methods, including greedy algorithms, approximate solutions, machine learning, heuristics, genetic algorithms, artificial fish swarm algorithms, and ϵ-bounded approximate algorithms, among others, have been employed to address these optimization challenges.

3   System Model

We are adopting a three-tier architecture for our MEC system, as depicted in Fig. 1. In this architecture, UE devices reside in the first layer, a cluster of base stations (DC) in the second layer, and a remote cloud operates in the third layer. To effectively manage the energy consumption of UE devices and adhere to task latency deadlines, we are incorporating DVFS-enabled UE devices [22], which enable us to control the CPU frequency [16]. The DCs in each of the BS that are part of a cluster cooperate with each other. Additionally, we have also considered the heterogeneity of MEC servers in terms of CPU capacity (in

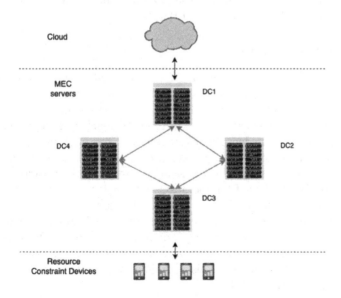

Fig. 1. System model

MIPS), memory size, and storage size. The UEs establish connections with the nearest base station through wireless communication links. These UE devices operate independently, giving them the flexibility to execute tasks locally or offload them to a remote server hosted in the base station. Consequently, MEC servers within these base stations receive tasks continuously from various UE devices.

The decision to adopt a 3-tier cooperative distributed architecture is grounded in two key factors. Firstly, the limited resource capacity of MEC servers compared to the central cloud necessitates a cooperative approach. Secondly, the increasing task sensitivity to latency in modern applications highlights the significance of an optimized cooperative architecture. By utilizing the resources of neighbouring MEC servers, we aim to meet latency deadlines, as the central cloud is often located far from the UE device. In situations where MEC servers in the nearest or neighbouring base stations cannot meet a task's resource requirements, we route the task to the cloud, assuming it possesses abundant computational resources. This 3-tier architecture achieves a balance between resource constraints, latency sensitivity, and resource availability, ensuring efficient task processing within latency requirements while optimizing resource utilization.

In each data center (BS), one of the nodes performs the coordinator function known as the coordinator node. The coordinator node ensures high availability, while the container for task execution is dynamically launched as needed. Periodically, every coordinator node updates its resource status to all other coordinators within the cluster. As part of its responsibilities, a coordinator node schedules a task to a compute node within its base station (DC) or forwards the task to another base station (DC). If a task cannot be executed in MEC, it will be forwarded to the remote cloud through a backhaul network. The set of base stations and UEs is denoted as B_n and W_n, respectively, with $n = 1, 2, 3, \cdots, n$.

4 Application Model

We consider an application comprising interdependent tasks, represented by a Directed Acyclic Graph (DAG) as the DAG representation is widely used in the literature to model various applications such as cognitive assistance [13], healthcare [11], data analytics [24] etc. In the DAG, each node represents a task, while the edges depict the dependencies between tasks. Each task in the DAG is characterized by a quadruplet $T_i = <d_i, c_i, IO_i, t_i^d>$, where d_i denotes the input data size, c_i indicates the CPU cycle requirement in million instructions (MI), IO_i represents the number of IO operations needed for the task, and t_i^d denotes the latency deadline. The application comes with a latency deadline of L_k^d. This deadline is distributed among all the tasks of that application (as explained in Sect. 9.2). To ensure a single terminal node in the application DAG when there are multiple terminal tasks, we create a dummy terminal task that depends on all the existing terminal nodes. This consolidation results in a single terminal node in each application DAG.

A scheduling plan for the DAG G is represented as $D_{i:n} = \delta1, \delta2, \delta3, \cdots, \delta_n$, where $n = |V|$ is the number of tasks, and δ_i indicates the offloading decision for task T_i. The decision variable $\delta_i = \{0, 1, 2, 3\}$, where 0 for local, 1 for the nearest BS, 2 for the neighbor BS, and 3 for the remote cloud execution. A task can be forwarded to another base station only once.

5   Energy Consumption Model for a UE

We adopt a power consumption model based on complementary metal-oxide semiconductor (CMOS) logic circuits [18] for the UE devices. Specifically, we focus on CMOS circuits-based UE devices, where the total power consumption consists of two main components: static and dynamic power consumption. Considering that dynamic power consumption significantly dominates the overall power usage [10, 16], we concentrate solely on it. The dynamic power consumption is directly related to the supply voltage and frequency, and since the frequency usually scales with the supply voltage, the processor's dynamic power consumption is expressed as $\rho_c = K.f^3$, where K is a proportional coefficient.

Let us consider a task in an application that takes an execution time of t when running on a CPU with a frequency of f_{max}. If the processor operates at a different frequency level f $(0 < f \leq f_{max})$, the execution time is defined as $t/\frac{f}{f_{max}}$. Thus, the dynamic power consumption during the task execution is defined by Eq. (1) as considered in [16].

$$E = \int_0^{t/\frac{f}{f_{max}}} \rho_c \, dt = K.t.f_{max}.f^2 = \omega.t.\lambda^2, \ where \ \lambda = \frac{f}{f_{max}} \tag{1}$$

where ω is a coefficient and λ is the relative processor speed for the CPU while running at frequency f.

6   Communication Model

Let B_w be the bandwidth between UE devices and the base station, and B_b be the bandwidth between two base stations. The backhaul network, facilitating task forwarding from a base station to the remote cloud, has a bandwidth of β_c. For wireless and wired links, we consider data rates R_u and R_p, respectively.

Let the latency to upload a task T_i from UEs to the nearest BS be T_i^u. The total latency T_i^{nb} for offloading a task to a neighbour base station will be the combination of task uploading latency T_i^u and the latency of forwarding a task to another BS. Similarly, T_i^{rc} is the latency of a task T_i when offloaded to the centralized remote cloud. It is the combination of latency of uploading tasks from UEs to BS and from BS to the remote cloud.

7   Computation Model

The task offloading decisions determine whether a task is executed locally at the UEs, at the Mobile Edge Computing (MEC) server, or at the remote cloud. Various computation models based on the task's offloading decision are elaborated in the following subsections.

7.1 Local Computation

During local task execution, the task utilizes the UE's local processing unit. Let f_l^k denote the computational capacity of the kth UE in million instructions per second (MIPS). Let IO_i^t be the time required for IO operations then local task execution time and the UE energy consumption for task T_i can be represented as $T_i^l = \frac{c_i}{f_l^k} + IO_i^t$ and $E_i^l = \alpha.T_i^l.\lambda^2$ respectively.

7.2 Remote Computation

When a task is offloaded by a UE device, it can be executed either in a MEC server or a remote central cloud. During task offloading, the UE device utilizes its processing unit to transfer the tasks to a remote server. As a result, the energy consumption of the UE is influenced by the CPU cycle required to upload the tasks to the remote server. Let T_i^{ul} represent the time taken by a UE device to offload a task to a remote server. The energy consumption for the offloaded task T_i can be expressed as $E_i^u = \alpha.T_i^u.\lambda^2$.

The latency computation model remains consistent for tasks executed at the nearest Base Station (BS), a remote BS, or in the cloud. If F_m^k and F_c^k represent the CPU capabilities of the kth MEC and the cloud servers then the latency at MEC and the cloud can be represented as in Eq. (2).

$$T_i^{mec} = \frac{c_i}{F_{m^k}} + IO_i^t , \quad T_i^c = \frac{c_i}{F_c^k} + IO_i^t \tag{2}$$

8 Problem Formulation

The primary goal is to minimize both the energy consumption of the UEs and the overall latency of the application. The total latency of a task T_i in a DAG for the application can be formulated using Eq. (3).

$$L_i = \frac{(1-\delta_i)(2-\delta_i)(3-\delta_i)}{6}T_i^l + \frac{\delta_i(2-\delta_i)(3-\delta_i)}{2}(T_i^u + T_i^{mec})$$
$$+ \frac{d_i(\delta_i-1)(3-\delta_i)}{2}(T_i^{nb} + T_i^{mec}) + \frac{\delta_i(\delta_i-1)(\delta_i-2)}{6}(T_i^{rc} + T_i^c) \tag{3}$$

The energy consumption for the UE remains constant regardless of whether a task is executed at the nearest Base Station (BS), a neighbouring BS, or the cloud, as the UE device always offloads the task to the nearest BS. Thus, the energy consumption of a task T_i can be expressed using Eq. (4) below.

$$E_i = \frac{(1-\delta_i)(2-\delta_i)(3-\delta_i)}{6}(E_i^l) + \frac{\delta_i(2-\delta_i)(3-\delta_i)}{2}(E_i^u)$$
$$+ \frac{d_i(\delta_i-1)(3-\delta_i)}{2}(E_i^u) + \frac{\delta_i(\delta_i-1)(\delta_i-2)}{6}(E_i^u) \tag{4}$$

The total latency and energy consumption of a UE for an application is represented as $L_{app} = L_{ft}$ and $E_{app} = \sum_{i=1}^n E_i$ respectively where the L_{ft}

is the completion time of the terminal task of an application. If there are N applications in the system, then the total energy consumption at UEs and the latency can be represented as in Eq. (5).

$$L_{tot} = \sum_{i=1}^{N} L_{app} \ , \ E_{tot} = \sum_{i=1}^{N} E_{app} \qquad (5)$$

The objective of the problem is to minimize the overall system cost, encompassing the total execution delay and UE energy consumption for all applications in the system. We express the total cost as a weighted sum of the total UE energy consumption and application latency. Thus, the minimization problem is represented as shown in Eq. (6) subject to the constraint defined in Equation (7).

$$minimize \ (AL_{tot} + BE_{tot}) \qquad (6)$$

$$\sum_{i=1}^{n} L_i \leq L_d \ , \ \sum_{i=1}^{n} c_i \leq F_l \ , \ c_i \leq F_m^i \ , \ \sum_{i=1}^{n} c_i \leq \sum_{i=1}^{B_i} \sum_{j=1}^{m} F_m^j \qquad (7)$$

The constraints presented in Eq. (7) apply to both the UE device and the MEC servers. The first constraint ensures that the total latency of an application must not surpass its latency deadline. The second constraint ensures that the total CPU cycle requirements of all the parallel tasks executing locally must not exceed the available CPU cycles of the UE. The third constraint guarantees that the CPU requirements for a task cannot exceed the available capacity of the MEC server. Lastly, the fourth constraint ensures that the total CPU cycle requirements of all tasks running in the MEC cluster at any given time must not surpass the total CPU capacity of the MEC cluster.

9   ELITE: The Task Offloading and Resource Allocation Strategy

The optimization problem stated in Eq. (6) is a challenging multi-objective mixed-integer programming (MIP) problem, proven to be NP-hard [31]. As a result, we propose an efficient heuristic algorithmic (Layered Scheduling Algorithm) approach to tackle this optimization problem. In the proposed strategy, we first rank the tasks of an application represented by a DAG for effective scheduling, as described in Sect. 9.1. Additionally, we compute the sub-deadline of all tasks within an application's DAG, using the total deadline for the entire application, as elaborated in Sect. 9.2

9.1   Task Ranking

We need to rank the tasks for scheduling and it is helpful in prioritizing multiple tasks that can be executed in parallel. Let CT_i^{nbs}, CT_i^{rbs}, and CT_i^c be the latency in worst case time for a task T_i if it executes in the nearest base station, remote base station, and remote cloud server respectively. So the rank of a task is calculated based on Eq. (8);

$$S_i^{avg} = \frac{CT_i^n bs + CT_i^r bs + CT_i^c}{3}, \quad T_i^{avg} = \frac{CT_i^m + S_i^{avg}}{2} \tag{8}$$
$$R(T_i) = T_i^{avg} + max(Pred_k T_k^{avg})$$

where $max(Pred_k T_k^{avg})$ represents the maximum of the average latency of all the predecessor tasks of T_i and CT_i^m is the local execution latency of task T_i.

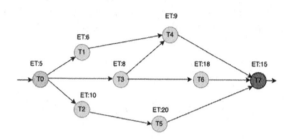

Fig. 2. An application DAG

9.2 Sub-deadline Calculation

In our approach, we divide the total latency deadline of an application and allocate sub-deadlines to its individual tasks. To achieve this, we compute the label-ratio ∂_l as in Eq. (9) and employ a modified version of the breadth-first traversal (MBFS) algorithm to assign ratios to each level in the DAG as depicted in Fig. 2. The label ratio signifies the maximum average execution time of tasks within a particular level. As tasks between levels can be executed in parallel, we determine the maximum waiting time for the next level based on the maximum latency of the previous level. Consequently, we assign equal sub-deadlines to all tasks within each level, taking into account the maximum average latency of tasks from the preceding level. The sub-deadline D_l of a task is calculated using Eq. (9), with D_{total} representing the total deadline of the application.

$$\partial_l = max_l(T_l^{avg}), \quad D_l = \frac{D_{total}}{\sum_{i=1}^l \partial_l} \partial_l \tag{9}$$

Let's consider the instance of level L1, encompassing three tasks: T1, T2, and T3. In accordance with the data presented in Fig. 2, the average execution times for T1, T2, and T3 are 6, 10, and 8 respectively. Consequently, the label ratio for level L1 becomes max(6, 10, 8), yielding 10. Analogously, the label ratios for L0, L2, and L3 are 5, 20, and 15 respectively. Utilizing Eq. (9), the sub-deadlines for tasks T1, T2, and T3 are calculated as $\frac{100*10}{(5+10+20+15)}$, resulting in 20. It's worth noting that the total deadline for the analyzed application is denoted as 100. The full calculation of the sub-deadline for the application represented by a DAG in Fig. 2 is given in Table 1.

Table 1. Sub deadline calculation

level	Tasks	Label ratio	Sub Deadline	Total Deadline
L0	T0	5	10	100
L1	T1, T2, T3	10	20	
L2	T4, T5, T6	20	40	
L3	T7	15	30	

9.3   Task Offloadability

We have categorized the tasks of a workflow into three categories as given below.

1. Remote Tasks: A task is called a remote task if it is compute-intensive or IO-intensive as described in Algorithm 2.
2. Local Tasks: Tasks that require the UE to interact directly with the environment such as mage capturing cannot be offloaded.
3. General Tasks: The third type of tasks can be executed either in UE devices or in remote servers, and we have the flexibility to schedule these tasks based on various parameters.

9.4   Layered Scheduling Algorithm

The layered scheduling algorithm involves two levels of scheduling algorithms: one operating at the UE and the other at the coordinator node of the MEC, hosted in the nearest base station.

Scheduling Algorithm at UE. The scheduling algorithm, outlined in Algorithm 1, handles the execution of an application on the UE device, that includes multiple tasks. The algorithm makes decisions to either schedule these tasks locally or offload them to the MEC server hosted in the nearest base station. Three queues are maintained in the algorithm: TaskPool, TaskReadyQueue, and TaskInProgress. Initially, the TaskPool contains all tasks (S_t) except for the entry task (T_{entry}) of the applications, while the entry tasks of all running applications at the UE are added to the TaskReadyQueue. The algorithm then selects one task from the TaskReadyQueue and schedules it either locally or offloaded to a remote server. Once a task is scheduled, whether locally or remotely, it is added to the TaskInProgress. The steps in the algorithm are summarized below.

Algorithm 1. Task Scheduling Algorithm at UE device

1: TaskInProgressl← ϕ
2: TaskPool← $S_t - T_{entry}$
3: $TaskReadyQueue \leftarrow T_{entry}$
4: **while** (TaskPool.size() > 0 or TaskReadyQueue.size() > 0 or TaskInProgress.size()> 0) **do**
5:    **while** $TaskReadyQueue.size() > 0$ **do**
6:       $Task_i \leftarrow$ dequeue from $TaskReadyQueue$
7:       **if** $Task_i$ is $remote$ **then**
8:          Offload the task to the nearest BS.
9:       **else if** $Task_i$ is $local$ **then**
10:          Schedule the task for local execution
11:       **else**
12:          $ET_i \leftarrow$ Worst-case execution time of the task in the MEC server.
13:          **if** $ET_i \leq$ Task deadline **then**
14:             Offload the tasks to the nearest BS.
15:          **else**
16:             Schedule the task for local execution
17:          **end if**
18:       **end if**
19:       TaskInProgress.$push(Task_i)$
20:    **end while**
21:    **for** $Task_j$ in $TaskInProgress$ **do**
22:       **if** $Task_j$ is $finished$ $executing$ **then**
23:          $ChildrenTasks_j \leftarrow$ get all children tasks of $Task_j$
24:          Sort the $ChildrenTasks_j$ based on the descending order of its rank
25:          **for** $k \leftarrow 0$ to $ChildrenTasks_j.size()$ **do**
26:             $child_k \leftarrow ChildrenTasks_j.get(i)$
27:             **if** All parent tasks of $child_k$ is finished executing **then**
28:                $TaskReadyQueue.Enqueue(child_k)$
29:                TaskPool.$Remove(child_k)$
30:             **end if**
31:          **end for**
32:          TaskInProgress.$remove(Task_j)$
33:       **end if**
34:    **end for**
35: **end while**

---

1. A task is offloaded to the nearest BS if it is a remote task.
2. A local task is scheduled for local execution.
3. A general tasks: Offload the task to the MEC server if the worst-case execution time of the task in the MEC server is less than the latency deadline or else schedule for local execution.

Upon completion of a task's execution, we iterate through all its child tasks. If all the parent tasks of a child task have also finished, we add the child tasks to the ReadyQueue and remove the current from the TaskPool and TaskExecutionProgressQueue.

Algorithm 2. Task Categorization Algorithm

Input: CPU time(CT_i), IO time (IO_i)
Output: Task category
$T_{tot} \leftarrow CT_i + IO_i$
if $\frac{CT_i}{T_{tot}} \geq 0.5$ **then**
    Return CPU-intensive
else if $\frac{IO_i}{T_{tot}} \geq 0.5$ **then**
    Return IO-intensive
else
    Return Normal
end if

Scheduling at MEC. The algorithm presented in Algorithm 3 is responsible for scheduling tasks to one of three locations: locally (nearest BS), neighbour BS, or a remote cloud. The coordinator node selects tasks from its task queue and checks if there is a suitable server in the current DC to execute the task. If a suitable server is found, the task is scheduled to the selected server. If no suitable server is available in the current DC, the coordinator node looks for a suitable server in the neighbouring DC. To determine the appropriate neighbour DC, we sort the neighbour DCs based on Euclidean distance and try to find the best-suited server, starting with the closest neighbour. If no suitable server is present in the MEC cluster, the task is forwarded to the central cloud. To find the best server in a particular DC we have used the following steps:

1. Enumerate the servers that have available CPU cores and a task latency less than the task deadline. If the list is not empty, return the server that executes a task with minimum latency.
2. Enumerate the servers where the task completion time is within the task deadline limit. If the list is not empty, return the server that executes a task with minimum latency.

Algorithm 3. Task Scheduling Algorithm at MEC coordinator node

---

function $GetFeasibleServer(serverList, Task_i)$
    for server in $serverList$ **do**
        $latency \leftarrow$ calculateLatency(server, $Task_i$)
        if $latency <=$ task deadline **then**
            return server
        end if
    end for
end function
function $GetBestServer$(Datacenter dc, $Task_i$)
    $svrsWithFreeCore \leftarrow$ get all servers with free available cores.
    $server \leftarrow GetFeasibleServer(svrsWithFreeCore, Task_i)$
    if $server \mathrel{!=} \phi$ **then**
        return server
    end if
    $otherServers \leftarrow$ get all servers with a free available core.
    $server \leftarrow GetFeasibleServer(otherServesr, Task_i)$
    if $server \mathrel{!=} \phi$ **then**
        return server
    end if
end function
dc $\leftarrow$ nearest DC
$server \leftarrow GetBestServer(dc, Task_i)$
if $server \mathrel{!} = \phi$ **then**
    $scheduleTask(Task_i, server)$
else
    $neighborDCs \leftarrow$ get all the neighbour MEC DCs in the cluster
    $neighborDCs \leftarrow$ sort $neighborDCs$ on the distance from the current DC
in ascending order.
    for dc in $neighborDCs$ **do**
        $server \leftarrow GetBestServer(dc)$
        if $server \mathrel{!} = \phi$ **then**
            $scheduleTask(Task_i, server)$
            Break
        end if
    end for
end if

---

10   Simulation and Result Analyses

Our proposed strategy was simulated using the PureEdgeSim simulator [21]. The simulation area covered a 2000 × 2000 square meter space, containing three edge data centers (DCs), each with three physical servers. We incorporated three types of edge devices in the simulation, namely smartphones, Raspberry Pi, and laptops. Each edge device is connected to its nearest edge DC based on Euclidean distance. To facilitate the simulation, we utilized the Zenodo dataset [3], which comprises 50,000 jobs containing 1.3 million tasks. This dataset represents various applications represented by DAGs generated by IoT nodes.

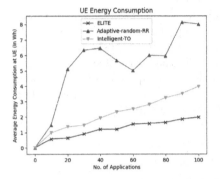

Fig. 3. UE Energy Consumption

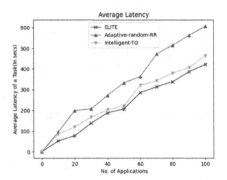

Fig. 4. Average Task Latency

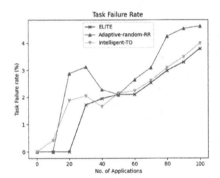

Fig. 5. Task Failure Rate

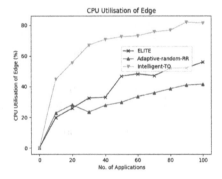

Fig. 6. Edge CPU Utilization

In order to assess the performance of our proposed layered algorithm, we conducted a benchmark comparison with two existing algorithms: "Intelligent task offloading for dependent tasks" presented by Chen et al. in [4] and the "Adaptive Random Round Robin Algorithm" described in Sect. 10.1.

10.1   State-of-Art Approach

1. **Intelligent task offloading for dependent tasks** [4]: In their work, researchers propose an energy and latency-optimized task offloading strategy for dependent tasks. They utilize a two-step process: organizing tasks

into layers based on dependencies using a layered algorithm and employing a cost function that considers task latency and UE device energy consumption for making offloading decisions. This approach allows for efficient task execution, choosing between local execution and offloading to a remote server based on the most favourable cost considerations.

2. **Adaptive Random Round Robin Scheme:** We adopted the same system model described in the ELITE algorithm except for the DVFS-enabled UE device. We offloaded all CPU-intensive and IO-intensive tasks to the MEC server, while normal tasks were randomly scheduled for either MEC execution or local execution. For MEC DC selection, we employed a Round-Robin algorithm, and the server selection within the DC was done randomly. The task categorization is the same as the ELITE algorithm.

Table 2. Simulation Parameters

Iteration	Applications	Total Tasks	UE devices
1	10	481	5
2	20	903	10
3	30	1314	15
4	40	1746	20
5	50	2194	25
6	60	2629	30
7	70	2973	35
8	80	3387	40
9	90	3855	45
10	100	4294	50

10.2 Results and Analyses

We performed the experiment using the parameters specified in Table 2. In Fig. 3, we plotted the average energy consumption of UE devices, which increases as the number of applications rises. This behaviour is attributed to the growing number of tasks executed on UE devices. Notably, our proposed layered algorithm outperforms the state-of-the-art by a factor of 2× in terms of UE energy consumption. This improvement can be attributed to two main factors: Firstly, our system model incorporates dynamic voltage and frequency scaling (DVFS) in UE devices, and secondly, our offloading decision algorithm demonstrates superior performance compared to others.

In Fig. 4, we presented the average latency of a task, which shows an increasing trend with the growing number of tasks. This increase is primarily due to the longer queue times experienced by both UE and MEC servers as the task load rises. Notably, our proposed model exhibits approximately 10% lower latency than the state-of-the-art algorithm. This improved performance can be attributed to two key factors: Firstly, our superior task offloading algorithm, and secondly, the resource allocation algorithm we introduced, which effectively reduces task latency by minimizing task waiting times.

As shown in Fig. 5, the task failure rate increases with the number of tasks, as the queue time for each task also increases, leading to task failures due to higher latency, considering the latency deadline of each task. In this aspect, our proposed layered algorithm outperforms the benchmarking algorithm. The CPU utilization of the MEC server is also plotted in Fig. 6, and it increases with the number of tasks. The results indicate that the average edge CPU utilization of the state-of-the-art model is approximately 55% higher than that of our proposed algorithm.

11   Conclusion

This research paper addresses the challenge of minimizing the latency of the applications and energy consumption of UE devices by employing dependent task modelling. Our proposed 3-tier system model incorporates a cluster of heterogeneous MEC servers in the MEC layer. In our model, we have considered DVFS-enabled UE devices, which aid in reducing their energy consumption by dynamically adjusting the CPU operating frequency. To optimize the problem, we formulate it as a bi-objective mixed integer programming (MIP), which is known to be NP-hard. To overcome this complexity, we introduce a near-optimal heuristic solution strategy that efficiently addresses both task offloading and resource allocation problems. Tasks are classified into local, remote, and general categories, with further subcategories based on their characteristics such as CPU-intensive, IO-intensive, and normal tasks. Our simulation results demonstrate the superior efficiency and performance of our approach compared to existing benchmarking algorithms.

References

1. Alameddine, H.A., Sharafeddine, S., et al.: Dynamic task offloading and scheduling for low-latency IoT services in multi-access edge computing. IEEE J. Sel. Areas Commun. **37**(3), 668–682 (2019)
2. Alfakih, T., Hassan, M.M., et al.: Task offloading and resource allocation for mobile edge computing by deep reinforcement learning based on SARSA. IEEE Access **8**, 54074–54084 (2020)
3. Ali Rezaee, S.A.: Jobs (DAG workflow) and tasks dataset with near 50k job instances and 1.3 millions of tasks (2020). https://doi.org/10.5281/zenodo.4667690
4. Chen, J., Leng, Y., Huang, J.: An intelligent approach of task offloading for dependent services in mobile edge computing. J. Cloud Comput. **12**(1), 1–14 (2023)

5. Chen, J., Chang, Z., et al.: Resource allocation and computation offloading for multi-access edge computing with fronthaul and backhaul constraints. IEEE Trans. Veh. Technol. **70**(8), 8037–8049 (2021)
6. Chouhan, S.: Energy optimal partial computation offloading framework for mobile devices in multi-access edge computing. In: International Conference on Software, Telecommunications and Computer Networks (SoftCOM), pp. 1–6. IEEE (2019)
7. Deka, V., Islam, A., Ghose, M.: Cloud-assisted dynamic and cooperative content caching in mobile edge computing. In: IEEE 19th India Council International Conference (INDICON), pp. 1–6 (2022)
8. Dinh, T.Q., Tang, J., et al.: Offloading in mobile edge computing: task allocation and computational frequency scaling. IEEE Trans. Commun. **65**(8), 3571–3584 (2017)
9. Ghose, M., Kaur, S., Sahu, A.: Scheduling real time tasks in an energy-efficient way using VMS with discrete compute capacities. Computing **102**(1), 263–294 (2020)
10. Ghose, M., Sahu, A., Karmakar, S.: Urgent point aware energy-efficient scheduling of tasks with hard deadline on virtualized cloud system. Sustain. Comput.: Inform. Syst. **28**, 100416 (2020)
11. Gia, T.N., Jiang, M., et al.: Fog computing in healthcare internet of things: a case study on ECG feature extraction. In: IEEE International Conference on Computer and Information Technology; Ubiquitous Computing and Communications; Dependable, Autonomic and Secure Computing; Pervasive Intelligence and Computing, pp. 356–363 (2015)
12. Guo, H., Liu, J., Zhang, J.: Computation offloading for multi-access mobile edge computing in ultra-dense networks. IEEE Commun. Mag. **56**(8), 14–19 (2018)
13. Ha, K., Chen, Z., et al.: Towards wearable cognitive assistance. In: Proceedings of the 12th Annual International Conference on Mobile Systems, Applications, and Services, MobiSys 2014, pp. 68–81. Association for Computing Machinery, New York (2014)
14. Islam, A., Debnath, A., et al.: A survey on task offloading in multi-access edge computing. J. Syst. Architect. **118**, 102225 (2021)
15. Ji, T., Luo, C., et al.: Energy-efficient computation offloading in mobile edge computing systems with uncertainties. IEEE Trans. Wirel. Commun. **21**, 5717–5729 (2022)
16. Kim, K.H., Beloglazov, A., et al.: Power-aware provisioning of virtual machines for real-time cloud services. Concurr. Comput.: Pract. Exp. **23**(13), 1491–1505 (2011)
17. Kuang, Z., Ma, Z., et al.: Cooperative computation offloading and resource allocation for delay minimization in mobile edge computing. J. Syst. Architect. **118**, 102167 (2021)
18. Lee, Y.C., Zomaya, A.Y.: Energy conscious scheduling for distributed computing systems under different operating conditions. IEEE Trans. Parallel Distrib. Syst. **22**(8), 1374–1381 (2010)
19. Liao, Z., Peng, J.O.: Adaptive offloading in mobile-edge computing for ultra-dense cellular networks based on genetic algorithm. J. Cloud Comput. **10**(1), 1–16 (2021)
20. Liu, B., Xu, X., et al.: Task scheduling with precedence and placement constraints for resource utilization improvement in multi-user MEC environment. J. Syst. Architect. **114**, 101970 (2021)
21. Mechalikh, C., Taktak, H., Moussa, F.: PureEdgeSim: a simulation framework for performance evaluation of cloud, edge and mist computing environments. Comput. Sci. Inf. Syst. **18**(1), 43–66 (2021)

22. Mokaripoor, P., Hosseini Shirvani, M.: A state of the art survey on DVFs techniques in cloud computing environment. J. Multidiscip. Eng. Sci. Technol **3**(5), 4740–4743 (2016)
23. Ranaweera, P., Jurcut, A.D., Liyanage, M.: Realizing multi-access edge computing feasibility: security perspective. In: IEEE Conference on Standards for Communications and Networking (CSCN), pp. 1–7. IEEE (2019)
24. Reza, H., Diyanat, A., et al.: MIST: fog-based data analytics scheme with cost-efficient resource provisioning for IoT crowdsensing applications. J. Netw. Comput. Appl. **82**, 152–165 (2017)
25. Song, F., Xing, H., et al.: Offloading dependent tasks in multi-access edge computing: a multi-objective reinforcement learning approach. Futur. Gener. Comput. Syst. **128**, 333–348 (2022)
26. Tran, T.X., Pompili, D.: Joint task offloading and resource allocation for multi-server mobile-edge computing networks. IEEE Trans. Veh. Technol. **68**(1), 856–868 (2018)
27. Vu, T.T., Van Huynh, N., et al.: Offloading energy efficiency with delay constraint for cooperative mobile edge computing networks. In: 2018 IEEE Global Communications Conference (GLOBECOM), pp. 1–6. IEEE (2018)
28. Wang, J., Hu, J., Min, G., et al.: Computation offloading in multi-access edge computing using a deep sequential model based on reinforcement learning. IEEE Commun. Mag. **57**(5), 64–69 (2019)
29. Wang, L., Deng, X., et al.: Microservice-oriented service placement for mobile edge computing in sustainable internet of vehicles. IEEE Trans. Intell. Transp. Syst. (2023)
30. Yu, H., Wang, Q., Guo, S.: Energy-efficient task offloading and resource scheduling for mobile edge computing. In: 2018 IEEE International Conference on Networking, Architecture and Storage (NAS), pp. 1–4. IEEE (2018)
31. Zhang, J., Liu, C., et al.: A survey for solving mixed integer programming via machine learning. arXiv preprint arXiv:2203.02878 (2022)

Parking Problem by Oblivious Mobile Robots in Infinite Grids

Abhinav Chakraborty[1]([✉]) and Krishnendu Mukhopadhyaya[2]

[1] Department of Computer Science and Engineering, Institute of Technical Education and Research, Siksha O Anusandhan University, Bhubaneswar, Odisha, India
`abhinav.chakraborty06@gmail.com`
[2] Advanced Computing and Microelectronics Unit, Indian Statistical Institute, Kolkata, India

Abstract. In this paper, the parking problem of a swarm of mobile robots has been studied. The robots are deployed at the nodes of an infinite grid, which has a subset of prefixed nodes marked as *parking nodes*. Each parking node p_i has a capacity of k_i which is given as input and equals the maximum number of robots a parking node can accommodate. As a solution to the parking problem, robots need to partition themselves into groups so that each parking node contains a number of robots that are equal to the capacity of the node in the final configuration. It is assumed that the number of robots in the initial configuration represents the sum of the capacities of the parking nodes. The robots are assumed to be autonomous, anonymous, homogeneous, identical and oblivious. They operate under an asynchronous scheduler. They neither have any agreement on the coordinate axes nor do they agree on a common chirality. All the initial configurations for which the problem is unsolvable have been identified. A deterministic distributed algorithm has been proposed for the remaining configurations, ensuring the solvability of the problem.

Keywords: Distributed Computing · Mobile Robots · Look-Compute-Move Cycle · Asynchronous · Infinite Grid · Parking Nodes

1 Introduction

Robot swarms are groups of generic mobile robots that can collaboratively execute complex tasks. Such systems of mobile robots are assumed to be simple and inexpensive and offer several advantages over traditional single-robot systems, such as scalability, robustness and versatility. A series of research on the algorithmic aspects of distributed coordination of robot swarms has been reported in the field of distributed computing (see [12] for a comprehensive survey). In the traditional framework of swarm robotics, the robots are assumed to be anonymous (no unique identifiers), autonomous (there is no centralized control), identical (no unique identifiers), homogeneous (each robot executes the same deterministic

© The Author(s), under exclusive license to Springer Nature Switzerland AG 2024
S. Devismes et al. (Eds.): ICDCIT 2024, LNCS 14501, pp. 68–84, 2024.
https://doi.org/10.1007/978-3-031-50583-6_5

distributed algorithm) and oblivious (no memory of past information) computational entities. The robots are represented as points in the Euclidean plane. They do not have access to any global coordinate system. However, each robot has its own local coordinate system, with the origin representing the current position of the robot. The robots do not have an explicit means of communication, i.e., they are assumed to be silent. They are disoriented, i.e., they neither agree on a common coordinate axes nor do they have any agreement on chirality. Each robot is equipped with visibility sensors, by which they can perceive the deployment region.

In this paper, the deployment region of the robots is assumed to be an infinite square grid, which represents a natural discretization of the plane. The robots are deployed at the nodes of the input grid graph. The graph also consists of some prefixed grid nodes, designated as parking nodes. When a robot becomes active, it operates according to the *Look-Compute-Move* cycle. A robot takes a snapshot of the entire graph, including the positions of the other robots and parking nodes in the *Look* phase. Based on the snapshot, it computes a destination node in the *Compute* phase according to a deterministic algorithm, where the destination node might be its current position as well. Finally, it moves towards the destination in the *Move* phase. In this paper, we have considered the most general model, which is the asynchronous model ($\mathcal{ASYNC}$). In this setting, there is no common notion of time, and all the robots are activated independently. Each of the Look, Compute and Move phases has a finite but unpredictable duration. In the initial configuration, it has been assumed that the robots are placed at the distinct nodes of the grid graph. During the look phase, the robots can perceive the parking nodes using their visibility sensors. Each parking node has a capacity, which is subjected to a constraint that it can accommodate a maximum number of robots equal to its capacity. The capacity of a parking node is given as an input to each robot. For simplicity, we have assumed that the number of robots in the initial configuration is equal to the sum of the capacities of the parking nodes. In this paper, we have assumed that the robots have *global-strong multiplicity detection capability*. This means the robots are able to determine the exact number of robots that make up the multiplicity in each node. It has been proved later that the parking problem is unsolvable if the robots do not have such capabilities.

1.1   Motivation

The fundamental motivation behind studying the parking problem is twofold. Firstly, the parking problem can be viewed as a special case of the partitioning problem [11], which requires the robots to divide themselves into m groups, each consisting of k robots while converging into a small area. Unlike the partitioning problem, the parking problem requires that each parking node must contain robots exactly equal to its given capacity in the final configuration. However, the capacities of the parking nodes may be different. Moreover, if the capacities of each of the parking nodes are assumed to be k, i.e., they are equal in the initial configuration; the problem is reduced to the k-epf problem [3], which is a generalized version of the embedded pattern formation problem, where each fixed point contains exactly k robots in the final configuration. Secondly, in the traditional models, the robots are assumed to be points that can move freely on the plane. The robots are assumed to move with high accuracy and by infinitesimal distance in the continuous domain. Even if the area of robot deployment is small, a dimensionless robot can move without causing any collision. In practice, it may not always be possible to perform such infinitesimal movements with infinite precision. However, in our paper, the robots are deployed at the nodes of an infinite grid. The movements of the robots are restricted along the grid lines, and a robot can move toward one of its neighbors at any instant of time. The restrictions imposed by the grid model on the movements of the robots make it challenging to design collision-less algorithms, as opposed to the movement of the robots in a continuous environment. In addition to the theoretical benefits, the parking nodes can also be seen as base stations or charging stations with some allowable capacities.

1.2 Related Works

Most of the theoretical studies on swarm robotics have been concentrated on *arbitrary formation problem* and *gathering* under different settings. The Arbitrary Pattern Formation or $\mathcal{APF}$ is a fundamental coordination problem in Swarm Robotics, where the robots are required to form any specific but arbitrary geometric pattern given as input. The study of $\mathcal{APF}$ was initiated in [16]. The authors characterized the class of formable patterns by using the notion of symmetricity, which is essentially the order of the cyclic group that acts on the initial configuration. The $\mathcal{APF}$ was first studied in the $\mathcal{ASYNC}$ by Flocchini et al. [13], where the robots are assumed to be oblivious. While all the previous studies considered the problem with unlimited visibility, Yamauchi et al. [17] studied the problem where the robots have limited visibility. Cicerone et al. [7] studied the $\mathcal{APF}$ problem without assuming common chirality among the robots. Bose et al. [4] were the first to study the problem in a grid-based terrain. D'Angelo et al. [9], studied the gathering problem on finite grids. Stefano et al. studied the optimal gathering problem in infinite grids [15]. In this paper, they proposed an optimal deterministic algorithm that minimizes the total distance traveled by all the robots. The concept of fixed points was first introduced by Fujinaga et al. [14] on the Euclidean plane. In this paper, the *landmark* covering problem was studied. The problem requires that each robot must attain a configuration where all the robots must occupy a single fixed point or landmark. They propose an algorithm based on the assumption that the robots agree on a common chirality. The proposed algorithm minimizes the total distance traveled by all the robots. In [8], Cicerone et al. studied the *embedded pattern formation* problem without assuming any common chirality among the robots. The problem necessitates a distributed algorithm in which each robot must occupy a unique fixed point within a finite amount of time. The *k-circle formation problem* [3,10] has been studied in the setting where the robots agree on the directions and orientations of the Y- axis and on the disoriented setting. Given a positive integer

k, the *k-circle formation problem* asks a swarm of mobile robots to form disjoint circles. Each of these circles must be centered at one of the pre-fixed points on the plane. Each circle must contain a total of k robots at distinct locations on the circumference of the circles. Bhagat et al. [3] also studied the *k- epf problem* in the continuous domain, which is a generalized version of the embedded pattern formation problem. This problem necessitates the arrival and retention of exactly k robots at each fixed point. Cicerone et al. [6] studied a variant of the gathering problem, where each robot must gather at one of the prefixed meeting points. The problem was defined as *gathering on meeting points* problem. The authors proposed a deterministic algorithm that minimizes the total distance traveled by all the robots and minimizes the maximum distance traveled by a single robot. *Gathering over meeting nodes* problem was studied by Bhagat et al. [1,2]. In this problem, the robots are deployed on the nodes of an infinite square grid, which has a subset of nodes marked as meeting nodes. Each robot must gather at one of the prefixed meeting nodes within a finite amount of time.

1.3 Our Contribution

This paper considers the parking problem over an infinite grid. The robots are deployed at the nodes of an infinite grid, which also consists of some prefixed parking nodes. Each parking node p_i has a capacity k_i, which is the maximum number of robots it can accommodate at any moment of time. We assume that the number of robots n is equal to $\sum_{i=1}^{m} k_i$, where m is the total number of parking nodes. We have characterized all the initial configurations and the values of k_i for which the problem is unsolvable. For the remaining configurations, a deterministic algorithm has been proposed that ensures the solvability of the problem.

2 Models and Definitions

2.1 Models

The robots are assumed to be dimensionless, anonymous, autonomous, identical, homogeneous and oblivious. The robots are assumed to be disoriented, i.e., they neither have any agreement on the coordinate axes nor have any agreement on a common chirality. They do not have an explicit means of communication, i.e., they are assumed to be silent. Let $P = (\mathbb{Z}, E')$ denote the infinite path graph with the vertex set V corresponding to the set of integers $\mathbb{Z}$ and the edge set is denoted by the ordered pair $E' = \{(i, i+1)|i \in \mathbb{Z}\}$. Let $\mathcal{R} = \{r_1, r_2 \ldots r_n\}$ denote the set of robots that are deployed at the nodes of G, where G is the input infinite grid graph defined as the usual *Cartesian Product* of the graph $P \times P$. Let $r_i(t)$ denote the node occupied by the robot $r_i \in \mathcal{R}$ at time t. Assume that $\mathcal{R}(t)$ denotes the set of all such distinct nodes occupied by the robots in $\mathcal{R}$ at time t. Since the robots are deployed at the nodes of an infinite square grid, they have an agreement on a common measure of unit distance.

The input grid graph also comprises some prefixed nodes designated as *parking nodes*. Let $\mathcal{P} = \{p_1, p_2, ..., p_m\}$ denote the set of parking positions. In the initial configuration, the parking nodes are located at the distinct nodes of the grid. A robot may be deployed at one of the parking nodes in the initial configuration. The movements of the robots are restricted along the grid lines. At any instant of time, a robot can move only to one of its four neighboring nodes. The movement of the robot is assumed to be instantaneous, i.e., the robot can be observed only at the nodes of the graph and not on the edges. In other words, no robot can be seen while moving. A robot's vision is assumed to be global, meaning that each robot is equipped with visibility sensors that allow it to observe the whole grid graph.

2.2   Terminologies and Definitions

- **Distance between two nodes:** Let $d(u, v)$ denote the distance between two nodes u and v.
- **Capacity of a parking node:** The *capacity* of a parking node given as an input is defined as the maximum number of robots the parking node can accommodate. A parking node is said to be *saturated* if it contains exactly the number of robots equal to its capacity. A parking node is said to be *unsaturated* if it is not saturated. Let $\mu : V \rightarrow \mathbb{N} \cup \{0\}$ be defined as a function, where:

$$\mu(v) = \begin{cases} 0 & \text{if } v \text{ is not a parking node} \\ capacity\ of\ the\ parking\ node & \text{otherwise} \end{cases}$$

  In the initial configuration, let k_i be the capacity of a parking node p_i, $\forall i = 1, 2, \ldots, m$.
- **Symmetry of a configuration $C(t)$:** Two graphs $G_1 = (V_{G_1}, E_{G_1})$ and $G_2 = (V_{G_2}, E_{G_2})$ are said to be isomorphic if there exists a bijection $\phi : V_{G_1} \rightarrow V_{G_2}$ such that any two nodes $u, v \in V_{G_1}$ are adjacent in G_1 if and only if $\phi(u), \phi(v) \in V_{G_2}$ are adjacent in G_2. An automorphism on a graph G is a permutation of its nodes mapping edges to edges and non-edges to non-edges. Let λ_t be defined as a function that denotes the number of robots residing on v at time t. Without any ambiguity, we denote the function λ_t by λ. $C(t) = (\mathcal{R}(t), \mathcal{P}, \lambda, \mu)$ denotes the *system configuration* at any time t. An automorphism of a graph can be extended to the automorphism of a configuration. Two configurations are said to be isomorphic if there exists an *automorphism* ϕ of the input grid graph such that $\lambda(v) = \lambda(\phi(v))$ and $\mu(v) = \mu(\phi(v))$, for all $v \in V$. The set of all automorphisms of a configuration forms a group which is denoted by $Aut(C(t), \lambda, \mu)$. If $|Aut(C(t), \lambda, \mu)| = 1$, then the configuration is asymmetric. Otherwise, the configuration is said to be symmetric. We assume that the infinite grid is embedded in the *Cartesian plane*. As a result, a grid can admit only three types of automorphism and combinations of them, *translation*: defined by the shifting of the nodes to the same extent, *reflection*: defined by the line of reflection axes and *rotation*:

defined by the angle of rotation and the center of rotation. The reflection axis can be horizontal, vertical or diagonal. It can either pass through the nodes or edges of the grid. If a configuration admits rotational symmetry, then the center of rotation can be either a node, the center of an edge or the center of the area surrounded by four nodes. The angle of rotation can be either 90° or 180°. Since the number of occupied nodes is finite, a translation symmetry is not admissible. Let MER be the *minimum enclosing grid* containing all the occupied nodes of $C(t)$. Assume that the dimension of MER is $a \times b$. The number of grid edges on a side of MER is used to define its length.

- **View:** Starting from a corner of MER, scan the entire grid in a direction parallel to the width of the rectangle. While scanning the grid, we associate the pair $(\lambda(v), \mu(v))$ to each node v that the string encounters. Similarly, we can define the string associated with the same corner and encounter the nodes of the grid in the direction parallel to the length of the grid. Consider the eight senary strings of length ab that are associated with the corners of MER, with two senary strings defined for each corner of MER. Let the two strings defined for a corner i be denoted by s_{ij} and s_{ik}.

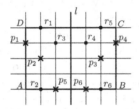

Fig. 1. The configuration is symmetric with respect to l. The crosses represent parking nodes and the black circles represent robot positions

If MER is a non-square rectangle, we can distinguish between the two strings associated with a given corner by looking at the string that runs parallel to the side with the shortest length. Consider any particular corner i of MER. Assume that $|ij| < |ik|$. We consider the direction parallel to ij as the *string direction* associated to i. We define $s_i = s_{ij}$ as the *string representation* associated to the corner i. The direction parallel to the larger side is defined as the *non-string direction* associated to the corner i. In the case of a square grid, between the two strings associated to a corner, the *string representation* is defined as the larger lexicographic string, i.e., $s_i = max(s_{ij}, s_{ik})$, where the maximum is defined according to the lexicographic ordering of the strings. If the configuration is asymmetric, we will always get a unique largest lexicographic string. Without loss of generality, let s_i be the largest lexicographic string among all the strings associated to the corners. Then we refer to i as the *key corner*. If the configuration is asymmetric, the robots can be ordered according to the key corner and the string direction. A *non-key corner* is defined as one that is not a key corner. In Fig. 1, assume that the capacity of each parking node is 1. The lexicographic string associated with the corners C and D are $s_{CB} = s_{DA} = ((0,0), (0,1), (0,0), (0,0), (0,0), (1,0), (0,0),$ $(0,1), (0,0), (1,0), (0,0), (1,0), (0,0), (0,0), (0,1), (0,0), (0,0), (0,0), (0,0), (0,0),$ $(0,0), (1,0), (0,0), (0,0), (0,1), (1,0), (0,0), (0,1), (0,0), (1,0), (0,0), (0,1), (0,0),$ $(0,0), (0,0))$. The strings $s_{CB} = s_{DA}$ are the maximum lexicographic strings associated and hence C and D are the key corners. The *configuration view* of a node is defined as the tuple (d', x), where d' denotes the distance of a node from the key corner in the string direction and x denotes the type of the node, i.e., x is either an empty node, parking node or a robot position.

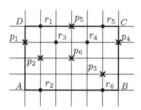

Fig. 2. Figure highlighting the definition of leading corner.

- **Symmetricity of the set** $\mathcal{P}$: We may define the symmetry of the set $\mathcal{P}$ in the same way as we define the symmetry of a configuration. The smallest grid-aligned rectangle that includes all the parking nodes is denoted as $M_{\mathcal{P}}$. We can define a string α_i similar to s_i. The only difference is that each node v is associated with $\mu(v)$ instead of the pair $(\lambda(v), \mu(v))$. If the parking nodes are asymmetric, a unique lexicographic largest string α_i always exists. If the parking nodes are not asymmetric, then the parking nodes are said to be symmetric. The corner with which the lexicographic largest string α_i is associated is defined as the *leading corner*. In Fig. 2, assume that the capacity of $p_1 = p_2 = p_3 = 3$ and $p_4 = p_5 = p_6 = 2$, $\alpha_{DA} = 03000003000000202000000000003002000$ is the largest lexicographic string among the $\alpha_i's$ and hence we have D as the leading corner. According to this definition of symmetricity of the set $\mathcal{P}$, the parking nodes that are located in the symmetric positions must have equal capacities.

Definition 1. *Let $C(0)$ be any given initial configuration. A parking node p_i is said to have a higher order than the parking node p_j if it appears after p_j in the string representation α_k, associated to some leading corner k of MER. Similarly, a robot r_i has a higher order or has a higher configuration view than r_j if it appears after r_j in the string representation s_k, associated to some key corner k of MER.*

3   Problem Definition and Impossibility Results

3.1   Problem Definition

Let $C(t) = (\mathcal{R}(t), \mathcal{P}, \lambda, \mu)$ denote the system configuration at any time t. Each parking node p_i has a capacity k_i. For each parking node p_i, the capacity k_i is given as an input. The number of robots is assumed to be equal to $\sum_{i=1}^{m} k_i$, where m is the total number of parking nodes. In an initial configuration, all the robots occupy distinct nodes of the grid. The goal of the parking problem is to transform any initial configuration at some time $t > 0$ into a configuration such that each parking node p_i is saturated, i.e., p_i contains exactly k_i robots on it and any robot taking a snapshot in the look phase at time t will decide not to move.

3.2   Partitioning of the Initial Configurations

All the initial configurations can be partitioned into the following disjoint classes.

1. $\mathcal{I}_1$: The parking nodes are asymmetric (Fig. 2).
2. $\mathcal{I}_2$: The parking nodes are symmetric with respect to a unique line of symmetry l. This class of configurations can be further partitioned into:
   $\mathcal{I}_{21}$: $C(t)$ is asymmetric (In Fig. 3(a), if the capacity of each parking node is the same, i.e., 1, the configuration is asymmetric with the parking nodes symmetric with respect to l).

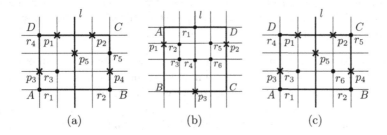

Fig. 3. Examples of $\mathcal{I}_{21}$, $\mathcal{I}_{221}$ and $\mathcal{I}_{223}$ configuration

   $\mathcal{I}_{22}$: $C(t)$ is symmetric with respect to l. This can be further partitioned into the following disjoint classes: (1) $\mathcal{I}_{221}$: There exists at least one robot position on l (In Fig. 3(b), with the assumption that the capacity of each parking node is 2, $C(t)$ is symmetric with respect to l with robots r_1 and r_4 on l). (2) $\mathcal{I}_{222}$: There does not exist any robot position on l. Also, there are no parking nodes on l. (3) $\mathcal{I}_{223}$: There does not exist any robot position on l, but there exists at least one parking node on l (In Fig. 3(c), if the capacity of each parking node not on l is 1, $C(t)$ is symmetric with respect to l and there exists parking node p_5 at l with capacity 2).
3. $\mathcal{I}_3$: The parking nodes are symmetric with respect to rotational symmetry, with c as the center of rotational symmetry. This class of configurations can be further partitioned into:
   $\mathcal{I}_{31}$: $C(t)$ is asymmetric (In Fig. 4(a) if the capacity of each parking node is 2, $C(t)$ is asymmetric with the parking nodes being symmetric with respect to rotational symmetry).

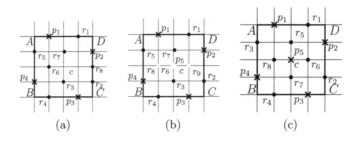

Fig. 4. Examples of $\mathcal{I}_{31}$ configuration, $\mathcal{I}_{321}$ configuration and $\mathcal{I}_{323}$ configuration.

$\mathcal{I}_{32}$: $C(t)$ is symmetric with respect to c. This can be further partitioned into the following disjoint classes: (1) $\mathcal{I}_{321}$: There exists a robot position on c (In Fig. 4(b), if the capacities of parking nodes p_1, p_2, p_3 and p_4 equal 1 and the capacity of the parking node p_5 equals 5, $C(t)$ is symmetric with respect to rotational symmetry. The robot r_6 is at the parking node p_5). (2) $\mathcal{I}_{322}$: There does not exist a robot position or parking node on c. (3) $\mathcal{I}_{323}$: There exists a parking node on c, but no robot on c (In Fig. 4(c) if the capacities of the parking nodes p_1, p_2, p_3 and p_4 equal 1 and the capacity of the parking node p_5 equals 4, $C(t)$ is symmetric with respect to rotational symmetry, with a parking node p_5 on c).

In the remainder of the paper, we assume that l is the line of symmetry if the parking nodes admit a single line of symmetry. If the parking nodes admit rotational symmetry, then c is the center of rotational symmetry. We also assume that if the parking nodes admit rotational symmetry, then l and l' are perpendicular lines passing through c, which divide the grid into four quadrants.

3.3   Impossibility Results

Lemma 1. *Let $\mathcal{A}$ be any algorithm for the parking problem in infinite grids. If there exists an execution of $\mathcal{A}$ such that the configuration $C(t)$ contains a robot multiplicity at a node that is not a parking node, then $\mathcal{A}$ cannot solve the parking problem.*

This lemma ensures that during the execution of any algorithm that solves the parking problem, the robots must perform a collision-less movement at all stages of the algorithm. Suppose the robots are oblivious and not endowed with global-strong multiplicity detection capability. In that case, they cannot detect whether exactly the k_i number of robots reaches the parking node p_i. We formalize the result in the following lemma:

Lemma 2. *Without the global-strong multiplicity detection capability of the robots, the parking problem is unsolvable.*

Lemma 3. *If the initial configuration $C(0) \in \mathcal{I}_{223}$ is such that the capacity of a parking node on l is an odd integer. Then the parking problem is unsolvable.*

It follows from Lemma 3 that if $C(t)$ admits multiple lines of symmetry and if there exists a parking node on l with odd capacity, then also the problem is unsolvable.[1]

Corollary 1. *If the initial configuration* $C(0) \in \mathcal{I}_{323}$, *then the parking problem is unsolvable if the capacity of the parking node at* c *is neither a multiple of 4 nor 2, depending on whether the angle of rotation is either* $90°$ *or* $180°$.

Let $\mathcal{U}$ be the set of all configurations that are unsolvable according to Lemma 3 and Corollary 1.

4   Algorithm

In this section, the parking problem is solved using a deterministic distributed algorithm *Parking ()* for all initial configurations except those belonging to $\mathcal{U}$. The fundamental strategy of the proposed algorithm is to identify a specific *target parking node* and permit a number of robots to move towards it, where the number of robots is equal to the parking node's capacity. The target parking node is selected in a sequential manner and the procedure executes unless each parking node becomes saturated. The proposed algorithm mainly consists of the following phases: *Guard Selection and Placement (GS)* phase, *Target Parking Node Selection (TPS)* phase, *Candidate Robot Selection (CR)* phase and *Guard Movement (GM)* phase.

Note that according to the definition of the symmetry of the set $\mathcal{P}$, there exists a unique lexicographic string α_i, when the parking nodes are asymmetric. From this, we can observe that if the parking nodes are asymmetric, the parking nodes can be ordered (say $\mathcal{O}_1$). Similarly, if the parking nodes are symmetric with respect to l, with at least one parking node on l, then the parking nodes on l are orderable (say $\mathcal{O}_2$). These orderings are necessary to identify a unique parking node, which will be selected by the robots in order to initialize the parking formation.

4.1   Guard Selection and Placement (GS)

Consider the case when the parking nodes are symmetric, but the configuration is asymmetric. In this phase, a unique robot is selected as a guard and placed in such a way that the configuration remains asymmetric during the execution of the algorithm. The following notations are used in describing this phase:

- Condition C_1: There exists at least one robot position outside the rectangle $M_\mathcal{P}$.
- Condition C_2: Each robot is inside the rectangle $M_\mathcal{P}$.
- Condition C_3: There exists a unique farthest robot from $l \cup \{c\}$.

---

[1] The proofs of the Lemmas 1 and 3 are in the arxiv version of the paper [5].

Depending on the class of configurations to which $C(t)$ belongs, the phase is described in Table 1. If there is more than one furthest robot from the key corner, then since the configuration is asymmetric, a unique robot can always be selected according to the view of the robots. Note that while the guard is selected and placed, the guard is the unique farthest robot from $l \cup \{c\}$. As a result, it does not have any symmetric image with respect to $l \cup \{c\}$, which implies that the configuration remains asymmetric during the execution of the algorithm.

Table 1. Guard Selection and Placement

Guard Selection and Placement		
Initial Configuration $(\mathcal{I}_{21} \cup \mathcal{I}_{31})$	Guard	Position of the guard
$C_1 \wedge C_3$	The unique robot farthest from $l \cup \{c\}$	Current position of the guard
$C_1 \wedge \neg C_3$	The unique robot furthest from $l \cup \{c\}$ and having the maximum configuration view among all the furthest robots	The unique robot moves towards an adjacent node away from $l \cup \{c\}$
$C_2 \wedge C_3$	The unique robot furthest from $l \cup \{c\}$	The guard continues its movement away from $l \cup \{c\}$, unless the condition C_1 becomes true
$C_2 \wedge \neg C_3$	The unique robot furthest from $l \cup \{c\}$ and having the maximum configuration view among all the furthest robots	The guard continues its movement away from $l \cup \{c\}$ until the condition C_1 becomes true

4.2   Half-Planes and Quadrants

First, consider the case when $C(0) \in \mathcal{I}_{21}$. The line of symmetry l divides the entire grid into two half-planes. We consider the open half-planes, i.e., the half-planes excluding the nodes on l. Let H_1 and H_2 denote the two half-planes delimited by l. The following definitions are to be considered.

1. $UP(t)$- Number of parking nodes which are unsaturated at time t.
2. *Deficit Measure of a parking node* p_i *($Df_{p_i}(t)$):* The deficit measure $Df_{p_i}(t)$ of a parking node p_i at time t is defined as the deficit in the number of robots needed to have exactly k_i robots on p_i.
3. $K_1 = \sum_{p_i \in H_1} Df_{p_i}(t)$ denotes the total deficit in order to have exactly $\sum_{p_i \in H_1} k_i$ number of robots at the parking nodes belonging to the half-plane H_1.
4. $K_2 = \sum_{p_i \in H_2} Df_{p_i}(t)$ denotes the total deficit in order to have exactly $\sum_{p_i \in H_2} k_i$ number of robots at the parking nodes belonging to the half-plane H_2.

Definition 2. *Let $C(t)$ be any initial configuration belonging to the set $\mathcal{I}_{21}$. $C(t)$ is said to be unbalanced if the two half-planes delimited by l contain an unequal number of robots. Otherwise, the configuration is said to be balanced.*

We next consider the following conditions.

1. Condition C_4- There exists a unique half-plane that contains the minimum number of unsaturated parking nodes.
2. Condition C_5- $K_1 \neq K_2$
3. Condition C_6- The configuration is unbalanced.
4. Condition C_7- The configuration is balanced and $\mathcal{R} \cap l \neq \emptyset$.
5. Condition C_8- The configuration is balanced and $\mathcal{R} \cap l = \emptyset$.

The half-plane $\mathcal{H}_{target}$ or $\mathcal{H}^+$ is defined according to Table 2, where the parking at the parking nodes initializes. The other half-plane is denoted by $\mathcal{H}^-$. In Fig. 5 (a), $ABCD$ is the $M_{\mathcal{P}}$ and $AB'C'D$ is the MER. Assume that the capacities of the parking nodes p_1, p_2, p_3 and p_4 are 2, 2, 1 and 1, respectively. The half-plane with more number of robots is selected as $\mathcal{H}^+$. In Fig. 5 (b), assume that the capacities of the parking nodes p_1, p_2, p_3 and p_4 are 3, 3, 2 and 2, respectively. Each of the half-planes contains the same number of robots. Therefore, the configuration is balanced. The half-plane not containing the guard r_5 is defined as $\mathcal{H}^+$. Due to space constraints, the case when the parking nodes are symmetric with respect to rotational symmetry has been included in the arxiv version of the paper [5]. The quadrant $\mathcal{Q}_{target}$ or $\mathcal{Q}^{++}$, where the parking is initialized, is defined according to Table 3 in the arxiv version of the paper [5].

Table 2. Demarcation of the half-planes

Demarcation of the half-planes for fixing the target	
Initial Configuration ($\mathcal{I}_{21}$)	$\mathcal{H}^+$
C_4	The unique half-plane which contains the minimum number of unsaturated parked nodes
$\neg\, C_4 \wedge C_5 \wedge K_1 < K_2$	H_1
$\neg\, C_4 \wedge C_5 \wedge K_2 < K_1$	H_2
$\neg\, C_4 \wedge \neg C_5 \wedge C_6$	The unique half-plane with the maximum number of robot positions
$\neg\, C_4 \wedge \neg C_5 \wedge \neg\, C_6 \wedge C_7$	The northernmost robot on l move towards an adjacent node away from l. The unique half-plane with the maximum number of robot positions is defined as $\mathcal{H}^+$
$\neg\, C_4 \wedge \neg C_5 \wedge \neg\, C_6 \wedge \neg\, C_7 \wedge C_8$	The unique half-plane not containing the guard

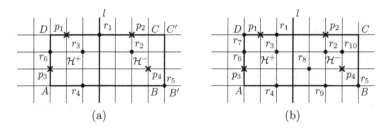

Fig. 5. Example configuration showing demarcations of half-planes.

4.3   Target Parking Node Selection (TPS)

In this phase, the target parking node for the parking problem is selected. Depending on the following classes of configurations, the phase is described in Table 3. Let p_{guard} be the closest parking node from the guard. If multiple such parking nodes exist, the parking node closest to the guard and having maximum order is selected as p_{guard}. We first assume that the target parking nodes are selected in $\mathcal{P} \setminus \{p_{guard}\}$. Due to space constraints, we have discussed the TPS phase in the arxiv version of the paper for the case when the parking nodes admit rotational symmetry [5]. We next consider the following conditions that are relevant in understanding this phase.

1. C_{14}- There exists an unsaturated parking node on l.
2. C_{16}- All the parking nodes belonging to $\mathcal{H}^+$ are saturated.
3. C'_{16}- All the parking nodes belonging to $\mathcal{H}^-$ are saturated.

While all the parking nodes belonging to the set $\mathcal{P} \setminus \{p_{guard}\}$ become saturated, p_{guard} becomes the target parking node. Note that $\neg C_{14}$ implies that the parking

Table 3. Target Parking Node Selection

Target Parking Node Selection	
Initial Configuration $C(0)$	Target Parking Node
$\mathcal{I}_1$	The parking node which is unsaturated and has the highest order with respect to $\mathcal{O}_1$
$\mathcal{I}_2 \wedge C_{14}$	The parking node on l which is unsaturated and has the highest order with respect to $\mathcal{O}_2$
$\mathcal{I}_{21} \wedge \neg C_{14} \wedge \neg C_{16}$	The parking node, which is unsaturated and has the highest order in $\mathcal{H}^+$ among all the unsaturated nodes in $\mathcal{H}^+$
$\mathcal{I}_{21} \wedge \neg C_{14} \wedge C_{16} \wedge \neg C'_{16}$	The parking node, which is unsaturated and has the highest order in $\mathcal{H}^-$ among all the unsaturated nodes in $\mathcal{H}^-$
$\mathcal{I}_{22} \wedge \neg C_{14}$	The two parking nodes that have the highest order among all the unsaturated parking nodes and lying on two different half-planes

nodes are symmetric with respect to l and there either does not exist any parking node on l or each parking node on l is saturated. In Fig. 5, A and B are the leading corners. p_1 is the parking node in $\mathcal{H}^+$ which has the highest order. The target parking nodes are selected in the order (p_1, p_3, p_2, p_4).

4.4 Candidate Robot Selection Phase

In view of Lemma 1, while a robot moves towards a parking node, it must ensure collision-free movement. Otherwise, the problem becomes unsolvable. As a result, a robot will move toward its target only when it has a path toward that target that does not contain any other robot positions.

Definition 3. *A path from a robot to a parking node is said to be free if it does not contain any other robot positions.*

A robot would move toward its target only when it has a free path toward it. In this phase, the *candidate robot* is selected and allowed to move toward the target parking node. Let $p \neq p_{guard}$ be the target parking node selected in the TPS phase. Depending on the different classes of configurations, the following cases are to be considered.

1. $C(t)$ is asymmetric. As a result, the robots are orderable. The robot that does not lie on any saturated parking node and has the shortest free path to p is selected as the candidate robot. If multiple such robots exist, the one with the highest order among such robots is selected as the candidate robot.
2. $C(t)$ is symmetric with respect to a single line of symmetry l. First, assume that p is on l. If at least one robot exists on l, then the symmetry can be broken by allowing a robot from l to move towards an adjacent node away from l. As a result, assume that there is no robot position on l. The two closest robots, which do not lie on any saturated parking node and have shortest free paths towards p, are selected as the candidates for p. If there are multiple such robots, the ties are broken by considering the robots that lie on different half-planes and have the highest order among all such robots. Next, assume that p is on the half-planes. The robot that does not lie on any saturated parking node and has a shortest free path toward p is selected as the candidate robot. Note that such candidates are selected in both half-planes.
3. $C(t)$ is symmetric with respect to rotational symmetry. First, assume that p is on c. If there exists a robot on c, the robot on c moves towards an adjacent node, and the configuration becomes asymmetric. Assume the case when there are no robots on c. The robots that are closest to p are selected as candidate robots. In this case, depending on whether the angle of rotational symmetry is 180° or 90°, two or four robots are selected as candidates. Next, assume that p is located either on a quadrant or on of the wedge boundaries. If the target parking node lies on a quadrant, the robot that does not lie on any saturated parking node and has a shortest free path toward p is selected as the candidate robot. It should be noted that such candidates are chosen from each of the four quadrants, for each target parking node. Otherwise, if the

target parking node is on a wedge boundary, the robot(s) not lying on any saturated parking node and having a shortest free path towards the target is (are) selected as candidate robot(s).

Next, assume that p_{guard} is the target parking node. The candidates are selected as the robot which has shortest free path towards p_{guard}. Finally, the guard moves towards p_{guard}. By the choice of p, there always exists a half-line starting from p, which does not contain any robot position. As a result, a free path always exists between the candidate robot and p.

4.5   Guard Movement

Assume the case when the parking nodes are symmetric and the configuration is asymmetric. In the GM phase, the guard moves toward its respective destination and the parking process is terminated. The guard moves only when it finds that, except for one, all the parking nodes have become saturated. It moves towards its destination p in a free path. The guard moves towards its destination and each parking node becomes saturated, transforming the configuration into a final configuration.

5   Correctness

Due to space constraints, the proofs of Lemmas 4–9 and Theorem 1 are mentioned in the arxiv version of the paper [5].

Lemma 4. *In the GS phase, the guard remains invariant while it moves towards its destination.*

Lemma 5. *During the execution of the algorithm Parking(), if the parking nodes admit a single line of symmetry l, then $\mathcal{H}^+$ remains invariant.*

Lemma 6. *During the execution of the algorithm Parking(), if the parking nodes admit rotational symmetry, then $\mathcal{Q}^{++}$ remains invariant.*

Lemma 7. *If the configuration is such that the parking nodes admit a unique line of symmetry l, then during the execution of the algorithm Parking(), the target parking nodes remain invariant.*

Lemma 8. *If the configuration is such that the parking nodes admit rotational symmetry, then during the execution of the algorithm Parking(), the target parking nodes remain invariant.*

Lemma 9. *During the CRS phase, the candidate robot remains invariant.*

Theorem 1. *Algorithm Parking() solves the Parking Problem in Infinite grids for all initial configurations not belonging to the set $\mathcal{U}$.*

6   Conclusion

This chapter proposed a deterministic distributed algorithm for solving the parking problem in infinite grids. We have characterized all the initial configurations and the values of k_i for which the problem is unsolvable, even if the robots are endowed with strong multiplicity detection capability. A deterministic algorithm has been proposed under the assumption that the robots are endowed with global-strong multiplicity detection capability. As a future work, it would be interesting to investigate the problem in case the number of robots is not equal to the sum of the capacities of the parking nodes. In case the number of robots in the initial configuration is less than the sum of the capacities of the parking nodes, one interesting study could be to investigate the problem with the objective of maximizing the number of saturated parking nodes.

References

1. Bhagat, S., Chakraborty, A., Das, B., Mukhopadhyaya, K.: Gathering over meeting nodes in infinite grid*. Fundam. Inform. **187**(1), 1–30 (2022)
2. Bhagat, S., Chakraborty, A., Das, B., Mukhopadhyaya, K.: Optimal gathering over weber meeting nodes in infinite grid. Int. J. Found. Comput. Sci. **34**(1), 25–49 (2023)
3. Bhagat, S., Das, B., Chakraborty, A., Mukhopadhyaya, K.: k-Circle formation and k-epf by asynchronous robots. Algorithms **14**(2) (2021)
4. Bose, K., Adhikary, R., Kundu, M.K., Sau, B.: Arbitrary pattern formation on infinite grid by asynchronous oblivious robots. Theor. Comput. Sci. **815**, 213–227 (2020)
5. Chakraborty, A., Mukhopadhyaya, K.: Parking problem by oblivious mobile robots in infinite grids (2023)
6. Cicerone, S., Stefano, G.D., Navarra, A.: Gathering of robots on meeting-points: feasibility and optimal resolution algorithms. Distrib. Comput. **31**(1), 1–50 (2018)
7. Cicerone, S., Stefano, G.D., Navarra, A.: Asynchronous arbitrary pattern formation: the effects of a rigorous approach. Distrib. Comput. **32**(2), 91–132 (2019)
8. Cicerone, S., Stefano, G.D., Navarra, A.: Embedded pattern formation by asynchronous robots without chirality. Distrib. Comput. **32**(4), 291–315 (2019)
9. D'Angelo, G., Stefano, G.D., Klasing, R., Navarra, A.: Gathering of robots on anonymous grids and trees without multiplicity detection. Theor. Comput. Sci. **610**, 158–168 (2016)
10. Das, B., Chakraborty, A., Bhagat, S., Mukhopadhyaya, K.: k-circle formation by disoriented asynchronous robots. Theor. Comput. Sci. **916**, 40–61 (2022)
11. Efrima, A., Peleg, D.: Distributed algorithms for partitioning a swarm of autonomous mobile robots. Theor. Comput. Sci. **410**(14), 1355–1368 (2009). structural Information and Communication Complexity (SIROCCO 2007)
12. Flocchini, P., Prencipe, G., Santoro, N.: Distributed computing by mobile entities. Curr. Res. Mov. Comput. **11340** (2019)
13. Flocchini, P., Prencipe, G., Santoro, N., Widmayer, P.: Arbitrary pattern formation by asynchronous, anonymous, oblivious robots. Theor. Comput. Sci. **407**(1–3), 412–447 (2008)

14. Fujinaga, N., Ono, H., Kijima, S., Yamashita, M.: Pattern formation through optimum matching by oblivious CORDA robots. In: Lu, C., Masuzawa, T., Mosbah, M. (eds.) OPODIS 2010. LNCS, vol. 6490, pp. 1–15. Springer, Heidelberg (2010). https://doi.org/10.1007/978-3-642-17653-1_1

15. Stefano, G.D., Navarra, A.: Gathering of oblivious robots on infinite grids with minimum traveled distance. Inf. Comput. **254**, 377–391 (2017)

16. Sugihara, K., Suzuki, I.: Distributed algorithms for formation of geometric patterns with many mobile robots. J. Field Robot. **13**(3), 127–139 (1996)

17. Yamauchi, Y., Yamashita, M.: Pattern formation by mobile robots with limited visibility. In: Moscibroda, T., Rescigno, A.A. (eds.) SIROCCO 2013. LNCS, vol. 8179, pp. 201–212. Springer, Cham (2013). https://doi.org/10.1007/978-3-319-03578-9_17

The Computational Landscape
of Autonomous Mobile Robots:
The Visibility Perspective

Archak Das$^{(\boxtimes)}$ⓘ, Satakshi Ghoshⓘ, Avisek Sharmaⓘ, Pritam Goswamiⓘ,
and Buddhadeb Sauⓘ

Department of Mathematics, Jadavpur University, Kolkata, India
{archakdas.math.rs,satakshighosh.math.rs,aviseks.math.rs,
pritamgoswami.math.rs,buddhadeb.sau}@jadavpuruniversity.in

Abstract. Consider a group of autonomous mobile computational entities called robots. The robots move in the Euclidean plane and operate according to synchronous *Look-Compute-Move* cycles. The computational capabilities of the robots under the four traditional mod-
els {$\mathcal{OBLOT}$, $\mathcal{FSTA}$, $\mathcal{FCOM}$, $\mathcal{LUMI}$} have been extensively investigated both when the robots had unlimited amount of energy and when
the robots were energy-constrained.

In both the above cases, the robots had full visibility. In this paper,
this assumption is removed, i.e., we assume that the robots can view up
to a constant radius V_r from their position (the V_r is same for all the
robots) and, investigates what impact it has on its computational capabilities.

We first study whether the restriction imposed on the visibility has
any impact at all, i.e., under a given model and scheduler does there exist
any problem which cannot be solved by a robot having limited visibility
but can be solved by a robot with full visibility. We find that the answer
to the question in general turns out to be positive. Finally, we try to get
an idea that under a given model, which of the two factors, *Visibility* or
Synchronicity is more powerful and conclude that a definite conclusion
cannot be drawn.

Keywords: Mobile Robots · Limited Visibility ·
Look-Compute-Move · Robots with Lights

1   Introduction

In this paper, we consider systems of *autonomous, anonymous, identical* and
homogenous computational entities called *robots* moving and operating in the
Euclidean plane. The robots are viewed as points and they operate according to
the traditional *Look-Compute-Move* (*LCM*) cycles in synchronous rounds. In
Look phase robots take a snapshot of the space, in the *Compute* phase the robots
execute its algorithm using the snapshot as input, then move to the computed

S. Devismes et al. (Eds.): ICDCIT 2024, LNCS 14501, pp. 85–100, 2024.
https://doi.org/10.1007/978-3-031-50583-6_6

destination in *Move* phase. The robots are collectively able to perform some tasks and solve some problems.

In recent times, exhaustive investigation has also been done [2,8] about the issues of *memory persistence* and *communication capability*, have on the solvability of a problem and computational capability of a system. In light of these facts, four models have been identified and investigated, $\mathcal{OBLOT}$, $\mathcal{LUMI}$, $\mathcal{FSTA}$ and $\mathcal{FCOM}$.

In the most common model $\mathcal{OBLOT}$, in the addition to standard assumptions of *anonymity* and *uniformity*, the robots are *silent*, i.e., without explicit means of communication and *oblivious*, i.e., they have no persistent memory to record information of previous cycles.

The other model which is generally considered as antithesis to $\mathcal{OBLOT}$ model, is the $\mathcal{LUMI}$ model first formally defined in [4,5], where the robots have both persistent memory and communication, although it must be noted that the remembering or communicating can be done only in limited capacity, i.e., the robots can remember or communicate finite number of bits.

Two new models have been introduced in [7] by eliminating one of the two capabilities of $\mathcal{LUMI}$ model, in each case. These two models are $\mathcal{FSTA}$ and $\mathcal{FCOM}$. In $\mathcal{FSTA}$ model the communication capability is absent while in $\mathcal{FCOM}$ model the robots do not have persistent memory. In [8] these models have been considered to investigate the question *is it better to remember or to communicate?*.

In this work we consider another factor, i.e., *visibility*, which helps to investigate the matter from a different angle and is of interest from both theoretical and practical point of view. If $\mathcal{M}$ denotes a model and σ is a scheduler then traditionally $\mathcal{M}^\sigma$ denotes a model $\mathcal{M}$ under scheduler σ. Here $\mathcal{M} \in \{\mathcal{OBLOT}, \mathcal{FSTA}, \mathcal{FCOM}, \mathcal{LUMI}\}$ and $\sigma \in \{FSYNCH, SSYNCH\}$. We here define $\mathcal{M}_\mathcal{V}^\sigma$ denotes a model $\mathcal{M}$ under scheduler σ and visibility state $\mathcal{V}$. Here $\mathcal{V} \in \{\mathcal{F}.\mathcal{V}., \mathcal{L}.\mathcal{V}.\}$. Here $\mathcal{F}.\mathcal{V}.$ denotes the full visibility model and $\mathcal{L}.\mathcal{V}.$ denotes the limited visibility model. In limited visibility model, each robot can view upto a constant radius of their position and the initial visibility graph is connected.

All the works done till now had given the full visibility power to the robots. So we try to answer a number of questions,

- Does restriction on visibility have a significant impact on the computational power of a model? In other words, is any problem which is solvable in full visibility model, solvable in limited visibility model also?
- If the answer to the second question mentioned above is no, then can the impairment be *always* adjusted by minor adjustments, i.e., by keeping the model intact but by making the scheduler more powerful?
- If the answer to the above question is also no, then what are the cases where the lack of full visibility can be compensated? Can all the cases be classified?

We have shown the answer to the first question is no, e.g., we have proved that $\mathcal{FSTA}_{\mathcal{L}.\mathcal{V}.}^\mathcal{F} < \mathcal{FSTA}_{\mathcal{F}.\mathcal{V}.}^\mathcal{F}$. This result turns out to be true for all the four models $\{\mathcal{OBLOT}, \mathcal{FSTA}, \mathcal{FCOM}, \mathcal{LUMI}\}$. After we got answer to our first question, we tried to answer our second question. A definite answer to the second question shall give us some insight about whether any one of the two parameters of *visibility* and *synchronicity* have any precedence over the other. But as we shall see this does not happen. For e.g., we got the result that $\mathcal{FCOM}^{\mathcal{F}}_{\mathcal{L}.\mathcal{V}.} \perp \mathcal{FCOM}^{\mathcal{S}}_{\mathcal{F}.\mathcal{V}.}$, which effectively shows that both the capabilities are important, and deficiency in one of the parameter cannot be compensated by making the other parameter stronger. In the process, we have defined a new problem *EqOsc* which we have shown to be unsolvable unless the scheduler is fully synchronous, but solvable if the scheduler is fully synchronous, even under limited visibility in $\mathcal{FSTA}$ and $\mathcal{FCOM}$ models. The third question as of now, yet remains unanswered, and subject to further investigations.

The results presented in this paper gives a whole new insight to the parameter of visibility and its relevance relative to the parameter of synchronicity, one that requires exhaustive analysis, even beyond the amount of investigation that had been done in this paper.

1.1 Related Work

Investigations regarding the computational power of robots under synchronous schedulers was done by the authors Flocchini et. al. in [8]. Main focus of the investigation in this work was which of the two capabilities was more important: *persistent memory* or *communication*. In the course of their investigation they proved that under fully synchronous scheduler communication is more powerful than persistent memory. In addition to that, they gave a complete exhaustive map of the relationships among models and schedulers.

In [2], the previous work of characterizing the relations between the robot models and three type of schedulers was continued. The authors provided a more refined map of the computational landscape for robots operating under fully synchronous and semi-synchronous schedulers, by removing the assumptions on robots' movements of *rigidity* and common *chirality*. Further authors establish some preliminary results with respect to asynchronous scheduler.

The previous two works considered that the robots was assumed to have unlimited amounts of energy. In [3], the authors removed this assumption and started the study of computational capabilities of robots whose energy is limited, albeit renewable. In these systems, the activated entities uses all its energy to execute an *LCM* cycle and then the energy is restored after a period of inactivity. They studied the impact that memory persistence and communication capabilities have on the computational power of such robots by analyzing the computational relationship between the four models $\{\mathcal{OBLOT}, \mathcal{FSTA}, \mathcal{FCOM}, \mathcal{LUMI}\}$ under the energy constraint. They provided a full characterization of this relationship. Among the many results they proved that for energy-constrained robots, $\mathcal{FCOM}$ is more powerful than $\mathcal{FSTA}$.

In all the three above mentioned works, the robots had full visibility. A robot uses its visibility power in the *Look* phase of the *LCM* cycle to acquire information about its surroundings, i.e., position and lights (if any) of other robots. The biggest drawback of full visibility assumption is that it is not practically feasible.

So, recently some of the authors [1,6,9,10] have considered limited visibility. For example, in [6] they considered that the robots can see up to a fixed radius V from it. So it was important to study the power of different robot models under limited visibility.

1.2 Our Contributions

We first examine the computational relationship under a constant model and scheduler between limited and full visibility conditions. We find that in both fully synchronous and semi-synchronous cases, a model under full visibility is strictly more powerful than a model under limited visibility. We get the following results:

1. $\mathcal{OBLOT}^{\mathcal{F}}_{\mathcal{F.V.}} > \mathcal{OBLOT}^{\mathcal{F}}_{\mathcal{L.V.}}$
2. $\mathcal{FSTA}^{\mathcal{F}}_{\mathcal{F.V.}} > \mathcal{FSTA}^{\mathcal{F}}_{\mathcal{L.V.}}$
3. $\mathcal{FCOM}^{\mathcal{F}}_{\mathcal{F.V.}} > \mathcal{FCOM}^{\mathcal{F}}_{\mathcal{L.V.}}$
4. $\mathcal{LUMI}^{\mathcal{F}}_{\mathcal{F.V.}} > \mathcal{LUMI}^{\mathcal{F}}_{\mathcal{L.V.}}$
5. $\mathcal{OBLOT}^{\mathcal{S}}_{\mathcal{F.V.}} > \mathcal{OBLOT}^{\mathcal{S}}_{\mathcal{L.V.}}$
6. $\mathcal{FSTA}^{\mathcal{S}}_{\mathcal{F.V.}} > \mathcal{FSTA}^{\mathcal{S}}_{\mathcal{L.V.}}$
7. $\mathcal{FCOM}^{\mathcal{S}}_{\mathcal{F.V.}} > \mathcal{FCOM}^{\mathcal{S}}_{\mathcal{L.V.}}$
8. $\mathcal{LUMI}^{\mathcal{S}}_{\mathcal{F.V.}} > \mathcal{LUMI}^{\mathcal{S}}_{\mathcal{L.V.}}$

We then examine the computational relationship between the four models $\{\mathcal{OBLOT}, \mathcal{FSTA}, \mathcal{FCOM}, \mathcal{LUMI}\}$ under limited visibility between fully synchronous and semi-synchronous schedulers. We find that under limited visibility conditions each of the three models are more powerful under fully synchronous scheduler.

9. $\mathcal{OBLOT}^{\mathcal{F}}_{\mathcal{L.V.}} > \mathcal{OBLOT}^{\mathcal{S}}_{\mathcal{L.V.}}$
10. $\mathcal{FSTA}^{\mathcal{F}}_{\mathcal{L.V.}} > \mathcal{FSTA}^{\mathcal{S}}_{\mathcal{L.V.}}$
11. $\mathcal{FCOM}^{\mathcal{F}}_{\mathcal{L.V.}} > \mathcal{FCOM}^{\mathcal{S}}_{\mathcal{L.V.}}$
12. $\mathcal{LUMI}^{\mathcal{F}}_{\mathcal{L.V.}} > \mathcal{LUMI}^{\mathcal{S}}_{\mathcal{L.V.}}$

Together with the three results mentioned immediately above, we also get an idea which of the capabilities, *visibility* or *synchronicity* is more powerful. From the previous results we generally conclude that $\mathcal{M}^{\mathcal{S}}_{\mathcal{L.V.}} < \mathcal{M}^{\mathcal{S}}_{\mathcal{F.V.}}$ and $\mathcal{M}^{\mathcal{S}}_{\mathcal{L.V.}} < \mathcal{M}^{\mathcal{F}}_{\mathcal{L.V.}}$. If we can prove that $\mathcal{M}^{\mathcal{F}}_{\mathcal{L.V.}} \geq \mathcal{M}^{\mathcal{S}}_{\mathcal{F.V.}}$, then it shall imply that by making the scheduler stronger, the limitation in visibility can be compensated. Similarly if we can prove that $\mathcal{M}^{\mathcal{S}}_{\mathcal{F.V.}} \geq \mathcal{M}^{\mathcal{F}}_{\mathcal{L.V.}}$, then it shall imply that by giving complete visibility, the weakness in terms of scheduler can be compensated. But after our detailed investigation it has been revealed that neither of the above cases happen and in general $\mathcal{M}^{\mathcal{F}}_{\mathcal{L.V.}} \perp \mathcal{M}^{\mathcal{S}}_{\mathcal{F.V.}}$. Specifically the results are:

13. $\mathcal{OBLOT}^{\mathcal{F}}_{\mathcal{L.V.}} \perp \mathcal{OBLOT}^{\mathcal{S}}_{\mathcal{F.V.}}$
14. $\mathcal{FSTA}^{\mathcal{F}}_{\mathcal{L.V.}} \perp \mathcal{FSTA}^{\mathcal{S}}_{\mathcal{F.V.}}$
15. $\mathcal{FCOM}^{\mathcal{F}}_{\mathcal{L.V.}} \perp \mathcal{FCOM}^{\mathcal{S}}_{\mathcal{F.V.}}$
16. $\mathcal{LUMI}^{\mathcal{F}}_{\mathcal{L.V.}} \perp \mathcal{LUMI}^{\mathcal{S}}_{\mathcal{F.V.}}$

1.3 Paper Organization

In Sect. 2 we define the computational model, visibility models and the other technical preliminaries. In Sects. 3, we discuss the computational relationships between the four models, $\mathcal{OBLOT}$, $\mathcal{FCOM}$, $\mathcal{FSTA}$ and $\mathcal{LUMI}$ models respectively, subject to variations in synchronicity and visibility. In Sect. 4, we try to compare the strength of the capabilities of *synchronicity* and *visibility*. In Sect. 5 we present the conclusion.

2 Model and Technical Preliminaries

2.1 The Basics

In this paper we consider a team $R = \{r_0, \ldots, r_n\}$ of computational entities moving and operating in the Euclidean Plane $\mathbb{R}^2$, which are viewed as points and called *robots*. The robots can move freely and continuously in the plane. Each robot has its own local coordinate system and it always perceives itself at its origin; there might not be consistency between these coordinate systems. The robots are *identical*: they are indistinguishable by their appearance and they execute the same protocol, and they are *autonomous*, i.e., without any central control.

The robots operate in $Look - Compute - Move$ (LCM) cycles. When activated a robot executes a cycle by performing the following three operations:

1. *Look*: The robots activate its sensors to obtain a snapshot of the positions occupied by the robots according to its co-ordinate system.
2. *Compute*: The robot executes its algorithm using the snapshot as input. The result of the computation is a destination point.
3. *Move*: The robot moves to the computed destination. If the destination is the current location, the robot stays still.

All robots are initially idle. The amount of time to complete a cycle is assumed to be finite, and the *Look* is assumed to be instantaneous. The robots may not have any agreement in terms of their local coordinate system. By *chirality*, we mean the robots agree on the same circular orientation of the plane, or in other words they agree on "clockwise" direction. In our paper, we do not assume the robots to have a common sense of chirality.

2.2 The Computational Models

There are four basic robot models which are considered in literature, they are namely, $\{\mathcal{OBLOT}, \mathcal{FSTA}, \mathcal{FCOM}, \mathcal{LUMI}\}$.

In the most common, $\mathcal{OBLOT}$, the robots are *silent*: they have no explicit means of communication; furthermore they are *oblivious*: at the start of the cycle, a robot has no memory of observations and computations performed in previous cycles.

In the most common model, $\mathcal{LUMI}$, each robot r is equipped with a persistent visible state variable $Light[r]$, called *light*, whose values are taken from a finite set C of states called *colors* (including the color that represents the initial state when the light is off). The colors of the lights can be set in each cycle by r at the end of its *Compute* operation. A light is *persistent* from one computational cycle to the next: the color is not automatically reset at the end of a cycle; the robots are otherwise oblivious, forgetting all other information from previous cycles. In $\mathcal{LUMI}$, the *Look* operation produces a colored snapshot; i.e., it returns the set of pairs (*position, color*) of the robots.

The lights provide simultaneously persistent memory and direct means of communication, although both limited to a constant number of bits per cycle. Two sub-models of $\mathcal{LUMI}$ have been defined and investigated, each offering only one of these two capabilities.

In the first model, $\mathcal{FSTA}$, a robot can only see the color of its own light; that is, the light is an *internal* one and its color merely encodes an internal state. Hence the robots are *silent*, as in $\mathcal{OBLOT}$, but are *finite-state*. Observe that a snapshot in $\mathcal{FSTA}$ is same as in $\mathcal{OBLOT}$.

In the second model, $\mathcal{FCOM}$, the lights *external*: a robot can communicate to the other robots through its colored light but forgets the color of its own light by the next cycle; that is, robots are *finite-communication* but are *oblivious*. A snapshot in $\mathcal{FCOM}$ is like in $\mathcal{LUMI}$ except that, for the position x where the robot r performing the *Look* is located, $Light[r]$ is omitted from the set of colors present at x.

2.3   The Schedulers

With respect to the activation schedule of the robots, and the duration of their *Look-Compute-Move* cycles, the fundamental distinction is between the *asynchronous* and *synchronous* settings.

In the *asynchronous* setting (ASYNCH), there is no common notion of time, each robot is activated independently of others, the duration of each phase is finite but unpredictable and might be different cycles.

In the *synchronous* setting (SSYNCH), also called semi-synchronous, time is divided into discrete intervals, called *rounds*; in each round some robots are activated simultaneously, and perform their *LCM* cycle in perfect synchronization.

A popular synchronous setting which plays an important role is the *fully-synchronous* setting (FSYNCH) where every robot is activated in every round; the is, the activation scheduler has no adversarial power.

In all two settings, the selection of which robots are activated at a round is made by an adversarial *scheduler*, whose only limit is that every robot must be activated infinitely often (i.e., it is fair scheduler). In the following, for all synchronous schedulers, we use round and time interchangeably.

2.4   The Visibility Models

In our work we do comparative analysis of computational models with robots having *full* and *limited* visibility. In *full visibility* model, denoted as $\mathcal{F}.\mathcal{V}.$, the robots have sensorial devices that allows it to observe the positions of the other robots in its local co-ordinate system.

In *limited visibility* model, denoted as $\mathcal{L}.\mathcal{V}.$, a robot can only observe upto a fixed distance V_r from it. Suppose, $r_p(t)$ denote the position of a robot r at the beginning of round t. Then we define the circle with center at $r_p(t)$ and radius V_r to be the *Circle of Visibility* of r at round t. Here the radius V_r is same for all the robots. The result of *Look* operation in round t will be the position of the robots and lights(if any) of the robots inside the circle of visibility.

We now define the *Visibility Graph*, $G = (V,E)$ of a configuration. Let C be a given configuration. Then all the robot positions become the vertices of G and we say an edge exists between any two vertices if and only if the robots present there can see each other. The necessary condition for the problems we have defined in the paper is that the *Visibility Graph* of the initial configuration must be connected.

2.5   Some Important Definitions

We define our computational relationships similar to that of [8]. Let $\mathcal{M} = \{\mathcal{OBLOT}, \mathcal{FSTA}, \mathcal{FCOM}, \mathcal{LUMI}\}$ be the robot models under investigation, the set of activation schedulers be $\mathcal{S} = \{FSYNCH, ASYNCH\}$ and the set of visibility models be $\mathcal{V} = \{\mathcal{F}.\mathcal{V}., \mathcal{L}.\mathcal{V}.\}$.

We denote by $\mathcal{R}$ the set of all teams of robots satisfying the core assumptions (i.e., they are identical, autonomous, and operate in LCM cycles), and $R \in \mathcal{R}$ a team of robots having identical capabilities (e.g., common coordinate system, persistent storage, internal identity, rigid movements etc.). By $\mathcal{R}_n \subset \mathcal{R}$ we denote the set of all teams of size n.

By *problem* we mean a task where a fixed number of robots have to form some configuration or configurations (which may be a function of time) subject to some conditions, within a finite amount of time.

Given a model $M \in \mathcal{M}$, a scheduler $S \in \mathcal{S}$, visibility $V \in \mathcal{V}$, and a team of robots $R \in \mathcal{R}$, let $Task(M, S, V; R)$ denote the set of problems solvable by R in M, with visibility V and under adversarial scheduler S.

Let M, $N \in \mathcal{M}$, S_1, $S_2 \in \mathcal{S}$ and V_1, $V_2 \in \mathcal{V}$. We define the relationships between model M with visibility V_1 under scheduler S_1 and model N with visibility V_2 under scheduler S_2:

- *computationally not less powerful* $(M_{V_1}^{S_1} \geq N_{V_2}^{S_2})$, if $\forall\ R \in \mathcal{R}$ we have $Task(M, S_1; R) \supseteq Task(N, S_2; R)$;
- *computationally more powerful* $(M_{V_1}^{S_1} > N_{V_2}^{S_2})$, if $M_{V_1}^{S_1} \geq N_{V_2}^{S_2}$ and $\exists R \in \mathcal{R}$ such that $Task(M, S_1, V_1; R) \setminus Task(N, S_2, V_2; R) \neq \emptyset$;
- *computationally equivalent* $(M_{V_1}^{S_1} \equiv N_{V_2}^{S_2})$, if $M_{V_1}^{S_1} \geq N_{V_2}^{S_2}$ and $M_{V_1}^{S_1} \leq N_{V_2}^{S_2}$;

– *computationally orthogonal or incomparable,* $(M_{V_1}^{S_1} \perp N_{V_2}^{S_2})$, if $\exists R_1, R_2 \in$ $\mathcal{R}$ such that $Task(M, S_1, V_1; R_1) \setminus Task(N, S_2, V_2; R_1) \neq \emptyset$ and $Task(N, S_2, V_2; R_2) \setminus Task(M, S_1, V_1; R_2) \neq \emptyset$.

For simplicity of notation, for a model $M \in \mathcal{M}$, let M^F and M^S denote M^{Fsynch} and M^{Ssynch}, respectively; and let $M_V^F(R)$ and $M_V^S(R)$ denote the sets $Task(M, FSYNCH, V; R)$ and $Task(M, SSYNCH, V; R)$, respectively.

2.6 Some Fundamental Comparisons

Trivially,

1. $\mathcal{LUMI} \geq \mathcal{FSTA} \geq \mathcal{OBLOT}$ and $\mathcal{LUMI} \geq \mathcal{FCOM} \geq \mathcal{OBLOT}$, when the *Visibility* and *Synchronicity* is fixed.
2. $\mathcal{FSYNCH} \geq \mathcal{SSYNCH} \geq \mathcal{ASYNCH}$ when the model and *Visibility* is fixed.
3. $\mathcal{F.V.} \geq \mathcal{L.V.}$ when the model and *Synchronicity* is fixed.

3 Angle Equalization Problem

Definition 1. *Problem Angle Equalization (AE):* *Suppose four robots* r_1, *r_2, r_3 and r_4 are placed in positions A, B, C and D respectively, as given in Configuration (I). The line AB makes an acute angle θ_1 with BC and the line CD makes an acute θ_2 with BC. Here $\theta_1 < \theta_2 < 90°$.*

The robots must form the Configuration (II) without any collision. The robots r_2 and r_3 must remain fixed in their positions.

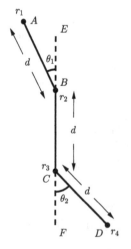

Fig. 1. Configuration (I) of Problem AE

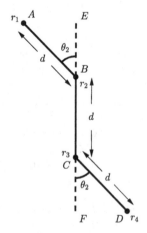

Fig. 2. Configuration (II) of Problem AE

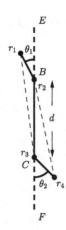

Fig. 3. Visibility Range Gap

3.1 Algorithm for AE Problem in $\mathcal{OBLOT}^{\mathcal{S}}_{\mathcal{F}.\mathcal{V}}$

Under full visibility conditions, each robot can see all the robot locations in the plane. Now each robot can uniquely identify its position in the plane. Therefore whenever the robot r_1 is activated, it will move to the position A' such that the $\angle A'BE = \theta_2$. The rest of the robots will not move. After the robot r_1 moves all the robots can perceive that Configuration (II) is obtained and henceforward there will be no further movement of the robots. Hence the problem is solved.

Lemma 1. $\forall\ R \in \mathcal{R}_4,\ AE \in \mathcal{OBLOT}^{\mathcal{S}}_{\mathcal{F}.\mathcal{V}}.$

Corollary 1. $\forall\ R \in \mathcal{R}_4,\ AE \in \mathcal{OBLOT}^{\mathcal{F}}_{\mathcal{F}.\mathcal{V}}.$

Proof. Follows from Lemma 1.

Corollary 2. $\forall\ R \in \mathcal{R}_4,\ AE \in \mathcal{FSTA}^{\mathcal{S}}_{\mathcal{F}.\mathcal{V}}.$

Proof. Follows from Lemma 1.

Corollary 3. $\forall\ R \in \mathcal{R}_4,\ AE \in \mathcal{FSTA}^{\mathcal{F}}_{\mathcal{F}.\mathcal{V}}.$

Proof. Follows from Corollary 1.

Corollary 4. $\forall\ R \in \mathcal{R}_4,\ AE \in \mathcal{FCOM}^{\mathcal{S}}_{\mathcal{F}.\mathcal{V}}.$

Proof. Follows from Lemma 1.

Corollary 5. $\forall\ R \in \mathcal{R}_4,\ AE \in \mathcal{FCOM}^{\mathcal{F}}_{\mathcal{F}.\mathcal{V}}.$

Proof. Follows from Corollary 1.

Corollary 6. $\forall\ R \in \mathcal{R}_4,\ AE \in \mathcal{LUMI}^{\mathcal{S}}_{\mathcal{F}.\mathcal{V}}.$

Proof. Follows from Lemma 1.

Corollary 7. $\forall\ R \in \mathcal{R}_4,\ AE \in \mathcal{LUMI}^{\mathcal{F}}_{\mathcal{F}.\mathcal{V}}.$

Proof. Follows from Corollary 1.

94   A. Das et al.

3.2 Impossibility of Solving AE Problem in Limited Visibility Model

Lemma 2. $\exists\, R \in \mathcal{R}_4,\ AE \notin \mathcal{LUMI}^{\mathcal{F}}_{\mathcal{L.V.}}$.

Proof. Let there exists an Algorithm $\mathcal{A}$ to solve the problem in $\mathcal{LUMI}^{\mathcal{F}}_{\mathcal{L.V.}}$. If Configuration (II) (see Fig. 2) has to be formed from Configuration (I) (see Fig. 1) then the robot r_1 must know the value of the angle it has to form. If r_1 has to move to the position A' such that the $\angle A'BE = \theta_2$, then the robot r_1 must know the position of two robots r_3 and r_4 respectively in the initial configuration, i.e., the positions C and D respectively. Unless the position C is known, the robot r_1 cannot perceive that it has to form the angle with respect to the extended line of the line segment. And unless it knows the position D, it cannot perceive the value θ_2 that it has to form. But if $V_r = BC + \epsilon$, then it is not possible for the robot r_1 to see them from the initial configuration. Also according the requirement of the problem the robots r_2 and r_3 cannot move. Therefore to solve the problem r_1 must move. Now, if r_1 has to move, unless r_1 performs the required move to form Configuration (II) in one move, it has to move preserving the angle θ_1. This is because r_1 does not know the fact that $\theta_1 < \theta_2$. The argument holds for r_4. And we have already seen that the initial configuration does not give the required information to form Configuration (II) in one move.

Now the only way the robot r_1 can move preserving the angle, is by moving along the line segment AB. Now note that if r_1 reaches B, the angle becomes 0. Also as collisions are not allowed the robot r_1 cannot cross B. Similarly, the robot r_3 can only move along line segment CD and it cannot cross the position C. Now, by moving along the line segments AB and CD respectively, however much the two robots r_1 and r_4 may come closer to B and C respectively, the adversary may choose the value of ϵ in such a way that the position C is outside the visibility range of r_1 and B is outside the visibility range of r_2 (see Fig. 3). Note that the robots r_2 and r_3 cannot see r_4 and r_1 respectively, therefore it is also unknown to them which robot should perform the required move to form Configuration (II). Though r_2 and r_3 can measure the angles θ_1 and θ_2 respectively. It is not possible to store the value of the angles with finite number of lights. Hence the problem cannot be solved.

From Lemma 2 follows:

Corollary 8. $\exists\, R \in \mathcal{R}_4,\ AE \notin \mathcal{LUMI}^{\mathcal{S}}_{\mathcal{L.V.}}$.

Corollary 9. $\exists\, R \in \mathcal{R}_4,\ AE \notin \mathcal{FST A}^{\mathcal{F}}_{\mathcal{L.V.}}$.

Corollary 10. $\exists\, R \in \mathcal{R}_4,\ AE \notin \mathcal{FST A}^{\mathcal{S}}_{\mathcal{L.V.}}$.

Proof. Follows from Corollary 8.

Corollary 11. $\exists\, R \in \mathcal{R}_4,\ AE \notin \mathcal{FCOM}^{\mathcal{F}}_{\mathcal{L.V.}}$.

Corollary 12. $\exists\, R \in \mathcal{R}_4,\ AE \notin \mathcal{FCOM}^{\mathcal{S}}_{\mathcal{L.V.}}$.

Proof. Follows from Corollary 8.

Corollary 13. $\exists\ R \in \mathcal{R}_4,\ AE \notin \mathcal{OBLOT}_{\mathcal{L}.\mathcal{V}}^{\mathcal{F}}$.

Corollary 14. $\exists\ R \in \mathcal{R}_4,\ AE \notin \mathcal{OBLOT}_{\mathcal{L}.\mathcal{V}}^{\mathcal{S}}$.

Proof. Follows from Corollary 8.

We get the following results:

Theorem 1. $\mathcal{OBLOT}_{\mathcal{F}.\mathcal{V}}^{\mathcal{F}} > \mathcal{OBLOT}_{\mathcal{L}.\mathcal{V}}^{\mathcal{F}}$.

Proof. From Corollary 1 and Corollary 13.

Theorem 2. $\mathcal{OBLOT}_{\mathcal{F}.\mathcal{V}}^{\mathcal{S}} > \mathcal{OBLOT}_{\mathcal{L}.\mathcal{V}}^{\mathcal{S}}$.

Proof. From Lemma 1 and Corollary 14.

Theorem 3. $\mathcal{FSTA}_{\mathcal{F}.\mathcal{V}}^{\mathcal{F}} > \mathcal{FSTA}_{\mathcal{L}.\mathcal{V}}^{\mathcal{F}}$.

Proof. From Corollary 3 and Corollary 9.

Theorem 4. $\mathcal{FSTA}_{\mathcal{F}.\mathcal{V}}^{\mathcal{S}} > \mathcal{FSTA}_{\mathcal{L}.\mathcal{V}}^{\mathcal{S}}$.

Proof. From Corollary 2 and Corollary 10.

Theorem 5. $\mathcal{FCOM}_{\mathcal{F}.\mathcal{V}}^{\mathcal{F}} > \mathcal{FCOM}_{\mathcal{L}.\mathcal{V}}^{\mathcal{F}}$.

Proof. From Corollary 5 and Corollary 11.

Theorem 6. $\mathcal{FCOM}_{\mathcal{F}.\mathcal{V}}^{\mathcal{S}} > \mathcal{FCOM}_{\mathcal{L}.\mathcal{V}}^{\mathcal{S}}$.

Proof. From Corollary 4 and Corollary 12.

Theorem 7. $\mathcal{LUMI}_{\mathcal{F}.\mathcal{V}}^{\mathcal{F}} > \mathcal{LUMI}_{\mathcal{L}.\mathcal{V}}^{\mathcal{F}}$.

Proof. From Corollary 7 and Lemma 2.

Theorem 8. $\mathcal{LUMI}_{\mathcal{F}.\mathcal{V}}^{\mathcal{S}} > \mathcal{LUMI}_{\mathcal{L}.\mathcal{V}}^{\mathcal{S}}$.

Proof. From Corollary 6 and Corollary 8.

4   Equivalent Oscillation Problem

Definition 2. *Problem Equivalent Oscillation (EqOsc):* *Let three robots* r_1, r_2 *and* r_3 *be initially placed at three points* B, A *and* C *respectively.* $AB = AC = d$. *Let* B', C' *be points collinear on the line such that* $AB' = AC' = \frac{2d}{3}$. *The robots* r_1 *and* r_3 *have to change their positions from* B *to* B' *and back to* B, C *to* C' *and back to* C *respectively, while always being equidistant from* r_2, *i.e.,* A *(Equidistant Condition).*

More formally speaking, if there is a round t *such that the robots* r_1 *and* r_3 *is at* B *and* C *respectively, then there must exist a round* $t' > t$, *such that* r_1 *and* r_3 *is at* B' *and* C' *respectively. Similarly if at round* t', r_1 *and* r_3 *is at* B' *and* C' *respectively, then there must exist a round* $t'' > t'$, *such that* r_1 *and* r_3 *is at* B *and* C *respectively (Oscillation Condition) (Fig. 4).*

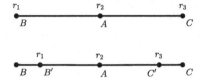

Fig. 4. Illustration of *EqOsc* problem

We prove that this problem is not solvable in $\mathcal{LUMI}^{\mathcal{S}}_{\mathcal{F}.\mathcal{V}}$.

Lemma 3. $\exists\ R \in \mathcal{R}_3,\ EqOsc \notin \mathcal{LUMI}^{\mathcal{S}}_{\mathcal{F}.\mathcal{V}}$.

Proof. Let the robots r_1, r_3 be able to successfully execute the movements satisfying the conditions of the problem till round t. Let at the beginning of round $t+1$ the robots r_1 and r_3 be at the points B and C respectively. So next the robots r_1 and r_3 must move to the points B', C' respectively. Note that the robots must move together or otherwise the equidistant condition is not satisfied. From round $t+1$ we activate only one of the terminal robots alternatively. Let at rounds $t+1$, $t+3$, $t+5$,......, the robot r_1 is activated and let at rounds $t+2$, $t+4$, $t+6$,......, the robot r_3 is activated.

Now whenever r_1 or r_3 makes a movement(when they are activated) the equidistant condition is violated. If neither r_1 nor r_3 makes any movement indefinitely then the oscillating condition is violated.

The problem cannot be solved in $\mathcal{LUMI}^{\mathcal{S}}_{\mathcal{F}.\mathcal{V}}$.

From Lemma 3 following result naturally follows,

Corollary 15. $\exists\ R \in \mathcal{R}_3,\ EqOsc \notin \mathcal{FSTA}^{\mathcal{S}}_{\mathcal{F}.\mathcal{V}}$ *and,* $\exists\ R \in \mathcal{R}_3,\ EqOsc \notin \mathcal{FCOM}^{\mathcal{S}}_{\mathcal{F}.\mathcal{V}}$.

4.1   Solution of Problem Equivalent Oscillation in $\mathcal{FSTA}^{\mathcal{F}}_{\mathcal{L}.\mathcal{V}}$

We now give an algorithm to solve the problem in $\mathcal{FSTA}^{\mathcal{F}}_{\mathcal{L}.\mathcal{V}}$. The pseudocode of the algorithm is given below.

Algorithm 1: Algorithm *AlgEOSTA* for Problem EqOsc executed by each robot r in $\mathcal{FSTA}^{\mathcal{F}}_{\mathcal{L}.\mathcal{V}}$.

---
1   d = distance from the closer robot;
2   A = Position of the middle robot;
3   **if** *not a terminal robot* **then**
4   Remain static
5   **else**
6   **if** *Light = Off or Light = F* **then**
7   Light $\leftarrow$ N
8   Move to a point D on the line segment such that $AD = \frac{2d}{3}$
9   **else**
10   Light $\leftarrow$ F
11   Move to a point D on the line segment such that $AD = \frac{3d}{2}$

Description and Correctness of $AlgEOSTA$. Let the three robots r_1, r_2 and r_3 be at B, A, and C respectively. Here $V_r > AB$, and $V_r > AC$, but $V_r < BC$. So there are three robots among which there is one robot which can see two other robots except itself, we call this robot the *middle robot*. The other two robots can see only one other robot except itself. We call each of these two robots *terminal robot*. The terminal robots are initially at a distance d from the middle robot. Whenever a robot is activated it can understand whether it is a terminal or a middle robot. Now, each of the robots save a light which is initially saved to Off. If a robot perceives that it is a middle robot it does not do anything. If it is a terminal robot and its light is set to Off or F, it changes its light to N and moves closer a distance two-third of the present distance from the middle robot, and if its light is set to N, it changes its light to F and moves further to a distance 1.5 times of the present distance from the middle robot. As we consider a fully synchronous system both the terminal robots execute the nearer and further movement alternatively together, and hence our problem is solved.

Hence we get the following result:

Lemma 4. $\forall\, R \in \mathcal{R}_3$, $EqOsc \in \mathcal{FSTA}^{\mathcal{F}}_{\mathcal{L}.\mathcal{V}.}$.

Theorem 9. $\mathcal{FSTA}^{\mathcal{F}}_{\mathcal{L}.\mathcal{V}.} > \mathcal{FSTA}^{\mathcal{S}}_{\mathcal{L}.\mathcal{V}.}$.

Proof. By Corollary 15 the problem cannot be solved in $\mathcal{FSTA}^{\mathcal{S}}_{\mathcal{L}.\mathcal{V}.}$, and, trivially $\mathcal{FSTA}^{\mathcal{F}}_{\mathcal{L}.\mathcal{V}.} \geq \mathcal{FSTA}^{\mathcal{S}}_{\mathcal{L}.\mathcal{V}.}$.

Theorem 10. $\mathcal{FSTA}^{\mathcal{F}}_{\mathcal{L}.\mathcal{V}.} \perp \mathcal{FSTA}^{\mathcal{S}}_{\mathcal{F}.\mathcal{V}.}$.

Proof. By Corollary 15 and Lemma 4, $EqOsc$ cannot be solved in $\mathcal{FSTA}^{\mathcal{S}}_{\mathcal{F}.\mathcal{V}.}$ but can be solved in $\mathcal{FSTA}^{\mathcal{F}}_{\mathcal{L}.\mathcal{V}.}$.

Similarly, by Corollary 9 and 2 AE cannot be solved in $\mathcal{FSTA}^{\mathcal{F}}_{\mathcal{L}.\mathcal{V}.}$ but can be solved in $\mathcal{FSTA}^{\mathcal{S}}_{\mathcal{F}.\mathcal{V}.}$. Hence the result.

4.2   Solution of Problem Equivalent Oscillation in $\mathcal{FCOM}^{\mathcal{F}}_{\mathcal{L}.\mathcal{V}.}$.

We now give an algorithm to solve the problem in $\mathcal{FCOM}^{\mathcal{F}}_{\mathcal{L}.\mathcal{V}.}$. The pseudocode of the algorithm is given below.

Algorithm 2: Algorithm $AlgEOCOM$ for Problem EqOsc executed by each robot r in $\mathcal{FCOM}^{\mathcal{F}}_{\mathcal{L}.\mathcal{V}.}$.

```
1   d = distance from the closer robot;
2   A = Position of the middle robot;
3   if not a terminal robot then
4   |     Remain static
5   |     if Visible light = NIL or FAR then
6   |     |  Light ← FAR
7   |     else if Visible light = NEAR then
8   |     |  Light ← NEAR
9   else
10  |     if Visible light = NIL or Visible light = NEAR then
11  |     |  Light ← NEAR
12  |     |  Move to a point D on the line segment such that AD = 2d/3
13  |     else if Visible light = FAR then
14  |     |  Light ← FAR
15  |     |  Move to a point D on the line segment such that AD = 3d/2
```

Description and Correctness of *AlgEOCOM*. Let the three robots r_1, r_2 and r_3 be at B, A, and C respectively. Here $V_r > AB$, and $V_r > AC$, but $V_r < BC$. So there are three robots among which there is one robot which can see two other robots except itself, we call this robot the *middle robot*. The other two robots can see only one other robot except itself. We call each of these two robots *terminal robot*. Whenever a robot is activated it can understand whether it is a terminal or a middle robot. Now, each of the robots has a light which is initially saved to NIL. If a robot perceives that it is a middle robot it can see the lights of the two terminal robots. If it perceives the lights of the terminal robots to be set to NIL or FAR, it sets its own light to FAR. And if it perceives the lights of the terminal robots to be set to $NEAR$, it sets its own light to $NEAR$. The middle robot only changes its light but does not change its position. If it is a terminal robot it can only see the light of the middle robot. If the light of the middle robot is set to NIL or $NEAR$, the terminal robot changes its light to $NEAR$ and moves closer to a distance which is two-third of the present distance from the middle robot. And if the light of the middle robot is set to FAR, it changes its light to FAR and moves away to a distance 1.5 times the present distance from the middle robot. As we consider a fully synchronous system both the terminal robots execute the nearer and further movement alternatively together, and hence our problem is solved.

Hence we get the following result:

Lemma 5. $\forall\ R \in \mathcal{R}_3,\ EqOsc \in \mathcal{FCOM}_{\mathcal{L.V.}}^{\mathcal{F}}$.

Theorem 11. $\mathcal{FCOM}_{\mathcal{L.V.}}^{\mathcal{F}} > \mathcal{FCOM}_{\mathcal{L.V.}}^{\mathcal{S}}$.

Proof. By Corollary 15 the problem cannot be solved in $\mathcal{FCOM}_{\mathcal{L.V.}}^{\mathcal{S}}$, and, trivially $\mathcal{FCOM}_{\mathcal{L.V.}}^{\mathcal{F}} \geq \mathcal{FCOM}_{\mathcal{L.V.}}^{\mathcal{S}}$. Hence our theorem.

Theorem 12. $\mathcal{FCOM}_{\mathcal{L.V.}}^{\mathcal{F}} \perp \mathcal{FCOM}_{\mathcal{F.V.}}^{\mathcal{S}}$.

Proof. By Corollary 15 and Lemma 5, $EqOsc$ cannot be solved in $\mathcal{FCOM}_{\mathcal{F.V.}}^{\mathcal{S}}$ but can be solved in $\mathcal{FCOM}_{\mathcal{L.V.}}^{\mathcal{F}}$.

Similarly, by Corollary 11 and 4 AE cannot be solved in $\mathcal{FCOM}_{\mathcal{L.V.}}^{\mathcal{F}}$ but can be solved in $\mathcal{FCOM}_{\mathcal{F.V.}}^{\mathcal{S}}$. Hence the result.

4.3   Similar Deductions in $\mathcal{OBLOT}$ and $\mathcal{LUMI}$

Theorem 13. $\mathcal{OBLOT}_{\mathcal{L.V.}}^{\mathcal{F}} \perp \mathcal{OBLOT}_{\mathcal{F.V.}}^{\mathcal{S}}$.

Proof. We have proved that the problem AE cannot be solved in $\mathcal{OBLOT}_{\mathcal{L.V.}}^{\mathcal{F}}$ but can be solved in $\mathcal{OBLOT}_{\mathcal{F.V.}}^{\mathcal{S}}$.

Now we consider the problem *Rendezvous* which was proved to be impossible in $\mathcal{OBLOT}_{\mathcal{F.V.}}^{\mathcal{S}}$ in [11]. Now we claim that in our model the problem is possible to solve in $\mathcal{OBLOT}_{\mathcal{L.V.}}^{\mathcal{F}}$. This is because in our model we assume the visibility graph of the robots in the initial configuration to be connected. Now when there are only two robots in the initial configuration this means, all the robots in the initial configuration can see each other. Hence in this case the problem reduces to $\mathcal{OBLOT}^{\mathcal{F}}$ model. Now it is well known that *rendezvous* problem is solvable in this model, as the robots just move to the mid-point of the line segment joining them. Hence the result.

Theorem 14. $\mathcal{OBLOT}^{\mathcal{F}}_{\mathcal{L}.\mathcal{V}} > \mathcal{OBLOT}^{\mathcal{S}}_{\mathcal{L}.\mathcal{V}}.$

Proof. Trivially $\mathcal{OBLOT}^{\mathcal{F}}_{\mathcal{L}.\mathcal{V}} \geq \mathcal{OBLOT}^{\mathcal{S}}_{\mathcal{L}.\mathcal{V}}$ and by Theorem 13 the problem *Rendezvous* is solvable in $\mathcal{OBLOT}^{\mathcal{F}}_{\mathcal{L}.\mathcal{V}}$ but not in $\mathcal{OBLOT}^{\mathcal{S}}_{\mathcal{L}.\mathcal{V}}$.

Lemma 6. $\forall\, R \in \mathcal{R}_3,\ EqOsc \in \mathcal{LUMI}^{\mathcal{F}}_{\mathcal{L}.\mathcal{V}}.$

Proof. From Lemma 4 and 5.

Theorem 15. $\mathcal{LUMI}^{\mathcal{F}}_{\mathcal{L}.\mathcal{V}} \perp \mathcal{LUMI}^{\mathcal{S}}_{\mathcal{F}.\mathcal{V}}.$

Proof. By Lemma 2 and Corollary 7 the problem AE cannot be solved in $\mathcal{LUMI}^{\mathcal{F}}_{\mathcal{L}.\mathcal{V}}$ but can be solved in $\mathcal{LUMI}^{\mathcal{S}}_{\mathcal{F}.\mathcal{V}}$.

By Lemma 3 and 6 , the problem $EqOsc$ cannot be solved in $\mathcal{LUMI}^{\mathcal{S}}_{\mathcal{F}.\mathcal{V}}$ but can be solved in $\mathcal{LUMI}^{\mathcal{F}}_{\mathcal{L}.\mathcal{V}}$. Hence, the result.

5   Conclusion

In this paper we have initiated the analysis of computational capabilities of mobile robots having limited visibility. Cross-model relationships under limited visibility conditions and computational relationships when the scheduler is asynchronous are interesting future directions.

Acknowledgement. The second author is supported by West Bengal State Government Fellowship scheme. The third and fourth authors are supported by UGC, Govt. of India.

References

1. Ando, H., Oasa, Y., Suzuki, I., Yamashita, M.: Distributed memoryless point convergence algorithm for mobile robots with limited visibility. IEEE Trans. Robot. Autom. **15**(5), 818–828 (1999). https://doi.org/10.1109/70.795787
2. Buchin, K., Flocchini, P., Kostitsyna, I., Peters, T., Santoro, N., Wada, K.: Autonomous mobile robots: refining the computational landscape. In: IEEE International Parallel and Distributed Processing Symposium Workshops, IPDPS Workshops 2021, Portland, OR, USA, 17–21 June 2021, pp. 576–585. IEEE (2021). https://doi.org/10.1109/IPDPSW52791.2021.00091
3. Buchin, K., Flocchini, P., Kostitsyna, I., Peters, T., Santoro, N., Wada, K.: On the computational power of energy-constrained mobile robots: algorithms and cross-model analysis. In: Parter, M. (ed.) Structural Information and Communication Complexity. SIROCCO 2022. LNCS, vol. 13298, pp. 42–61. Springer, Cham (2022). https://doi.org/10.1007/978-3-031-09993-9_3

4. Das, S., Flocchini, P., Prencipe, G., Santoro, N., Yamashita, M.: The power of lights: synchronizing asynchronous robots using visible bits. In: 2012 IEEE 32nd International Conference on Distributed Computing Systems, Macau, China, 18–21 June 2012, pp. 506–515. IEEE Computer Society (2012). https://doi.org/10.1109/ICDCS.2012.71

5. Das, S., Flocchini, P., Prencipe, G., Santoro, N., Yamashita, M.: Autonomous mobile robots with lights. Theor. Comput. Sci. **609**, 171–184 (2016). https://doi.org/10.1016/j.tcs.2015.09.018

6. Flocchini, P., Prencipe, G., Santoro, N., Widmayer, P.: Gathering of asynchronous robots with limited visibility. Theor. Comput. Sci. **337**(1–3), 147–168 (2005). https://doi.org/10.1016/j.tcs.2005.01.001

7. Flocchini, P., Santoro, N., Viglietta, G., Yamashita, M.: Rendezvous with constant memory. Theor. Comput. Sci. **621**, 57–72 (2016). https://doi.org/10.1016/j.tcs.2016.01.025

8. Flocchini, P., Santoro, N., Wada, K.: On memory, communication, and synchronous schedulers when moving and computing. In: Felber, P., Friedman, R., Gilbert, S., Miller, A. (eds.) 23rd International Conference on Principles of Distributed Systems, OPODIS 2019, December 17–19, 2019, Neuchâtel, Switzerland. LIPIcs, vol. 153, pp. 25:1–25:17. Schloss Dagstuhl - Leibniz-Zentrum für Informatik (2019). https://doi.org/10.4230/LIPIcs.OPODIS.2019.25

9. Goswami, P., Sharma, A., Ghosh, S., Sau, B.: Time optimal gathering of myopic robots on an infinite triangular grid. In: Devismes, S., Petit, F., Altisen, K., Di Luna, G.A., Fernandez Anta, A. (eds.) Stabilization, Safety, and Security of Distributed Systems. SSS 2022. LNCS, vol. 13751, pp. 270–284. Springer, Cham (2022). https://doi.org/10.1007/978-3-031-21017-4_18

10. Poudel, P., Sharma, G.: Time-optimal gathering under limited visibility with one-axis agreement. Inf. **12**(11), 448 (2021). https://doi.org/10.3390/info12110448

11. Suzuki, I., Yamashita, M.: Distributed anonymous mobile robots: formation of geometric patterns. SIAM J. Comput. **28**(4), 1347–1363 (1999). https://doi.org/10.1137/S009753979628292X

Coverage Criteria Based Testing of IoT Applications

S. R. Nagalakshmi$^{(\boxtimes)}$ and Meenakshi D'Souza

International Institute of Information Technology, Bangalore, India
{nagalakshmi,meenakshi}@iiitb.ac.in

Abstract. IoT applications are ubiquitous and many of them are large in scale, involving processing and storage of real-time sensor data and various events. Many such applications are safety-critical in nature demanding rigorous testing to eliminate as many errors as possible. We propose a coverage criteria-based white-box testing framework for large-scale IoT applications. Our criteria are derived from the underlying architecture of these applications. We present two different views of the IoT applications architecture and coverage criteria are defined based on these two views Event coverage, functionality coverage, and end-to-end flow coverage are some of the proposed criteria, we illustrate their use in detecting subtle errors in the underlying IoT applications. Our framework has been prototyped on the AWS IoT free-tier services, one of the most popular IoT application development frameworks.

Keywords: Large-scale IoT applications · White-box testing · Coverage criteria

1 Introduction

Internet of Things (IoT) is an emerging paradigm that is growing to be ubiquitous amongst our everyday lives. A recent report by Gartner [6] predicts that IoT technologies and applications are set to grow exponentially in the coming decade with several million devices connected to the internet. IoT applications deal with devices called *things* that are connected to the internet and are capable of transmitting data. Using the data from a range of such connected devices, a suite of applications has been developed in the areas of smart homes, smart transportation, industrial IoT, etc. These systems interact with human users and provide functionality to aid their various activities.

There are several platforms that are available for developing IoT applications [7]— AWS IoT [1], Samsung SmartThings [5], Google Cloud IoT [3], Azure platform [2] etc. Many of them provide features that replicate the functionality of

---

This work is sponsored by a cluster project on Interdisciplinary Cyber-Physical systems, Department of Science and Technology, Government of India.

things and a serverless application development platform to design and implement a full-fledged IoT application. The applications developed on the serverless cloud platform can then be ported to an IoT platform seamlessly. Such applications have been developed in several domains ranging from health care, agriculture, smart homes, smart transport, industries etc. [1]. Apart from basic functionality involving decision making based on sensor inputs, many IoT applications also provide sophisticated features like machine learning, signal/image processing, and data analytics algorithms to make them adaptive in nature.

Many IoT applications are safety critical in nature and hence testing and verification of these systems is of utmost importance. They deal with data that is secure and need to satisfy several stringent security and privacy requirements [8]. Typically, IoT applications are developed using different kinds of technologies including but not limited to, hardware devices like sensors and actuators, communication protocols of different kinds, security policies and mechanisms, programming languages like Java, JavaScript, Python, etc. databases, and their supporting query languages like SQL, etc. Such a complex mix of technologies makes it difficult to reuse existing testing and verification techniques smoothly.

There have been several different efforts toward formally verifying safety critical IoT applications and the underlying technologies. Techniques for formally verifying IoT applications have been proposed using abstraction and model checking [7,8], theorem proving [10,11] etc. Most of these techniques are good but, one needs a strong mathematical background in one or more formal methods based techniques and an IoT application developer using these techniques is still far from becoming a reality.

Testing is a time-tested technique to find errors in software applications. It can be used directly by developers and hence can scale to practical use. Testing of IoT applications can be challenging due to the mix of technologies involved in application development. In this paper, we propose a testing framework for IoT applications based on their architectures. Our architecture framework is generic and includes the various IoT application development platforms mentioned earlier [1,5], and [3]. We define two views of such a generic IoT applications architecture and propose coverage criteria based on the two views of this architecture. The coverage criteria are defined to capture the unique features of IoT applications and can be used to generate test cases for system level functionality testing of the applications. A test case generation framework that automatically generates test cases to test against the proposed coverage criteria is also presented.

We have prototyped our framework to work on the architecture entities derived from the AWS IoT platform. AWS IoT is one of the most popular IoT application development platforms and provides several free-tier applications [6]. Our prototype can be easily generalized to other platforms too. Our testing framework and the associated coverage criteria are strong enough to detect errors that occur due to complex interactions across IoT components [8].

The paper is structured as follows. We introduce large-scale IoT applications in the next section and list the important commonalities of the underlying platforms. Section 2.1 describes our generic architecture and the two views that we discuss. Related work is presented in Sect. 3. Section 4 defines the proposed coverage criteria for white-box testing based on the generic IoT architecture. The test case generation framework along with the prototype implementation is described in Sect. 5. We conclude the paper and describe the plans for future work in Sect. 6.

2 Large-Scale IoT Applications

IoT applications work with several different kinds of sensors/sensor-embedded devices that transfer telemetry data and take decisions/provide functionality using programs that work on it. Such large-scale IoT applications are typically built using (serverless) cloud computing platforms where the developers can focus solely on writing code to implement the desired functionality using a standard programming language, while the platform takes care of provisioning, scaling, and managing the underlying infrastructure. This approach allows developers to build and deploy applications without having to worry about traditional server management tasks. As mentioned in the Introduction, several such cloud infrastructure and platform service providers are available— [1,2,5]. Some of these platforms provide a set of free-tier services that help developers to design IoT applications including the sensors, computation, and actuation paradigm.

2.1 IoT Architecture

The IoT application platforms cater to the common goal of developing IoT applications and provide mostly similar features for application development. We identify and list the common features below, with the aim of using them to derive an IoT application architecture.

- IoT devices or *things*, (sensor, sensor-embedded devices, actuators) connect using *communication protocols* (like MQTT or HTTP) to send and/or receive data. The protocols also help to connect and communicate the device's data throughout the IoT architecture for providing basic functionality including storage and handling through user-defined rules.
- *Data* in an IoT application is the information generated by interconnected devices as they interact with their surroundings. Data is represented using the JSON format.
- An *event* refers to a significant occurrence or happening that takes place within the system. Events are used to represent changes in the state of a device, environment, or system, and they trigger specific actions or responses. Events often come with associated data that provides context about the event, e.g., a temperature sensor event might include the temperature reading, timestamp, and the sensor identifier. The data values measured are typically embedded in the event and transmitted as JSON objects.
- Security of data is managed through Identity and Access Management (IAM) policies and through standard SSL/TLS X.509 certificates.

- The platform is typically serverless and provides computing functions and supports a variety of programming languages.

An *IoT applications architecture*, or IoT architecture or application architecture, in short, is one framework that includes all the above components and depicts several details regarding their interactions encompassing the functionality of the application. We consider two **views** of the architecture, the two views will facilitate defining various coverage criteria for testing.

2.2   Component-Based View of IoT Architecture

In the component-based view, the architecture of an IoT application I is given by $\mathcal{A}_{\mathcal{I}} = (C_I, Cn_I, Int_I, Cf_I)$ where

- C_I is the set of all components of I. Each component in C_I can have *subcomponents* which again, are in C_I. For e.g., in AWS IoT, C_I contains the devices, API gateways that send and receive data, IoT core entities like rule engine (RE), Lambda functions written by application developers, databases (DynamoDB), storage entities (S3 and queues in SQS), cloud platform services, and the third-party apps connected to the platform. Most of the components are executable and put together with the connectors, define the functionality of the underlying IoT application I.
- Cn_I is the set of all connectors of I. Connectors link components for providing data and control transfer and can be communication channels, protocols, etc. Connectors in IoT application architectures typically follow a publish-subscribe mechanism (e.g. MQTT protocol with appropriate topics acting as a channel to carry data).
- Int_I is the set of all interfaces of I. They are used by connectors to connect with one or more components. Message broker (MB), device-shadow service (DSS), and simple notification services (SNS) are typical interfaces to attach things to the cloud platform services. Message brokers are used to manage communication by establishing publish-subscribe matches for data. Device shadow holds the updated state, which can be retrieved by the actuator device at any time. Notification services are used to notify end users/actuators/apps regarding various alerts or actions through messages or emails.
- Cf_I represents the *configuration* information that describes the properties and structure of the data, the components, and the connectors. The configuration also includes the descriptions of IoT core topic rules (TR), event-source-mappings (ESM), event bridge rules (EBR), cloud watch logs, policies, and their permissions attached to each service. They specify details on integration and accessibility for using other authorized services.

After analyzing different IoT platforms, we observe that AWS IoT [1] comprehensively encompasses the fundamental building blocks of an IoT architecture. We use the free-tier services of AWS IoT to describe our work in detail. As given in Fig. 1, data sent from the things (associated with a unique topic name) are transferred through a message broker and the rule engine sub-components of the

IoT core using the MQTT communication protocol (a connector). In the core, the *shadows* (virtual replica) of the things/devices are created. Rules are associated with the IoT core (*rule engine*) and *event bridge* service to filter and route data to invoke and execute *Lambda* functions that connect to cloud platform services like database/storage (DynamoDB/S3/SQS), image/signal processing components (Kinesis, in the case of AWS), and notification services that communicate back with the things.

Several large-scale IoT applications also involve components (signal/image processing, machine learning components) that process the data to make inferences involving perception, object detection, etc. We do not explicitly consider the algorithms that run as a part of these components in this work.

2.3   Event-Driven View of IoT Architecture

An event-driven architecture pattern [15] is also well-suited for IoT systems because it aligns with the real-time, dynamic, and interconnected nature of these applications. For IoT applications, event generation, routing, and consumption are fundamental concepts that help manage the flow of information and actions within the ecosystem of connected devices and services.

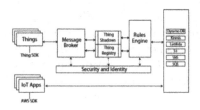

Fig. 1. AWS IoT Generic Architecture

Generally, an event-driven architecture has the following components: An *event generator* is a component responsible for initiating events based on specific conditions or triggers. An *event router* is responsible for directing events from their source to appropriate destinations or consumers. An *event consumer* is a component or service that receives, processes, and acts upon the events.

A publish-subscribe model is typically used in IoT applications for the distribution of events. In this model, event generators (publishers) emit events, and event consumers (subscribers) subscribe to specific types of events. An event router or MB handles the distribution of events to appropriate subscribers. For the AWS IoT application architecture, sensors generating and sending various kinds of data (measurements, readings, status updates, etc.) are the event generators, MB generates/routes the events based on the underlying publish-subscribe matches, and the subscribers react to the events by processing the data and taking appropriate actions. AWS also features TR and ESM services, cloud watch events (EBR) services, step functions, and HTTP, to help connect event origins to their destinations. Here, computational entities encompass Lambda functions ensuring a cohesive flow.

Considering other service providers, in the Azure ecosystem [2], the IoT hub serves as a data collection point, seamlessly integrating with Azure Event Grid to initiate the subsequent processes. This orchestration facilitates event matching through subscriptions, while the responsibility of computation lies with Azure functions and logic apps. Samsung SmartThings [5] also employs a subscription management layer, forging connections between event generators, like device-type handlers, and their corresponding consumers, Smart apps, resulting in a harmonious interaction. The IoT proposed architecture is versatile enough to seamlessly accommodate both component-based and event-driven views.

2.4   Paths in an IoT Architecture

Paths in an architecture $\mathcal{A}_\mathcal{I}$ typically start at a *source component*, pass through one or more connectors using the interfaces, to a *next* component, and so on, always ending in a *destination component*. Source components in IoT applications are things (sensor devices or applications triggering the flow), and destination components are actuators or applications performing some actions.

These are *control flow* paths that depict the transfer of control from one component to another. We say that a particular component c_i is *reachable* if there is a control flow path that originates from one of the source components and ends at c_i. Similarly, *data flow reachability* involves the transfer of data originating from the things to one or more components. It is important that the data does not get modified during the transfer unless an application is meant to do so. With the event-driven view, *event flow reachability* involves event paths that originate from event generators, go through one or more event routers, and end at an event consumer.

We propose a set of coverage criteria considering both the views that impose test requirements on the various features and paths of an IoT application architecture. Our coverage criteria can be used for system-level testing of IoT applications and

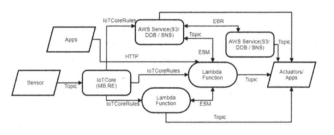

Fig. 2. Paths in an AWS IoT Architecture

interestingly, find errors in IoT applications that result from non-trivial interactions between components [8,9].

Coverage Criteria-Based White-box Testing. White-box testing is a powerful testing methodology that can discover several coding and design errors in software artifacts. It is typically applied to code to ensure that the desired portions of the code (like statements, decisions, loops, function calls, etc.) are executed by designing appropriate test cases with the aim of finding errors, if any. A test requirement is specified as a coverage criterion and test cases are designed to meet the coverage criterion. For example, statement coverage is a test requirement, and test cases that meet statement coverage will execute every reachable statement in the program under test. Such coverage criteria are defined for software artifacts like requirements, design models [13], and architecture entities too [12].

For IoT applications, the architecture contains all the necessary information for complete application development. The configuration information and the executable components can be parsed to extract the necessary information for defining the test requirements for the various coverage criteria.

3   Related Work

Since several IoT applications are safety-critical in nature, there is prior work available on testing and formal verification of IoT applications. [7,8] are on formal verification and program analysis of IoT applications against security and privacy properties. Their prototype is based on the Samsung SmartThings platform which involves a proprietary language (Groovy) and they verify different properties related to security violations. Our proposed coverage criteria can precisely check for the same properties that involve complex interactions between components. Our work also can be used to detect several of the scenarios that have been identified to be problematic in the context of IoT applications [9]. Other papers consider specific properties of IoT applications and work on elaborate models using EventB theorem prover [10] and Maude verifier [11] and verify properties of IoT communication protocols and applications respectively.

Our definition of IoT applications architecture and the test case generation based on coverage over the architecture model is motivated by prior work on formalizing event-driven behavior of serverless applications [15], the architecture coverage criteria defined in [12] and applicability of coverage-criteria-based testing on serverless applications [16]. Our proposed framework is specific to IoT applications and our coverage criteria are motivated by some of the concepts proposed in the above papers. Our framework also includes coverage criteria for all the possible scenarios in IoT applications, as against specific paths considered in [16]. Table 1 given in Sect. 5 includes applications that illustrate that our coverage criteria can find errors shown in [9] and also includes scenarios not considered in [16].

4   Coverage Criteria for IoT Applications Architecture

We propose the following specific test requirements for coverage criteria-based testing of IoT applications. Given an IoT application $\mathcal{I}$, we consider the underlying architecture of I, $\mathcal{A}_{\mathcal{I}}$. Test cases are defined based on the two views and the paths of $\mathcal{A}_{\mathcal{I}}$. For each of the coverage criteria below, a description of the test requirement of the criterion is provided, followed by details regarding how a set of test cases will *satisfy* the respective criterion.

1. *Lambda coverage*: Lambda functions run on the serverless cloud platform and provide the main functionality of an IoT application. Execution of Lambda

functions in response events results in specific actions like actuating one or more devices, sending notifications to users, updating the database, or storing data, etc. The test requirement of Lambda coverage specifies that each Lambda function be executed once at least by one of its *invoker* resources. The test case is a path that includes at least one of the Lambda functions used in an IoT application. We say that Lambda coverage is *met* or *satisfied* by a set of test cases T if, for each Lambda function in the application under test, there is at least one test case $t \in T$ that executes the function.

2. *End-to-end flow coverage*: A behaviour of an IoT application is a *flow* from the sensor end to the actuator end through at least one of the Lambda functions (Sensor-Computation(Lambda)-Actuator). The test requirement of end-to-end flow is a path/set of control flow paths from a sensor device, through one or more computation components to an actuator device or another output. We say that end-to-end flow coverage is *met* or *satisfied* by a set of test cases T if there is at least one test case $t \in T$ for each end-to-end path in the architecture of the application under test.

3. *Event coverage*: The test requirement of event coverage is a path from the event generator to the event consumer through at least one of the event routers along with the event (represented as JSON object) that flows through the router. We say that event coverage is *met* or *satisfied* by a set of test cases T if there is at least one test case $t \in T$ that contains each such path of the application under test.

4. *Decision coverage*: As discussed earlier, events drive the interactions and flows in an IoT applications. Different decisions are taken based on the arrival of events. Lambda functions, acting as event handlers, receive events from multiple sources and take decisions based on the nature of the events. The underlying decisions can also originate from topic rules in the rule engine, ESM criteria, etc., and play a crucial role in orchestrating the event flow across the various components. The test requirement of decision coverage is to list and write a set of test cases to execute all such decision statements. A set of test cases *satisfies* a particular decision statement if the outcome of the decision on executing a test case is true once and false once.

The above coverage criteria are defined considering the architecture models and views as described in Sect. 2.1. In addition, we can consider the coverage criteria involving individual components, their connectors, etc. along the lines proposed in [12]. In fact, the end-to-end flow coverage criterion proposed above subsumes the coverage criterion of "all-connected-components-path" (which in turn, is a combination of "direct component-to-component path" and "indirect component-to-component path") defined in [12]. Every test case that satisfies the end-to-end flow coverage criterion proposed above will also satisfy the all connected components path criterion proposed in [12].

5   Coverage Criteria-Based Test Case Generation Framework

Figure 3 provides an overview of our proposed coverage criteria-based test case generation framework. The framework is presented as per a generic IoT application architecture described in the earlier section. Our prototype of the framework and certain terminologies are specific to the AWS IoT application architecture [1].

Input to the test generation framework is an IoT application, $\mathcal{I}$, a collection of files consisting of executable code typically written in JavaScript along with configuration information files (in JSON format). Configuration information includes

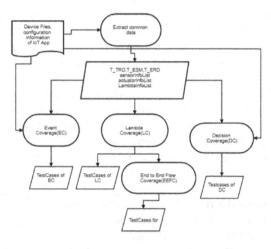

Fig. 3. Test case generation framework

information on TR, ESM, and EBR descriptions as below, sample files are available in https://github.com/NagalakshmiAthreya/TestCase-Generation-Parser

- *TR Description (TRD)* file containing the descriptions of all IoT core Topic Rules used in $\mathcal{I}$. TR acts as the bridge between the source (MQTT topics where devices publish messages) and the destination. Actions are taken at the destination on satisfying conditions in the SQL rules.
- *ESM Description (ESMD)* file containing the descriptions of all the ESMs associated with every Lambda function in $\mathcal{I}$. An ESM defines the link between an event source (like a stream or queue) and a Lambda function. It may include filter criteria to impose conditions on events to trigger Lambda.
- *EBR Description (ERD)* file with the descriptions of all the EBR rules used in $\mathcal{I}$, in the context of showing the connection between event sources and targets. It also contains an event pattern, which includes the constraints imposed on the event.
- A list of all (AWS) services used, along with their associated policies and exported cloud watch logs of the Lambda functions are also provided.

As shown in Fig. 3, to start with, specific parsers are invoked to extract the common data required by the coverage criteria. The extracted information is used to generate the test cases as per the chosen test requirement. The generated test cases can be executed by using a tool like Mocha [4], a widely used JavaScript testing framework for Node.js and browsers. Algorithms 1 and 2 describe the process for extraction of common data from configuration information like source, destinations, and data constraints from TRD, ESMD, ERD, and the component information like deviceName, topics, JSON data (params) from the sensors and actuator files. The Lambda functions connect to the actuator directly by publishing data on MQTT topics to the device or the device shadow or an app controlling some devices (HTTP). Algorithm 4 parses the Lambda functions of I to extract information like `sdkObject` (connects with Lambda destinations), `params` sent or received by querying `cloudWatchlogs`. The algorithms for Lambda coverage, end-to-end flow coverage, event coverage, and decision coverage criteria are executed based on the tester's choice. The pseudo code for Lambda coverage is given here, details regarding the other algorithms can be found in https://github.com/NagalakshmiAthreya/TestCase-Generation-Parser. Algorithm 3 maps the topic names and the attributes (`params`) of SQL statements of $\mathcal{T}_{TRD}$ with device data and sensor information to extract the triggering values to be used as test inputs.

Algorithm 1. Parser to extract common data

Require: *TRD* file,*ESMD* file, *ERD* file
Ensure: $\mathcal{T}_{TRD}, \mathcal{T}_{ESM}, \mathcal{T}_{ERD}$
 1: Initialize $\mathcal{T}_{TRD}$ with empty column entries for **RuleName, ActionDestination,** and **SQLQuery**
 2: **for** each *description* in *TRD* file **do**   ▷ Extract $\mathcal{T}_{TRD}$
 3:     Extract *ruleName, actions & SQLStmt* from *TRD file*
 4:     Append (*RuleName, ActionDestination, SQLQuery*) to $\mathcal{T}_{TRD}$
 5: **end for**
 6: **return** $\mathcal{T}_{TRD}$
 7: Initialize $\mathcal{T}_{TRD}$ with empty column entries for **EventSource, EventDestination,** and **FilterCriteria**
 8: **for** each *description* in *ESMD* file **do**   ▷ Extract $\mathcal{T}_{ESM}$
 9:     Extract *EventSourceArn, FunctionName & FilterCriteria* from *ESMD* file
10:     Append (*EventSource, EventDestination, FilterCriteria*) to $\mathcal{T}_{ESM}$
11: **end for**
12: **return** $\mathcal{T}_{ESM}$
13: Initialize $\mathcal{T}_{TRD}$ with empty column entries for **EventSource, EventDestination,** and **Event**
14: **for** each *description* in *ERD* file **do**   ▷ Extract $\mathcal{T}_{ERD}$
15:     Extract *eventSource, eventName from EventPattern & Targets* from *ERD* file
16:     Append (*EventSource, Event, EventDestination*) to $\mathcal{T}_{ERD}$
17: **end for**
18: **return** $\mathcal{T}_{ERD}$

Lambda Coverage (LC). Lambda functions play a significant role in IoT architectures, enabling event-driven processing, data transformation, and seamless integration with other services. A Lambda function can be invoked by the rules

---

Algorithm 2. Parser to extract device information

Require: List of sensor.js, actuator.js files in the application
Ensure: A list of extracted sensor and actuator information
 1: **function** PARSESENSORFILES(*sensorFiles*)
 2:     Initialize *sensorInfoList* with (*deviceName, topic, params*) as empty list
 3:     **for** each *sensorFile* in *sensorFiles* **do**
 4:         Extract device name, topic-names & attributes sent
 5:         Append the entry to *sensorInfoList*
 6:     **end for**
 7:     **return** *sensorInfoList*
 8: **end function**
 9: **function** PARSEACTUATORFILES(*actuatorFiles*)
10:     Initialize *ActuatorInfoList* with (*deviceName, topic, params*) as empty list
11:     **for** each *actuatorFile* in *actuatorFiles* **do**
12:         Extract device name, subscriptions
13:         **for** each *subscription* in *subscriptions* **do**
14:             Extract topic, attributes sent
15:             Append the entry to *actuatorInfoList*
16:         **end for**
17:     **end for**
18:     **return** *actuatorInfoList*
19: **end function**

---

of the rule engine, by several other services, or even by another Lambda function. Towards exercising the various Lambda functions, we need to fetch the data attributes or events or the parameters between two services in a particular control flow path. For services connected to the IoT core through a rule, we use Algorithm 3. For dealing with events through EBR or ESM, we execute the Lambda functions and get a query of the logs to extract the event formats.

Algorithm 3. Parser to get Core_data

Require: *sensorInfoList, Device-Data file* and $\mathcal{T}_{TRD}$
Ensure: *Core_Data_Values file*
 1: **for** each *SQLQuery* in $\mathcal{T}_{TRD}$ **do**
 2:     Extract *Topics*, & *params* from *SQLQuery*,
 3:     **if** *Topics* ∈ *sensorInfoList*(*topic*) **then**
 4:         Extract value V for *params* from *Device-Data* file.
 5:         Append (*RuleName, Topics, params, V*) to $\mathcal{T}_{TRD}$
 6:     **end if**
 7: **end for**
 8: **return** *Core_Data_Valuesfile*

Algorithm 5 starts with the list of Lambda functions provided and does backward traceability to find the services that trigger those Lambda functions (Lambda Invoker (LI)) in the first parse, later keeps looping to find the invoker's invoker till it *reaches* the invoker as IoT core Topic Rule. The IoT Core component routes sensor data (as it arrives) on selected topics of a rule, establishing a connectivity to find source components. Such a traceability is done on a case-by-case basis using the various features of the serverless framework, considering all possible ways of executing Lambda functions to enable different kinds of functionality. This way, the complete flow of control and data across the IoT application architecture is taken into consideration by our framework. The same represented in Fig. 4. The algorithm outputs LCtable ($\mathcal{T}_{LC}$), and each tuple of $\mathcal{T}_{LC}$ yields a test case for Lambda coverage.

Algorithm 4. Lambda Information Extraction

Require: *LambdaFiles* and *Lambda_logs* file
Ensure: LambdaInfoList
 1: **function** PARSELAMBDACODE(*LambdaFiles*)   ▷ Parse Lambda code
 2:     Initialize *LambdaInfoList* as empty
 3:     **for** each *LambdaFile* in *LambdaFiles* **do**
 4:         *LambdaName* ← Name of Lambda in *LambdaFiles*
 5:         *sdkObjects* ← Extract Objects of AWS-SDK class
 6:         **for** *sdkObject* in *sdkObjects* **do**
 7:             *targetService* ← Identify target service in *sdkObject*
 8:             *paramsSent* ← Extract parameters sent with *sdkObject*
 9:             *paramsRecieved* ← Extract event_info from *Lambda_logs* file
10:             Append (*LambdaName, targetService, paramsSent, paramsRecieved*) to *LambdaInfoList*
11:         **end for**
12:     **end for**
13:     **return** *LambdaInfoList*
14: **end function**

End-to-end Flow Coverage. The IoT application architecture, if visualized from an event-driven view, provides us with paths that flow through the IoT application, resulting in different behaviors. Control flow paths in the architecture from sensor devices pass through interfaces, message handlers, and rules to reach one or more

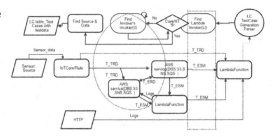

Fig. 4. Lambda Coverage

Lambda functions and finally reach actuator devices as control commands or notification services. This end-to-end flow coverage criteria helps us to generate test cases for system-level testing of an IoT application.

Algorithm 5. Test Case Generation for Lambda Coverage

Require: $\mathcal{T}_{TRD}, \mathcal{T}_{ESM}, \mathcal{T}_{ERD}$
Require: $\mathcal{L}_{LC}$: List of Lambda Functions
Ensure: Table of test requirements for Lambda coverage $\mathcal{T}_{LC}$
1: Initialize Table $\mathcal{T}_{LC}$ with columns LambdaFunctionName, LambdaInvoker (LI) and TriggerInfo
2: **for** each Lambda function l in $\mathcal{L}_{LC}$ **do**
3:    **if** $l \in ActionDestination(\mathcal{T}_{TRD})$ **then**
4:        Mark $Invoker = IoTCore$
5:        LI of $l = RuleName(\mathcal{T}_{TRD})$,
6:        TriggerInfo of $l = SQLQuery(\mathcal{T}_{TRD})$,
7:        Update $\mathcal{T}_{LC}$
8:        Call Parser to get Core_data with TriggerInfo of l
9:    **else**
10:        **if** $l \in EventDestination(\mathcal{T}_{ESM})$ **then**
11:            Mark $Invoker = AWSService$
12:            LI of $l = EventSource(\mathcal{T}_{ESM})$
13:            Execute Procedure to find Invoker's Invoker ($\mathcal{II}$)
14:            Update $\mathcal{T}_{LC}$
15:        **else**
16:            $Invoker = HTTPRequest$
17:            LI of $l =$ source of the HTTP request,
18:            Querying logs of l Extract TriggerInfo
19:            Update $\mathcal{T}_{LC}$
20:        **end if**
21:    **end if**
22: **end for**
23: Procedure to find Invoker's Invoker ($\mathcal{II}$)
24: **for** each $LI \in \mathcal{T}_{LC}$ **do**
25:    **if** $LI \in AWSService$ **then**
26:        **if** $LI \in ActionDestination(\mathcal{T}_{TRD})$ **then**
27:            Mark $Invoker = IoTCore$
28:            $II = RuleName(\mathcal{T}_{TRD})$,
29:            TriggerInfo of $l = SQLQuery(\mathcal{T}_{TRD})$,
30:            Update $\mathcal{T}_{LC}$
31:            Call Parser to get Core_data,
32:        **else**
33:            **if** $LI \in EventDestination(\mathcal{T}_{ESM})$ **then**
34:                Mark $Invoker = AWSService$
35:                $II = EventSource(\mathcal{T}_{ESM})$
36:                Extract TriggerInfo by querying logs of l
37:            **else**
38:                **if** $LI \in EventDestination(\mathcal{T}_{ERD})$ **then**
39:                    Mark $Invoker = AWSService$,
40:                    $II = EventSource(\mathcal{T}_{ERD})$
41:                    Extract TriggerInfo by querying logs of l
42:                **end if**
43:                Update $\mathcal{T}_{LC}$
44:            **end if**
45:        **end if**
46:    **end if**
47: **end for**
48: **return** $\mathcal{T}_{LC}$
49: **repeat** Procedure to find Invoker's Invoker
50: **until** $\mathcal{II}$ of each $\mathcal{LI} \in RuleName(\mathcal{T}_{TRD})$

The algorithm for generating test cases for such paths uses the tables used for Lambda coverage, invokes Algorithm 5 to get a path from the source end to every Lambda used in the I, and for each such Lambda function it searches T_{ESM}, T_{ERD} and *LambdaInfoList* to trace their successors (*Lambda Successor (LS)*) in the first parse. This is followed by forward traceability for finding *successors' successor (SS)* until we reach one of the actuator services (device shadow/device/SNS) as the *final successor (FS)*.

Event Coverage. The end-to-end flow coverage has been designed to identify paths that incorporate at least one Lambda function as a part of the execution. Basic IoT applications can exhibit simple behavior scenarios where a sensor directly sends data to IoT Core for storage in DynamoDB and subsequently triggers an SNS notification to a client, Lambda functions need not be integrated. We introduce event coverage to include these scenarios. It uncovers all such pathways that might have been unnoticed within the comprehensive end-to-end flow. The configuration information outlines the way by which Event Consumers (EC) and Event Generators (EG) are interconnected. Considering all possible ways in which they can get connected in an event-driven architectural style, our test case generation algorithm for event coverage finds every possible pair of EG and EC along with events connecting them and returns a table with this information. The table is then used to construct paths in the architecture that span all the events.

Decision Coverage. We finally consider decision coverage criteria. Decisions come as a part of executable components like Lambda functions, in the query statements of TRD tables, in the filter criteria of the events in the event source mapping tables, and in the event pattern ERD tables. Testing decision points across various components and resources helps us to validate the end-to-end behavior of an IoT application, ensuring that the desired outcomes are achieved. We first extract the predicates that span the decisions present in the various components. The predicates are then used to define black-box test cases for Lambda coverage based on standard black-box testing techniques like equivalence partitioning and boundary value analysis [13].

We end this section with Fig. 5 that presents details on the expressiveness of the four proposed coverage criteria.

Prototype Implementation. The framework proposed in Sect. 5 above has been implemented within the NodeJS framework using JavaScript for IoT applications hosted on the AWS IoT framework [1]. All the architecture components considered in this paper for test case generation are supported in the free-tier AWS IoT framework and several other IoT application development platforms also provide the same features. The definition of our generic IoT architecture closely correlates with the architecture of serverless AWS IoT applications.

The TestCase-Generation-Parser extracts the relevant information for each coverage criterion, and all the steps as described in the algorithms above are implemented for each of the coverage criteria. The source code is available for use on the page https://github.com/NagalakshmiAthreya/TestCase-Generation-Parser.

We have also developed several in-house examples on the AWS IoT application development platform and tested our coverage criteria-based framework on them. Table 1 provides a summary of our experimental results. All the generated test cases were executed using the Mocha tool [4]. Mocha is an open-source tool for executing JavaScript test cases, both client-side and server-side applications.

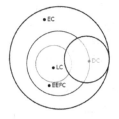

Fig. 5. Subsumption of Coverage Criteria

Table 1. Applications used for experimentation

IoT Application	LoC	Coverage Criteria	Errors found
Smart lighting	220	All the coverage criteria	No error
Smart vehicles [9]	172	All the coverage criteria	Conflicting actions
Temp-pressure monitor [9]	175	All the coverage criteria	Event chaining actions
Orphan event [14]	86	Event Coverage	No event consumer
Useless Lambda [14]	28	Lambda Coverage	No event source
Consecutive Lambda	175	All the coverage criteria	No error
Consecutive data stores	144	All the coverage criteria	No error
Trivial paths	70	Event Coverage	No error

Event coverage plays a crucial role in identifying events that may lack consumers, often referred to as *orphan* events. The identification of these orphan events holds particular significance, especially in the context of safety-critical systems, where the proper handling of every event is very important. Lambda coverage ensures that any unreachable Lambda indicates the absence of a source-generating event for that function, rendering it useless for the current application. Eliminating such unreachable Lambdas can prove to be beneficial in terms of optimizing costs and conserving resources.

6 Conclusion and Future Work

We have proposed a generic architecture for large-scale IoT applications and a test case generation framework based on coverage criteria over the generic architecture. Our coverage criteria are expressive enough to discover subtle errors that arise from complex interactions of architecture components and connections as explained in Sect. 3.

We are currently working on expanding the framework to include asynchronous events in NodeJS based IoT applications. We are also working on a testing framework that includes image and signal processing algorithms that are integrated as a part of the IoT application.

References

1. AWS IoT Core Documentation, June 2022. https://docs.aws.amazon.com/iot/index.html
2. Azure IoT Documentation (2022). https://azure.microsoft.com/en-in/solutions/iot/#overview
3. Google Cloud IoT Documentation (2022). https://cloud.google.com/iot/docs
4. Mocha - The fun, simple, flexible JavaScript test framework (2022). https://mochajs.org
5. Samsung SmartThings Developers Documentation (2022). https://developer-preview.smartthings.com/
6. Bala, R., Gill, B., Smith, D., Wright, D., Ji, K.: Magic quadrant for cloud infrastructure and platform services, July 2021. https://www.gartner.com/doc/reprints?id=1-271OE4VR&ct=210802&st=sb
7. Celik, Z.B., Fernandes, E., Pauley, E., Tan, G., McDaniel, P.: Program analysis of commodity IoT applications for security and privacy: challenges and opportunities. ACM Comput. Surv. **52**(4) (2019). https://doi.org/10.1145/3333501
8. Celik, Z.B., McDaniel, P., Tan, G.: SOTERIA: automated IoT safety and security analysis. In: Proceedings of the 2018 USENIX Conference, pp. 147–158. USENIX ATC '18, USENIX Association, USA (2018)
9. Chi, H., Zeng, Q., Du, X., Yu, J.: Cross-app interference threats in smart homes: categorization, detection and handling. In: 50th Annual IEEE/IFIP International Conference on Dependable Systems and Networks (DSN), pp. 411–423 (2020). https://doi.org/10.1109/DSN48063.2020.00056
10. Diwan, M., D'Souza, M.: A framework for modeling and verifying IoT communication protocols. In: Larsen, K.G., Sokolsky, O., Wang, J. (eds.) SETTA 2017. LNCS, vol. 10606, pp. 266–280. Springer, Cham (2017). https://doi.org/10.1007/978-3-319-69483-2_16
11. Fortas, A., Kerkouche, E., Chaoui, A.: Formal verification of IoT applications using rewriting logic: an MDE-based approach. Sci. Comput. Program. **222**(C) (2022). https://doi.org/10.1016/j.scico.2022.102859
12. Jin, Z., Offutt, J.: Deriving tests from software architectures. In: 12th International Symposium on Software Reliability Engineering (ISSRE), China, pp. 308–313. IEEE Computer Society (2001). https://doi.org/10.1109/ISSRE.2001.989484
13. Jorgensen, P.C.: Software Testing: A Craftsman's Approach, 4th edn. Auerbach Publications, Boca Raton (2014)
14. Madsen, M., Tip, F., Lhoták, O.: Static analysis of event-driven node.js javascript applications **50**(10) (2015). https://doi.org/10.1145/2858965.2814272
15. Obetz, M., Das, A., Castiglia, T., Patterson, S., Milanova, A.: Formalizing event-driven behavior of serverless applications. In: Brogi, A., Zimmermann, W., Kritikos, K. (eds.) ESOCC 2020. LNCS, vol. 12054, pp. 19–29. Springer, Cham (2020). https://doi.org/10.1007/978-3-030-44769-4_2
16. Winzinger, S., Wirtz, G.: Applicability of coverage criteria for serverless applications. In: 2020 IEEE International Conference on Service Oriented Systems Engineering (SOSE), pp. 49–56 (2020). https://doi.org/10.1109/SOSE49046.2020.00013

An Online Algorithm for Cost Minimization of Amazon EC2 Burstable Resources

Sharmistha Mandal[1], Sanjeet Lal[1], Soumik Sensarma[1], Srijoyee Saha[1], Giridhar Maji[2(✉)], Sunirmal Khatua[1], and Rajib K. Das[1]

[1] Department of Computer Science and Engineering, University of Calcutta, Kolkata, India
[2] Department of Electrical Engineering, Asansol Polytechnic, Asansol, India
giridhar.maji@gmail.com

Abstract. Many computational workloads do not require a constantly high CPU. They generally have occasional peak computation needs with low CPU utilization most of the time. Cloud service providers have started providing *burstable* instances to cater to such workloads. Burstable instances allow users occasional surges in utilization provided the job's CPU utilization remains below a certain baseline usage most of the time. Instead of running a job by provisioning regular instances based on peak usage, using burstable instances can significantly reduce costs. Amazon EC2 provides t-instances (T2/T3/T4g etc.) with different baseline usage (like 5%, 10%, 20%, 30%) to the users with two modes – (*standard* and *unlimited*). Burstable instances have a credit mechanism with a maximum capacity limit. When the usage is below the baseline, a credit is earned that can be utilized later during peak demands. In the present work, we attempt to utilize different types of burstable instances for workloads with a provision to migrate from one baseline to another to optimize (i) (minimize) surplus charges and (ii) (maximize) the use of credit earned. We have implemented the proposed migration approach on AWS burstable instances with real PlanetLab demand traces. We show that even without prior knowledge of future CPU utilizations of a job, our proposed online algorithm can achieve cost comparable to a hypothetical future-aware algorithm that assumes future knowledge of utilization values.

Keywords: AWS Burstable Instances · Cost Minimization · baseline usage · VM migration · standard and unlimited mode

1 Introduction

Cloud services are now well accepted and used by users for various types of applications. Due to the large number of well-established global and local cloud service providers (CSPs), the service offerings have become more competitive and user-centric. Several types of virtual machines (VM) are provisioned and offered

S. Devismes et al. (Eds.): ICDCIT 2024, LNCS 14501, pp. 117–132, 2024.
https://doi.org/10.1007/978-3-031-50583-6_8

to the cloud service users (CSUs) with different combinations of resources like vCPU, RAM, and bandwidth. Based on the availability guarantee and long-term commitment, Amazon EC2 offers *reserved, on-demand* and *spot* VM instances. Reserved instances are for long-term users with large upfront payments, while on-demand instances are available on demand without any long-term commitment or upfront payments but with a higher price per hour. Spot instances are available with a much discounted hourly rate but with the risk of revocation. With many types of VMs and pricing schemes, it becomes challenging for a CSU to choose a proper mix of VMs that reduce cost without compromising other aspects like QoS or SLA.

Many researchers have proposed numerous job provisioning schemes to reduce the cost of CSUs by mixing different VMs, check-pointing, and migration of jobs [4,5,7–9,12,13,15].

Recently, CSPs offered another kind of VM known as *burstable* instances [6] that does not provide a fixed amount of resources such as CPU or memory. Instead, they have a baseline amount of CPU with the provision to burst for a short time above the baseline utilization. It may be suitable for jobs with low usage most of the time but an occasional requirement of higher resources. Burstable instances are comparatively cheaper than the corresponding non-burstable ones and come with a baseline percentage. If resource usage is less than the baseline, then CSU earns net credit, and during any burst (sudden peak usage of cloud resources), earned credit can be utilized. However, the credits cannot accumulate beyond a certain limit [16] as fixed by the provider (Table 1). Amazon EC2 offers two modes for burstable instances, namely, *standard* and *unlimited*. In the unlimited mode, the user application does not suffer any resource constraint, but a surcharge may build up if the credit earned cannot satisfy the demand in the burst period. In standard mode, once the earned credits finish, CSP automatically limits the resource usage to the baseline, and the application suffers SLA violation or QoS degradation. So, the unlimited mode is preferable to users who are ready to pay the extra cost but are unwilling to sacrifice performance degradation. For this reason, in the proposed scheme, we only consider the unlimited mode of burstable instances.

The burstable instances offered by Amazon EC2, also known as *T-instances*, are listed in Table 1. These instances are categorized based on the maximum resource (RAM/CPU) and baseline usage percentage. The table also shows the hourly cost when average utilization remains below baseline. It also shows the applicable surcharge amount that has to be paid by the CSU if the job runs on surplus credit in unlimited mode. We have also tabulated the corresponding non-burstable VM instances and their prices. We observe that burstable instances are much cheaper than equivalent regular instances if average usage remains within the baseline with occasional peaks. It is worth mentioning that spot instances also provide significantly reduced cost but with the unbounded risk of complete failure and SLA violation due to revocation.

In the present work, we have used burstable instances with a flexible migration policy based on estimated resource utilization variation that allows work-

Table 1. Amazon EC2 Burstable Instance attributes. s_{od} denotes the On-demand hourly rate of normal instances, s_{od}^b denotes the On-demand hourly rate of burstable instances

T-instances	vCPU	Memory	Baseline	Corresponding M-instances	s_{od}	s_{od}^b	Surplus credit price	Accrued credit limit	Credit validity
T3.nano	2	0.5 GiB	5%	M6g.large	$0.077	$0.0052		144	
T3.micro	2	1 GiB	10%	M6g.large	$0.077	$0.0104		288	
T3.small	2	2 GiB	20%	M6g.large	$0.077	$0.0208		576	
T3.medium	2	4 GiB	20%	M6g.large	$0.077	$0.0416	$0.05 per vCPU-Hour for Linux, RHEL and SLES, and $0.096 per vCPU-Hour for Windows and Windows with SQL Web	576	7 days (credits persist for 7 days after an instance stops)
T3.large	2	8 GiB	30%	M6g.large	$0.077	$0.0832		864	
T3.xlarge	4	16 GiB	40%	M6g.xlarge	$0.154	$0.1664		2304	
T3.2xlarge	8	32 GiB	40%	M6g.2xlarge	$0.308	$0.3328		4608	
T3a.nano	2	0.5 GiB	5%	M6g.large	$0.077	$0.0047		144	
T3a.micro	2	1 GiB	10%	M6g.large	$0.077	$0.0094		288	
T3a.small	2	2 GiB	20%	M6g.large	$0.077	$0.0188		576	
T3a.medium	2	4 GiB	20%	M6g.large	$0.077	$0.0376		576	
T3a.large	2	8 GiB	30%	M6g.large	$0.077	$0.0752		864	
T3a.xlarge	4	16 GiB	40%	M6g.xlarge	$0.154	$0.1504		2304	
T3a.2xlarge	8	32 GiB	40%	M6g.2xlarge	$0.308	$0.3008		4608	

loads to self-migrate to new VMs to reduce the overall cost without impacting QoS. We decide on migration heuristically. We compare the cost incurred over a past window with the cost that may have occurred if the same job had run on an alternative instance. Our technique monitors the cost of the workload and places it in the appropriate *burstable VM instance*. It attempts to balance the number of migrations and cost. We avoid using cheaper spot resources in the proposed scheme due to its severe negative impact on SLA, deadline, and QOS.

The rest of the paper goes as follows. Section 2 discusses recent studies on cost optimizations using burstable instances, followed by the problem formulation in Sect. 3.2. The proposed scheme is discussed in Sect. 4 followed by the implementation details in Sect. 5.1. Section 5 presents the performance evaluation on real data, and finally, Sect. 6 concludes the paper.

2 Related Work

Wei et al. [17] proposed a stochastic resource rate-based revenue model with dynamic provisioning of the burstable instances. They employed a differential evolution (DE) based solution approach to search for the optimal solution for the resource scheduling problem with the objective of cost minimization for fluctuating demands. The work focused on using demand as a distribution instead of a mean value. They achieved a significant reduction in overall cost compared to traditional VMs.

Park et al. [10] focused on the burstable storage use cases (based on data longevity) for performance improvement without incurring extra costs. They have showcased results on AWS gp2 volumes with more than a 90% reduction in cost. Sharma et al. [11] proposed a token bucket-based approach named credit aware resource scheduling (CASH) as a middleware cluster manager that uses rough knowledge of expected resource utilization during scheduling. They report up to 22% cost savings on AWS t3 instances.

Teylo et al. [14] combined multiple tasks and scheduled using a mix of spot, on-demand, and burstable resources with their proposed Burst-HADS (Burst Hibernation-Aware Dynamic Scheduler). They considered job-mix with fixed deadlines and minimized execution time and cost by employing their proposed scheduler. Wang et al. [15] suggested burstable resources as a high-availability backup while running jobs on failure-prone spot instances. It improves performance, but still, revocations remain a concern.

Dantas et al. [3] proposed the BIAS auto scaler that combines regular and burstable resources to cater to sudden queueing caused by traffic and flash crowds. They applied it to real microservice demands and evaluated it on Google's compute engine to show up to 25% cost savings.

Ali et al. [1] proposed CEDULE for scheduling jobs in burstable instances using quantile regression for workload profiling and prediction. They employed a throttling mechanism that optimally used spare resources synergistically.

Jian et al. [6] have comprehensively modeled burstable resources and identified some key metrics. They have characterized the equilibrium behind CSU's responses to the CSP-provided prices for different burstable instances, considering the impact of CSU's actions on the performance achieved by each service category.

3   Preliminary Ideas and Problem Formulation

We first explain the charge a CSU has to pay while running a burstable instance of a given base type and then formulate our problem. Table 2 mentions all the notations and definitions ysed throughout the paper.

3.1   Cost Model for Burstable Resources

The burstable instances like t3-nano, t3-micro, and t3-small vary in resources and costs. Let cr_h^i denote the credit earned per hour when we execute a job on a burstable instance of type i. An instance of type i gets an initial credit of max_c^i. The credit balance increases at every hour t by cr_h^i and decreases by $u_t * v^i * 0.60$ where u_t is the average utilization percentage at the tth hour, and v^i is the number of vCPUs, for instance type i. So, if the credit balance at the start of hour t is c_b^i, the credit balance at the end of hour t is given by the equation

$$c_b^i(t+1) = c_b^i(t) + cr_h^i - u_t * v^i * 0.60 \tag{1}$$

The baseline utilization percentage b^i of instance type i is related to cr_h^i by the equation $b^i * v^i * 0.60 = cr_h^i$. So, when the utilization u_t is the same as b^i, credit earned equals credit spent, and the user has to pay only the hourly cost co_h^i. If $u_t < b^i$, credit earned exceeds credit spent, and the credit balance increases, and if $u_t > b^i$, the credit balance decreases. Also, the credit balance c_b^i cannot

Table 2. Notations

Symbol	Definition
T	Total number of submission hours
u_t	The CPU utilization at time t, $1 \leq t \leq T$
I	Set of burstable instances
cr_h^i	Credit earned per hour for instance type i
v^i	Number of v-cpus for instance type i
b^i	Baseline CPU utilization for instance type i
co_h^i	Cost per hour for using instances type i
max_c^i	Maximum CPU credit hours for instance type i
cb_t^i	Credit balance of instant type i at time t
p^i	penalty per hour for negative credit balance for instance type i
dt^i	downtime for instance type i
$time^i$	number of hours the instant i is continuously running

exceed $2 * max_c^i$ as the credit earned can be maximum max_c^i [16]. According to the Amazon EC2 model, for burstable instances, at every hour, the user may have to pay one, two, or three types of costs according to the following rules:

1. **Rule a:** Regular cost $Cost_R$ given by

$$Cost_R = co_h^i \qquad (2)$$

2. **Rule b:** Immediate negative balance cost caused by a sudden burst in utilization. If credit balance c_b^i becomes negative at hour t, the cost $Cost_B$ due to burst is given by

$$Cost_B = -c_b^i * p^i \qquad (3)$$

where p^i is the penalty per credit hour for a negative balance. The credit balance c_b is then reset to 0.

3. **Rule c:** Long-term low balance cost. As the initial value of c_b^i, max_c^i is given as credit, at the end of 24 h, if c_b^i is below max_c^i, the user has to pay a long-term cost $Cost_L$ given by

$$Cost_L = (max_c^i - c_b^i) * p^i \qquad (4)$$

After settling the long-term cost R_L, c_b^i increases to max_c^i. If $c_b^i \geq max_c^i$, $Cost_L$ is zero, and the credit balance (not reset to max_c^i) carries forward to the next hour.

In our case, the instance types vary from 0 to 3, 0 corresponding to the smallest, i.e., T3.nano, 1 to T3.micro, 2 to T3.small, and 3 to T3.large. We illustrate the cost model with the following example.

Example 1. Let us assume the instance type selected is 0, i.e., T3.nano. Then $v^0 = 2$, $b^0 = 5\%$, $p^0 = 0.1$, $cr_h^0 = 5 * 2 * 0.60 = 6$, and initially $c_b^0 = max_c^0 = 144$. If for the first hour, $u_t = 2\%$, credit earned is 6, credit spent is $2 * 2 * .60 = 2.4$, and the credit balance will increase by $6 - 2.4 = 3.6$. If u increases in the next hour to 9%, the credit balance will decrease by $9 * 2 * .60 - 6 = 4.8$. If sometimes, c_b^0 becomes negative, say, -2, the user has to pay $2 * 0.1 = 0.2$\$ immediately as per Eq. 3. If $c_b^0 = 140$ after 24 h, the user has to pay a long-term cost $Cost_L = (144 - 140) * 0.1 = 0.4$\$ (Eq. 4), and c_b^0 will increase to 144.

3.2   Problem Statement

We have a set of computational jobs to run on the cloud with different job profiles (compute-intensive/intermittent/fluctuating). At the time of submission, the future utilization values of a job are unknown. The objective is to select a suitable instance type for a job and, if required, switch instance types to reduce the cost. When a job runs on an instance of $i \in I$, the credit balance and cost at every hour are computed by applying Eqs. 1 to 4. Even though $Cost_L$ is to be paid at the end of every 24 h, if we switch to another instance before that, and $c_b < max_c^i$, we need to pay $(max_c - c_b^i) * p^i$ to the CSP. The cost optimization problem for burstable instances (**COB**) can be formally stated as follows:

Definition 1. COB: *Given a job with utilization values* $u_j, j \in \{1, 2, \cdots, T\}$, *while at any time* t, $u_j, j \geq t$ *are unknown, and a set of instances* $I = \{i_1, i_2, \ldots i_k\}$, *with their corresponding parameters, find the best instance* $i \in I$ *to use at time* t *to minimize the total cost of executing the job.*

The problem COB is challenging because we must decide the best instance at time t without knowing the utilization u_j for $j \geq t$, and the value of u_j may fluctuate unpredictably from hour to hour.

4   Proposed Scheme

Algorithm 3 decides the instance type on which to run the job at the next hour every hour and also computes the total cost of executing the job. It takes the help of Algorithm 1 and Algorithm 2. The first algorithm assumes knowledge of u_t over a window $w = [start, end)$ and finds the cost if the job ran unchanged over a given instance type i. The second algorithm takes as input the instance type i and runs the job for one hour on that instance. It finds the cost at the end of the hour. We now give a brief explanation of both algorithms.

Algorithm Calculate Cost: This algorithm first checks if the instance i was down for more than 24 h. The variable dt^i denotes the downtime for the instance i. If $dt^i > 0$, the credit balance c_b is set to max_c^i (lines 7,8). Inside the for loop, it computes the credit balance c_b at every $t \in [start, end)$ (Line 9) applying Eq. 1. Since every instance starts with a credit of max_c^i and the maximum credit earned cannot exceed max_c^i, c_b^i cannot be more than $2 * max_c^i$. Line 10 of the

---

Algorithm 1: Calculate Cost

---

    input : window : $w = [start, end)$, utilizations : $u_t, start \leq t < end$;
               instance-type: i

1 $Cost_{total}, hour \leftarrow$ all initialized to 0 ;
2 $c_b \leftarrow c_b^i$;
3 **if** $dt^i > 24 * 7$ **then**
4 | $c_b \leftarrow max_c^i$
5 **end**
6 **foreach** $t \in [start, end)$ **do**
7 | $Cost_B \leftarrow 0; Cost_L \leftarrow 0$;
8 | $hour \leftarrow hour + 1$;
9 | $c_b \leftarrow c_b + co_h^i - u_t * v^i * 0.6$;
10 | $c_b \leftarrow min(c_b, 2 * max_c^i)$;
11 | $Cost_R \leftarrow co_h^i$;   /* (Rule a) */
12 | **if** $c_b^i < 0$ **then**
13 | | $Cost_B \leftarrow (-1) * c_b^i * p^i$;
14 | | $c_b \leftarrow 0$;   /* (Rule b) */
15 | **end**
16 | **if** $hour$ mod $24 = 0$ **then**
17 | | Apply Rule c to compute $Cost_L$ and c_b
18 | **end**
19 | $Cost_{total} \leftarrow Cost_{total} + Cost_R + Cost_B + Cost_L$
20 **end**
21 **if** $c_b < max_c^i$ **then**
22 | $Cost_L \leftarrow (max_c^i - c_b) * p^i$
23 **end**
24 **return** $(Cost_{total} + Cost_L)$

---

algorithm sets c_b to $2 * max_c^i$ if it exceeds $2 * max_c^i$. Then, it applies Rules a and b to compute regular cost $Cost_R$ and negative balance cost $Cost_B$. It also updates c_b if it is negative and $Cost_B > 0$. Also, Rule c is applied every 24 h to compute the long-term cost $Cost_L$. If the window size is not a multiple of 24 h, it computes the long-term cost $Cost_L$ outside the for loop (lines 17, 18) as the cost to pay if we switch instances after completing execution over the window.

Algorithm Hourly Cost: This Algorithm runs the job for the next hour on the given instance i. It increments the variable $time^i$ to keep track of the number of hours it is currently executing in instance i. At the end of the hour, it computes $Cost_R$, $Cost_B$ and the credit balance c_b^i. It returns two values, $Cost_h$ and due, where $Cost_h$ is the cost of running the job over that hour and due is the amount to be paid to the CSP if we switch to another instance after completing the current hour.

Alternative Instances. When a job is running on instance type $i \in I$, the set of alternative instances $Alt(i)$ are instances immediately above and below

---

Algorithm 2: Hourly Cost

---

   input : utilization: u_t; instance-type: i
   output: hourly cost : $Cost_h$; Due:due
1 $time^i \leftarrow time^i + 1$;
2 **if** $dt^i > 24 * 7$ **then**
3 | $c_b^i \leftarrow max_c^i$
4 **end**
5 Run the job for next 1 hour on instance type i
6 $Cost_B \leftarrow 0$; $Cost_L \leftarrow 0$;
7 $c_b^i \leftarrow c_b^i + co_h^i - u_t * v^i * 0.6$;
8 $c_b^i \leftarrow min(c_b^i, 2 * max_c^i)$;
9 Apply Rules a,b to compute $Cost_R$, $Cost_B$, and c_b^i
10 **if** $time^i$ mod $24 = 0$ **then**
11 | Apply Rule c to compute $Cost_L$ and c_b^i
12 **end**
13 $Cost_h \leftarrow Cost_R + Cost_B + Cost_L$
14 **if** $c_b^i < max_c^i$ **then**
15 | $due \leftarrow (max_c^i - c_b^i) * p^i$
16 **end**
17 return $(Cost_h, due)$

---

provided they exist. That is if $I = \{0, i, \ldots k\}$ where 0 is the smallest instance (smallest baseline, least co_h etc.) and k is the largest instance, then $Alt(i)$ is defined as follows:

$$Alt(i) = \begin{cases} \{i+1\} & \text{if } i = 0 \\ \{i-1, i+1\} & \text{if } i \in \{1, \ldots k-1\} \\ \{i-1\} & \text{if } i = k \end{cases} \quad (5)$$

Algorithm Burst Optimizer. This algorithm chooses instances for optimizing the cost of running a job over burstable instances. During the lifetime of a job, it may switch to an alternative instance at the end of each hour of its execution. It uses a sliding window $[start, end)$ of past utilizations to decide to switch. For the first hour of the job's execution, it chooses a random instance i_type from the pool of available burstable instance I to start the execution of the job (line 5). It calculates the *cost* and *due* of running the job for the first hour over the random instance i_type (line 7). The *due* is the cost one pays if she switches to another instance in the next hour. At the end of each hour, it calculates the cost of running the job for the past window on all the alternate instances (line 13) determined as per Eq. 5. The variable w_{cost} stores the cost incurred in the current window. If the cost of running the job with the best alternate instance (in terms of minimum cost) is less than w_{cost} plus *due* (if any), it decides to switch to that alternate instance (line 14–20). It updates the downtime dt^i, credit balance cb^i, and the total cost $cost_{total}$ accordingly.

Algorithm 3: Burst Optimizer

---

    input   : w_size : window size in hours; u_t: cpu utilization for hour t
    parameters : set of instances : I
    output   : Total cost of running the job

1 **foreach** $i \in I$ **do**
2 | $c_b^i \leftarrow max_c^i$; $time^i \leftarrow 0$; $dt^i \leftarrow 0$
3 **end**
4 $Cost_{total} \leftarrow 0$
5 $i\_type \leftarrow$ random instance from I
6 $k \leftarrow 0$
7 $(cost_0, due) \leftarrow HourlyCost(u_0, i\_type)$;   /* $cost_0$: cost at hour 0 */
8 $w_{cost} \leftarrow cost_0$
9 **while** $job \neq terminated$ **do**
10 | $k \leftarrow k + 1$
11 | $end \leftarrow k$; $start \leftarrow max(k - w\_size, 0)$; $window \leftarrow [start, end)$
12 | $Alternatives \leftarrow Alt(i\_type)$
13 | $Cost_{alt} \leftarrow \{CalculateCost(window, u, j) : j \in Alternatives\}$
14 | **if** $min(Cost_{alt}) < w_{cost} + due$ **then**
15 | | $time^{i\text{-}type} \leftarrow 0$
16 | | $i\_type \leftarrow j$ where $j \in Alternatives$ and
                          $CalculateCost(window, u, j) = min(Cost_{alt})$
17 | | **if** $due > 0$ **then**
18 | | | $Cost_{total} \leftarrow Cost_{total} + due$
19 | | | $c_b^i \leftarrow max_c^i$
20 | | **end**
21 | **end**
22 | $(cost_k, due) \leftarrow HourlyCost(u_k, i\_type)$;   /* $cost_k$: cost at hour k */
23 | $Cost_{total} \leftarrow Cost_{total} + cost_k$
24 | $dt^i \leftarrow dt^i + 1$ for $i \in I - \{i\_type\}$
25 | $dt^i \leftarrow 0$ for $i = i\_type$
26 | $w_{cost} = w_{cost} + cost_k$
27 | **if** $k \geq w\_size$ **then**
28 | | $w_{cost} = w_{cost} - cost_{start}$
29 | **end**
30 **end**
31 **return** $(cost_{total} + due)$

4.1 Benchmark Results for Comparison with the Proposed Online Algorithm

We consider two other algorithms whose costs act as a benchmark for comparison with the proposed method. In one, we assume that utilization values of the next W (window size) hours are known. In another, we assume that the utilization values averaged over the entire simulation period is known.

Algorithm Where Future Utilization Values Are Known: Here, at every hour, we apply Algorithm 1 (*Calculate Cost*) to find the total cost if the job runs on instance type $i \in I$. If the cost is minimum for a particular instance type i', the job runs for the next hour in the instance type i'. In the next hour, the window slides forward by one hour, and we repeat the process. The total cost is the sum of the costs over all hours plus the cost to be paid as *due* whenever we switch instances.

Algorithm Where the Average Utilization over the Entire Period is Known: Let the job duration be D days and average utilization over the entire period is $\sum_{t=1}^{24*D} u_t/(24*D) = u_{av}$. Here, based on u_{av}, we select a specific instance type and run the job throughout on that instance type. We call the cost for this approach *Fixed Instance Cost*. For the instance types $i \in \{0, 1, 2, \cdots k\}$ we have the baseline utilizations b^i where $b^0 < b^1 < \cdots < b^k$. We find a set of boundaries $br^i, b^i < br^i < b^{i+1}$ for $i = 0, 1, \cdots k - 1$ and for a job with average utilization u_{av}, the instance type chosen is $Choice(u_{av})$ given as follows:

$$Choice(u_{av}) = \begin{cases} 0, & \text{if } u_{av} < br_0 \\ i, & \text{if } br^{i-1} \le u_{av} < br^i, 1 \le i \le k - 1 \\ k, & \text{if } u_{av} \ge br^{k-1} \end{cases}$$

Suppose $b^i < u_{av} < b^{i+1}$. Then we decide the instance to be i or $i + 1$ depending on $u_{av} < br^i$ or $u_{av} \ge br^i$. We get an estimate of br^i on the following assumptions:

1. The credit balance never becomes negative ($Cost_B$ is always zero).
2. The average utilization over every 24 h remains between b^i and b^{i+1}.

Let us denote by TC_i the total cost if the instance remains i throughout the D days. The cost of running the job on instance i for hours 1 to 24 is
$$= \sum_{t=1}^{24} Cost_R + Cost_L$$
$$= co_h^i * 24 + \sum_{t=1}^{2} 4(u_t * v^i * .6 - cr_h^i) * p^i.$$
This is because the credit spent per hour is $u_t * v^i * .6$, and the credit per hour is cr_h. So, at the end of 24 h, the credit balance will fall below max_c^i by $\sum_t (u_t * v^i * .6 - cr_h^i)$, and the penalty is p^i per credit hour.
If the simulation period is D days then total cost for instance i is
$$TC_i = co_h^i * 24 * D + \sum_{t=1}^{24*D} u_t * v^i * .6 * p^i - cr_h^i * p^i * 24 * D$$
$$= (24 * D)[co_h^i + u_{av} * v^i * 0.6 * p^i - cr_h^i * p^i]$$
As $u_{av} < b_{i+1}$, and if we assume average utilization over every 24 h is less than b_{i+1}, there will be no long-term cost if we choose instance $i + 1$.
So, $TC_{i+1} = 24 * D * co_h^{i+1}$.
Hence, $TC_i < TC_{i+1}$, if $co_h^i + u_{av} * v^i * .6 * p^i - cr_h^i * p^i] < co_h^{i+1}$
$$\implies u_{av} < \frac{co_h^{i+1} - co_h^i + cr_h^i * p^i}{v^i * .6 * p^i}.$$
Thus, br_i is given by the equation :

$$br^i = \frac{co_h^{i+1} - co_h^i + cr_h^i * p^i}{v^i * .6 * p^i} \tag{6}$$

As $cr_h^i = b^i * v^i * .6$, $br^i = b^i + \frac{co_h^{i+1} - co_h^i}{v^i * .6 * p^i}$, i.e., slightly more than b^i. We can compute br^i from the parameters of the instances i and $i + 1$ and run the job on $Choice(u_{av})$ assuming u_{av} is known.

5   Results and Discussion

5.1   Implementation and Data Preparation

We use Python (Python v 3.5) to implement the proposed online algorithm (only the cpu utilizations of the past hours are known), future known algorithm (future utilizations are known), and the fixed instance algorithm (average utilization over the entire job duration is known).

In a real-time scenario, a broker handles custom API calls for reallocation and monitoring. The broker periodically computes the cost incurred in a past window and the possible costs in alternative instances for the same window. The broker compares these costs, decides if any change of instance is needed, and if so, informs the VM provisioner which in turn executes the reallocation or migration decision.

Data Preparation. This prototype is simulated and evaluated on a set of Planetlab [2] node (instance) workload traces. PlanetLab is a global research network that allows researchers to deploy and experiment with their applications on a geographically distributed set of nodes. These workload traces represent datasets of actual workload measurements collected from the PlanetLab network. It captures the resource usage patterns of applications running on the PlanetLab nodes over a certain period of time.

Ten workload folders are available under Planetlab in CloudSim for March and April 2011. Each node's raw workload traces contain 288 rows of usage percentages separated by a time frame of 5 min for 24 h (daily). Joining all the daily datasets from each day's folders, we obtain the penultimate aggregated workload datasets of a time duration of 10 days each. Hence, such a dataset will contain $288 * 10 = 2880$ rows of CPU usage percentages. Now, as per AWS's official documentation of burstable instances, the cost is calculated hourly. Hence, the final aggregated dataset is created by taking the hourly average of the penultimate dataset, i.e., combining a window of 12 rows each time by taking their mean (since $12 * 5\,\text{min} = 60\,\text{min}$, i.e., 1 h). So, the final hourly usage dataset contains $2880/12 = 240$ rows, where each row is now a representation of the average CPU usage % per hour for the entirety of 10 days. There are 21 such instance workload CSV files formed that are used for the simulation of our prototype and cost computation.

Performance of the Proposed Online Algorithm. We measure the performance of the proposed online cost minimization algorithm in terms of two metrics - the total cost of executing a job over ten days and the total number of migrations. Algorithm 3 uses a parameter w_size (size of the window in hours). Since the long-term cost $Cost_L$ is to be paid every 24 h, it is logical to use $w\_size = 24$. We have computed the cost by varying window size from 12 to 36 and found that $w\_size = 24$ gives minimum costs. Hence, we have presented the results of Algorithm 3 only for $w\_size = 24$.

Table 3. Statistical description of the datasets used during experiments

Dataset#	AVG	MAX	MIN	STD	Dataset#	AVG	MAX	MIN	STD
1	2.21	4.92	0.5	0.85	12	9.08	26.83	1.83	4.47
2	2.53	7.08	0.83	0.97	13	9.56	30	1.5	6.04
3	2.91	8.33	0.67	1.18	14	10.05	25.42	2.42	4.57
4	4.58	8.67	0.17	2.02	15	10.77	24.33	2.08	3.63
5	4.59	7.83	0	1.68	16	10.79	28.5	1.5	5.13
6	4.78	22.25	0.83	2.30	17	12.02	32.33	1.5	4.52
7	5.46	21.33	0.83	4.31	18	12.91	29.75	2.42	4.27
8	6.4	13.5	1.17	2.30	19	13.54	44	0.17	12.30
9	7.06	13.17	3.5	1.67	20	15.32	34.08	9.33	4.50
10	8.1	14.42	1.5	2.37	21	22.39	47.58	6.08	8.15
11	8.36	19.83	2.5	3.02	–	–	–	–	–

Total Cost: For 21 different data sets, we computed the costs for the proposed algorithm. We also have the costs corresponding to two benchmarks - *future-aware* and *fixed instance*. Figure 1 shows the plot of all three costs. The set of instances I is equal to $\{0, 1, 2, 3\}$, corresponding to T3.nano, T3.micro, T3.small and T3.large. The values of base rates are $b^0 = 5\%$, $b^1 = 10\%$, $b^2 = 20\%$ and $b^3 = 30\%$. By applying Eq. 6, we compute boundary values $br^0 = 5.04\%$, $br^1 = 10.09\%$, and $br^2 = 20.52\%$. For computing *fixed instance* cost, we compute the average u_{av} over ten days and select the instance by comparing u_{av} with boundary values. As expected, the future-aware algorithm has the minimum costs. Even though while computing the *fixed instance* cost, we assume the knowledge of the average utilization over the entire ten days and the proposed online algorithm has no such knowledge, the total cost for fixed instances is sometimes much higher than the proposed one (data sets 4, 5, 19, and 20). This indicates that the proposed algorithm that switches instances is better suited to handle the occasional surge in utilization values.

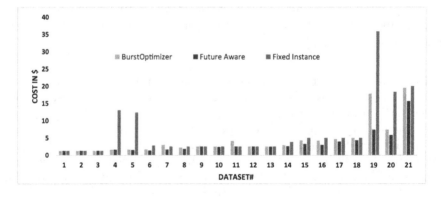

Fig. 1. Cost comparison between future aware and proposed and fixed approach

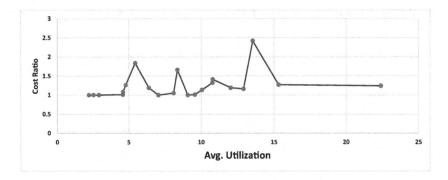

Fig. 2. Variation of average utilization and cost ratio (BurstOptimizer/Future Aware) for all dataset

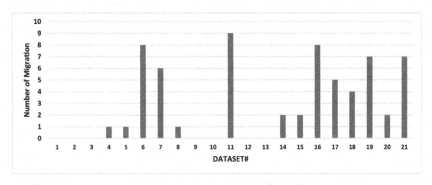

Fig. 3. Number of migrations using the proposed BurstOptimizer for all datasets

Figure 2 plots the ratio of the cost for the proposed algorithm to that from the benchmark corresponding to future known. This ratio is 2.42 for data set 19 and less than 2 for all other data sets. If we look at the statistics of data set 19 in Table 3, it has an average of 13.54 and a maximum of 44, i.e., the maximum is more than three times the average. That means this data set has frequent surges in cpu utilization that cause negative balances so that $Cost_B$ and $Cost_L$ are high. As the proposed algorithm only makes decisions based on past costs, it pays for such bursts before it can switch instances. So, we can conclude that if the data set does not exhibit such a high variation, the performance of the proposed algorithm is acceptable, considering it does not have prior knowledge of the utilization values.

Table 4 shows the cost for each job and the total cost of running all 21 jobs in the bottom row. We see that the total cost of the proposed algorithm is only

Table 4. Cost comparison between future-aware, fixed instance and the proposed BurstOptimizer

Dataset#	BurstOptimizer	Future Aware	Fixed burstable cost	Cost Ratio	# of Migrations
1	1.25	1.25	1.25	1.00	0
2	1.25	1.25	1.25	1.00	0
3	1.25	1.25	1.25	1.00	0
4	1.60	1.58	13.01	1.01	1
5	1.64	1.52	12.31	1.08	1
6	1.69	1.34	2.80	1.26	8
7	3.00	1.63	2.50	1.84	6
8	2.19	1.83	2.50	1.19	1
9	2.50	2.50	2.50	1.00	0
10	2.50	2.37	2.50	1.05	0
11	4.14	2.50	2.50	1.66	9
12	2.50	2.50	2.50	1.00	0
13	2.50	2.46	2.50	1.01	0
14	2.96	2.62	3.84	1.13	2
15	4.30	3.25	5.02	1.32	2
16	4.22	3.00	5.02	1.41	8
17	4.71	3.95	5.02	1.19	5
18	5.03	4.32	5.02	1.16	4
19	17.85	7.36	35.89	2.42	7
20	7.38	5.82	18.35	1.27	2
21	19.52	15.68	20.04	1.24	7
Total	**93.96**	**69.97**	**147.52**	**1.34**	**63 (Avg. = 3)**

1.34 times that of the hypothetical future-aware algorithm. The corresponding total cost for a fixed instance is more than two times that of the future-aware one.

Migrations: Figure 3 shows the number of migrations between instances for each data set. We observe that the values vary between 0 to 9. Considering that we ran each job for 240 h and there is a chance of migration at each hour based on cost comparison, the number 9 is acceptable. Too many migrations can lead to QoS violations because they may add delay. Table 4 shows that the average number of migrations is only 3. We can conclude that the proposed algorithm can handle variations in cpu utilization to reduce cost without causing too many changes in instances.

6   Conclusion

This study presents an online algorithm for cost minimization by switching between burstable instances of different base utilization rates. The algorithm monitors the cost of resources for the current instance type and takes a reallocation decision to another instance type it deems appropriate. We have taken a window of 24 h, computed the cost incurred in that period, and compared it with the cost if run on an alternative instance type. We perform this comparison at the end of every hour and switch to an alternative option if that seems more economical. Simulation of this algorithm on numerous real-life workloads shows that our approach of switching between instances is more cost-effective than running the entire job on a fixed base rate. However, it is difficult to give an overall measure or metric of this cost minimization as the actual reduction in cost depends on the specific workload and the selected instance types. We can also safely ignore the overhead due to migration time, as the frequency of switching over our simulation period (10 days) is negligibly small.

References

1. Ali, A., Pinciroli, R., Yan, F., Smirni, E.: CEDULE: a scheduling framework for burstable performance in cloud computing. In: 2018 IEEE International Conference on Autonomic Computing (ICAC), pp. 141–150. IEEE (2018)
2. Cloudslab: Planetlab workload traces retrieved from: Cloudslab (n.d.). Release cloudsim-3.0 (2023). https://github.com/Cloudslab/cloudsim/releases/tag/cloudsim-3.0
3. Dantas, J., Khazaei, H., Litoiu, M.: Bias autoscaler: leveraging burstable instances for cost-effective autoscaling on cloud systems. In: Proceedings of the Seventh International Workshop on Serverless Computing (WoSC7) 2021, pp. 9–16 (2021)
4. Harlap, A., Chung, A., Tumanov, A., Ganger, G.R., Gibbons, P.B.: Tributary: spot-dancing for elastic services with latency SLOs. In: 2018 USENIX Annual Technical Conference (USENIX ATC 2018), pp. 1–14 (2018)
5. Huang, B., Jarrett, N.W., Babu, S., Mukherjee, S., Yang, J.: Cümülön: matrix-based data analytics in the cloud with spot instances. Proc. VLDB Endow. 9(3), 156–167 (2015)
6. Jiang, Y., Shahrad, M., Wentzlaff, D., Tsang, D.H., Joe-Wong, C.: Burstable instances for clouds: performance modeling, equilibrium analysis, and revenue maximization. IEEE/ACM Trans. Netw. 28(6), 2489–2502 (2020)
7. Mandal, S., Khatua, S., Das, R.K.: Bid selection for deadline constrained jobs over spot VMs in computational cloud. In: Krishnan, P., Radha Krishna, P., Parida, L. (eds.) ICDCIT 2017. LNCS, vol. 10109, pp. 118–128. Springer, Cham (2017). https://doi.org/10.1007/978-3-319-50472-8_10
8. Mandal, S., Maji, G., Khatua, S., Das, R.K.: Cost minimizing reservation and scheduling algorithms for public clouds. IEEE Trans. Cloud Comput. 11(2), 1365–1380 (2021). https://doi.org/10.1109/TCC.2021.3133464
9. Mandal, S., Saify, S.S., Ghosh, A., Maji, G., Khatua, S., Das, R.K.: An approach to cost minimization with EC2 spot instances using VM based migration policy. In: Bapi, R., Kulkarni, S., Mohalik, S., Peri, S. (eds.) ICDCIT 2022. LNCS, vol. 13145, pp. 96–110. Springer, Cham (2022). https://doi.org/10.1007/978-3-030-94876-4_6
10. Park, H., Ganger, G.R., Amvrosiadis, G.: More IOPS for less: exploiting burstable storage in public clouds. In: Proceedings of the 12th USENIX Conference on Hot Topics in Cloud Computing, p. 18 (2020)
11. Sharma, A., Dhakshinamurthy, S., Kesidis, G., Das, C.R.: CASH: a credit aware scheduling for public cloud platforms. In: 2021 IEEE/ACM 21st International Symposium on Cluster, Cloud and Internet Computing (CCGrid), pp. 227–236. IEEE (2021)
12. Shastri, S., Irwin, D.: HotSpot: automated server hopping in cloud spot markets. In: Proceedings of the 2017 Symposium on Cloud Computing, pp. 493–505 (2017)

13. Subramanya, S., Guo, T., Sharma, P., Irwin, D., Shenoy, P.: SpotOn: a batch computing service for the spot market. In: Proceedings of the Sixth ACM Symposium on Cloud Computing, pp. 329–341 (2015)
14. Teylo, L., Arantes, L., Sens, P., Drummond, L.M.A.: Scheduling bag-of-tasks in clouds using spot and burstable virtual machines. IEEE Trans. Cloud Comput. **11**(1), 984–996 (2021). https://doi.org/10.1109/TCC.2021.3125426
15. Wang, C., Urgaonkar, B., Gupta, A., Kesidis, G., Liang, Q.: Exploiting spot and burstable instances for improving the cost-efficacy of in-memory caches on the public cloud. In: Proceedings of the Twelfth European Conference on Computer Systems, pp. 620–634 (2017)
16. Wang, C., Urgaonkar, B., Nasiriani, N., Kesidis, G.: Using burstable instances in the public cloud: why, when and how? Proc. ACM Measur. Anal. Comput. Syst. **1**(1), 1–28 (2017)
17. Wei, W., Yang, W., Xu, H.: Burstable resource compatible general resource scheduling for stochastic demands in heterogeneous cloudsU+ 2605. Ain Shams Eng. J. **13**(1), 101503 (2022)

A Practical and Efficient Key-Aggregate Cryptosystem for Dynamic Access Control in Cloud Storage

Gaurav Pareek[1,2]([✉]) [ID] and B. R. Purushothama[2] [ID]

[1] Indian Institute of Information Technology Vadodara, International Campus Diu (U.T.), Diu, India
gaurav_pareek@diu.iiitvadodara.ac.in
[2] Department of Information Technology, National Institute of Technology Karnataka, Surathkal, India
puru@nitk.edu.in

Abstract. Dynamically changing access rights of users in large-scale secure data sharing is an important challenge which designers of the secure systems have to address. We focus efficient enforcement of the dynamic access control using key-aggregate cryptosystem (KAC), an efficient solution to secure data sharing. In this paper, we present a novel KAC construction that, in addition to satisfying all key-aggregate efficiency requirements, allows a data owner to enforce dynamic updates in access rights of a user much more efficiently than the existing ones. In particular, the proposed KAC construction handles the dynamic updates at the level of public parameters, and does not require the data owner to carry out any secure transmissions. This further means that none of the data users, including the one(s) whose access rights are updated, has to update their secrets. Thus, the dynamic update operation of the proposed KAC scheme is free from the one-affects-all problem. We present a formal security proof of the proposed KAC scheme and analyze its performance to further support our claims.

Keywords: Dynamic Access Control · Secure Data Sharing · Key-Aggregate Cryptosystem · Cloud Computing

1 Introduction

With the advent of distributed computing, especially cloud computing, Internet of Things (IoT), and Edge Computing, the world is generating and consuming very large amount of data on a daily basis. At the center of technologies like these is the "always online" enormous distributed storage and resourceful distributed computing facility that performs the dual task of storing its users' data and allowing its users to share the data with selected parties in a secure manner. It is practical to assume the cloud storage server to be semi-trusted [5]. So, the data is usually encrypted by the user who owns the data, also called the *data*

© The Author(s), under exclusive license to Springer Nature Switzerland AG 2024
S. Devismes et al. (Eds.): ICDCIT 2024, LNCS 14501, pp. 133–148, 2024.
https://doi.org/10.1007/978-3-031-50583-6_9

owner, before storing on to the cloud server. As a result, the task of data sharing is reduced to selectively and securely sharing the decryption keys of the stored data with the data users who the data owner wishes to authorize.

Each data user is authorized for a subset of data items stored by the data owner on the cloud server. For all practical reasons, this authorization may keep changing depending upon the system's requirements. So, the data owner employs a cryptosystem that efficiently enforces dynamic updates in the access authorizations of the data users. One of the important and efficient public-key cryptographic primitives suitable for this purpose is Key-Aggregate Cryptosystem (KAC) [2,16]. Using a KAC, the data owner encrypts its data under different classes $1, 2, \ldots, n$. In a practical setting, these classes correspond to the various types of data items a person may own, e.g., personal, medical, educational etc. Now suppose that the data owner wishes to authorize a user u to access a subset $Auth(u) \subseteq \{1, 2, \ldots, n\}$ of the data classes. Using KAC, the data owner generates a constant-size aggregate key denoted as $\mathcal{K}_u$ that is capable of successfully decrypting the data encrypted under any class $i \in Auth(u)$. This aggregate key is securely transmitted to the user and acts as the only constant-size secret required by the user to decrypt a collection of data items for which the user is authorized. The efficiency of KAC comes from the constant-size secret aggregate key capable of decrypting a large subset of shared data items. However, we stress that updating the authorization of any given user using a KAC is inefficient.

Suppose that the authorization of the user u is updated and it is no more authorized for data class i. In other words, update $Auth(u) = Auth(u)\backslash\{i\}$. As a result, the data owner should carry out updates such that the user u is not able to decrypt the data encrypted under data class i. This is called the KAC's forward secrecy [14]. The schematic representation of the operation and *forward secrecy* requirement is presented in Fig. 1. In case user u, who was initially unauthorized for a data class, say j, is now authorized for it, the updates carried out by the data owner must be such that the user u can decrypt all future data encrypted under class j. A KAC scheme satisfying this requirement is said to satisfy *backward secrecy*.

A KAC should address the dynamically changing access rights of users and allow the data owner to update the authorization set $Auth(u)$ with minimal effort. Ideally, it should not require the data owner to re-compute a large number of aggregate keys and securely transmit them to the users. Indeed, for a highly dynamic environment, each user should not have to update their secret aggregate key just because authorization of one among the large population of users has changed. In other words, the KAC should be free from the one-affects-all problem. However, we stress that there is no KAC construction in the literature that does not require at least a "few" aggregate key updates. We also emphasize that in most cases, this "few" is loosely bounded from the upper side by the number of users in the system.

The contribution of this paper is summarized as follows. In this paper, we address the problem of dynamic updates in key-aggregate cryptosystems and present a novel construction that efficiently enforces dynamic updates in the authorization sets of data users without compromising on the key-aggregate

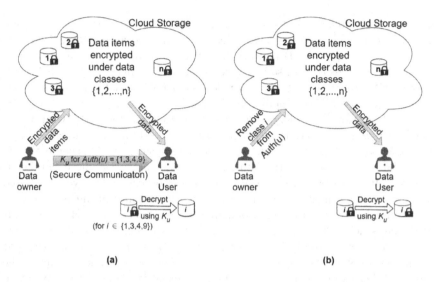

Fig. 1. (a) User can obtain plaintext encrypted under data class i using $\mathcal{K}_u$ as $i \in Auth(u)$. (b) Forward secrecy in KAC: After removing the class i from $Auth(u)$, the user cannot obtain plaintext encrypted under data class i.

efficiency requirements. In particular, the proposed KAC for dynamic access control requires no secret aggregate keys to be updated in case one or more authorized sets are updated based on the data owner's requirements. The proposed construction works in the public-key setting and satisfies all key-aggregate efficiency requirements, namely constant ciphertext size, constant-size aggregate key, and linear (in the number of data classes) total public storage required. We present the formal security proof and compare the performance of the proposed construction with the state-of-the-art KAC schemes to support our claims.

The organization of the remainder of the paper is as follows. Section 2 summarizes some important research in the area of KAC and its applications. Section 3 contains the basic definitions related to the proposed scheme. Section 4 defines the mathematical and cryptographic tools along with complexity assumptions used to design the proposed scheme. In Sect. 5, we present our proposed concrete construction along with its correctness, security and performance analysis. We conclude the paper in Sect. 6.

2 Related Work

The concept of key-aggregate cryptosystem (KAC) was first proposed by Chu et al. [2]. The formal security definitions and security analysis were given by Patranabis et al. [15,16]. Due to its efficiency, it became an immediate choice for secure data sharing and access control [1,9]. There are several works in which KAC is augmented or combined with other known cryptographic primitives to achieve the functional goals of various target application scenarios. KAC is combined with searchable encryption to achieve fine-grained access control for outsourced data [3,7,8,10,11]. Broadcast encryption was used in conjunction with KAC to design access control solutions for scalable systems [16]. Also, KAC was combined with proxy re-encryption for designing flexible data sharing solution tailor-made for distributed cloud scenario [13].

One of the major and widely addressed issues is enhancing the KAC primitive so that it can enforce dynamic access control. The need for a dynamic KAC was first realized by Patranabis et al. [15]. They designed a KAC scheme that is dynamic but requires secure transmissions of aggregate keys whose number is not too loosely upper bounded by the total number of aggregate keys distributed in the system. Also, the cihertext size does not remain constant in case the KAC operates in a highly dynamic environment. Later, Pareek et al. [14] overcame some of the issues and designed a dynamic KAC with constant ciphertext size. However, their scheme still requires large-size secure transmission to carry out from the data owner to various data users in case of dynamic updates. The scheme in [12] claims constant secure communication size, constant computation cost of dynamic updates and constant ciphertext size in case all the authorized sets are disjoint. The work further mentions that in case there are overlapping (non-disjoint) authorized sets, both secure communication size and computation cost in an event of dynamic update is upper bounded by the number of aggregate keys in the system. Furthermore, we stress that the scheme in [12] is not designed for public-key setting. Indeed, the encryption function takes the master-secret keys as input to produce any valid ciphertext.

Several other schemes were proposed to address the dynamic access control requirements in KAC. Guo et al. [6] claimed their scheme to be dynamic. However, Alimohammadi et al. [1] proved the scheme in [6] to be insecure. Gan et al. [4] designed a dynamic KAC that requires no secure communication to enforce dynamic access control. However, their scheme uses multilinear maps, which limits the practical applicability of their scheme.

It is clear from the review of the literature given above that there is no KAC construction that is suitable for efficiently enforcing dynamic access control. In the process of making the KAC scheme dynamic, the existing schemes either have to compromise on the storage efficiency or have to carry out a large number of secure transmissions or both. We intend to design a KAC in a public key setting and using bilinear maps that is secure and features dynamic update operations in which there is no secure transmission required. It also satisfies all the key-aggregate efficiency requirements, that is constant size aggregate key, constant ciphertext size and public storage linear in the number of data classes.

3 Proposed Key-Aggregate Cryptosystem for Dynamic Access Control

We present the construction syntax, and the formal definitions of correctness and security of the proposed KAC for dynamic access control.

3.1 Construction Syntax

We define the proposed KAC for dynamic access control Π as a collection of procedures Π = {Initialize, Gen, Extract, Enc, Dec, UpdateSet} as follows:

1. **Initialize**$(1^\lambda, n) \to$ **params:** This procedure takes as an input the security parameter λ and the maximum number of data classes n supported by the KAC. It outputs the set of public parameters **params** required for the remaining of the operations in the KAC.
2. **Gen(params)** $\to$ {**msk, mpk, dynK**}: This procedure outputs the master secret key **msk**, master public key **mpk** and dynamic key **dynK**. Here, the master-public key and dynamic key are published and the master-secret key is kept as secret.
3. **Extract(params,msk, dynK,** $Auth(u)) \to$ {$\mathcal{K}_u, pub(u)$}: This procedure has two sub-procedures **AggExtract** and **PubExtract**. It takes as input the public parameters, master-secret, dynamic key and the authorized set. While the sub-procedure **AggExtract** outputs the aggregate key $\mathcal{K}_u$ to be securely transmitted to the users authorized for the set $Auth(u)$, the sub-procedure **PubExtract** outputs $pub(u)$, the public parameter corresponding to the authorized set $Auth(u)$.
4. **Enc**$(i,$ **mpk, dynK,** $M) \to C_i$: This procedure takes the data class i under which the message M is encrypted. It also takes public parameters **params** and the dynamic key **dynK** as input to produce the ciphertext C_i corresponding to the input message M under data class i.
5. **Dec**$(C_i, \mathcal{K}_u, pub(u), Auth(u)) \to M$: This procedure takes the ciphertext to be decrypted, and aggregate key $\mathcal{K}_u$, public parameter corresponding to the authorized set $Auth(u)$ and the set $Auth(u)$ itself. The output is the underlying plaintext message M if and only if $i \in Auth(u)$.
6. **UpdateSet**$(i, Auth(u),$ **params, type**$) \to$ {**dynK'**$, pub'(u), C_i'$} : This procedure adds or removes the data class i to/from the aggregate set $Auth(u)$ as indicated by the input **type** to the procedure. To ensure backward/forward secrecy outputs the updated dynamic key **dynk'**, updated public parameters $pub'(u)$ corresponding to $Auth(u)$ and all future ciphertexts under the data class i are computed as $C_i' \leftarrow$ **Enc**$(i,$ **mpk, dynK'**).

3.2 Correctness

The correctness requirement of the proposed dynamic KAC scheme requires that given that the data class $i \in Auth(u)$, the decryption procedure must output the correct underlying plaintext message M encrypted under i. Formally,

$$\Pr\left[\begin{array}{l} \mathbf{Dec}(C_i, \mathcal{K}_u, pub(u), Auth(u)) \\ = M \end{array} \middle| \begin{array}{l} C_i \leftarrow \mathbf{Enc}(i, \mathbf{mpk}, \mathbf{dynK}), \\ \{\mathcal{K}_u, pub(u)\} \leftarrow \mathbf{Extract} \\ (\mathbf{params}, \mathbf{msk}, Auth(u)), \\ i \in Auth(u) \end{array} \right] = 1$$

3.3 Security Definition

Chosen-Plaintext Attack (CPA) security of the proposed KAC is defined as a game between a probabilistic polynomial time (PPT) adversary $\mathcal{A}$ and challenger $\mathcal{C}$ as follows:

1. **Init:** $\mathcal{A}$ outputs a target authorized set $Auth(u) \subseteq \{1, 2, \ldots, n\}$ and sends to the challenger $\mathcal{C}$. Then, the challenger $\mathcal{C}$ randomly selects a target data class $i^* \in Auth(u)$.
2. **Setup:** The challenger $\mathcal{C}$ uses **Initialize** and **Gen** of the proposed KAC construction Π and publishes **params, mpk** and **dynK**. It keeps the master secret key **msk** secret.
3. **Query-Phase-1:** $\mathcal{A}$ issues to $\mathcal{B}$ **Extract** queries for sets $Auth(k) \subseteq \overline{Auth(u)}$. Here, $\overline{Auth(u)}$ denotes an aggregate set containing all data classes which are not in $Auth(u)$.
4. **Challenge:** $\mathcal{A}$ picks two random messages M_0, M_1 from the message space and sends them to $\mathcal{B}$. Now, $\mathcal{B}$ chooses a random bit $b \in \{0, 1\}$ and uses the procedure **Enc** of the proposed construction Π to output the challenge $\{C_{i^*}, M_0, M_1\}$, where C_{i^*} is the ciphertext corresponding to M_b under the target data class i^*. That is, $C_{i^*} \leftarrow \textbf{Enc}(i^*, \textbf{mpk}, \textbf{dynK})$.
5. **Query-Phase-2:** $\mathcal{A}$ can further continue to issue **Extract** queries for all authorized sets $Auth(k) \subseteq \overline{Auth(u)}$, to which $\mathcal{B}$ responds in the same way as in Query-Phase-1.
6. **Guess:** $\mathcal{A}$ outputs the guess b' and wins if $b = b'$.

We define the advantage of the adversary $\mathcal{A}$ of winning the game described above against the challenger $\mathcal{C}$ as follows:

$$Adv_{\mathcal{A},n}^{(\epsilon,t,n)\text{-CPA-sec}} = \left| \Pr[b = b'] - \frac{1}{2} \right|.$$

Definition 1 ((ϵ, t, n)-CPA Secure KAC). *A KAC construction over n data classes is said to be (ϵ, t, n)-CPA-secure against all t-time non-adaptive PPT adversaries if the advantage of such an adversary $\mathcal{A}$ is upper bounded by ϵ, i.e., $Adv_{\mathcal{A},n}^{(\epsilon,t,n)\text{-CPA-sec}} < \epsilon$.*

4 Mathematical Preliminaries and Assumptions

Definition 2 (Bilinear Pairing). *Consider a cyclic multiplicative group $\mathbb{G}_1$ of prime order 'p', $g \in \mathbb{G}_1$ its generator and $\mathbb{G}_2$ another cyclic multiplicative group with order same as that of $\mathbb{G}_1$. A symmetric and efficiently computable bilinear map $e : \mathbb{G}_1 \times \mathbb{G}_1 \rightarrow \mathbb{G}_2$ satisfies the following:*

a) Bilinearity: $e(g^l, g^k) = e(g, g)^{lk} = e(g^k, g^l) = e(g, g)^{kl}$, $\forall g \in \mathbb{G}_1$, $l, k \in \mathbb{Z}_p$,
b) Non-degeneracy: $e(g, g) \neq 1$.

Definition 3 (Decision n-BDHE problem). *Given an input $(h, P = (g, g_1, \ldots, g_n, g_{n+2}, \ldots, g_{2n}), Z)$, where $h \in \mathbb{G}_1, g \in \mathbb{G}_1$, $g_i = g^{\alpha^i} \in \mathbb{G}_1$ (for $\alpha \in \mathbb{Z}_p$ and $i = 1, 2, \ldots, n, n+2, \ldots, 2n$), $Z \in \mathbb{G}_2$ and $e(.,.)$ is an efficiently computable bilinear pairing, decide if $Z = e(h, g_{n+1})$.*

Let $\mathcal{A}$ be an algorithm that runs in time τ and takes as input an n-BDHE tuple. We say $\mathcal{A}$ has advantage ϵ in solving the decision n-BDHE problem if:

$$|\Pr\left[\mathcal{A}\left(h, P, e(h, g_{n+1})\right) = 0\right] - \Pr\left[\mathcal{A}\left(h, P, Z\right) = 0\right]| \geq \epsilon.$$

Definition 4 (Decision (τ, ϵ, n)-BDHE Assumption). *The (τ, ϵ, n)-BDHE assumption holds in $(\mathbb{G}_1, \mathbb{G}_2)$ if no τ-time algorithm has advantage of at least ϵ in solving the Decision n-BDHE problem in $(\mathbb{G}_1, \mathbb{G}_2)$.*

5   Concrete Proposed KAC for Dynamic Access Control

We present the concrete mathematical construction, correctness analysis and security analysis of the proposed KAC for dynamic access control. We also analyze the computational and storage performance of the proposed scheme with the important existing ones.

5.1   Basic Idea Behind Our Construction

In the proposed construction, the data owner outputs both public and private parameter corresponding to an authorized set $Auth(u)$. The public parameter is denoted by $pub(u)$, whereas the private parameter is nothing but the aggregate key $\mathcal{K}_u$ which is securely transmitted to the user authorized for the set $Auth(u) \subseteq \{1, 2, \ldots, n\}$. In the decryption procedure, $pub(u)$ is used to partially decrypt the ciphertext and the remaining partial decryption is done by the $\mathcal{K}_u$ kept securely by the authorized user to obtain the underlying plaintext message.

To accomplish this, the proposed scheme outputs total $2n$ different g_i's for identifying n data classes (total $4n$ different g_i's at the setup time). Out of these, $g_1, \ldots, g_n$ are used to identify n data classes and computing $pub(u)$. The remaining $g_{n+1}, \ldots, g_{2n}$ are used for generating $\mathcal{K}_u$. Note that in this case, g_{2n+1} is not published along with **params** as opposed to g_{n+1} not being published in traditional KAC schemes. When the dynamic updates are to be made to any authorized set, the data owner updates the public parameter $pub(u)$ corresponding to the set while the $\mathcal{K}_u$ remains unchanged. This way, the proposed scheme requires updating only the public parameters and none of the secret aggregate keys of any user. This means that there is no need for secure transmission of any keys in an event of dynamic updates to authorized set(s).

5.2   Concrete Construction

As discussed earlier in Sect. 5.1, the proposed construction uses twice the number of public parameters g_i's as the number of data classes it handles. We describe our concrete construction for a KAC that handles $n/2$ data classes. This is because by doing so, the parts of the proposed construction will look comparable to the traditional construction, which will facilitate better readability and understanding of the construction. While $g_1, \ldots, g_{n/2}$ identify the $n/2$ data classes and ar used for computing the public parameter $pub(u)$, the remaining $g_{n/2+1}, \ldots, g_n$ are used to compute the secret aggregate key $\mathcal{K}_u$. Note that it is straightforward to extend the construction to a case of n data classes by simply doubling the subscripts of all g_i's.

In short, to handle n data classes the proposed scheme uses twice the public parameters as used in the traditional KACs. Note however that this number is still a constant multiple of n and does not cause any significant overhead. The only difference is seen in the security proof where we prove $(\epsilon, t, n/2)$-CPA security of the proposed construction, under the n–BDHE assumption. This is because the number of data classes for which the KAC can be proved secure under n–BDHE assumption has halved.

In what follows, we describe the proposed KAC for dynamic access control handling $n/2$ data classes $\Pi = \{\text{Initialize, Gen, Extract, Enc, Dec, UpdateSet}\}$:

1. **Initialize**$(1^\lambda, n/2) \rightarrow$ **params:** Sets up the KAC as follows:
   - Select bilinear groups $\mathbb{G}_1$ and $\mathbb{G}_2$ both with prime order p where $2^\lambda \leq p \leq 2^{\lambda+1}$ and a generator $g \in \mathbb{G}_1$ at random.
   - Choose random $\alpha \in \mathbb{Z}_p$ secretly and for all $i \in \{1, 2, \ldots, n, n+2, \ldots, 2n\}$, compute $g_i = g^{\alpha^i}$ and remove α.
   - Select a target collusion-resistant (TCR) hash function $H : \mathbb{G}_2 \rightarrow \mathbb{G}_1$.
   - Store **params** $\leftarrow \langle g, p, \mathbb{G}_1, \mathbb{G}_2, H, g_1, g_2, \ldots, g_n, g_{n+2}, g_{n+3}, \ldots, g_{2n} \rangle$

2. **Gen**(**params**) $\rightarrow$ **{msk, mpk, dynK}:** Generates the master-public and master-secret keys along with the dynamic key as follows:
   - Select two numbers $\gamma_1, \gamma_2 \in \mathbb{Z}_p$ uniformly at random.
   - Store **msk**$\leftarrow \{\gamma_1, \gamma_2\}$, **mpk** $\leftarrow g^{\gamma_1}$ and **dynK** $= g^{\gamma_2}$.

3. **Extract**(**params, msk, dynK**, $Auth(u)$) $\rightarrow \{\mathcal{K}_u, pub(u)\}$: Generates the aggregate key using the sub-procedure **AggExtract** and public key corresponding to the authorized set $Auth(u) \subseteq \{1, 2, \ldots, n\}$ using the sub-procedure **PubExtract** as follows:

   (a) **AggExtract:** Compute $\mathcal{K}_u = \left(\prod_{b \in Auth(u)} g_{n/2+1-b} \right)^{\gamma_1}$ and send it to the authorized user over a secure communication channel. Also, compute and publish $pub_{0,u} = \prod_{j \in Auth(u)} g_{n/2+j}$. Both $\mathcal{K}_u$ and $pub_{u,0}$ remain unchanged throughout the system operation.

   (b) **PubExtract:** Choose random values $r, s \overset{\$}{\leftarrow} \mathbb{Z}_p$, another random value $R_1 \overset{\$}{\leftarrow} \mathbb{G}_2$ and use them to compute the public parameters $pub(u) = (pub_1, \ldots, pub_5)$ corresponding to the aggregate key $\mathcal{K}_u$ as follows:

   $$pub_1 = \left(\prod_{a \in Auth(u)} g_{n+1-a} \right)^{\gamma_1} \cdot (\textbf{dynK})^s, \quad pub_2 = (g_{n/2})^r$$

   $$pub_3 = (\textbf{mpk} \cdot pub_{0,u})^r, \quad pub_4 = R_1.e(g_1, g_n)^r, \quad pub_5 = g^s.H(R_1)$$

4. **Enc**$(i, \mathbf{mpk}, dynK, M) \rightarrow C_i$: Encrypts the plaintext message M under a data class i to produce ciphertext $C_i \langle C_1, C_2, C_3, C_4, C_5 \rangle$ as follows:

   - Choose a random value $t \xleftarrow{\$} \mathbb{Z}_p$, a random value $R_2 \xleftarrow{\$} \mathbb{G}_2$ and compute:

$$C_1 = g^t, \; \dot{C}_2 = (\mathbf{mpk}.g_i)^t, \; C_3 = R_2.e(g_1, g_n)^t, \; C_4 = (\mathbf{dynK})^t,$$
$$C_5 = M \oplus H(R_2)$$

5. **Dec**$(C_i, \mathcal{K}_u, pub(u), Auth(u)) \rightarrow M$: Use the aggregate key $\mathcal{K}_u$ and decrypt the ciphertext $C_i = \langle C_1, C_2, C_3, C_4, C_5 \rangle$ to obtain the underlying plaintext message M as follows:
   - Compute **A** as:

$$\mathbf{A} = \frac{C_3.e(pub_1 \prod_{\substack{a \in Auth(u) \\ a \neq i}} g_{n+1-a+i}, C_1)}{e(C_2, \prod_{a \in Auth(u)} g_{n+1-a})} = R_2.e(g^{\gamma_2 s}, g^t)$$

   - Compute **B** as:

$$\mathbf{B} = \frac{pub_4.e(\mathcal{K}_u, pub_2).e(\prod_{j \in Auth(u)} \prod_{\substack{b \in Auth(u) \\ b \neq j}} g_{n/2+1-b+j}, pub_2)}{e(pub_3, \prod_{b \in Auth(u)} g_{n/2+1-b})}$$

   - Use **A** and **B** computed above to obtain M as follows:

$$M = H\left(\mathbf{A}.e(pub_5.(H(\mathbf{B}))^{-1}, C_4)^{-1}\right)^{-1} \oplus C_5.$$

6. **UpdateSet**$(i, Auth(u), \mathbf{params}, \mathbf{type}) \rightarrow \{\mathbf{dynK'}, pub'(u), C_i'\}$: Removes/ adds the data class i from/to the aggregate set $Auth(u)$ and outputs the updated dynamic key, public key and updated ciphertext to ensure forward/backward security as follows:
   - If **type** = 'Revoke', then set $Auth'(u) \leftarrow Auth(u) \backslash \{i\}$. Otherwise, if **type** = 'Add', then set $Auth'(u) = Auth(u) \cup \{i\}$
   - Select a random value $\gamma_2' \xleftarrow{\$} \mathbb{Z}_p$, compute the updated dynamic key **dynK'**$= g^{\gamma_2'}$ and update the master-secret key component γ_2 with γ_2'. The component γ_1 of the master-secret key remains the same.
   - Invoke **Extract.PubExtract**$(\mathbf{params}, \mathbf{msk}, \mathbf{dynk'}, Auth'(u))$ with the updated dynamic key **dynK'** and the updated authorized set $Auth'(u)$ as input. It outputs the updated public parameter $pub'(u)$ corresponding to the authorized set that undergoes the update operation.
   - All future ciphertexts under i are encrypted using the updated dynamic key **dynK'**. That is, $C_i \leftarrow \mathbf{Enc}(i, \mathbf{mpk}, \mathbf{dynK'})$.

Noteworthy is that the procedure for revoking the data class does not update or securely transmit the aggregate key of the affected user.

5.3 Correctness Analysis

We present the analysis of correctness of the proposed construction under the correctness definition given in Sect. 3.2. Firstly, the value **A** defined in the description of the **Dec** procedure of the proposed KAC construction as follows:

$$
\mathbf{A} = \frac{C_3.e(pub_1 \prod_{\substack{a \in Auth(u) \\ a \neq i}} g_{n+1-a+i}, C_1)}{e(C_2, \prod_{a \in Auth(u)} g_{n+1-a})}
$$

$$
= \frac{R_2.e(g_1, g_n)^t e(\prod_{a \in Auth(u)} g_{n+1-a}^{\gamma_1} \cdot g^{\gamma_2 s} \cdot \prod_{\substack{a \in Auh(u) \\ a \neq i}}, g^t)}{e(g^{\gamma_1 t} g_i^t, \prod_{a \in Auth(u)} g_{n+1-a})}
$$

$$
= \frac{R_2.e(g_1, g_n)^t e(g^{\gamma_2 s}, g^t).e(g^t, \prod_{\substack{a \in Auth(u) \\ a \neq i}} g_{n+1-a+i})}{e(g^t, \prod_{a \in Auth(u)} g_{n+1-a+i})}
$$

$$
= \frac{R_2.e(g_1, g_n)^t . e(g^{\gamma_2 s}, g^t)}{e(g^t, g_{n+1})}
$$

$$
= R_2.e(g^{\gamma_2 s}, g^t)
$$

Next, the procedure **Dec** computes the value **B**, which simplifies as follows:

$$
\mathbf{B} = \frac{R_1.e(g_1, g_n)^r e(\prod_{b \in Auth(u)} g_{n/2+1-b}^{\gamma_1}, g_{n/2}^r).e(\prod_{j \in Auth(u)} \prod_{\substack{b \in Auth(u) \\ b \neq j}} g_{n/2+1-b+j}, g_{n/2}^r)}{e(g^{\gamma_1 r} \prod_{j \in Auth(u)} g_{n/2+j}^r, \prod_{b \in Auth(u)} g_{n/2+1-b})}
$$

$$
= \frac{R_1.e(g_1, g_n)^r e(\prod_{j \in Auth(u)} \prod_{\substack{b \in Auth(u) \\ b \neq j}} g_{n/2+1-b+j}, g_{n/2}^r)}{e(\prod_{j \in Auth(u)} g_{n/2+j}^r, \prod_{b \in Auth(u)} g_{n/2+1-b})}
$$

$$
= \frac{R_1.e(g_1, g_n)^r \prod_{j \in Auth(u)} e(\prod_{\substack{b \in Auth(u) \\ b \neq j}} g_{n/2+1-b+j}, g_{n/2}^r)}{\prod_{j \in Auth(u)} e(g_{n/2+j}^r, \prod_{b \in Auth(u)} g_{n/2+1-b})}
$$

$$
= R_1.e(g_1, g_n)^r . \prod_{j \in Auth(u)} \left(\frac{e(\prod_{\substack{b \in Auth(u) \\ b \neq j}} g_{n/2+1-b+j}, g_{n/2}^r)}{e(g_{n/2+j}^r, \prod_{b \in Auth(u)} g_{n/2+1-b})} \right)
$$

$$
= R_1.e(g_1, g_n)^t . e(g_1, g_n)^{-t} = R_1.
$$

Finally, compute the following:

$$H\left(\mathbf{A}.e(pub_5.(H(\mathbf{B}))^{-1}, C_4)^{-1}\right)^{-1} \oplus C_5$$
$$= H\left(R_2.e(g^{\gamma_2 s}, g^t).e(g^s.H(R_1).H(R_1)^{-1}, g^{\gamma_2 t})^{-1}\right)^{-1} \oplus M \oplus H(R_2)$$
$$= H(R_2.e(g^{\gamma_2 s}, g^t).e(g^{\gamma_2 s}, g^t)^{-1}) \oplus M \oplus H(R_2)$$
$$= H(R_2) \oplus M \oplus H(R_2) = M.$$

Therefore, based on the analysis given above, we conclude that the proposed KAC construction is correct.

5.4 Security Analysis

Theorem 1. *The proposed KAC construction given in Sect. 5.2 is secure under the $(\epsilon, t, n/2)$-CPA-Security of Definition 1 given that the (ϵ, t, n)-BDHE assumption holds in $\mathbb{G}_1, \mathbb{G}_2$ and a target collusion-resistant (TCR) hash function $H : \mathbb{G}_2 \to \mathbb{G}_1$ exists.*

Proof. Let $\mathcal{A}$ be a t-time PPT adversary such that $Adv_{\mathcal{A},n}^{(\epsilon,t,n/2)\text{-CPA-sec}} > \epsilon$ for an instance of the proposed dynamic KAC construction handling $n/2$ data classes. We build another adversary $\mathcal{B}$ that can decide the n-BDHE tuple with an advantage at least ϵ'. The input for adversary $\mathcal{B}$ is (h, Q, Z) where $h \in \mathbb{G}_1$, $Q = \{g_i | i \in [1, n] \text{ and } i \neq n+1\}$ and Z is either $e(h, g_{n+1})$ or a random element from $\mathbb{G}_2$.

During various stages of game simulation, the adversary issues queries and stores the query results in an indexed table to maintain the state information and use it in future. The table is defined as follows:

- *AggPub*^{List}: Set of all aggregate keys and the corresponding public parameter queried by the adversary $\mathcal{A}$ and computed by the challenger $\mathcal{B}$. Each entry is indexed by the authorized set identifier. For example, if the set queried is $Auth(u)$, then the entry is a 4-tuple $\langle u, Auth(u), \mathcal{K}_u, pub(u) \rangle$.

The execution of $\mathcal{B}$ proceeds as follows:

- **Init:** $\mathcal{B}$ invokes $\mathcal{A}$ to obtain the set $Auth(u^*)$ over which $\mathcal{A}$ wishes to be challenged. Then, $\mathcal{B}$ chooses an index (data class) $i^* \in Auth(u^*)$ at random.
- **Setup:** $\mathcal{B}$ computes **params**, **mpk** and **dynK** and sends to $\mathcal{A}$ as follows:
  - Choose a random $\alpha \in \mathbb{Z}_p$ and outputs the **params** $= \langle g, p, \mathbb{G}_1, \mathbb{G}_2, H, g_1,$ $g_2, \ldots, g_n, g_{n+2}, \ldots, g_{2n} \rangle$ where each $g_i = g^{\alpha^i}$.
  - Select a target collusion-resistant hash function $H : \mathbb{G}_2 \to \mathbb{G}_1$.
  - Choose a random $\gamma_1 \in \mathbb{Z}_p$ and compute **mpk** $= g^{\gamma_1} g_{i^*}^{-1}$. This means that the master-secret key **msk** $= (\gamma_1 - \alpha^{i^*})$. This master-secret is stored secretly by $\mathcal{B}$.
  - $\mathcal{B}$ now selects a random $x_1 \in \mathbb{Z}_p$ and sends the dynamic key as **dynK** $= h_1 = g^{x_1}$ to $\mathcal{A}$.

- **Query-Phase-1:** $\mathcal{A}$ queries the collusion aggregate keys $\mathcal{K}_u$ by sending the authorized set $Auth(u) \subseteq \{1, \ldots, n\} \backslash Auth(u^*)$ to $\mathcal{B}$. To this, $\mathcal{B}$ responds after computing $\mathcal{K}_u$ and $pub(u)$ as follows:

$$\mathcal{K}_u = \prod_{b \in Auth(u)} \left(g_{n/2+1-b}^{\gamma_1} \cdot g_{n/2+1-b+i^*}^{-1} \right)$$

Here, the value $r \in \mathbb{Z}_p$ is selected at random. $\mathcal{B}$ further selects a random value $s \in \mathbb{Z}_p$, a random $R_1 \in \mathbb{G}_2$, and sets $h_2 = h_1^s$, $h_3 = g^r$,

$$h_4 = \left(g.(\prod_{j \in Auth(u)} g_{n/2+j} \cdot g_{i^*}^{-1})^{1/\gamma_1} \right)^r \text{ and } h_5 = H(R_1). \text{ Then, } \mathcal{B} \text{ computes}$$

the public key parameter corresponding to $\mathcal{K}_u$ as:

$$pub(u) = \langle pub_1, \ldots, pub_5 \rangle$$

$$pub_1 = \left(\prod_{a \in Auth(u)} g_{n+1-a}^{\gamma_1} \cdot g_{n+1-a+i^*}^{-1} \right) h_2$$

$$pub_2 = h_3^{\alpha^{n/2}}, \quad pub_3 = h_4^{\gamma_1}, \quad pub_4 = R_1.e(h_3, g_{n+1}), \quad pub_5 = h_2^{1/x_1}.h_5$$

It is straightforward to verify that the values $\mathcal{K}_u$ and $pub(u)$ computed above are valid and can be computed by $\mathcal{B}$ using information available in its view. These computed values are now stored in the list $AggPub^{\mathrm{List}}$. Since all the values are chosen by $\mathcal{B}$ uniformly at random, the distribution of all the computed $\mathcal{K}_u$ and $pub(u)$ is the same as in the original construction.

- **Challenge:** When $\mathcal{A}$ decides to end the query phase, it chooses two random messages M_0, M_1 and sends them to $\mathcal{B}$. Then, $\mathcal{B}$ selects a bit b uniformly at random and encrypts the message M_b under the target data class i^* to obtain $C_{i^*} = \langle C_1, C_2, C_3, C_4, C_5 \rangle$ as follows. Compute $y_1 = g^t$ for a random $t \in \mathbb{Z}_p$, select a random $R_2 \in \mathbb{G}_2$ and set the ciphertext components using the information in $\mathcal{B}$'s view as follows:

$$C_1 = y_1, \quad C_2 = y_1^{\gamma_1}, \quad C_3 = R_2.Z, \quad C_4 = y_1^{x_1}, \quad C_5 = M_b \oplus H(R_2)$$

We can verify that all ciphertext components, if computed as above, take the same form as in the actual construction.

- **Query-Phase-2:** $\mathcal{A}$ continues to issue **Extract** queries to $\mathcal{B}$ under the same condition as the one mentioned in **Query-Phase-1**. $\mathcal{B}$ responds to these queries in the same way as in **Query-Phase-1** and sends valid $\mathcal{K}_u$ and publishes a valid $pub(u)$ every time.

- **Guess:** The adversary $\mathcal{A}$ outputs a guess b' of the guess b. If the guess b' equals the bit b, then $\mathcal{B}$ outputs 0 indicating that $Z = e(y_1, g_{n+1})$. Otherwise, it outputs 1 indicating that Z is a uniform and random element from $\mathbb{G}_2$. This concludes the description of the game.

It can be seen that the algorithm $\mathcal{B}$ successfully simulates $\mathcal{A}$'s view in the attack. Also, it can be seen that the problem of deciding the (h, Q, Z) nicely reduces to the problem of distinguishing the challenge ciphertext C_{i^*}. Formally, if Z is an element chosen uniformly at random from $\mathbb{G}_2$, then $\Pr\left[\mathcal{B}(Q, Z) = 0\right] = \frac{1}{2} - Adv_{\mathcal{A},H}^{\text{TCR}}$, where $Adv_{\mathcal{A},H}^{\text{TCR}}$ is the advantage for $\mathcal{A}$ of getting a collision in the hash function H. On the other hand, if $Z = e(h, g_{n+1})$, then the same probability is at least $\frac{1}{2} + \epsilon' - Adv_{\mathcal{A},H}^{\text{TCR}}$, i.e., $\Pr\left[\mathcal{B}(Q, Z) = 0\right] \geq \frac{1}{2} + \epsilon' - Adv_{\mathcal{A},H}^{\text{TCR}}$ or, $Adv_{\mathcal{A},n}^{(\epsilon,t,n/2)\text{-CPA-sec}} \geq \epsilon' - Adv_{\mathcal{A},H}^{\text{TCR}}$. Hence, the proposed KAC construction is $(\epsilon, t, n/2)$-CPA-secure if the (ϵ, t, n)-BDHE assumption is hard in $\mathbb{G}_1, \mathbb{G}_2$.

5.5 Performance Analysis

In this section, we analyze and compare the efficiency of the proposed KAC with respect to the existing constructions. In particular, we target the very first KAC construction bu Chu et al. [2], a few works that claim to be dynamic [4,12,14,15], and a recent construction by Alimohammadi et al. [1] that points out the security issues with Guo et al.'s scheme [6] The analysis presented here focuses both computational and storage efficiencies of the KAC constructions.

Table 1. Comparison of storage overhead

Scheme	Private Storage Owner	Private Storage User	Public Storage	Ciphertext Size	Dynamic?/ Assumption
[2]	$\lvert \mathbb{Z}_p \rvert$	$\lvert \mathbb{G}_1 \rvert$	$(n+1)\lvert \mathbb{G}_1 \rvert$	$2\lvert \mathbb{G}_1 \rvert + \lvert \mathbb{G}_2 \rvert$	No/n-BDHE
[15]	$\lvert \mathbb{Z}_p \rvert$	$(\lvert Auth(u) \rvert + 1)\lvert \mathbb{G}_1 \rvert$	$(n+1)\lvert \mathbb{G}_1 \rvert$	$2\lvert \mathbb{G}_1 \rvert + \lvert \mathbb{G}_2 \rvert$	Yes/n-BDHE
[4]	$2\lvert \mathbb{Z}_p \rvert$	$2\lvert \mathbb{G}_1 \rvert$	$\log n(\lvert \mathbb{G}_i \rvert) + \lvert \mathbb{G}_{2n} \rvert + 2\lvert \mathbb{G}_n \rvert$	$2\lvert \mathbb{G}_n \rvert + \lvert \mathbb{G}_{2n} \rvert$	Yes/Multilinear Maps
[1]	$\lvert \mathbb{Z}_p \rvert$	$\lvert \mathbb{G}_1 \rvert$	$(3n+1)\lvert \mathbb{G}_1 \rvert$	$2\lvert \mathbb{G}_1 \rvert + \lvert \mathbb{G}_2 \rvert$	No/n-BDHE
[14]	$2\lvert \mathbb{Z}_p \rvert$	$3\lvert \mathbb{G}_1 \rvert$	$(2 + poly(\lambda))\lvert \mathbb{G}_1 \rvert$	$3\lvert \mathbb{G}_1 \rvert + \lvert \mathbb{G}_2 \rvert$	Yes/$poly(\lambda)$ public storage
[12]	$(n+2)\lvert \mathbb{Z}_p \rvert$	$\lvert \mathbb{G}_1 \rvert$	$(4n+1)\lvert \mathbb{G}_1 \rvert$	$n_{max}(3\lvert \mathbb{G}_1 \rvert + \lvert \mathbb{G}_2 \rvert)$	Yes/requires **msk** to encrypt
Ours	$\lvert \mathbb{Z}_p \rvert$	$\lvert \mathbb{G}_1 \rvert$	$n(6\lvert \mathbb{G}_1 \rvert + \lvert \mathbb{G}_2 \rvert)$	$3\lvert \mathbb{G}_1 \rvert + 2\lvert \mathbb{G}_2 \rvert$	Yes/TCR Hash function

n denotes the number of data classes
n_{max} denotes the maximum number of authorized sets of which any given data class can belong to. Loosely, $n_{max} = \mathcal{O}(m)$
$\lvert X \rvert$ denotes the maximum size in bits of an element in the set X

Table 1 presents analysis of the storage performance of the proposed KAC construction. Except the scheme in [12], all schemes including the proposed one require constant private storage for data owner. The private storage requirements for data user reflects the size of aggregate key. It can be seen that all schemes require a constant size aggregate key to be stored by the data user except the dynamic KAC given in [15], where the size of the aggregate key is upper bounded by a linear function of the size of the authorized set $Auth(u)$. Total public storage is an important requirement as it may impact the total effective cost

Table 2. Comparison of computation overhead

Scheme	Enc cost	Decrypt Public cost	Decrypt Private cost	Dynamic Updates	Secure Communication size
[2]	$3t_e + 2t_m$	$(2n+1)t_m + t_p$	$t_p + 2t_m$	Not Supported	NA
[15]	$3t_e + 2t_m$	$(2n+1)t_m + t_p$	$t_p + 2t_m$	$n_{max}t_e$	$n_{max}|\mathbb{G}_1|$
[4]	$3t_{e*} + 2t_{m*}$	$(2n+2)t_{m*} + t_{mp}$	$t_{mp} + t_{m*}$	$\log mt_{m*} + 2\log mt_{e*}$	Not required
[1]	$(3t_e + 2)t_m$	$(3n+2)t_m + t_e + t_p$	$t_p + t_m$	Not Supported	NA
[14]	$4t_e + 2t_m$	$(2n+1)t_m + t_p$	$3(t_p + t_m)$	$2t_e + n_{\max}(3t_e + (n+2)t_m)$	$3n_{max}|\mathbb{G}_1|$
[12]	$4t_e + 2t_m$	$(2mn + n + 2)t_m + t_p$	$t_p + t_m$	$3n_{max}(t_e + t_m)$	$n_{max}|\mathbb{G}_1|$
Ours	$4t_e + 2t_m$	$(n^2 + 2n + 5)t_m + 4t_p$	$t_p + t_m$	$m(6t_e + 4t_m)$	**Not required**

n and m denote the number of data classes and number aggregate keys, respectively.

t_m, t_e and t_p denote the time-costs of performing one modulo multiplication, exponentiation and bilinear pairing operation, respectively.

t_{mp}, t_{te*} and t_{m*} are time-costs of computing one multilinear pairing, one exponentiation in multilinear group, and one multiplication in multilinear group.

of outsourcing an owner's data to the Cloud storage. All the schemes, including ours, require linear total public storage except [4] and [14]. Gan et al.'s scheme [4] requires logarithmic public storage, which may seem efficient. However, their scheme is constructed using multilinear maps. Since there is no known practical instantiation of multilinear maps existing in the literature, Gan et al.'s scheme [4] is less practical compared to the other schemes. Further, Pareek et al.'s KAC [14] requires public storage which is upper bounded by a polynomial in the number of data classes n. It can be seen that the proposed KAC construction for dynamic access control satisfies all state-of-the-art key-aggregate efficiency requirements.

In Table 2, we compare the time-costs of various operations involved in the proposed scheme with those involved in the existing ones. It can be seen that in all the schemes compared in Table 2, majority of decryption operation is out-sourceable to a semi-trusted third-party. Note that only those computations can be outsourced that involve either publicly available components or the cipher-text components. The user will have to perform the operations that involve its secret, in this case the aggregate key $\mathcal{K}_u$. We refer to the cost of the outsourceable computational steps as public cost and those that have to be performed by the data user as private cost of decryption. It is clear from Table 2 that all schemes including the proposed one incur only a constant private cost for decryption. An important cost depicted here is the cost of enforcing dynamic updates. This includes the computation cost of the dynamic update and the size of the secure communication required to complete the update. While former gives a fair idea of computation overhead, the latter is an indication of the extent of the one-affects-all problem in the scheme. For comparison, we consider the cost involved in deletion of one data class from an aggregate set with forward secrecy. It is clear that in all KAC schemes, the data owner has to perform roughly the same amount of computations and secure communications. However, there are only two works that do not require any secure transmissions, namely Gan et al. [4] and the proposed KAC scheme. As we have already pointed out, the scheme in [4] is based on the multilinear maps, which makes it less practical than ours which is designed using bilinear pairings. To conclude, the proposed scheme supports secure and efficient dynamic updates. Ours is the only KAC construction so far that requires zero secure communication to ensure dynamic security while not compromising on the key-aggregate computational efficiency requirements.

6   Conclusions and Future Work

Key-aggregate cryptosystems (KAC) have attracted attention in recent times due to their efficiency and simplicity of enforcing access control on data outsourced to a cloud storage. However, enforcing dynamic updates in access rights of users using the existing KAC constructions is computationally inefficient. In this paper, we have successfully mitigated this problem by designing the first key-aggregate cryptosystem using bilinear pairings that does not require any secure communications to securely enforce dynamic updates in access rights. The aggregate keys are assigned to the users only once. Any dynamic updates in access rights of the users ar handled by only modifying the public parameters thereby making the dynamic update procedure very efficient. We have proved security of the proposed construction and compared its performance with the existing KAC constructions. Our analyses have indicated that the proposed KAC satisfies all key-aggregate efficiency requirements despite having the most efficient dynamic update procedure of all the KAC constructions. An important future direction is to use the notion of KAC and design lightweight authentication protocols that suit the requirements of highly dynamic and pervasive computing environments.

References

1. Alimohammadi, K., Bayat, M., Javadi, H.H.: A secure key-aggregate authentication cryptosystem for data sharing in dynamic cloud storage. Multimed. Tools Appl. **79**, 2855–2872 (2020). https://doi.org/10.1007/s11042-019-08292-8
2. Chu, C.K., Chow, S.S., Tzeng, W.G., Zhou, J., Deng, R.H.: Key-aggregate cryptosystem for scalable data sharing in cloud storage. IEEE Trans. Parallel Distrib. Syst. **25**(2), 468–477 (2013)
3. Cui, B., Liu, Z., Wang, L.: Key-aggregate searchable encryption (KASE) for group data sharing via cloud storage. IEEE Trans. Comput. **65**(8), 2374–2385 (2015)
4. Gan, Q., Wang, X., Wu, D., et al.: Revocable key-aggregate cryptosystem for data sharing in cloud. Secur. Commun. Netw. **2017**, 2508693 (2017)
5. Goh, E.J., Shacham, H., Modadugu, N., Boneh, D.: SiRiUS: securing remote untrusted storage. In: NDSS, vol. 3, pp. 131–145. Citeseer (2003)
6. Guo, C., et al.: Key-aggregate authentication cryptosystem for data sharing in dynamic cloud storage. Future Gener. Comput. Syst. **84**, 190–199 (2018)
7. Lee, J., Kim, M., Oh, J., Park, Y., Park, K., Noh, S.: A secure key aggregate searchable encryption with multi delegation in cloud data sharing service. Appl. Sci. **11**(19), 8841 (2021)

8. Li, T., Liu, Z., Li, P., Jia, C., Jiang, Z.L., Li, J.: Verifiable searchable encryption with aggregate keys for data sharing in outsourcing storage. In: Liu, J.K., Steinfeld, R. (eds.) ACISP 2016. LNCS, vol. 9723, pp. 153–169. Springer, Cham (2016). https://doi.org/10.1007/978-3-319-40367-0_10

9. Liu, L., Huang, C., Zhu, D., Liu, D., Ni, J., Shen, X.S.: Secure and distributed access control for dynamic pervasive edge computing services. In: GLOBECOM 2022–2022 IEEE Global Communications Conference, pp. 5487–5492. IEEE (2022)

10. Liu, Z., Li, T., Li, P., Jia, C., Li, J.: Verifiable searchable encryption with aggregate keys for data sharing system. Future Gener. Comput. Syst. **78**, 778–788 (2018)

11. Padhya, M., Jinwala, D.C.: BTG-RKASE: privacy preserving revocable key aggregate searchable encryption with fine-grained multi-delegation & break-the-glass access control. In: ICETE (2), pp. 109–124 (2019)

12. Pareek, G., Maiti, S.: Efficient dynamic key-aggregate cryptosystem for secure and flexible data sharing. Concurr. Comput. Pract. Exp. **35**(19), e7553 (2023)

13. Pareek, G., Purushothama, B.: KAPRE: key-aggregate proxy re-encryption for secure and flexible data sharing in cloud storage. J. Inf. Secur. Appl. **63**, 103009 (2021)

14. Pareek, G., Purushothama, B.: Secure and efficient revocable key-aggregate cryptosystem for multiple non-predefined non-disjoint aggregate sets. J. Inf. Secur. Appl. **58**, 102799 (2021)

15. Patranabis, S., Shrivastava, Y., Mukhopadhyay, D.: Dynamic key-aggregate cryptosystem on elliptic curves for online data sharing. In: Biryukov, A., Goyal, V. (eds.) INDOCRYPT 2015. LNCS, vol. 9462, pp. 25–44. Springer, Cham (2015). https://doi.org/10.1007/978-3-319-26617-6_2

16. Patranabis, S., Shrivastava, Y., Mukhopadhyay, D.: Provably secure key-aggregate cryptosystems with broadcast aggregate keys for online data sharing on the cloud. IEEE Trans. Comput. **66**(5), 891–904 (2016)

Intelligent Technology

Prediction of Failure in Scania Truck Due to Air Pressure System Failure

Prasoon Singh and Lalatendu Behera$^{(\boxtimes)}$

Department of CSE, NIT Jalandhar, Jalandhar, India
{prasoons.cs.21,beheral}@nitj.ac.in

Abstract. This paper addresses the prediction of failures in the air pressure system of Scania trucks to minimize associated operating costs. A custom ensemble model is proposed combining random forest, XGBoost, and multi-layer perceptron algorithms. By optimizing the classification threshold, false positives and false negatives are reduced, effectively minimizing costs. In comparison to previous studies, the model's performance is evaluated using metrics like accuracy, AUC, precision, recall, etc., and it demonstrates superior performance across all these measures. This research significantly contributes to predictive maintenance in the automotive industry by offering valuable insights for effective failure management, cost reduction, and enhanced operational efficiency.

Keywords: Scania trucks · ensemble model · classification threshold · cost optimization · predictive maintenance

1 Introduction

Scania vehicles are renowned for their dependability, durability, and performance in the transportation industry. Heavy-duty applications, construction, and long-distance transportation are just a few industries that use these trucks extensively. An essential part of Scania trucks, the air pressure system is crucial to these vehicles' safe and effective running. Further, the air pressure system is significant in ensuring Scania trucks' smooth operation and safety. It maintains the proper air pressure within the braking system, which is crucial for efficient braking performance and overall vehicle stability. However, failures in the air pressure system can lead to severe consequences, such as accidents, increased maintenance expenses, and vehicle downtime, etc. [1]. In response to these challenges, this research undertakes the development of a specialized failure prediction model tailored specifically for the air pressure system of Scania trucks. This involves leveraging advanced machine learning algorithms and predictive maintenance techniques to anticipate potential failures before they occur accurately.

The prediction of air pressure system failures holds immense value in terms of proactive maintenance planning and cost reduction. By identifying potential issues ahead of time, fleet managers and maintenance teams can take prompt actions to prevent failures, minimize downtime, and optimize maintenance schedules. This approach significantly enhances operational efficiency, reduces maintenance costs, and ultimately improves the overall safety of the vehicles.

Our paper's main contribution.

– This study presents an ML-based approach to predict failure and minimize the cost defined by $C(t) = 10*FP + 500*FN$, where FP is number of instances with type 1 error and FN is number of instances with type 2 error.
– We applied different imputation techniques and came up with the best techniques for handling missing values.
– Along with Hyperparameter tuning, we applied threshold tuning to optimize our failure prediction model.
– The model is evaluated using hybrid ML algorithms, and the results show that our model outperforms other approaches in failure prediction by reducing cost along with higher AUC, accuracy, sensitivity, and specificity scores.

2   Literature Review

Costa and Nascimento (2016) [5] propose a model with a more significant penalty for false negatives than false positives, reducing misclassification costs. They compare several classification techniques and find that the Random Forest algorithm outperforms others, significantly reducing misclassification costs.

Ozan *et al.* (2016) [11] introduce an improved K-NN classification method for missing data and unbalanced datasets. Their approach incorporates missing value estimation and optimization strategies, outperforming conventional techniques like SVM, AdaBoost, and Random Forests.

Gondek *et al.* (2016) [6] suggest various strategies for managing missing values, including median imputation, feature engineering, and feature selection. Lastly, the Random Forest algorithm is employed for modeling, and the classification threshold is 95.

Cerqueira *et al.* (2016) [4] present a data mining methodology for preventive maintenance in heavy truck air pressure systems. Their approach involves missing value filtering, meta-feature engineering, class imbalance correction, and learning with boosted trees. Experimental results demonstrate the effectiveness of XGBoost with meta-features.

Syed *et al.* (2021) [17] propose a method for binary classification issues, combining Logistic Regression with SVM to optimize the AUC criteria. The goal is to minimize the gap between the true positive rate (TPR) and the false positive rate (FPR) by pushing them as close as possible to the points (0, 1). They evaluate several performance criteria to assess the approach's performance.

Selvi et al. *et al.* (2022) [15] explore resampling techniques such as undersampling, oversampling, and SMOTE to preprocess unbalanced data to balance the data distribution. They assess and compare the outcomes of various machine learning algorithms using accuracy, precision, recall, and f1 score metrics.

Rafsunjani *et al.* (2019) [12] investigate missing value imputation methods and compare the performance of classifiers such as Naive Bayes, KNN, SVM,

Random Forest, and Gradient Boosted Tree. The study finds that random under-sampling and MICE imputation enhance prediction accuracy.

Lokesh *et al.* (2020) [8] propose a methodology that combines the SMOTE class imbalance technique with feature selection, missing data imputation, and PCA. They evaluate the performance of Random Forest, SVM, Xgboost, and Catboost, aiming to reduce maintenance costs.

Shivakarthik *et al.* (2021) [16] develop a system using OBD-II sensors, a microcontroller, and a machine learning model for real-time defect prediction in cars. They compare logistic regression, random forest, and gradient-boosting tree classifiers with the gradient-boosting tree model, yielding the best results.

Akarte and Hemachandra (2018) [2] use the gradient boosting method to apply predictive maintenance to Scania trucks' air pressure systems. They emphasize cost-sensitive learning to address the dataset's imbalance and find that the cost-sensitive classifier outperforms the cost-insensitive one regarding maintenance costs.

Jose and Gopakumar (2019) [7] discuss the Random Forest (RF) method to solve a classification problem and suggest tweaks to boost performance. It investigates the elements that affect RF accuracy and overfitting, makes improvements to strengthen and decrease correlation between trees, discusses missing value imputation, and offers performance data demonstrating the suggested approach's viability.

Nguyen and Bui (2019) [10] focus on blast-induced air overpressure forecasting, developing a hybrid model called ANNs-RF that combines artificial neural networks and random forests. The hybrid model outperforms other AI models in terms of accuracy.

Nabwey (2020) [9] investigates the effective brake system defect diagnosis for driverless vehicles and enhanced driver support systems. The paper suggests employing artificial neural networks, decision trees, and rough set theory to diagnose defects to overcome current approaches' shortcomings. A flaw detection strategy for air brake systems is created using wheel speed sensor data to improve road safety and vehicle health monitoring.

Raveendran *et al.* (2020) [13] propose a fault diagnosis method for brake systems based on machine learning and wheel speed sensor data. They use decision trees and random forest algorithms to classify air brake system faults.

Raveendran *et al.* (2019) [14] introduce a method for predicting pushrod stroke in air brake systems of heavy commercial vehicles using artificial neural networks (ANN). Experimental data from a Hardware-in-Loop system is used to train and test the network. The prediction system demonstrates remarkable accuracy with a forecast error of no more than 15% for manual slack adjusters and 8% for automatic slack adjusters.

3   Proposed Methodology

The main aim of our proposed approach is to improve the performance of our failure prediction model and minimize the cost of misclassification. The proposed architecture is shown below (Fig. 1).

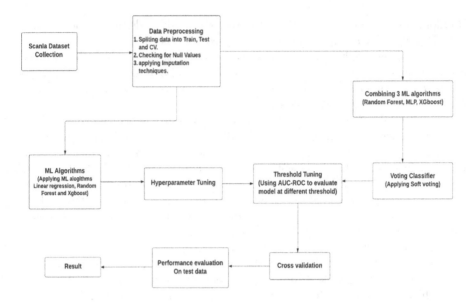

Fig. 1. Flowchart of proposed methodology

3.1 Data Collection and Preprocessing

The information comes from the University of California [1], specifically from the Scania competition dataset. The dataset consists of two main files: the training and test files. The training file contains 60,000 rows and 171 columns. In addition, the training data is split 75:25, with 75% used for training and 25% for cross-validation purposes, in contrast to the test file's 16,000 rows and 171 columns. Various imputation approaches, including mean, median, mode, k-nearest neighbors (k-NN), linear regression, etc., are used to handle these missing data. The mean imputation technique involves replacing the missing values with the mean of the available data for that feature. Similarly, the median imputation approach replaces missing values with the median of the available data for the respective feature. It is often preferred when dealing with data that has outliers or is not normally distributed. The missing values are replaced by the mode (the most frequently occurring value) of the feature in the mode imputation technique. The K-NN imputation technique finds the K most similar records based on other available features and uses their values to impute the missing values. The linear regression imputation technique involves predicting the missing values based on the relationship between the target variable and other variables through a linear regression model. It was discovered through recurrent investigation that imputation produced the most excellent forecast precision and performance outcomes.

3.2 Model Construction

This study employed multiple algorithms, including linear regression, Random forest, and XGBoost. Then, a hybrid model is built using three machine learning algorithms, i.e., Random forest, XGBoost, and MLP, as a base model. The algorithms are chosen based on their performance ability, e.g., Linear Regression provides easy interpretability of the relationship between the dependent and independent variables, Random forest is robust to overfitting and can handle a large number of input variables without variable deletion, and Xgboost is highly scalable and can efficiently handle large datasets due to its parallel and distributed computing. Further, Hybrid model leverages the strengths of multiple algorithms, combining different models to improve overall predictive performance. We use a voting classifier on the hybrid model to create a robust framework for failure prediction.

3.3   Classification Threshold Optimization

In the context of failure prediction, choosing the right classification threshold is crucial to find a suitable trade-off between false positives (FP) and false negatives (FN). Hyperparameters are the configuration settings of an algorithm that govern the learning process. They are not learned during the training phase but are set before the learning process begins. Examples of hyperparameters include the learning rate in neural networks, the depth of a decision tree, the number of clusters in a k-means clustering algorithm, and the regularization parameter in regression models. Hyperparameter Tuning refers to the process of finding the optimal values for these hyperparameters to achieve the best possible model performance. The goal is to find the hyperparameter values that minimize the error or maximize the performance metric on a validation set or through cross-validation. This study's classification threshold was fine-tuned to minimize costs using a dedicated cost-minimization formula.

3.4   Threshold Tuning

Threshold tuning is an important technique used in imbalanced classification to adjust the decision threshold, which is the point at which the predicted probabilities are converted to class labels. This technique is crucial in cases where the default threshold (usually 0.5) may not be optimal, especially in the presence of severe class imbalance or when the cost of misclassifications is asymmetric.

Threshold tuning involves the following steps:

1. Fit Model on the Training Dataset: Train your chosen machine learning model on the training dataset, allowing it to learn patterns and relationships within the data.
2. Predict Probabilities on the Test Dataset: After training the model, use it to make predictions on a separate test dataset. The output of the model will be probabilities of class membership for each sample in the test dataset.
3. Convert Probabilities to Class Labels Using Various Thresholds: Try different threshold values for converting these probabilities into class labels. For instance, if the threshold is 0.5, predicted probabilities above 0.5 are classified as one class, and those below 0.5 are classified as the other.

4. Evaluate Class Labels: Evaluate the performance of the class labels generated by applying different thresholds. This evaluation is done using a chosen evaluation metric, which could be related to the specific requirements of the problem, such as precision, recall, F1 score, or a custom cost-sensitive metric.
5. Adopt Optimal Threshold: Select the threshold that maximizes the chosen evaluation metric or strikes the right balance between trade-offs. This optimal threshold is then used for making predictions on new, unseen data in the future.

Generalised Mathematical Proof for Optimal Threshold. We aim to find the ideal threshold value while considering a fixed model, which reduces the overall operating cost. To do this, we will create a cost function called $C(t)$, which includes the expenses related to various classification error kinds. It's crucial to weigh the costs involved with examining warned instances against the possible rewards of accurately classifying a case, such as potential revenue generating. A prepared dataset with N examples will be subjected to this cost function, and the threshold value, designated by the letter f, will be selected to have an impact on the cost computation [3].

$$S(f) = L_{FP}M_{FP}(f) + L_{FN}M_{FN}(f) - L_{TP}M_{TP}(f) \\ - L_{TN}M_{TN}(f) + L_{exp}[M_{TP}(f) + M_{FP}(f)] \tag{1}$$

where,

- L_z: the cost of single error of type $z \in \{FP, FN\}$.
- $M_z(f)$: the number of instances that, for a particular operating threshold f, our model is incorrectly labeled as z errors.
- L_{TP}: the advantage that each TP case offers.
- L_{TN}: the advantage that each TN case offers.
- L_{exp}: expense associated with going over each flagged (predicted-positive) case.

To simplify differentiation, we shall restate the formulas of $M_z(f)$ in terms of differentiable values. To accomplish this, we will add an additional function named $g(x)$, which represents the probability density distribution of the model output results that would be observed if the model were applied to a representative dataset.

In line with the definition of a probability distribution, the integral of the function $g(x)$ over all feasible output scores is 1.

$$1 = \int_{-\infty}^{+\infty} g(x)\,dx \tag{2}$$

Similarly, integrating the marginal distribution $g(x, v = 1)$ over whole possible results is the fraction of the total M samples that have a positive class label (i.e., $v = 1$).

$$\frac{M_{\text{pos}}}{M} = \int\limits_{-\infty}^{+\infty} g(x, v = 1)\, dx \tag{3}$$

By dividing the marginal distribution $g(x, v = 1)$ by the probability density distribution g, the probability calibration curve for the model is obtained. Given a model score of x, this calibration curve tells us what the likelihood is that an example will have a genuine label of 1:

$$d(x) = \frac{g(x, v = 1)}{g(x)} \tag{4}$$

The number of *FN* cases can be calculated by performing integration of the positive label distribution $g(x, v = 1)$ up to the cutoff value f. These "*FN* cases" allude to situations where the model indicates a bad result, but the cases really show a good result:

$$M_{FN}(f) = M \int\limits_{-\infty}^{f} g(x, v = 1)\, dx = M \int\limits_{-\infty}^{f} d(x) g(x)\, dx \tag{5}$$

Similarly, we get an expression each for the quantity of FP, TP, and TN cases:

$$M_{FP}(f) = M \int\limits_{f}^{\infty} g(x, v = 0)\, dx \;\;= M \int\limits_{f}^{\infty} (1 - d(x)) g(x)\, dx \tag{6}$$

$$M_{TP}(f) = M \int\limits_{f}^{\infty} g(x, v = 1)\, dx = M \int\limits_{f}^{\infty} d(x) g(x)\, dx \tag{7}$$

$$M_{TN}(f) = M \int\limits_{-\infty}^{f} g(x, v = 0)\, dx = M \int\limits_{-\infty}^{f} (1 - d(x)) g(x)\, dx \tag{8}$$

Differentiating equations (5), (6), (7), and (8), we get:

$$M_{FN}'(f) = M \cdot d(f) g(f) \tag{9}$$
$$M_{FP}'(f) = -M \cdot (1 - d(f)) g(f) \tag{10}$$
$$M_{TP}'(f) = -M \cdot d(f) g(f) \tag{11}$$
$$M_{TN}'(f) = M \cdot (1 - d(f)) g(f) \tag{12}$$

The derivatives of the TP and FN formulas, as you can see, add up to zero:

$$M'_{TP}(f) + M'_{FN}(f) = 0 \qquad (13)$$

This result demonstrates that the threshold selection does not impact the number of cases with an actual positive class label. With equal and opposing rates of change, true positive (TP) and false negative (FN) circumstances are directly related to each other when the threshold is raised. This justification also supports the link between true negative (TN) and false positive (FP) situations:

$$M'_{FP}(f) + M'_{TN}(f) = 0 \qquad (14)$$

Now we differentiate $S(f)$ and use the relationships indicated in Eq. 14 to reduce $S'(f)$ to an equivalent form that is easily recognizable:

$$
\begin{aligned}
S'(f) &= L_{FP} M'_{FP}(f) + L_{FN} M'_{FN}(f) - L_{TP} M'_{TP}(f) \\
&\quad - L_{TN} M'_{TN}(f) + L_{exp}[M'_{TP}(f) + M'_{FP}(f)] \\
&= L_{FP} M'_{FP}(f) + L_{FN} M'_{FN}(f) + L_{TP} M'_{FN}(f) + L_{TN} M'_{FP}(f) \qquad (15) \\
&\quad + L_{exp}[-M'_{FN}(f) + M'_{FP}(f)] \\
&= (L_{FP} + L_{TN} + L_{exp}) M'_{FP}(f) + (L_{FN} + L_{TP} - L_{exp}) M'_{FN}(f)
\end{aligned}
$$

From this point, we can rearrange terms and enter the $M_z(f)$ derivatives.

$$
\begin{aligned}
S'(f) &= (L_{FP} + L_{TN} + L_{exp})[-M \cdot (1 - d(f))g(f)] \\
&\quad + (L_{FN} + L_{TP} - L_{exp})[M \cdot d(f)g(f)] \\
&= M \cdot g(f)[(L_{FP} + L_{FN} + L_{TN} + L_{TP})d(f) - (L_{FP} + L_{TN} + L_{exp})] \\
&\qquad\qquad\qquad\qquad\qquad\qquad\qquad\qquad\qquad\qquad\qquad\qquad (16)
\end{aligned}
$$

Now we get two different solutions by equating $S'(f)$ to zero, but only one of these solutions is really reliant on our cost coefficients:

$$
\left\{
\begin{aligned}
g(\theta_0) &= 0 \\
d(\theta_1) &= \frac{L_{FP} + L_{TN} + L_{exp}}{L_{FP} + L_{FN} + L_{TN} + L_{TP}}
\end{aligned}
\right\} \qquad (17)
$$

To determine the nature of these solutions as critical points, it is necessary to examine the curvature of $S(f)$ at each of these locations. To achieve this, another derivative is required. To simplify the notation, we'll introduce two new nonnegative constants: i and j.

$$i = L_{FP} + L_{FN} + L_{TN} + L_{TP} \qquad (18a)$$

$$j = L_{FP} + L_{TN} + L_{exp} \qquad (18b)$$

Rewriting $S'(f)$ with the constants in Eqs. (18a) and (18b), we get:

$$S'(f) = M \cdot g(f)[i \cdot d(f) - j] \tag{19}$$

Then we differentiate $S'(f)$ using the product rule:

$$S''(f) = M \cdot g'(f)[i \cdot d(f) - j] + M \cdot g(f)[i \cdot d'(f)] \tag{20}$$

When evaluating this expression at our first solution in Eq. 17, we obtain a rather intricate result:

$$\begin{aligned} S''(\theta_0) &= M \cdot g'(\theta_0)[i \cdot d(\theta_0) - j] + M \cdot 0 \cdot [i \cdot d'(\theta_0)] \\ &= M \cdot g'(\theta_0)[i \cdot d(\theta_0) - j] \end{aligned} \tag{21}$$

However, the slope of $g(x)$ at the extrema may not always be zero if the function is specified within a constrained range and becomes zero at the extrema of x. Consideration of the behavior of the probability calibration function in such circumstances becomes critical. Higher score values always translate into increased probabilities, a property of a trustworthy probability calibration function called monotonicity. If the model scores do not show this behavior, then the model is not doing a good enough job capturing how the labeled data is distributed. Furthermore, $d(x)$ should ideally approach, or at least nearly approximate, 0 and 1, respectively, at the lowest and largest x values.

When we analyze our second derivative S'' solution at x_{min} (the smallest conceivable value of x), taking into account our hypotheses regarding suitable probability calibration functions, the following findings come to light:

$$S''(\theta_0 = x_{min}) \approx -j \cdot M \cdot g'(x_{min}) \tag{22}$$

$g'(x)$ must be greater than or equal to 0 at x_{min} in order to hold the result. j is higher than or equal to 0 and $g(x_{min}) = 0$. Therefore S'' is lower than or equal to 0.

In other words, treating every scenario favorably, the scenario will only lead to the cost function to reach its maximum value or inflection point. Let's explore the case where $g(x)$ is zero at x maximal at the other end of the distribution (the maximum possible value of x). We can observe the following by replacing S'' with $d(x_{max}) \approx 1$.

$$\begin{aligned} S''(\theta_0 = x_{max}) &\approx -M \cdot g'(x_{max}[i - j]) \\ &\approx -M \cdot g'(x_{max}[L_{FN} + L_{TP} - L_{exp}] \end{aligned} \tag{23}$$

As $g'(x) <= 0$ at x_{max}, the following must be true

$$S''(\theta_0 = x_{max}) > 0 \quad iff \quad L_{exp} > L_{FN} + l_{TP} \tag{24}$$

It is evident from this that, even after accounting for the potential benefit of correctly predicting the true positive (TP), estimating every specific instance as negative can only lower overall operating costs if the expense of reviewing a real positive case is greater than the expense of a false negative (FN) brought on by ignoring it.

Let us now concentrate on the non-trivial answer at θ_1. We can simplify the expression for S$''$ at the critical point by substituting the value of $\frac{j}{i}$ for $d(1)$ as follows:

$$S''(\theta_1) = M \cdot g'(\theta_1)[i \cdot \frac{j}{i} - j] + i \cdot N \cdot g(\theta_1)d'(\theta_1)$$
$$= i \cdot M \cdot g(\theta_1)d'(\theta_1) \tag{25}$$

The probability distribution that is the function $f(t)$ ensures that it is always non-negative. Now that we've assumed that the critical point has some data density, we can state the concavity condition as follows:

$$S''(\theta_1) > 0 \quad iff \quad d(\theta_1) > 0 \tag{26}$$

Our chosen threshold value will always minimize the cost because a reasonable probability calibration function is strictly rising. As a result, this requirement serves as the standard for choosing the best threshold.

Hence we set the parameters for the ideal threshold as follows

$$d(\theta) = \frac{L_{FP} + L_{TN} + L_{exp}}{L_{FP} + L_{FN} + L_{TN} + L_{TP}} \tag{27}$$

Our cost minimization formula C(t) = 10 * FP + 500 * FN can be rewritten in the general form as follows

$$S(f) = L_{FP}M_{FP}(f) + L_{FN}M_{FN}(f) \tag{28}$$

So, by using the same general formula, we can derive the condition for the optimal threshold for a given cost function as follows

$$d(\theta) = \frac{L_{FP}}{L_{FP} + L_{FN}} \tag{29}$$

Hence, when we choose to run a model at a probability decision limit of $d(\theta) = 0.5$, it signifies that we assign equal importance to both types of misclassification costs. But as in our cost function, FN is 50 times more costly than FP. Hence, we can tune our threshold value as close to zero as possible to minimize the cost.

4   Result and Discussion

4.1   Performance Evaluation

The following performance metrics are used to evaluate our algorithm:

- **AUC:** The AUC measures how well a model can classify data into two categories (Area Under the Curve). It demonstrates the probability that the model will assign a greater value to a randomly picked positive instance than to a negatively sampled case.

- **Accuracy:** A common way to measure how well a classification model works is by how accurate it is. It shows how many of the total number of instances in the dataset have been correctly categorized.
  Accuracy = (Number of Cases That Were Correctly Classified)/(Total Number of Instances)
- **Precision:** It measures how well a classification model can pick out true positives from the cases it thinks are true positives. It looks at how accurate the good predictions were.
  Precision = (True Positives)/(True Positives + False Positives)
- **Recall:** It is also called sensitivity or true positive rate and is a performance metric that measures a classification model's ability to identify all positive cases in a dataset correctly. It focuses on how well the model can capture all good things.
  Recall = (True Positives)/(True Positives + False Negatives)
- **Misclassification Cost:** Formula used to calculate the cost

$$C(t) = 10 * FP + 500 * FN \qquad (30)$$

Here we consider Hybrid Model, xgboost, Random Forest, and Logistic Regression for comparison based on their respective strengths like Linear Regression provides easy interpretability of the relationship between the dependent and independent variables. Random forest is robust to overfitting and can handle a large number of input variables without variable deletion. Xgboost is highly scalable and can efficiently handle large datasets due to its parallel and distributed computing. Hybrid model leverages the strengths of multiple algorithms, combining different models to improve overall predictive performance (Table 1).

Table 1. Performance of the Hybrid Model, Xgboost, Random Forest and Logistic Regression on the Train and Test Dataset of APS Failure Detection

Performance metric	Hybrid Model		Xgboost		Random Forest		Logistic Regression	
	Train	Test	Train	Test	Train	Test	Train	Test
AUC	0.997	**0.996**	0.996	0.995	0.994	0.995	0.933	0.942
Sensitivity	0.985	0.971	0.988	**0.984**	0.963	0.944	0.901	0.909
Specificity	0.980	0.974	0.960	0.962	0.984	**0.979**	0.922	0.923
Accuracy	0.979	0.973	0.960	0.962	0.983	**0.978**	0.921	0.922
TP	985	364	988	**369**	963	354	901	341
TN	57814	15212	56650	15027	58035	**15302**	54373	14418
FP	1186	413	2350	598	965	**323**	4627	1207
FN	15	11	12	**6**	37	21	99	34

1. **Hybrid Model:**

    The Hybrid Model received strong AUC ratings from both the training (0.99732) and test (0.99619) datasets, demonstrating how well it could distinguish between the two groups. It did a fantastic job of identifying both positive and negative instances thanks to its high sensitivity (0.985 on the train and 0.971 on the test) and specificity (0.980 on the train and 0.974 on the test). The hybrid model was similarly quite accurate with training set values of 0.97998 and test set values of 0.9735. In contrast to the 57, 814 true negatives on the train and 15, 212 true positives on the test, there were 985 true positives on the train and 364 on the test.

2. **Xgboost:**

    Compared to the Hybrid Model, Xgboost had slightly lower AUC values (0.99696 on train and 0.99556 on test). It was able to distinguish between good and bad instances because of its excellent sensitivity (0.988 on the train and 0.984 on the test) and specificity (0.960 on the train and 0.962 on the test). With training set values of 0.96063 and test set values of 0.96225, Xgboost's accuracy was similarly quite high. There were 988 true positives on the train, while 369 people tested positive. There were 56, 650 genuine negatives on the train, and on the test, there were 15, 027.

3. **Random Forest:**
    With AUC values of 0.994431 on the train and 0.99578 on the test, Random Forest performed marginally worse than Xgboost. It exhibited a reduced sensitivity (0.963 on train and 0.944 on test) compared to the earlier models, but it still had a high specificity (0.984 on train, 0.979 on test). Random Forest was also quite accurate with training set values of 0.9833 and test set values of 0.9785. There were 963 true positives on the train, while 354 people tested positive. There were 58, 035 genuine negatives on the train, whereas on the test, there were 15, 302.

4. **Logistic Regression:** Logistic Regression had the lowest AUC scores among the other models, with 0.93370 on the train and 0.94244 on the test. Compared to earlier models, its sensitivity was reduced (0.901% on train and 0.909% on test), but its specificity remained moderate (0.922 on train, 0.923 on test). Logistic Regression lacked the precision of competing models. On the training set, its values were 0.92123, whereas, on the test set, they were 0.92243. The train contained 901 genuine positives, while 341 failed the test. 14, 418 test results and 54, 373 authentic negatives were discovered.

4.2   Comparision with Base Model

We considered the model in [17] as the base model for comparison with our models. The base model has moderate performance across all metrics, with values ranging from approximately 0.78 to 0.80. The hybrid model outperforms the base model significantly in all metrics, achieving high values close to 1.0, as shown in Fig. 2.

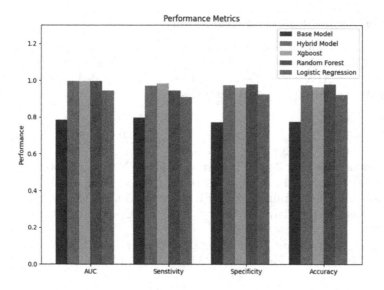

Fig. 2. Comparision of Performance of our models with Base model

Table 2. Threshold values for different classifiers

Classifier	Threshold value
Hybrid Model	0.031998
Xgboost	0.00775
Random Forest	0.081930
Logistic regression	0.011349

4.3   Optimal Threshold Obtained

Table 2 shows the optimal threshold values obtained on different classifiers after performing threshold tunning at which the misclassification cost defined by the cost function is minimum,

Table 3. Cost calculation of Hybrid Model, Xgboost, Random Forest and Logistic Regression on the Train and Test Dataset of APS Failure Detection

Classifier	Training data			Test Data		
	FP Cost	FN Cost	Total Cost	FP Cost	FN Cost	Total Cost
Hybrid Model	11860	7500	19360	4130	5500	9630
XGboost	23500	6000	29500	5980	3000	8980
Random Forest	9650	18500	28150	3230	10500	13730
Logistic Regression	46270	49500	95770	12070	17000	29070

4.4 Misclassification Cost Evaluation

As Shown in Table 3 the cost calculations are for four different classifiers (Hybrid Model, XGBoost, Random Forest, and Logistic Regression) on the train and test datasets of APS Failure Detection. The costs are divided into False Positive (*FP*), False Negative (*FN*), and Total Costs.

- **Hybrid Model:**
  Training data: FP Cost = 11,860, FN Cost = 7,500, Total Cost = 19,360 Test data: FP Cost = 4,130, FN Cost = 5,500, Total Cost = 9,630
- **XGBoost:** Training data: FP Cost = 23,500, FN Cost = 6,000, Total Cost = 29,500 Test data: FP Cost = 5,980, FN Cost = 3,000, Total Cost = 8,980
- **Random Forest:** Training data: FP Cost = 9,650, FN Cost = 18,500, Total Cost = 28,150 Test data: FP Cost = 3,230, FN Cost = 10,500, Total Cost = 13,730
- **Logistic Regression:** Training data: FP Cost = 46,270, FN Cost = 49,500, Total Cost = 95,770 Test data: FP Cost = 12,070, FN Cost = 17,000, Total Cost = 29,070

4.5 Cost Comparison with Base Model

From Fig. 3, we can observe that Xgboost showed the lowest total cost, but the FN cost is less than the Base model. The Hybrid Model has the lowest both FP Cost and FN Cost compared to the base model while maintaining Lower total misclassification cost, indicating better performance in minimizing false positives and false negatives compared to the other models.

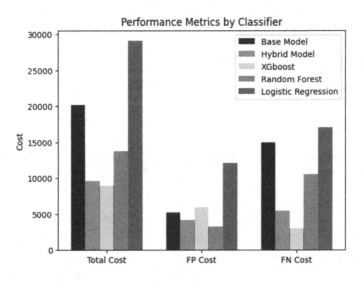

Fig. 3. Comparision of misclassification cost of our models with Base model

5 Conclusion

In conclusion, the study analyzed the effectiveness of various machine learning algorithms, emphasizing failure prediction in the air pressure system of Scania trucks. The Hybrid Model was found to be the most efficient with its extraordinary discrimination abilities, high accuracy, sensitivity, and specificity, and low total cost in terms of false positives and false negatives. While Logistic Regression performed poorly, XGBoost and Random Forest models performed well.

The research findings have significant implications for the field of failure prediction in the automotive industry, particularly for the air pressure systems of trucks. The precise failure prediction provided by the models can result in improved maintenance strategies, cost savings through optimized restorations, increased safety and reliability, and a more comprehensive application for predicting failures in other automotive components. In addition, the study contributes to advancements in predictive maintenance research and offers valuable insights for developing cutting-edge strategies.

However, the study has limitations, such as the small dataset size, the limited feature selection due to anonymized data, and the choice of particular machine learning models. Future research directions are suggested, including the incorporation of advanced machine learning techniques, the incorporation of real-time sensor data, and the incorporation of external data sources in order to improve the accuracy and reliability of failure prediction models.

References

1. APS Failure at Scania Trucks. UCI Machine Learning Repository (2017). https:// doi.org/10.24432/C51S51
2. Akarte, M.M., Hemachandra, N.: Predictive maintenance of air pressure system using boosting trees: a machine learning approach. In: ORSI (2018)
3. Bryant, C.: Choosing-the-Right-Model-Threshold. UCI Machine Learning Repository (2020)
4. Cerqueira, V., Pinto, F., Sá, C., Soares, C.: Combining boosted trees with metafeature engineering for predictive maintenance. In: Boström, H., Knobbe, A., Soares, C., Papapetrou, P. (eds.) IDA 2016. LNCS, vol. 9897, pp. 393–397. Springer, Cham (2016). https://doi.org/10.1007/978-3-319-46349-0_35
5. Costa, C.F., Nascimento, M.A.: IDA 2016 industrial challenge: using machine learning for predicting failures. In: Boström, H., Knobbe, A., Soares, C., Papapetrou, P. (eds.) IDA 2016. LNCS, vol. 9897, pp. 381–386. Springer, Cham (2016). https:// doi.org/10.1007/978-3-319-46349-0_33
6. Gondek, C., Hafner, D., Sampson, O.R.: Prediction of failures in the air pressure system of Scania trucks using a random forest and feature engineering. In: Boström, H., Knobbe, A., Soares, C., Papapetrou, P. (eds.) IDA 2016. LNCS, vol. 9897, pp. 398–402. Springer, Cham (2016). https://doi.org/10.1007/978-3-319-46349-0_36
7. Jose, C., Gopakumar, G.: An improved random forest algorithm for classification in an imbalanced dataset. In: 2019 URSI Asia-Pacific Radio Science Conference (AP-RASC), pp. 1–4. IEEE (2019)

8. Lokesh, Y., Nikhil, K.S.S., Kumar, E.V., Mohan, B.G.K.: Truck APS failure detection using machine learning. In: 2020 4th International Conference on Intelligent Computing and Control Systems (ICICCS), pp. 307–310. IEEE (2020)
9. Nabwey, H.A.: A method for fault prediction of air brake system in vehicles. Int. J. Eng. Res. Technol. 13(5), 1002–1008 (2020)
10. Nguyen, H., Bui, X.-N.: Predicting blast-induced air overpressure: a robust artificial intelligence system based on artificial neural networks and random forest. Nat. Resour. Res. 28(3), 893–907 (2019). https://doi.org/10.1007/s11053-018-9424-1
11. Ozan, E.C., Riabchenko, E., Kiranyaz, S., Gabbouj, M.: An optimized k-NN approach for classification on imbalanced datasets with missing data. In: Boström, H., Knobbe, A., Soares, C., Papapetrou, P. (eds.) IDA 2016. LNCS, vol. 9897, pp. 387–392. Springer, Cham (2016). https://doi.org/10.1007/978-3-319-46349-0_34
12. Rafsunjani, S., Safa, R.S., Al Imran, A., Rahim, M.S., Nandi, D.: An empirical comparison of missing value imputation techniques on APS failure prediction. Int. J. Inf. Technol. Comput. Sci. 2, 21–29 (2019)
13. Raveendran, R., Devika, K., Subramanian, S.C.: Intelligent fault diagnosis of air brake system in heavy commercial road vehicles. In: 2020 International Conference on COMmunication Systems & NETworkS (COMSNETS), pp. 93–98. IEEE (2020)
14. Raveendran, R., Suresh, A., Rajaram, V., Subramanian, S.C.: Artificial neural network approach for air brake pushrod stroke prediction in heavy commercial road vehicles. Proc. Inst. Mech. Eng. Part D J. Autom. Eng. 233(10), 2467–2478 (2019)
15. Selvi, K.T., Praveena, N., Pratheksha, K., Ragunanthan, S., Thamilselvan, R.: Air pressure system failure prediction and classification in Scania trucks using machine learning. In: 2022 Second International Conference on Artificial Intelligence and Smart Energy (ICAIS), pp. 220–227. IEEE (2022)
16. Shivakarthik, S., et al.: Maintenance of automobiles by predicting system fault severity using machine learning. In: Karuppusamy, P., Perikos, I., Shi, F., Nguyen, T.N. (eds.) Sustainable Communication Networks and Application. LNDECT, vol. 55, pp. 263–274. Springer, Singapore (2021). https://doi.org/10.1007/978-981-15-8677-4_22
17. Syed, M.N., Hassan, M.R., Ahmad, I., Hassan, M.M., De Albuquerque, V.H.C.: A novel linear classifier for class imbalance data arising in failure-prone air pressure systems. IEEE Access 9, 4211–4222 (2020)

A Multi-class Classification for Detection of IoT Network Attacks Using Machine Learning Models

Gadde Ashok, Kommula Serath, and T. Gireesh Kumar[(✉)]

Department of Computer Science and Engineering, Amrita School of Computing, Coimbatore,
Amrita Vishwa Vidyapeetham, Coimbatore, India
{cb.en.u4cse20020,cb.en.u4cse20631}@cb.students.amrita.edu,
t_gireeshkumar@cb.amrita.edu

Abstract. The adoption of IoT devices is growing due to their versatility and simplicity. The number of security risks associated with these devices has increased as a result of their increased popularity. Therefore, it is crucial to have a reliable IoT network intrusion monitoring system. In order to identify IoT network attacks using machine learning models, this study suggests a multi-class classification method. It includes contemporary attacks that enabled us to categorize them into more than two classes. In this study, we looked at 9 different IoT network assault variations using the UNSW-NB15 dataset and 6 of these 9 attacks are given higher importance during the classification process. The suggested approach includes data preparation, feature selection, and the creation of synthetic data using the CTGAN methodology. After generating synthetic records, the final dataset is used to train and evaluate the efficacy of various machine-learning designs, such as Random forests, Extra trees, Decision trees, and XG Boost, with XGBoost outperforming them all with an accuracy of 96.71. The findings of this study will help to create a more reliable and effective IoT network assault detection system, which will aid in the prevention of possible security vulnerabilities in IoT networks.

Keywords: Network intrusion · Multiclass · XGBoost · Machine learning · UNSW-NB15 · Conditional Generative Adversarial Networks (CTGAN) · Population-Based Training (PBT)

1 Introduction

1.1 IoT Attack

The Internet of Things (IoT) is a network of devices that connect with one another and over the internet [1]. IoT devices are vulnerable to a wide range of assaults, including viruses, botnets, and denial-of-service (DoS) attacks, which might jeopardise their security [2]. Attacks like this can take many different forms, DDoS, malware, and man-in-the-middle (MITM) attacks are examples of such threats [3]. Several studies have highlighted the need of protecting IoT devices from these assaults [4, 5]. Kolias et al.

© The Author(s), under exclusive license to Springer Nature Switzerland AG 2024
S. Devismes et al. (Eds.): ICDCIT 2024, LNCS 14501, pp. 167–178, 2024.
https://doi.org/10.1007/978-3-031-50583-6_11

(2017) [6] said that IoT security is a critical problem owing to these devices susceptibility to DDoS, botnets, and malware attacks. The Mirai botnet assault on Dyn, for example, caused major internet disruption in the United States and Europe. In a similar way the Reaper botnet [7] infected more than one million IoT devices and could launch DDoS assaults and steal data. Another example is the VPNFilter virus, which infected over 500,000 routers and IoT devices throughout the world [8], allowing attackers to steal data, launch DDoS assaults, and render equipment inoperable. As a result, it is critical to put in place strong security measures to safeguard IoT devices from these risks (refer Fig. 1).

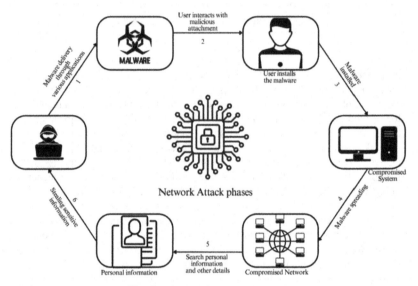

Fig. 1. Phases of a network attack

1.2   Types of IoT Attacks

The surge in Internet of Things (IoT) devices usage has raised concerns about network security and reliability due to their vulnerability to various attacks, including fuzzers, analysis, backdoors, DoS, exploits, generic attacks, reconnais-sance, Shellcode and worms [9–17]. IoT devices, such as smart homes, smart watches, and industrial control systems, are frequently plagued by insufficient security standards and a lack of upgrades. Fuzzing attacks include the use of fuzzers to find weaknesses in a system by entering random or erroneous data [9]. Analysis attacks collect and analyse data from connected devices in order to extract sensitive information [10]. Backdoor attacks on IoT devices enable unauthorized access and control for malicious purposes [11], such as the 2017 IoT camera backdoor incident. Denial-of-service (DoS) attacks aim to overwhelm networks with excessive data, rendering them inaccessible, with IoT devices often targeted due to their weak security [12]. Exploits take advantage of software vulnerabilities to gain unauthorized system access, with the 2019 Ripple20 exploit impacting millions of IoT devices worldwide [13]. Generic attacks encompass a broad range of methods, including social engineering and phishing, to obtain unauthorized network access, as seen in the 2018 IoT hotel room lock system attack [14]. Reconnaissance attacks involve gathering information about networks or devices to identify potential vulnerabilities, with IoT devices commonly targeted [15], like the 2018 IoT CCTV company incident. Shellcode attacks introduce malicious software for unauthorized access, as evidenced by the 2020 IoT smart home shellcode exploit [16]. Worms, a type of malware, replicate and spread by exploiting system weaknesses, with IoT devices frequently targeted due to their poor security and lack of updates, as demonstrated by the 2018 IoT Reaper worm [17].

2 Related Works

Various feature extraction and classification techniques have been used in a number of studies to classify IoT network threats. Examples include Moustafa et al. [18] created the UNSW-NB15 dataset in 2015. This dataset uses the IXIA tool to simulate attacks and actual benign traffic. Koroniotis and others [19] made the Bot-IoT dataset available in 2018, which includes both legitimate and malicious traffic that was generated through actual experimentation. Faruki and co. In 2017, [20] proposed a hybrid feature selection and random forest classifier-based intrusion detection system for IoT networks. Al-Smadi and co. [21] delivered the IoT-Botnet dataset in 2020, comprising of traffic created by different IoT gadgets, and they utilized AI strategies, for example, choice tree and arbitrary woodland figuring out how to classify the traffic as malware or not. Goyal et al. in 2021 [22] combined methods for feature selection and extraction to propose a novel strategy for classifying IoT network intrusions. Be that as it may, these datasets have restricted measures and may not cover all possible IoT network assault circumstances. Furthermore, not all IoT networks or attack scenarios can benefit from the feature selection and extraction techniques described in [22]. Kumar et al. [25] proposed a methodology that includes data preprocessing with label encoding, feature selection using chi-square analysis, data split (80% training, 20% testing), model construction (SVM, LR, XGB, DT, RF), and evaluation based on AUC, F1 score, and FAR. Fuat et al. [26] proposed a methodology that involves data preprocessing, the application of various machine learning algorithms, including Logistic Regression, K-Nearest Neighbors, Random Forest, and Decision Trees, as well as deep learning architectures such as Multi-Layer Perception (MLP) and Long-Short-Term Memory (LSTM). Model evaluation is conducted using key performance metrics. Khorzom et al. [27] proposed a machine learning-based system for the intrusion detection system. The proposed system is a dynamically scalable multi-class machine learning-based network IDS. The outputs of the extreme learning machine classifier are used as the inputs of a fully connected layer followed by a logistic regression layer to make smooth decisions for all classes. The results show that it outperforms the related studies in terms of accuracy.

The general goal of this study is to develop a multiclass classifier that accurately identifies an IoT network attack while also having characteristics and data that are scalable enough to be categorised into different groups of IoT attack variants. Our contribution, in particular, has three goals, which are listed below:

1. A multi-class model that accurately focusses on worms, analysis, shellcode, espionage, backdoor, and normal attacks, which are usually regarded more serious attacks as they entail intentional and focused efforts to infiltrate and damage a system.
2. Use CTGAN to produce additional dynamic data for testing the accuracy of the built classifiers and alleviating the data scarcity issue for Analysis, Backdoor, Shellcode, and Worms. As a result, machine learning algorithms for classifying IoT network threats performed better. When compared to using only the original dataset, the addition of synthetic data improved the precision of their models.
3. On the basis of the aforementioned data, compare several models and choose the best match classifier.

The methodology and architecture designed for our study is shown in Fig. 2.

3 Data Collection and Preprocessing

3.1 Details About UNSW-NB15 Dataset

The UNSW-NB15 dataset is a labeled dataset for network intrusion detection systems, containing over 2 million instances with 48 features each, developed by Nour Moustafa et al. [18]. It encompasses diverse attacks and benign traffic recorded using Bro and Argus simulators [18]. Features were selected from literature recommendations [1, 23], and an annotated ground truth file aids model comparison [18, 23]. This dataset is essential for evaluating and advancing intrusion detection systems.

3.2 Data Pre-processing and Clamping

To preprocess the dataset, the 'id' and 'label' columns were removed, and highly correlated columns were eliminated, identified by a correlation threshold of >0.8. Extreme values were pruned to reduce skewness, using the logic that features with a maximum value more than ten times the median were pruned to the 95th percentile. Clamping was only applied to features with a maximum greater than 10 times the median to prevent excessive pruning of small value distributions. Then scaling and transforming numerical and categorical features is done. The mathematical columns are chosen first, which include only columns with data types of integer and float. Similarly, the categorical columns are selected with the data type as object, and all necessary pre-processing is performed.

3.3 Samples and Features Considered

Table 1 provides information about the samples evaluated for creating a classifier. Although, substantial work was done to increase the scalability of our work, we added a big number of samples. We identified the 24 top features from the dataset's 49 features based on parameters such as correlation and feature relevance.

The dataset features that we considered are: The features include dur, service, spkts, dpkts, rate, sttl, dttl, sload, dload, sinpkt, dinpkt, sjit, djit, swin, stcpb, dtcpb, smean, dmean, trans_depth, response_body_len, ct_srv_src, ct_state_ttl, is_ftp_login, ct_flw_http_mth and attact_cat.

Table 1. Count of each attack

S. No	Attack name	Attack count
1	Normal	56000
2	Generic	40000
3	Reconnaissance	10491
4	Analysis	2000
5	Backdoor	1746
6	Shellcode	1133
7	Worms	130

4 Data Collection and Preprocessing

4.1 Hyperparameter Training with Grid Search

The XGBoost classifier in terms of accuracy, beats other models, according to Table 2. We used Grid Search hyperparameter training to identify the best XGBoost hyperparameters, including number of trees, maximum tree depth, subsample ratio, and learning rate. The optimal set of hyperparameters was determined by employing a method provided by a specific library, known as 'GridSearchCV.best_params_.' This method, available in the GridSearchCV module, was utilized to identify the best hyperparameter configuration for our experiments. The code is implemented to map integer values to attack categories, and a dataframe is generated that shows the count of each unique value in the test and predicted values. Another dataframe is created to analyze where accuracy can be improved for each model by displaying the number of correctly predicted and wrongly predicted values for each class. We decided to increase the number of records for attacks causing imbalance in the dataset based on the analysis of the number of records for different attacks in Table 1.

4.2 Applying Conditional Generative Adversarial Networks (CTGAN)

Generative Adversarial Networks (GANs) are a two-stage process that includes building additional samples from existing data using a generator model and a discriminator model that forecasts whether the samples are genuine or false. CTGAN is a generative adversarial network (GAN) model designed for generating synthetic tabular data [28]. It is specifically tailored to address the challenges of generating structured, tabular data commonly found in applications like financial datasets, healthcare records, and more. CTGAN utilizes conditional GANs to capture the complex relationships and distributions present in tabular data, allowing it to generate realistic synthetic data that closely resembles the original dataset.

GANs are widely used in image processing and can even create synthetic human faces that have never appeared before.In this study, to solve the data imbalance issue in the UNSW15 network attack dataset, we used CTGAN, a variant of GAN, to produce

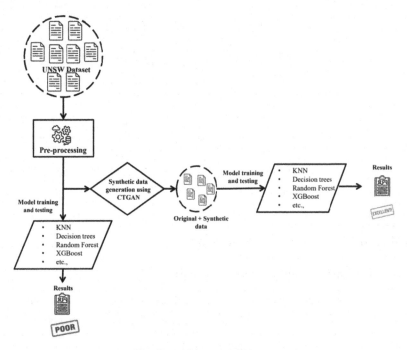

Fig. 2. Architectural Diagram

synthetic tabulated data from a combination of quantitative and categorical origins [24]. By using the conditional generator and resampling training data, CTGAN generates column-wise synthetic data using fully connected networks, rather than long short-term memory networks [24]. We utilized this approach to increase the records for classes with data scarcity and merged the generated records with the original dataset, as shown in Fig. 3 and Table 2. After pre-processing, the newly generated data was split into train and test sets by stratified train-test split, ensuring that each class is adequately represented in the training and testing sets and the train data was fed to all the classification algorithms mentioned, and the models were trained with hyper-parameter tuning and tested. We had added synthetically generated data for whole data and then split it into train-test sets. We had used stratified train-test sampling to avoid imbalance in training data and testing data.

4.3   Population-Based Training (PBT) for Enhanced Individual Attack Detection

In order to improve the accuracy of individual attack detection models, we employ Population-Based Training (PBT), to dynamically fine-tune hyperparameters for each attack type's detection model, hence maximizing their performance, by building on the foundation built by CTGAN-generated synthetic data.

Table 2. Statistics of GAN Data

S. No	Attack name	Attack count
1	Normal	56000
2	Generic	40000
3	Reconnaissance	10491
4	Analysis	12000
5	Backdoor	11746
6	Shellcode	11133
7	Worms	10130

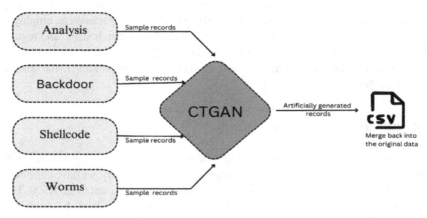

Fig. 3. Implementation of CTGAN

4.3.1   PBT Initialization and Hyperparameter Configuration

We began the Population-Based Training (PBT) procedure by launching a broad collection of individual assault detection models. Each model was painstakingly developed with unique hyperparameter settings that included critical variables like as learning rates, batch sizes, and regularization factors. The introduction of a variety of hyperparameter values into the models strategically established the groundwork for a fruitful environment amenable to intricate study and optimization.

4.3.2   Model Exchange and Diversity Maintenance on a Regular Basis

The incorporation of periodic hyperparameter exchange among individual models within the cohort was a defining feature of our research path. PBT's inherent orchestration of knowledge exchange among models served as a bulwark against the dangers of converging to local optima. The maintenance of variety, a fundamental premise of PBT, echoed throughout the training process, encouraging the study of hyperparameter dimensions and fostering the formation of attack detection models that exemplified both resilience and accuracy. PBT dynamically explored hyperparameter choices during training by iteratively assessing the efficacy of each individual model. Depending on the reported model performance, hyperparameters are disturbed and changed.

4.3.3 Constant Refinement and Improved Accuracy

As the pace of our research accelerated, the PBT architecture remained firm in its dedication to the constant refining of hyperparameters inside specific attack detection models. A continual state of adaptation guaranteed that these models stayed tuned in to the dataset's ever-changing subtleties. This commitment to ongoing refining unlocked the latent potential for refinement, resulting in levels of accuracy that exceeded traditional standards. PBT automatically altered and modified hyperparameters with each iteration depending on model performance input. This flexibility is a response to the subtleties brought by the dataset's ever-changing properties, which inevitably includes a range of attack methods, variances, and complexity.by tweaking hyperparameters, employing PTB, and recalibrating crucial settings such as learning rates, batch sizes, and regularisation factors to correspond with the current data landscape. As a result, the models were fine-tuned to effectively identify patterns and anomalies, responding to the nuanced complexities that may occur over time.

5 Results and Discussion

The entire execution of the accompanying models is finished in Python programming language utilizing Scikit-learn, TensorFlow and Pandas etc. Initially, we have considered 1,11,500 records and applied CTGAN and increased the record count to 1,51,500. Then we have split the data into training and testing sets and have trained the models. In Table 2, all of the initial results are listed with their respective accuracies. On the other hand, after CTGAN all the 5 models performed exceptionally well with best accuracy for XGBoost Classifier with 96.71%, which consumed around 60 min for training, then Random Forest with accuracy of 96.66%, which took 45 min followed by Extra Tree Classifier with 96.31%, Decision Tree with 95.10% and KNN model with accuracy of 89.58%, which took around 35 min each, which are mentioned in Table 3.

A synergistic combination of CTGAN-generated synthetic data and PBT's adaptive optimization prowess unfolded in front of us, providing a riveting story of exponential increases in the accuracy of individual attack detection models. Our experimental analysis' annals echo with the clear declaration of PBT's dominance, extolling its function as the spearhead in magnifying the overall efficacy of our painstakingly constructed approach. This unrelenting dedication to pushing the boundaries of IoT network threat detection manifests itself through the integration of Population-Based Training.Additionally, we had obtained the best accuracy for prediction over all the models. Worms are best predicted with accuracy of 99.63, then Generic with accuracy of 99.62, Normal with accuracy of 98.62, Shellcode with accuracy of 97.30, Backdoor with accuracy of 92.43 and Analysis with accuracy of 90.70 as shown in Table 4.

Furthermore, our study offers a granular insight into the capabilities of various machine learning models in recognizing specific types of attacks as detailed in Table 4.

For instance, our Random Forest model achieved an accuracy of 99.72% in detecting 'Generic' attacks and 97.22% for 'Shellcode' attacks, which suggests a high degree of precision and reliability that surpasses the general performance metrics provided in previous literature. While Kumar et al. [25] and Fuat et al. [26] reported general performance metrics like accuracy, precision, and F1-score, they did not delve into the performance of individual attacks. Our detailed breakdown offers a more comprehensive view, facilitating a nuanced understanding of how well each model performs in different intrusion scenarios. In our study, the use of CTGAN as a data augmentation technique significantly improved the performance of our machine learning models across various metrics. For example, the Extra Trees model saw a dramatic improvement in accuracy, rising from 83.94% to 96.31%. Additionally, the models excelled in identifying specific types of network-attacks, with the XGBoost model achieving an outstanding 99.63% accuracy rate in detecting 'Worms.' This high degree of precision underscores the versatility and reliability of our models in different intrusion detection contexts. Compared to existing research, our work stands out for its exceptional performance, especially after the application of CTGAN, reinforcing the value of using data augmentation in enhancing intrusion detection systems (Fig. 4).

Table 3. Results before and after CTGAN

S. No	Model name	Before			After		
		Accuracy (in %)	Precision (in %)	F1-score (in %)	Accuracy (in %)	Precision (in %)	F1-score (in %)
1	KNN	80.03	78.00	78.62	89.58	89.56	89.49
2	Decision Tree	82.32	82.35	82.20	95.10	95.12	95.09
3	Extra Trees	83.94	82.75	83.05	96.31	96.32	96.29
4	Random Forest	84.67	83.54	83.58	96.66	96.77	96.66
5	XGBoost	85.34	84.20	84.63	96.71	96.74	96.70

Table 4. Accuracy of individual attack

S. No	Model name	Accuracy of each attack per model						
		Normal	Generic	Reconnaissance	Analysis	Backdoor	Shellcode	Worms
1	KNN	94.06	99.30	67.07	66.92	65.06	81.63	91.13
2	Decision Tree	98.30	99.18	83.13	77.87	84.26	91.60	95.55
3	Extra Trees	98.37	99.68	83.57	84.71	90.81	96.02	97.61
4	Random Forest	98.42	99.72	80.74	90.70	92.43	97.22	99.45
5	XGBoost	98.62	99.62	83.06	87.67	91.19	97.30	99.63

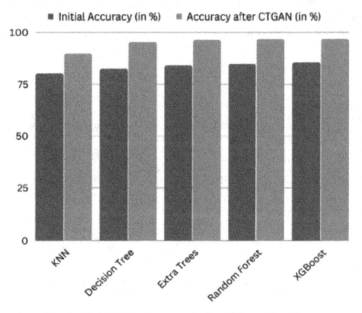

Fig. 4. Variations in accuracy rise for different classifiers

6   Conclusion

Finally, we demonstrated the efficacy of using CTGAN for synthetic data creation to improve the accuracy of intrusion detection systems. As we demonstrated that each of the five machine learning models performed considerably better after CTGAN, with the XGBoost classifier getting the best accuracy. PBT actively travelled the landscape of hyperparameter settings during our research endeavor, experiencing iterative evaluation of the performance of each unique model. Hyperparameters were exposed to computed perturbations and adaptive adjustments based on observed model performance. Models that produced promising results were given hyperparameters similar to those used by their more experienced counterparts. This adaptive process aided in the path to ideal hyperparameter settings, culminating in the highest level of accuracy for individual attack detection. Our research also found that worms, which are considered significant security risks, were the best-predicted attacks with the highest accuracy, followed by generic attacks with the next highest accuracy, as shown in Table 3. These findings highlight the significance of our multi-class model, which accurately examines worms, analysis, shellcode, generic, normal and backdoor attacks, that are usually more serious than fuzzers and DoS attacks with respect to the accuracy of models. Predicting these attacks accurately can help organizations in taking proactive measures to mitigate their effect and avoid possible harm to their systems and networks. Overall, our findings emphasize the significance of employing sophisticated machine learning methods such as CTGAN and PBT optimizer to improve the accuracy and efficacy of systems that detect intrusions.

References

1. Kumar, M., Yadav, S., Sharma, S.: Security in Internet of Things (IoT) using machine learning algorithms. In: Proceedings of the International Conference on Automation, Computational and Technology Management (ICACTM), pp. 232–236 (2019)
2. Thomas, A., Kumar, T.G., Mohan, A.K.: Neighbor attack detection in Internet of Things. In: 2020 2nd International Conference on Advances in Computing, Communication Control and Networking (ICACCCN), pp. 262–267. IEEE (2020)
3. Chunduri, H., Kumar, T.G., Sai Charan, P.V.: A multi class classification for detection of IoT botnet malware. In: 2021 IEEE 11th Annual Computing and Communication Workshop and Conference (CCWC), pp. 0458–0462. IEEE (2021). https://doi.org/10.1007/978-3-030-767 76-1_2
4. Pallavi, S., Anantha Narayanan, V.: An overview of practical attacks on BLE based IoT devices and their security. In: 2020 IEEE 7th Uttar Pradesh Section International Conference on Electrical, Electronics and Computer Engineering (UPCON), pp. 1–6 (2020). https://doi.org/10.1109/icaccs.2019.8728448
5. Raakesh, M., Ananthanarayanan, V.: Machine learning based prediction analysis in intrusion detection. In: 2022 International Conference on Electronics and Renewable Systems (ICEARS), pp. 1153–1159. IEEE (2022)
6. Kolias, C., Kambourakis, G., Stavrou, A., Gritzalis, D.: DDoS in the IoT: Mirai and other botnets. Computer 50(7), 80–84 (2017)
7. Cho, H., Kim, H., Kim, J., Lee, D., Kim, J.: A comprehensive survey on Internet of Things security: Review, taxonomy, and open research issues. J. Inf. Secur. Appl. 38, 9–31 (2018)
8. Cisco Talos: New VPNFilter malware targets at least 500K networking devices worldwide. https://blog.talosintelligence.com/2018/05/VPNFilter.html. Accessed 29 Mar 2023
9. Vanhoef, M., Piessens, F.: Key reinstallation attacks: forcing nonce reuse in WPA2. In: Proceedings of the ACM SIGSAC Conference on Computer and Communications Security, pp. 1313–1328 (2017)
10. Roman, R., Najera, P., Lopez, J.: Securing the Internet of Things. Computer 46(2), 30–38 (2013). https://doi.org/10.1109/MC.2012.368
11. Al-Fuqaha, A., Guizani, M., Mohammadi, M., Aledhari, M., Ayyash, M.: Internet of Things: a survey on enabling technologies, protocols, and applications. IEEE Commun. Surv. Tutor. 17(4), 2347–2376 (2015). https://doi.org/10.1109/COMST.2015.2444095

12. Krebs, B.: Who is Anna-Senpai, the Mirai Worm Author? KrebsOnSecurity (2016). https:// krebsonsecurity.com/2016/10/who-is-anna-senpai-the-mirai-worm-author/
13. Rajkumar, V.S., Stefanov, A.: Exploiting ripple20 to compromise power grid cyber security and impact system operations. In: 2021 IEEE Power & Energy Society Innovative Smart Grid Technologies Conference (ISGT), pp. 1–6. IEEE (2021)
14. Suo, H., Wan, J., Zou, C., Liu, J.: Attack on an IoT hotel room lock system. Security in the Internet of Things: a review. IEEE Internet Things J. **6**(1), 49–70 (2019)
15. Leevy, J.L., Hancock, J., Khoshgoftaar, T.M.: IoT reconnaissance attack classification with random undersampling and ensemble feature selection. Comput. Secur. **68**, 81–93 (2017)
16. Cui, A., Kataria, J., Stolfo, S.J.: Killing the Myth of Cisco IOS diversity: recent advances in reliable shellcode design. In: Proceedings of the 15th ACM Conference on Computer and Communications Security, pp. 245–254 (2008)
17. Edwards, S., Profetis, I.: Hajime: analysis of a decentralized internet worm for IoT devices. In: 2017 IEEE Symposium on Computers and Communication (ISCC), pp. 1034–1039 (2017)
18. Moustafa, N., Slay, J., Creech, G., Hu, W.: UNSW-NB15: a comprehensive data set for network intrusion detection systems (UNSW-NB15 network data set). In: Military Communications and Information Systems Conference (MilCIS) (2015)
19. Koroniotis, N., Syed, T., Schäfer, G.: Bot-IoT: evaluating the impact of DDoS attacks on IoT devices. In: International Conference on Cyber Security and Protection of Digital Services (2018)
20. Faruki, P., Bharmal, A., Laxmi, V., Ganmoor, V., Gaur, M.S.: IoT intrusion detection system using hybrid feature selection and random forest classifier. IEEE Access **5**, 19148–19160 (2017)
21. Al-Smadi, M., Al-Khateeb, W., Jararweh, Y., Al-Ayyoub, M.: IoT botnet detection using machine learning techniques. In: 15th International Conference on Innovations in Information Technology (IIT), pp. 50–55. IEEE (2020). https://doi.org/10.1109/iit50501.2020.9299061
22. Nazir, A., Memon, Z., Sadiq, T., Rahman, H., Khan, I.U.: A novel feature-selection algorithm in IoT networks for intrusion detection. Sensors. **23**, 8153 (2023). https://doi.org/10.3390/s23 198153
23. Chen, C.-L., Lai, J.L.: An experimental detection of distributed denial of service attack in CDX 3 platform based on snort. Sensors. **23**, 6139 (2023). https://doi.org/10.3390/s23136139
24. Navidan, H., Fard Moshiri, P., Nabati, M., Shahbazian, R., Ghorashi, S.A.: Generative Adversarial Networks (GANs) in networking: a comprehensive survey & evaluation. Comput. Netw. **193**, 108003 (2021)
25. Kumar, S., Pathak, N.K.: Evaluation of machine learning algorithms for intrusion detection utilizing UNSW-NB15 dataset. J. Pharm. Negative Res. **13**, 4819–4832 (2022)
26. Fuat, T.Ü.R.K.: Analysis of intrusion detection systems in UNSW-NB15 and NSL-KDD datasets with machine learning algorithms. Bitlis Eren Üniversitesi Fen Bilimleri Dergisi **12**(2), 465–477 (2023)
27. Moualla, S., Khorzom, K., Jafar, A.: Improving the performance of machine learning-based network intrusion detection systems on the UNSW-NB15 dataset. Comput. Intell. Neurosci. **2021** (2021). https://doi.org/10.1155/2021/5557577
28. Xu, L., Skoularidou, M., Cuesta-Infante, A.: Modeling tabular data using conditional GAN. In: Proceedings of the International Conference on Machine Learning (ICML) (2019)

Optimizing Sentiment Analysis on Twitter: Leveraging Hybrid Deep Learning Models for Enhanced Efficiency

Gadde Ashok, N. Ruthvik, and G. Jeyakumar$^{(\boxtimes)}$

Department of Computer Science and Engineering, Amrita School of Computing, Coimbatore, Amrita Vishwa Vidyapeetham, Coimbatore, India
{cb.en.u4cse20020,cb.en.u4cse20442}@cb.students.amrita.edu,
g_jeyakumar@cb.amrita.edu

Abstract. Sentiment analysis has emerged as a prominent and critical research area, particularly in the realm of social media platforms. Among these platforms, Twitter stands out as a significant channel where users freely express opinions and emotions on diverse topics, making it a goldmine for understanding public sentiment. The study presented in this paper delves into the profound significance of sentiment analysis within the context of Twitter, with a primary focus on uncovering the underlying sentiments and attitudes of users towards various subjects. To achieve it, this study presents a comprehensive analysis of sentiment on Twitter, leveraging a diverse range of advanced deep learning and neural network models, including Convolutional Neural Network (CNN) and Recurrent Neural Network (RNN). Moreover, investigates the effectiveness of Hybrid Ensemble Models in enhancing sentiment analysis accuracy and optimized time. The proposed architecture (HCCRNN) puts forward a sophisticated deep learning model for sentiment analysis on Twitter data, achieves great accuracy whilst considering computational efficiency. Standard models such as Multinomial-NB, CNN, RNN, RNN-LSTM, and RNN-CNN, as well as hybrid models such as HCCRNN (2CNN-1LSTM), CATBOOST, and STACKING (RF-GBC), were examined CNN and RNN-CNN had the best accuracy (82%) and F1-score (81%), with appropriate precision and recall rates among the conventional models. RNN-CNN surpassed other models in terms of analysis time, requiring just 22.4 min. For hybrid models, our suggested model, HCCRNN (2CNN-1LSTM), attained high accuracy in 59 s and an accuracy of 82.6%. It exhibits the capability of real-time sentiment analysis with extraordinary precision and efficiency. This comprehensive exploration of sentiment analysis on Twitter enriches the knowledge base of the community and the application of sentiment analysis across diverse domains.

Keywords: Sentiment Analysis · Twitter · Social media · Natural Language Processing · Deep Learning · Hybrid Ensemble Models · Text Classification · Emotion Analysis · Text Mining

1 Introduction

In the contemporary digital age, social media platforms have revolutionized communication, offering individuals an unprecedented means to express their opinions, emotions, and reactions on a myriad of topics. Among these platforms, Twitter emerges as a prominent channel where users freely share their thoughts and feelings, making it a virtual goldmine for understanding public sentiment. The exponential increase of user-generated material on Twitter brings possibilities as well as problems in collecting relevant insights from this huge body of data. As a result, sentiment analysis has arisen as an important study subject within the wider domain of natural language processing (NLP) [1–4]. Sentiment analysis, often known as opinion mining, is a technique for automatically extracting and categorizing sentiments, attitudes, and emotions expressed in text data. The ultimate objective is to gain a better understanding of how different themes and settings affect people's perceptions and reactions. Sentiment analysis is valuable in many sectors, including advertising, brand management, political evaluation, and public perception monitoring. In the context of social media, sentiment analysis is crucial for measuring user involvement, brand perception, and growing trends. Because of its real-time and vast nature, Twitter has proven to be an important tool for sentiment research. Users actively discuss their opinions on social, political, economic, and cultural matters, transforming it into a microcosm of public opinion. Traditional sentiment evaluation algorithms, however, are hampered by the particular characteristics of posts on Twitter, such as shortness, informality, and the usage of emoticons and hashtags. As a result, to capture the intricacies and complexities of thoughts conveyed in tweets, researchers have resorted to highly sophisticated machine learning techniques, notably deep learning models.

This paper presents a comprehensive study on sentiment analysis of Twitter data using advanced deep learning and neural network models with an essential goal to reveal the basic feelings and perspectives of clients towards different subjects and occasions on Twitter. To accomplish this, the study presented in this paper influence a different scope of profound learning models, including Convolu-tional Brain Organizations (CNN) and Repetitive Brain Organizations (RNN), which have shown promising outcomes in taking care of regular language handling errands. Moreover, investigated the adequacy of Mixture Troupe Models in improving opinion examination exactness while enhancing handling time. Predictions made using ensemble techniques are more reliable and accurate. By incorporating the qualities of various models, desire to work on the general execution of opinion investigation on Twitter information. By providing insights into the efficacy of deep learning models for sentiment classification, this study adds to the existing body of knowledge in sentiment analysis. Moreover, we shed light on the potential of Hybrid Ensemble Models in improving sentiment analysis outcomes. The findings from this research hold practical implications for businesses, policymakers, and researchers. For marketers, understanding public sentiment on Twitter allows for targeted marketing strategies, enabling them to tailor their campaigns to resonate with their audience's emotions and preferences. This study emphasises the necessity of researching the technical basis of sentiment classification, pushing the boundaries of what is feasible within the discipline by exploring the research side of sentiment analysis. Researchers gain access to real-time public sentiment on a wide range of topics, unlocking opportunities for

sociological and behavioral studies. In subsequent sections, the study presents methodologies employed, experimental results obtained, and a comprehensive analysis of the
research findings. By integrating advanced deep learning techniques and Hybrid Ensemble Models, this research aims to foster a deeper understanding of human emotions and
opinions within the dynamic landscape of social media platforms, particularly Twitter.

2 Related Works

Over the past years, sentiment analysis on Twitter data has garnered significant attention
among researchers, leading to the exploration of various methodologies and techniques
to effectively classify sentiments expressed in tweets. The studies mentioned above
have been pivotal in advancing the field, each contributing unique insights and showcasing the effectiveness of different approaches. Go et al. [5] presented a novel approach
known as distant supervision for Twitter sentiment classification. Their method leveraged
emoticons present in tweets as noisy labels for training a sentiment classifier. Despite
the inherent noise in the training data, their approach achieved remarkable accuracy
in sentiment classification. This study highlighted the potential of utilizing large-scale,
crowd-sourced data for training sentiment classifiers, an aspect that has become more
relevant with the increasing availability of massive social media datasets. In a similar
vein, Pak and Paroubek [6] conducted a comprehensive exploration of machine learning
techniques for sentiment analysis on Twitter. By evaluating several classifiers, including Support Vector Machines (SVM), Naive Bayes, and Maximum Entropy, they shed
light on the strengths and weaknesses of each model in capturing tweet sentiments. The
exceptional performance of SVM stood out, showcasing the importance of selecting
appropriate machine learning algorithms for sentiment analysis tasks. Deep learning
models have also emerged as powerful tools for sentiment analysis on Twitter. Zhang
et al. [7] introduced a Convolutional Neural Network (CNN) model tailored for text
classification tasks, including sentiment analysis. The CNN model demonstrated competitive performance in capturing local textual features, thus highlighting the potential
of deep learning in handling sequential data like tweets. Ensemble methods, such as
the stacking model proposed by Wang et al. [8], have gained popularity for improving
sentiment analysis accuracy. By combining the predictions of multiple classifiers, the
stacking model demonstrated enhanced performance compared to individual classifiers.
This work emphasized the importance of leveraging the complementary strengths of
different classifiers to boost overall sentiment classification results. Furthermore, Dos
Santos and Gatti [9] delved into the impact of word embeddings on sentiment analysis.
Their model, which integrated word embeddings with Convolutional Neural Networks,
showcased the importance of capturing semantic information in tweets for more accurate
sentiment classification. Dhanya and Harish [10] used machine learning techniques to do
sentiment analysis on Twitter data pertaining to demonetization. A deep learning-based
approach for predicting noise in audio recordings was proposed in a paper by K. P. V.
    S. M. S. and Jeyakumar [11]. Although the application differed from our study on
Twitter data sentiment analysis, the implementation of deep learning techniques inspired
us. Their work's architecture and methodology served as the foundation for constructing
deep learning model suited for sentiment analysis on Twitter data. Similarly, Uthayasuriyan et al. [12] investigated impact maximization models in social networks. While

their goal was to evaluate the effectiveness of various models using certain measures. This prompted us to take a similar approach in our research, in which we compared several sentiment analysis algorithms for Twitter data. G. A. J. Nair et al. [13] conducted a comparison-research using COVID-19 tweet sentiment analysis. Furthermore, Naveenkumar et al. [14] published a Twitter dataset for sentiment analysis using traditional machine learning and deep learning methodologies. These previous studies provided the groundwork for understanding sentiment analysis in the context of Twitter data, and their findings give useful insights for this research article. In the light of these remarkable contributions, our research seeks to expand the knowledge base and address specific challenges in sentiment analysis on Twitter data. By focusing on a diverse range of advanced deep learning and neural network models, including Convolutional Neural Networks (CNN) and Recurrent Neural Networks (RNN), aimed to harness the strengths of these models to achieve more precise sentiment classification. Additionally, explored the effectiveness of Hybrid Ensemble Models, combining the best features of multiple models, to enhance sentiment analysis accuracy while optimizing runtime. Through this study of extensive analysis and experimentation to contribute further to the field of sentiment analysis on Twitter data, providing valuable insights that can be applied across various domains and applications. By building upon the foundations laid by previous studies, this research strives to create a more comprehensive understanding of human emotions and opinions within the dynamic landscape of social media platforms, particularly Twitter.

In particular, the contribution of this study has three main objectives mentioned below:

1. Investigate and Compare Advanced Models: The first objective is to conduct a comprehensive investigation and comparison of advanced deep learning and neural network models, including Convolutional Neural Networks (CNN) and Recurrent Neural Networks (RNN), for sentiment analysis on Twitter data. By evaluating the strengths and limitations of each model, aim to identify the most effective approach for accurately capturing sentiments expressed in tweets.
2. Develop and Optimize Hybrid Ensemble Models: The second objective is to propose and optimize Hybrid Ensemble Models that combine the strengths of different deep learning and neural network architectures. By blending the best features of multiple models, seek to achieve improved sentiment classification accuracy and efficiency. These ensemble models have the potential to outperform individual models and yield more robust sentiment analysis results.
3. Validate and Benchmark Performance: The third goal is validating and benchmarking the suggested models' performance utilizing the Senti-ment140 dataset, consisting of 1.6 million tweets tagged with sentiment labels. To demonstrate the success of proposed technique and give insights into the possible uses of sentiment evaluation in real-world contexts through rigorous testing and assessment.

This study contributes valuable insights and advancements to the field of sentiment analysis on Twitter data by encouraging researchers, organizations, and policy makers with more precise, accurate and effective tools for comprehending public sentiment, brand perception, and emerging trends on social media platforms by achieving these goals.

3 Methodology

In this segment, the technique embraced in exploration to accomplish the targets framed in the past area is presented depicting the information prepro-cessing steps, model designs, and assessment measurements used for opinion examination on the Twitter dataset.

3.1 Data Preprocessing

Data preparation is an important stage in sentiment analysis because it sets the groundwork for developing successful models that can identify sentiment from the Twitter dataset [8, 9]. In this part, various procedures taken to clean the data, tokenize it, remove stopwords, and lemmatize the Sentiment140 dataset are mentioned.

3.1.1 Data Cleaning

The analysis begin with data pre-processing phase by cleaning the tweets in order to guarantee the text data's consistency and quality [6]. This includes eliminating unessential data, like URLs, makes reference to, exceptional characters, and accentuation. By disposing of these components, we make a normalized design for the text, empowering better examination and model execution [7].

3.1.2 Stopword Removal

Certain terms in the tokenized text, which include "and", "the", "is", and so on, are frequent across numerous tweets and do not contain substantial sentiment information. Stopwords are words like these. Also removed stop-words as part of data preparation to decrease noise and focus on significant words that contain sentiment information [6]. This step improves the performance of sentiment classification models.

3.1.3 Lemmatization

Lemmatization is another essential data preprocessing technique employed in this study to convert words into their base or root form [7]. This step reduces the dimensionality of the text and captures the essence of the sentiments expressed [8]. By transforming words to their canonical form, we ensure that variations of the same word do not affect the sentiment analysis results.

The Sentiment140 dataset used in this research study contains 1.6 million tweets, annotated with sentiment labels (0 = negative, 2 = neutral, 4 = positive). The dataset includes fields such as target, ids, date, flag, user, and text. With the data preprocessing steps detailed above, aim to create a clean and standardized dataset suitable for training and evaluating the sentiment analysis models [8, 9]. By preparing the data meticulously, we ensure that the subsequent steps in this research produce reliable and meaningful results in understanding public sentiment on Twitter.

3.2   Model Architecture

To achieve accurate sentiment analysis on Twitter data, this research propose an approach called the Hybrid Contextual Convolutional Recurrent Neural Network (HCCRNN). The HCCRNN model is designed to leverage the strengths of Convolutional Neural Networks (CNNs) and Long Short-Term Memory (LSTM) layers to enhance sentiment classification performance and capture contextual information in tweets. Samples and Features considered. The various layers are explained as shown in Fig. 1.

Input Layer: The HCCRNN model takes the preprocessed tweets as input, represented as sequences of word embeddings.

First CNN Layer: The initial CNN layer captures local features and patterns within the tweet representations through convolution operations, identifying key features.

Second CNN Layer: The output from the first CNN layer is further refined by passing it through the second CNN layer, identifying more complex patterns.

LSTM Layer: The output from the second CNN layer is then fed into the LSTM layer, which captures sequential dependencies and context within the tweet, enabling a broader understanding of sentiment.

Contextual Fusion: After the LSTM layer, a contextual fusion mechanism is introduced to merge outputs from both CNNs and the LSTM layer. This fusion process combines local features from CNNs with the contextual understanding from LSTM, creating a comprehensive representation of tweet sentiment.

Output Layer: The final output layer produces sentiment predictions (positive, negative, or neutral) based on the learned features from the contextual fusion step.

The proposed Hybrid Contextual Convolutional Recurrent Neural Network (HCCRNN) model for sentiment analysis on Twitter data consists of several interconnected components to effectively capture sentiment information from tweets. The entire process begins with the input layer, where preprocessed tweets are taken as input. These tweets are then tokenized into individual words or tokens, creating a structured input for the model. Common stopwords, which do not carry significant sentiment information, are removed, while lemmatization is applied to reduce dimensionality and capture essential sentiment expressions as shown in Fig. 1.

To achieve accurate sentiment analysis on Twitter data, this study propose a novel approach called the Hybrid Contextual Convolutional Recurrent Neural Network (HCCRNN) for sentiment analysis, inspired by the works of Go et al. [8], Pak and Paroubek [6]. The HCCRNN model combines the strengths of Convolutional Neural Networks (CNNs) and Long Short-Term Memory (LSTM) layers to enhance sentiment classification performance and capture contextual information in tweets. We preprocess the tweets using techniques inspired by dos Santos and Gatti [9]. The tweets are cleaned to remove irrelevant information, tokenized to create structured input, and stop words are removed to focus on meaningful words. Lemmatization is applied to reduce dimensionality and capture essential sentiment expressions. Drawing inspiration from the works of Wang et al. [8] and dos Santos and Gatti [9], the HCCRNN model architecture consists of an input layer, followed by two 1D CNN layers with 32 filters each. These layers capture local features and patterns within the tweet representations. MaxPooling1D layers follow each CNN layer to reduce spatial dimensions. Next, our research introduce an

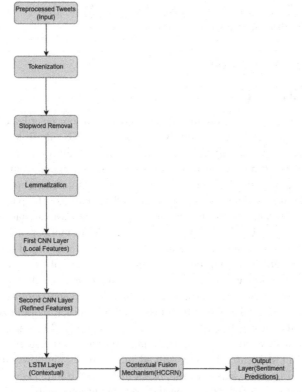

Fig. 1. HCCRNN Model Architecture

LSTM layer with 64 units, inspired by the work of Zhang et al. [7], to capture sequential dependencies and contextual information within the tweet. Dropout and recurrent dropout rates are set to 0.5 to prevent overfitting. Inspired by the work of Wang et al. [7], introducing a contextual fusion mechanism that combines the outputs from the CNN and LSTM layers. This fusion process merges local features from the CNNs with the contextual understanding from LSTM, creating a comprehensive representation of tweet sentiment. The model concludes with a dense layer with the number of classes as the output dimension and 'softmax' activation, inspired by the work of Zhang et al. [8]. This layer performs the sentiment classification and outputs the predicted probabilities for each class.

The distinguishing aspect of the HCCRNN model lies in the Contextual Fusion Mechanism. This method is implemented following the LSTM layer and is intended to contextually integrate the outputs of both CNNs and the LSTM layer. The model derives a richer representation of the tweet's sentiment by combining local characteristics from the CNNs with contextual understanding from the LSTM, increasing the accuracy of sentiment predictions. Finally, in the output layer, sentiment predictions are generated, categorizing tweets as either positive or negative based on the contextual fusion step's learnt properties. The design of the HCCRNN model combines the benefits of CNNs in collecting local characteristics with the capacity of LSTMs to grasp context, giving in a new method to sentiment analysis on Twitter data.

4 Results and Discussion

4.1 Experimental Setup

The experimental setup utilized to test the performance of our postulated Hybrid Contextual Convolutional Recurrent Neural Net-work (HCCRNN) algorithm for sentiment analysis on Twitter data is described in this section. Initially divided the sentiment-labeled Twitter dataset into two distinct sections at first: a training set and a testing set. To minimize bias, the split of both positive and negative emotion samples was ensured to be equal in both sets. The training set was used to optimize the parameters of the model, while the test data set was used as an independent assessment dataset to examine the model's capacity to generalize. Then set the maximum number of features for the model architecture to 20,000 and the embedding dimension to 128. These parameters were selected to establish a compromise between complexity of the model and performance. The Adam optimizer was used to train the suggested HCCRNN model, which has been shown to be successful for multi-class classification applications. During training, we used the categorical cross-entropy loss function in order to optimize the model's parameters. The model was trained across two epochs with 128 batches. These hyperparameters were developed using empirical data and past field research. In this study utilized a sufficient hardware platform with adequate processing power to perform the training process efficiently. This platform meant that model training went smoothly and on schedule, allowing to concentrate on the assessment and analysis of the findings. Various parameters, including as accuracy, loss, and validation accuracy, were tracked during the training process. Moreover, able to analyze the model's development and assure its convergence to an ideal state using these indicators. Following training, used numerous assessment criteria to assess the effectiveness of the model on the testing set. These measures comprised accuracy, precision, recall, and F1-score, which provided a thorough grasp of the model's prediction skills as well as its capacity to perform sentiment categorization tasks. Then created a confusion matrix to acquire insight into the way the model performed across different sentiment classes.

In this work randomly generated seed was adjusted to a predetermined value to assure the repeatability of studies. This practice enabled to acquire consistent and dependable outcomes over several research runs. Overall, with carefully structured experimental setup to evaluate the usefulness and efficiency of the postulated HCCRNN approach to sentiment analysis on Twitter data and able to draw informed conclusions regarding the model's performance and prospective contributions to sentiment evaluation tasks on social networking platforms thanks to the selection of hyperparameters, optimization approaches, and assessment measures.

4.2 Evaluation Metrics and Analysis

As shown below the findings of the comparison analysis in Table 1 which comprised assessing several sentiment analysis models using Twitter data. The primary goal of this study was to develop a model that finds a compromise between high accuracy and fast execution time. To do this, thoroughly evaluated each model's performance in terms of accuracy, execution time as shown in Table 2 and efficiency-to-accuracy ratio to determine the best strategy for sentiment analysis on Twitter data. Each models effectiveness was assessed according to accuracy, time required for execution, and the effectiveness to correctness ratio.

Table 1. Results for standard and ensemble deep learning models

Model	Accuracy	F1-Score	Precision	Recall
Multinomial-NB	0.76	0.77	0.76	0.77
CNN	0.82	0.82	0.83	0.81
RNN	0.81	0.82	0.80	0.84
RNN – LSTM	0.81	0.82	0.80	0.84
RNN – CNN	0.82	0.81	0.85	0.78

Table 2. Time taken for standard and ensemble deep learning models

Model	Accuracy	Time
CNN	82.6	45.6 min
RNN	81.8	35.2 min
RNN-CNN	82.2	22.4 min
RNN – GRU	81.4	32 min
Lexicon-approach	67.6	12 min
Multinomial-NB	76	26 s (<1 min)

The traditional lexicon-based approach using the VADER sentiment analysis tool obtained an accuracy of 67.6%. Moving to machine learning models, the Multinomial Naive Bayes model demonstrated improved performance, achieving an accuracy of 76% in a mere 26 s. This model showcased a commendable efficiency-to-accuracy ratio, making it an appealing choice.

Deep learning approaches were further explored, starting with the Convolutional Neural Network (CNN). The CNN model exhibited promising accuracy of 82%, but it required 45 min for execution. Additionally, a Recurrent Neural Network (RNN) was employed, achieving an accuracy of 81.4% in 32 min, with results comparable to the CNN. To enhance efficiency, the Gated Recurrent Unit (GRU) model was explored, producing a similar accuracy of around 81.4% to the RNN. However, the GRU model significantly reduced the execution time to 25 min, showcasing better efficiency as shown in Fig. 2(a). Inspired by these findings, then devised a hybrid model combining the strengths of CNN and RNN. The fusion resulted in an accuracy of 82% and an execution time of only 22 min, making it the preferred choice for sentiment analysis on Twitter data when standard deep learning models are considered as shown in Table 2. This combined model demonstrated the highest accuracy and significant efficiency improvements. In this research, attempted to the use of a pre-trained BERT (Bidirectional Encoder Representations from Transformers) model for sentiment analysis on Twitter data. BERT is a state-of-the-art deep learning model that has demonstrated impressive performance in various natural language processing tasks, including sentiment analysis. However, when attempted to employ the pretrained BERT model for sentiment analysis task, encountered certain challenges related to its extensive training requirements. BERT is a large model with a substantial number of parameters, which makes its training computationally expensive and timeconsuming, especially when dealing with sizable datasets like the one we used for our experiments.

The training process for the BERT model on Twitter dataset took an exceptionally long time, exceeding 13 h. Due to the substantial time required for training, had to terminate the process prematurely to ensure the feasibility of our research within the allocated time frame. Despite the shortened training period, the pre-trained BERT model did show some promising potential. At the beginning of the training, the model achieved an accuracy of 62%. This initial accuracy indicated that the model was able to capture certain patterns and features related to sentiment in the tweets. However, it's important to note that the accuracy at the beginning of training is typically lower than the final performance of the model, as the optimization process is still in its early stages. To fully realize the potential of the pre-trained BERT model for sentiment analysis on Twitter data, a longer training period would have been necessary. Longer training would allow the model to fine-tune its parameters and learn more intricate patterns and representations from the data, potentially leading to improved accuracy. While the pre-trained BERT model's extensive training requirements posed challenges in our research, it remains a powerful option for sentiment analysis when computational resources and time are not a limiting factor. Future research with a focus on leveraging BERT's capabilities through more extended training could lead to even more accurate sentiment analysis results on Twitter data. However, given the constraints of this research, to prioritize other models that offered a good balance of accuracy and execution time, such as the hybrid models mentioned earlier.

Table 3. Accuracy for hybrid deep learning models

Model	Accuracy	Time
HCCRNN (2CNN-1LSTM)	82.6	59 s
RNN – GRU	81.4	32 min
RNN-LSTM	81.2	120 s
CATBOOST	74.78	1 m 38 s
STACKING (RF-GBC)	74.75	2 min

Whereas the approach to hybrid ensemble models as shown in Table 3 presents the accuracy and execution time for various hybrid deep learning models. The HCCRNN (2CNN-1LSTM) model achieved the highest accuracy of 82.6%, completing in just 59 s.

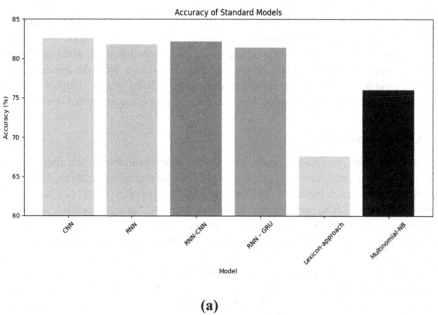

(a)

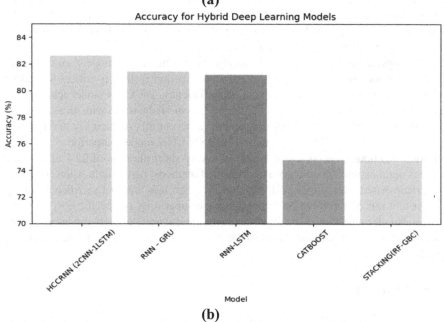

(b)

Fig. 2. Accuracy comparison for a. Standard models and b. Hybrid models.

The RNN – GRU model obtained an accuracy of 81.4%, with a training time of 32 min. The RNN-LSTM model demonstrated an accuracy of 81.2% and required only 120 s (2 min) for training. The CATBOOST model achieved an accuracy of 74.78% and took 1 min 38 s to train. Lastly, the STACKING model of Random Forest and Gradient Boost Classifier obtained an accuracy of 74.75%, with a training time of 2 min as shown in Fig. 2(b). Thus, the combined 2 CNN and 1LSTM Layered model emerged as the most efficient and accurate choice, achieving an accuracy of 82% in just 21 min. This model strikes an optimal balance between performance and execution time, making it well-suited for sentiment analysis tasks on Twitter data. The results from the hybrid model emphasize the potential of our proposed model can be utilized to gain valuable insights from public sentiments and enhance decision-making processes in various domains.

4.3 Comparative Analysis

We did a rigorous comparison study with the methods available in the literature in order to offer a full assessment of our suggested sentiment analysis methods. Our deep learning models, which include Convolutional Neural Networks (CNN) [7], Recurrent Neural Networks (RNN), and Hybrid Ensemble Models, have competitive accuracy, F1-Score, precision, and recall values, as shown in Table 1. Notably, the CNN model outperforms the others with an accuracy of 82%, demonstrating its usefulness in collecting local textual elements in Twitter data, which is consistent with the findings of Zhang et al. [7], who established the promise of CNNs for text classification tasks. Furthermore, our Hybrid Ensemble Models, such as HCCRNN (2CNN-1LSTM), attain an accuracy of 82.6%, demonstrating the value of integrating several models' capabilities [8]. In terms of accuracy, our hybrid model beats previous models such as RNN-LSTM, CATBOOST, and STACKING (RF-GBC) [13], emphasizing the benefit of employing ensemble approaches in boosting sentiment analysis findings.

In alongside performance measurements, we examined our models' runtime efficiency, as shown in Table 2. While our models function well, it is critical to strike a balance between accuracy and computational efficiency. The CNN model achieves this equilibrium in 45.6 min by performing the sentiment analysis job with an accuracy of 82%. RNN models, on the other hand, provide a decent mix of accuracy and runtime, processing the data in about 35.2 min. The RNN-CNN model outperforms the competition, obtaining an accuracy of 82.2% in a very short duration of 22.4 min. These findings demonstrate the utility of our suggested methods, particularly when compared to Lexicon-based alternatives [14], which need much less time but sacrifice accuracy. As a result, our research not only highlights the superiority of specific deep learning models, but also emphasizes the importance of a careful trade-off between accuracy and real time efficiency in sentiment analysis on Twitter data, contributing to the continuing debate in the area.

5 Conclusion

In this research an extensive comparative analysis of various models was conducted for sentiment analysis on Twitter data. The primary objective was to identify a model that achieves high accuracy while maintaining reasonable execution time. This study explored different approaches, including lexicon-based methods, traditional machine learning models, and deep learning architectures. The lexicon-based approach, implemented using the VADER sentiment analysis tool, provided valuable insights into sentiment classification. However, it demonstrated limitations in terms of execution time and scalability, which may hinder its applicability to real-time or large-scale sentiment analysis tasks. Moving to machine learning models, Multinomial Naive Bayes exhibited commendable performance, combining acceptable accuracy with rapid execution time. It emerged as a promising choice for certain sentiment analysis applications. In the realm of deep learning, Convolutional Neural Networks (CNN) and Recurrent Neural Networks (RNN) were evaluated. The CNN model demonstrated impressive accuracy, albeit with a longer execution time. Conversely, the RNN model offered slightly faster processing with a marginally lower accuracy.

To address efficiency concerns, we explored the Gated Recurrent Unit (GRU) model, which achieved competitive accuracy while significantly reducing execution time. A key contribution of this research is the development of a hybrid ensemble model that fuses the strengths of CNN and RNN. This model achieved high accuracy while demonstrating improved efficiency, making it a promising solution for sentiment analysis on Twitter data.

In the future, researchers may explore advanced pre-trained models and transfer learning techniques to improve sentiment analysis accuracy on Twitter data. Fine-tuning pre-trained models on domain-specific Twitter datasets could potentially lead to enhanced performance and efficiency. Efforts should be directed towards optimizing hyper-parameters and model architectures for sentiment analysis. Conducting systematic hyper-parameter tuning experiments can help uncover the best configuration for each model, maximizing accuracy while minimizing execution time. Further research could investigate the use of hybrid models that combine multiple deep learning architectures, as well as ensemble techniques, to achieve even higher predictive performance. Moreover, investigating the impact of data preprocessing techniques, including text normalization and feature engineering, could contribute to the overall performance of sentiment analysis systems. By addressing these avenues for future research, we can advance the field of sentiment analysis and facilitate the development of more accurate and efficient sentiment analysis systems for various applications.

References

1. Gupta, S., Chopra, C.: Impact Of Social Media On Consumer Behaviour (2020). https://doi.org/10.13140/RG.2.2.26927.15527
2. Brown, L., Williams, E.: Analyzing user-generated content: opportunities and challenges. In: Proceedings of the International Conference on Natural Language Processing, pp. 45–58 (2020)
3. Liu, B.: Sentiment analysis and opinion mining. Synth. Lect. Hum. Lang. Technol. 5(1), 1–167 (2012). https://doi.org/10.2200/S00416ED1V01Y201204HLT016
4. Pang, B., Lee, L.: Opinion mining and sentiment analysis. Found. Trends® Inf. Retr. 2(12), 1–135 (2008). https://doi.org/10.1561/1500000011
5. Go, A., Bhayani, R., Huang, L.: Twitter sentiment classification using distant supervision. CS224N Project Report, Stanford 1, p. 12 (2009)

6. Pak, A., Paroubek, P.: Twitter as a corpus for sentiment analysis and opinion mining. In: Proceedings of the International Conference on Language Resources and Evaluation, pp. 1320–1326 (2010)
7. Zhang, Y., Zhang, L., Chen, H.: Sentence-level sentiment classification with convolutional neural networks. In: Proceedings of the 56th Annual Meeting of the Association for Computational Linguistics (Volume 1: Long Papers), pp. 1–10 (2018)
8. Wang, Y., Huang, M., Zhu, X., Zhao, L., Zhang, X.: Attention-based stacked ensemble for twitter sentiment classification. In: Proceedings of the 56th Annual Meeting of the Association for Computational Linguistics (Volume 2: Short Papers), pp. 231–236 (2018)
9. Dos Santos, C., Gatti, M.: Deep convolutional neural networks for sentiment analysis of short texts. In: Proceedings of COLING 2014, the 25th International Conference on Computational Linguistics: Technical Papers, pp. 69–78 (2014)
10. Dhanya, N.M., Harish, U.C.: Sentiment analysis of twitter data on demonetization using machine learning techniques. In: Hemanth, D.J., Smys, S. (eds.) Computational Vision and Bio Inspired Computing. LNCVB, vol. 28, pp. 227–237. Springer, Cham (2018). https://doi.org/10.1007/978-3-319-71767-8_19
11. Kartik, P.V.S.M.S., Jeyakumar, G.: A Deep learning based system to predict the noise (disturbance) in audio files. In: Proceedings of 3rd International Conference on Emerging Current Trends in Computing and Expert Technologies (COMET-2020). Advances in Parallel Computing, Intelligent System and Computer Technology, Chennai, vol. 37, pp. 154–160. COMET-2020 (2020)
12. Uthayasuriyan, A., Chandran, G.H., Kavvin, U., Mahitha, S.H., Jeyakumar, G.: Influence maximization models in social networks: a comparative analysis. In: 2023 International Conference on Advancement in Computation & Computer Technologies (InCACCT), Gharuan, India, pp. 1–5. IEEE (2023). https://doi.org/10.1109/InCACCT57535.2023.10141772
13. Nair, A.J., Veena, G., Vinayak, A.: Comparative study of twitter sentiment on COVID - 19 tweets. In: 2021 5th International Conference on Computing Methodologies and Communication (ICCMC), pp. 1773–1778 (2021). https://doi.org/10.1109/ICCMC51019.2021.9418320
14. Naveenkumar, K.S., Soman, K.P., Vinayakumar, R.: Amrita-CEN-Senti-DB: twitter dataset for sentimental analysis and application of classical machine learning and deep learning (2020). https://doi.org/10.36227/techrxiv.12058968

Identification of Onset and Progression of Alzheimer's Disease Using Topological Data Analysis

Harshitha Bingi and T. Sobha Rani[✉]

School of Computer and Information Sciences, University of Hyderabad,
Hyderabad, India
sobharani@uohyd.ac.in

Abstract. Structural changes that can occur in a network as time progresses are difficult to capture. To handle such data, one of the methods used is Topological Data Analysis(TDA), which can transform the data, in order to extract and analyze the data. Alzheimer's disease networks show the changes that happen in the brain network as the disease progresses. Methods should be devised to capture these changes efficiently. In this work, two powerful tools of Topological data analysis, "persistent homology" and "mapper algorithm" are applied on the disease networks to gain insights about the changes happening during onset and progression of the disease. From the results, it can be concluded that more fragmentation is happening within the brain network as the disease progresses. The interconnections within the community(or cluster) are stronger as compared to the connections with other communities(or clusters). This may lead to difficulties in various cognitive functions such as attention, memory, language, and problem-solving.

Keywords: Node2vec · Persistent homology · Mapper algorithm

1 Introduction

Various methods have been/are being proposed to analyze the data generated in different domains. The analysis may provide insights about the underlying structures, complex processes, or interactions that are responsible for generating such data. In literature, statistics, machine learning algorithms, and artificial intelligence are some techniques that are used for this purpose.

Scenarios where the interactions can be modeled using networks are even more complex than data, where there is no influence between individual instances of data. Network analysis can be carried out on such data using graph theory, social network concepts such as centrality measures, influence maximization, community discovery, topological data analysis, and so on.

In various domains [5], topological data analysis is yielding encouraging and promising results. Topological data analysis(TDA) is specifically about studying

S. Devismes et al. (Eds.): ICDCIT 2024, LNCS 14501, pp. 193–205, 2024.
https://doi.org/10.1007/978-3-031-50583-6_13

the topology of the data and extracting the topological features from it. These may be much more robust than the features extracted from the raw data when noise may distort the original data.

The key focus of this paper is to analyze the high-dimensional and complex structures without the risk of data loss using the tools provided by TDA and how these methods may provide a different perspective of the Alzheimer's network data specifically. Alzheimer's disease is a neurological disorder case, where the formation of tangles and plaques inhibits the communication between various parts of the brain network, thereby causing issues in the functionalities of memory, mobility, comprehension, and so on. Since there is a structural change in the brain network as the disease progresses, we would like to capture these changes using topological data analysis.

2 Background

There are two main approaches used in TDA to capture the topological changes: Persistent homology and mapper algorithm. Persistent homology helps to identify and quantify the persistence of topological features across scales. Persistent homology, which is based on simplicial complexes, also includes betti numbers and plots as they are useful analytical tools for TDA. Mapper algorithm provides a simplified representation of clusters and their relationships. It uses dimensionality reduction, and clustering methods to help in understanding the network at a deeper level.

2.1 Persistent Homology

Persistent Homology(PH) is a powerful method that is used to identify topological features of simplicial complexes. It also tracks the changes and encodes the evolution in the homology across different scales [5]. To compute these changes in the features, PH uses simplicial complexes.

Simplicial Complex. A simplex is the generalization of a triangle in all dimensions. 0-simplex is a point. 1-simplex is a line segment. 2-simplex is a triangle. 3-simplex is a tetrahedron and so on. The collection of these simplexes is called simplicial complex [10, 16, 20] (Fig. 1).

Homology. Homology of a topological space is characterized as connected components, holes, voids, etc., and it can be decomposed into degrees: degree 0 homology corresponds to connected components, degree 1 homology encodes the presence of a cycle, degree 2 stands for a void. As simplexes, homology is also generalized to more than one dimension and it is known as homology groups [16]. Homology is denoted as $H_k(\sum)$ where k denotes the degree or dimension and $\sum$ denotes the simplicial complex. Zero-dimensional homology (H_0) represents connected components, one-dimensional homology (H_1) denotes loops, two-dimensional homology (H_2) denotes voids or cavities, and so on.

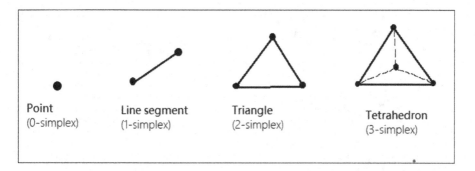

Fig. 1. First few simplexes.

Betti number [14] is defined as the rank of the homology group. It is denoted by β and k^{th} Betti number β_k is the rank of $H_k(\sum)$.

Betti numbers quantify the number of connected components, loops, and voids present in the data, revealing its underlying topological characteristics.

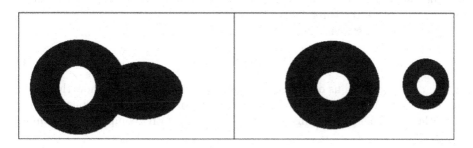

Fig. 2. Two sets of components.

In Fig. 2, the left set has one connected component and has one loop hence, $\beta_0 = 1$ and $\beta_1 = 1$. The right set has two connected components and two loops thus, $\beta_0 = 2$, $\beta_1 = 2$. Clearly β_0 denotes number of connected components, β_1 denotes number of loops, β_2 represents number cavity spaces and so on [20].

Building Simplicial Complexes. There are two main approaches to build simpilicial complexes [2]:

– Čech complex
– Vietoris-Rips complex

For both methods, the process starts by initiating the balls around every node in the dataset with the same radius, where we get the data points with the balls overlapping with each other as shown in Fig. 3. From this overlap, simplexes

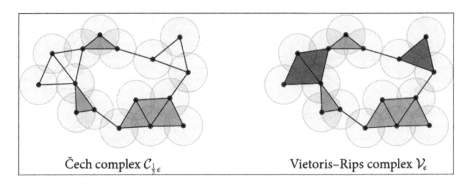

Čech complex $C_{\frac{1}{2}\varepsilon}$ Vietoris–Rips complex V_ε

Fig. 3. Čech in the left, Vietoris in the right [13].

are found like an edge or a triangular or a tetrahedron, etc., but there are two ways of considering a cavity [2].

In Fig. 3, the difference between Čech complex and Vietoris-Rips complex is shown in the blue color filling(the left one has 2-simplexes whereas the right one has 3-simplexes at the same place), that is because there is no point of intersection of all the three balls.

The relation between Čech and Vietoris-Rips complex is:

$$C_\varepsilon \subseteq VR_\varepsilon \subseteq C_{2\varepsilon} \tag{1}$$

where ε is a fixed radius of the balls. These two methods differ in how they treat the collection of balls [14]. Also Čech complex is computationally expensive than the other available algorithms. Hence Vietoris-Rips(VR) complex is used more often.

Computing Persistent Homology. Computation of persistent homology involves the utilization of simplicial complexes as a key component. The input for this process is represented as point cloud data. The process is initiated by applying balls at each data point with radius $\epsilon = 0$. As the radius starts to increase the balls start to overlap to form edges where we consider the balls as vertices. As more and more balls overlap, new simplexes are formed and some are merged with others to form new simplexes.

Persistent homology encodes, at what radii the topological features appear or born as ϵ_{birth} and at what radii the topological features disappear(merging with other simplexes) or dead as ϵ_{death}. The outputs of the PH are real number pairs [10,16]. The output is represented as $< \epsilon_{birth}, \epsilon_{death} >$ tuple and is called the persistent interval of the topological feature. The difference between ϵ_{death} and ϵ_{birth} is called the lifespan of the topological feature [16].

These pairs are generally represented with set of lines called bar codes or as set of points in persistent diagrams.

2.2   Mapper Algorithm

Mapper algorithm is another tool to extract, study, and analyze topological features of high-dimensional datasets [15]. The fundamental concept of mapper is to create a simplicial complex from high-dimensional noisy data without data loss [6]. Mapper has many real applications compared to persistent homology. It is being used in lot of industries for biotech/healthcare through Ayasdi [4](a software platform and company that specializes in TDA and machine learning) and also by many individual data scientists. Mapper has been applied to data in breast cancer patients [11], NLP training data [21], topic detection in twitter [17] etc.

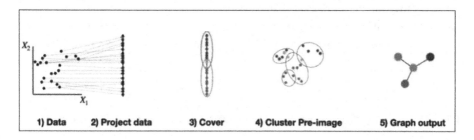

Fig. 4. Mapper algorithm example [16].

Computation of Mapper Algorithm. The idea of mapper algorithm is illustrated in Fig. 4. Firstly, the high-dimensional dataset is projected onto an axis through dimensionality reduction methods, to reduce the complexity of the noisy data. This projection is directed by *"filter* or *lens function"* [16].

Next a *cover function* is applied on the projected data so that we get overlapping subsets as shown in Fig. 4. Then we apply a clustering algorithm on all the subsets to get clusters and these clusters act as nodes. These nodes are connected if any two clusters share a data point(this is due to the cover function with the "overlapping subsets") [18,19].

Thus nodes and edges are formed for the resultant graph based on the clusters. It is very flexible due to the choice of functions for lens, cover, and clustering algorithms for different datasets, but it is also difficult to choose the best functions.

3   Experiments and Results

Persistent homology and mapper algorithms are applied to the Alzheimer's disease network [1]. This dataset of Alzheimer's disease network is provided by Alzheimer Disease Neuroimaging Initiative(ADNI) [1]. In this dataset, the brain network is divided into 70 major regions where the brain will be the most affected as the disease progresses. This is an adjacency matrix of the dataset with 70 rows and 70 columns. If there is an edge between two nodes(regions in the brain) then the matrix entry is 1 otherwise it is 0. This dataset contains the data that is monitored through four stages of the disease to study the changes in the network from normal, early, late, and Alzheimer's stages. Pre-processing of the data is done by converting these data matrices into graphs using networkx [7] (Table 1).

Table 1. Dataset matrix [1].

S No.	Stages	number of nodes	number of edges
1	Normal	70	3048
2	Early mild cognitive impairment(emci)	70	3088
3	Late mild cognitive impairment(lmci)	70	2828
4	Alzheimer's disease	70	2796

3.1 Persistent Homology on the Alzheimer's Disease Network

Using **R** studio, after loading the datasets, the homology for each matrix is calculated and the outputs, the birth and death radii of the topological features and their dimensions are generated. But from the bar codes and persistent diagrams we are not able to actually analyze or compare the changes as the disease progresses. Here we can use the idea of **Betti number plot** or **Betti curves**.

Betti number plot is the plot between betti-numbers and the radius of the ball that is Vietoris-Rips radius [9]. For every betti number, there will be a betti plot. In this dataset, the dimensions came out to be either 0 or 1. So for our dataset, there will be two betti curves for each stage. So, we have plotted all the betti curves in two graphs for all the stages of the disease, that is, the 0-betti curve and the 1-betti curve.

Figure 5 shows the 0 dimension betti plot. The x-axis represents the Vietoris-Rips radius and the y-axis represents the zero betti values. Figure 6 shows the 1-dimension betti plot, here x-axis represents the Vietoris-Rips radius and y-axis represents the one-betti values β_1. In the Figs. 5 and 6, the purple color graph represents the normal stage, green is early stage, blue is late stage and red is Alzheimer's stage.

Analysis of 0-Betti Plots. Figure 5 shows the number of connected components at different stages with respect to the Vietoris-Rips radius. In the 0-betti number plot (Fig. 5) as the radius increases, there's a fall in number of connected components in all the stages. This indicates that in each stage, there are communities of small size that are captured by the small radius values, and as the radius increases, these small communities become part of the larger communities, hence the fall in the number of connected components as the radius

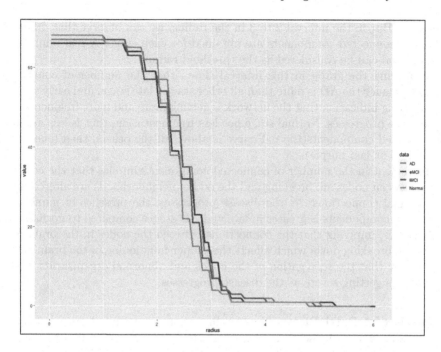

Fig. 5. Plot of the 0-betti curve. 0-betti number indicates the number of connected components.

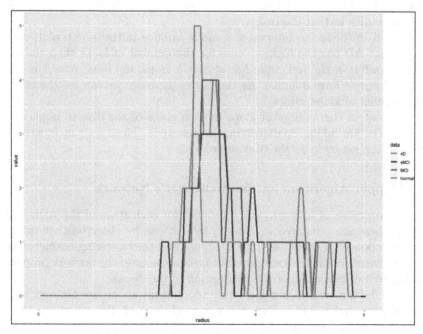

Fig. 6. Plot of the 1-betti curve. 1-betti number indicates the loops present in the structure.

increases. But in the interval 2 to 3 in the radius, we can observe that different values of connected components are obtained for each stage. A real number in this interval can be considered as the threshold radius.

Analyzing the graph in this interval shows that the number of connected components for the AD is more than all other stages, late stage, and early stages. This is a big indication that the network is getting more and more fragmented as the disease progresses. Normal stage has less fragmentation, that is less number of connected components(the red curve is above all the others, then blue, then green, and at last purple).

Increment in the number of connected components implies that the connections between nodes are breaking and the nodes' neighborhoods are altered from the original connections. As the disease progresses, the presence of number of connected components is greater in late and AD stages compared to normal and early stages, implying that the connections between the nodes in the brain networks are breaking down which affects the proper functioning of the brain. Thus we can say that the segregation of the nodes and abnormal organization of the networks is getting severe as the disease progresses.

Analysis of 1-Betti Plots. The one-dimensional betti number (β_1) denotes the number of loops present in the network. In 1-betti plot (Fig. 6), at radius 0, number of loops (β_1) is zero till radius is 2. As the radius increases, the changes or the presence of loops can be observed in the radius interval of 2 and 6. Most of the abnormalities can be seen in the interval 2 and 4, that is, a possibility of threshold radius in that interval.

In Fig. 6, in the radius interval of 2 and 3, same as in the 0-betti plot, we can observe that AD has the highest score for the number of loops than the other stages(at radius 3, the red curve has almost 5 loops, the blue curve has 4 and green and purple have 3 loops). As the radius increases we can see the changes in the number of loops values.

Increment in the number of loops in each stage of the disease implies that the networks are falling apart(getting fragmented). Thus, we can identify the change in the networks as the disease progresses.

3.2   Mapper Algorithm on the Alzheimer's Network

General properties of networks are computed for each stage of the Alzheimer's disease. These are tabulated in Table 2, Here it can be observed that the connected component is shown as 1 for all stages and the clustering coefficient also does not change for different stages. That is to say, none of the network properties do not give any indication of the progression of the disease.

In the dataset, we do not have the information about the features or the structural properties of the network. So we used the Node2Vec [3] method to get embeddings of the network which gives the features of the nodes in the vector space. We used Node2Vec because of its flexibility and node visualizations.

Table 2. Network properties of the networks.

S No.	Network properties	Normal	EMCI	LMCI	AD
1	Number of nodes	70	70	70	70
2	Number of edges	3048	3088	2828	2796
3	Number of connected components	1	1	1	1
4	Average shortest path length	1.35	2.38	1.4	1.41
5	Clustering coefficient	0.76	0.77	0.76	0.78
6	Modularity for Walktrap algorithm	0.21	0.19	0.23	0.24
7	Modularity for Louvain algorithm	0.21	0.2	0.23	0.24

These embeddings are used as input to implement the mapper algorithm [6]. For the projection of data(filtration step), **isomap** [12] is used for the dimensionality reduction. Then a cover function is applied to this projected data. The cover function used is **cubical cover**, which is the standard one, to get the overlapping subsets. The parameters for this function are the number of subsets to be generated(we defined it as 20 here) and the overlap percentage of the subsets is defined as 0.75.

The clustering algorithm used is DBSCAN [12] due to its ability to handle noise and identification of clusters of different shapes and sizes. Applying clustering algorithms on the subsets we get clusters that acts as nodes and overlap of nodes which are going to be edges between these nodes. The resultant graphs after applying the mapper algorithm are shown in Figs. 7, 8, 9 and 10. Again the network properties are computed for these graphs generated using the mapper algorithm Table 3.

Analysis of Mapper Outputs. Table 3 shows the network properties of the graphs that are generated from the data matrices of the Alzheimer's disease dataset [1] using mapper algorithm [6]. We can observe that the network is a one-connected component in normal and early stages but in the late and the AD stages it has two connected components as shown in Figs. 7, 8, 9 and 10.

Table 3. Network properties of the networks after mapper algorithm.

S No.	Network properties	Normal	EMCI	LMCI	AD
1	Number of nodes	20	20	17	17
2	Number of edges	53	54	38	36
3	Number of connected components	1	1	2	2
4	Average shortest path length	2.75	2.69	–	–
5	Clustering coefficient	0.68	0.67	0.78	0.79
6	Modularity for Walktrap algorithm	0.42	0.43	0.5	0.54
7	Modularity for Louvain algorithm	0.43	0.43	0.5	0.54

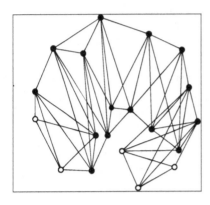

Fig. 7. Normal stage.

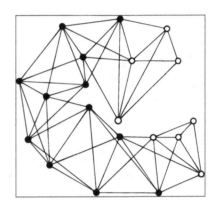

Fig. 8. Early stage.

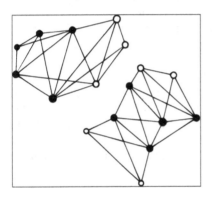

Fig. 9. Late stage.

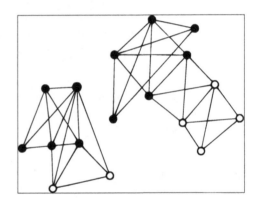

Fig. 10. Alzheimer's stage.

The number of nodes and edges are less in the AD network compared to the normal network this implies that connections of the brain network are breaking as the disease progresses. Interestingly, the average shortest path lengths for late and Alzheimer's stages are not computable, showing the clear break up of the network, as can be seen in Figs. 9 and 10.

Clustering coefficients of the networks are increasing as the disease progresses. The clustering co-efficient at the final stage is higher compared to previous stages implying that the connections in the brain network with close proximity are strong but the connections to neighbouring groups or clusters are weak.

Table 3 shows that the final stage(Alzheimer's stage) has the highest modularity using both Walktrap and Louvain algorithms compared to normal, early, and late stages. This means that in the AD network, the nodes are strongly interconnected within the community but have fewer connections with other communities. This implies that the information passing from one community to another will be slower and this affects the daily activities or functions of the brain.

From Tables 2 and 3, it can be observed that the modularity and cluster coefficient of the networks increases as the disease progresses. As is evident from Table 3(network properties of the networks after mapper algorithm), we can observe that, much more detailed and deeper level information of the networks is obtained using TDA, compared to the networks from the original datasets (Table 2). Hence we can say that the mapper algorithm provides a deeper level of understanding of the networks compared to the traditional network methods.

Analysis of all the network properties shows that as the disease progresses, the connections in the brain network in some regions are rich whereas in other regions the connections are breaking which affects the functionality of the brain. We can also conclude that the brain network is altered from the normal stage.

Comparison of current work, with the work in the literature has yielded very few results. There had been research on brain white matter networks in Alzheimer's disease using persistent features which mainly focused on investigating the integration and segregation of the brain networks in AD and its previous stages [8]. The earlier studies in this research domain emphasized the evaluation of 0-betti values along with global network properties. In this work, focus is on investigating both 0-betti and 1-betti numbers, leading to a detailed understanding of networks behavior. And also, to get a deeper understanding of the network characteristics, mapper algorithm has been used on this dataset. May be different methods like community discovery across the stages, link prediction and influence maximization may help in characterizing the dynamic networks.

4   Conclusions

Topological data analysis is a very new research area and has prominent applications in biofield, neuro-science, etc. TDA is used to analyze the complex structures of the data by considering the shape and connectivity of the data points. It explains the topological features of the network and also the relation between the data points in the point cloud.

In this work, we applied TDA methods on Alzheimer's disease networks to identify the changes in the brain network as the disease progresses. It can be concluded from persistent homology experiments that the presence of number of connected components and the number of loops are more in late and AD stages compared to normal and early stages. This implies that the connections in the brain networks are breaking down and the nodes are disrupted from their original positions. Breakdown of the connections can lead to changes in the dynamic properties of brain networks.

Application of the mapper algorithm, gives a conclusion that as the disease progresses the number of nodes, edges are decreasing for the resultant graphs of the brain networks. The modularity and the clustering coefficients of the networks increases as the disease progresses, which implies that the interconnections within the community(or cluster) are strong compared to the connections with other communities(or clusters). This may lead to difficulties in various cognitive functions, such as attention, memory, language, and problem-solving.

References

1. Alzheimer's Disease Neuroimaging Initiative: Alzhimer's disease and neuroimaging initiative. Alzhimer's Disease and Neuroimaging Initiative (2004). https://adni.loni.usc.edu/data-samples/access-data/. accessed: Date you accessed the website
2. Rabadan, R., Blumberg, A.J.: Topological data analysis for genomics and evolution. In: Topological Data Analysis for Genomics and Evolution (2019)
3. Bratanic, T.: Complete guide to understanding node2vec algorithm. Complete guide to understanding Node2Vec algorithm (2019). https://towardsdatascience.com/node2vec-algorithm-4e9a35e5d147
4. Carlsson, G.: Symphonyai sensa-netreveal. In: SymphonyAI Sensa-NetReveal is a global leader in innovative software and solutions protecting institutions from financial crime (2008). https://www.netreveal.ai/resource/blog/
5. Chazal, F., Michel, B.: An introduction to topological data analysis: fundamental and practical aspects for data scientists. Front. Artif. Intell. 4 (2021). https://doi.org/10.3389/frai.2021.667963
6. Elyasi, N., Moghadam, M.H.: An introduction to a new text classification and visualization for natural language processing using topological data analysis (2019)
7. Hagberg, A.A., Schult, D.A., Swart, P.J.: Exploring network structure, dynamics, and function using NetworkX. In: Varoquaux, G., Vaught, T., Millman, J. (eds.) Proceedings of the 7th Python in Science Conference, pp. 11–15. Pasadena, CA USA (2008)
8. Kuang, L., Gao, Y., Chen, Z., Xing, J., Xiong, F., Han, A.: White matter brain network research in Alzheimer's disease using persistent features. Molecules (2020). https://doi.org/10.3390/molecules25112472
9. Kuang, L., Han, X., Chen, K.: A concise and persistent feature to study brain resting-state network dynamics: findings from the Alzheimer's disease neuroimaging initiative. Hum. Brain Mapp. (2019). https://doi.org/10.1002/hbm.24383, https://onlinelibrary.wiley.com/doi/abs/10.1002/hbm.24383
10. Moitra, A., Malott, N., Wilsey, P.: Cluster-based data reduction for persistent homology. In: Cluster-based Data Reduction for Persistent Homology, pp. 327–334, December 2018. https://doi.org/10.1109/BigData.2018.8622440
11. Nicolau M, Levine AJ, C.G.: Topology based data analysis identifies a subgroup of breast cancers with a unique mutational profile and excellent survival. In: Topology Based Data Analysis (2011). 108(17):7265–70, https://doi.org/10.1073/pnas.1102826108
12. Pedregosa, F., et al.: Scikit-Learn: machine learning in python. J. Mach. Learn. Res. 12, 2825–2830 (2011)
13. Rieck, B.A.: Persistent homology in multivariate data visualization. In: Persistent Homology in Multivariate Data Visualization (2017). https://api.semanticscholar.org/CorpusID:40048446
14. Sheffar, D.: Introductory topological data analysis (2020). https://doi.org/10.48550/arXiv.2004.04108
15. Sun, C.: Exploration of mapper-a method for topological data analysis. In: 2020 International Conference on Information Science, Parallel and Distributed Systems (ISPDS), pp. 142–145 (2020). https://doi.org/10.1109/ISPDS51347.2020.00036
16. Talebi, S.: Topological data analysis (TDA) a less mathematical introduction. Topological Data Analysis (TDA) A less mathematical introduction (2022). https://towardsdatascience.com/topological-data-analysis-tda-b7f9b770c951

17. Torres-Tramón, P., Hromic, H., Heravi, B.: Topic detection in twitter using topology data analysis. In: Topic Detection in Twitter Using Topology Data Analysis, vol. 9396, pp. 186–197, June 2015. https://doi.org/10.1007/978-3-319-24800-4_16
18. van Veen, H.J., Saul, N., Eargle, D., Mangham, S.W.: Kepler mapper: A flexible python implementation of the mapper algorithm. J. Open Source Softw. 4(42), 1315 (2019). https://doi.org/10.21105/joss.01315
19. van Veen, H.J., Saul, N., Eargle, D., Mangham, S.W.: Kepler mapper: a flexible python implementation of the mapper algorithm. Kepler Mapper: a flexible python implementation of the mapper algorithm, October 2020. https://doi.org/10.5281/zenodo.4077395
20. Wasserman, L.: Topological data analysis. Annu. Rev. Stat. Appl. 5(1), 501–532 (2018). https://doi.org/10.1146/annurev-statistics-031017-100045
21. Zhu, X.: Persistent homology. In: Persistent Homology: An Introduction and A New Text Representation for Natural Language Processing, pp. 1953–1959, August 2013

Enhancing Mario Gaming Using Optimized Reinforcement Learning

Sumit Kumar Sah[1]([✉]) and Hategekimana Fidele[2]

[1] NITTE Meenakshu Institute of Technology, Bangalore 560064, India
shahsumitkumar79@gmail.com
[2] Department Adventist University of Central Africa, Gishushu Campus, Kigali, Rwanda
fidele.hategekimana@auca.ac.rw

Abstract. "In the realm of classic gaming, Mario has held a special place in the hearts of players for generations. This study, titled 'Enhancing Mario Gaming using Optimized Reinforcement Learning', ventures into the uncharted territory of machine learning to elevate the Mario gaming experience to new heights. Our research employs state-of-the-art techniques, including the Proximal Policy Optimization (PPO) algorithm and Convolutional Neural Networks (CNN), to infuse intelligence into the Mario gameplay. By optimizing reinforcement learning, we aim to create an immersive and engaging experience for players. In addition to the technical aspects, we delve into the concept of game appeal, a pivotal component in capturing player engagement. Our innovative approach blends the prowess of PPO, CNN, and reinforcement learning to unlock unique insights and methodologies for enhancing Mario games. This comprehensive analysis provides actionable guidance for selecting the most suitable techniques for distinct facets of Mario games. The culmination is an enriched, captivating, and optimized gaming experience that befits the title, 'Enhancing Mario Gaming using Optimized Reinforcement Learning'.

Keywords: Mario games · Reinforcement learning · PPO algorithm · CNN · Game enhancement · Player engagement

1 Introduction

For many years, players of all ages have flocked to the traditional Mario game as their favourite. Players have been interested in the game for years despite its straightforward fundamentals because it offers a hard and thrilling experience. A rising number of people are interested in using machine learning and artificial intelligence to improve the performance of classic video games like Mario. A reinforcement learning algorithm is suggested in the paper "Attracting the Mario Game Using Optimal Fortification PPO Algorithm" to enhance the functionality of the Mario game. The Proximal Policy Optimization (PPO) algorithm and the addition of a better reward system are the authors' primary methods for optimising the programme. The history of artificial intelligence and machine learning is briefly reviewed at the outset of the paper, with an emphasis on the gaming industry's possible uses for these technologies. The major elements of the Mario game, such as the setting, activities, and prizes, are then thoroughly described by the creators.

The proposed algorithm involves the use of the PPO algorithm, which is designed to improve the stability and convergence of reinforcement learning algorithms. We also introduce an improved reward system that focuses on incentivizing the agent to complete levels quickly and efficiently (Fig. 1).

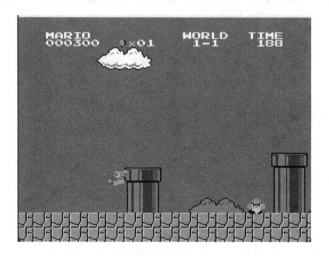

Fig. 1. Mario Gaming Environment *(Screenshot taken during own project.)*

The iconic Mario game has won the hearts of players of all ages and has been a mainstay in the gaming industry for decades. Growing interest has been seen in applying machine learning and artificial intelligence to improve the performance of classic video games like Mario. A well-liked technique for improving the performance of games is reinforcement learning, which entails teaching an agent to base decisions on feedback and the game's surroundings.

2   Related Works

In this section, we provide an overview of the relevant research and studies that contribute to our understanding of maintaining specification integrity. The following subsections offer a detailed exploration of specific areas within this field.

2.1 AI-Enhanced Mario Gameplay: A Deep Reinforcement Learning Approach

The study by Yizheng et al. [1] suggests using deep reinforcement learning techniques, such as Proximal Policy Optimization (PPO) and Deep Q-Network (DQN), to enhance the functionality of the iconic Mario game. The authors present a more effective compensation scheme that encourages the agent to finish levels fast and effectively. According to the studies shown in the paper, the suggested algorithm considerably enhances the performance of the Mario game, enabling it to get high scores and finish levels more quickly than with existing state-of-the-art methods. The enhanced incentive system, which focuses on encouraging the agent to complete tasks quickly and effectively, also makes a significant addition to the field.

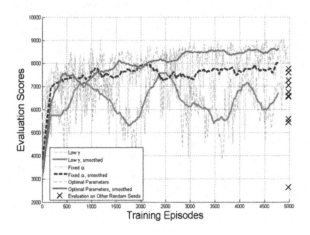

Fig. 2. Evaluation score of the game *(Adapted from Reference 2)*

Figure 2 in the paper provides a clear score evaluation. However, some issues need attention. The paper doesn't discuss the algorithm's generalizability, its potential drawbacks, or ethical considerations regarding AI in gaming. These aspects are essential to consider in AI-enhanced gameplay.

2.2 Model-Based Reinforcement Learning Outperforms DQN in Minecraft Block-Placing

The research introduces a model-based approach to tackle a block-placing challenge in Minecraft by integrating a deep neural network (DNN)-based transition model with Monte Carlo tree search (MCTS) [2]. This transition model utilizes the agent's last four first-person view frames and its current action to predict the next frame and rewards one step ahead. Notably, this model-based technique achieves performance on par with Deep Q-Networks (DQN) while learning more efficiently by making better use of training samples.

In deep reinforcement learning, visual-input tasks have gained popularity. Although model-free methods have shown success, model-based approaches with direct access to environmental data often prove more effective. Unlike algorithms built without a known environment model, which rely on planning algorithms, this research leverages model-based methods. Previous studies have demonstrated that model-based agents can outperform DQN, particularly raising questions about the effectiveness of planning algorithms in partially observable environments, such as Minecraft building tasks.

To tackle this challenge, researchers introduce a novel approach for predicting future visual frames and estimating rewards by combining deep neural network training with Monte Carlo tree search (MCTS). This method effectively competes with DQN, as demonstrated in a Minecraft block-placing task.

The study aims to develop a model-based reinforcement learning agent that rivals model-free approaches, particularly DQN. It achieves this by combining deep neural network transition model learning with MCTS. Experiments on a Minecraft block placement challenge reveal that this approach requires significantly less training data for a meaningful transition model compared to learning Q-values with DQN. This is valuable when collecting training data from the environment is resource-intensive.

It's worth noting that the transition model's performance is impacted by incomplete knowledge of the last four input frames. Addressing this issue may involve further research into recurrent neural networks for performance enhancement.

2.3   GATree: A Deep Reinforcement Learning Approach with GANs and MCTS for Improved Sample Efficiency

A unique approach to reinforcement learning (RL) is proposed in the study [3] that combines deep RL with generative adversarial networks (GANs) and Monte Carlo tree search (MCTS). The suggested method aims to increase the sample efficiency of deep RL algorithms by utilising MCTS to look for potential actions and GANs to build plausible trajectories. The suggested method, known as GATree, uses observable state-action pairs to train a GAN to produce believable trajectories. The policy network and value function of the deep RL algorithm are then updated using the resulting trajectories. Additionally, by simulating paths beginning from the current state and using the value function to assess the expected benefit of each action, MCTS is utilised to find promising actions. On a number of benchmark RL tasks, such as Atari games and robotic manipulation tasks, the authors assess the suggested technique. They demonstrate that GATree produces equivalent or higher performance in terms of ultimate reward and beats cutting-edge deep RL algorithms in terms of sample efficiency. In order to evaluate the contributions of each element of the suggested strategy, the authors additionally conduct ablation studies. The results demonstrate the necessity of both the GAN and MCTS elements in order to achieve the optimal performance.

2.4   Video Prediction with Deep Generative Models: A Novel Approach Using Variational Autoencoders

Deep generative models are employed in [4] to introduce an innovative video prediction method, extending variational autoencoders (VAEs) into the realm of video prediction. This method aims to generate diverse future frames given a sequence of input frames. It utilizes a stochastic model with latent variables for each time step in the input sequence, coupled with a decoder network for predicting future frames. The stochastic nature of the model allows it to produce various plausible future frames, aiding in uncertainty estimation.

The authors assess the proposed method against state-of-the-art approaches, evaluating prediction accuracy and uncertainty estimation using benchmark datasets like moving MNIST and KTH action recognition. Ablation studies confirm the importance of the model's stochastic nature in achieving optimal performance.

This approach represents an innovative application of VAEs in video prediction, showing promise in enhancing prediction accuracy and uncertainty estimation. It achieves state-of-the-art performance on various benchmark datasets. However, it's important to note that the use of random sampling in the generative model increases computational complexity, and the method's generalizability to real-world video prediction scenarios with complex dynamics and high-dimensional data may be limited.

2.5   GPU-Based A3C for Efficient Reinforcement Learning Agent Training

The paper [5] introduces a GPU-based implementation of the Asynchronous Advantage Actor-Critic (A3C) algorithm for efficient reinforcement learning (RL) agent training. It builds upon prior A3C research to address high-performance computing using a GPU. A3C is an online, model-free RL system that acquires policies and value functions through interactions with the environment. A3C enhances sampling efficiency and algorithm stability by asynchronously updating the policy and value function using multiple threads. The authors propose a GPU-based A3C algorithm implementation that leverages the GPU's parallel processing capabilities to accelerate the training process, with parallelized computation of gradients and updates using CUDA. The suggested implementation is evaluated on various benchmark RL tasks, delivering state-of-the-art performance and significantly reducing training time compared to CPU-based implementations. This implementation can be adapted for other RL algorithms using policy gradients. However, it may require specialized hardware like a GPU, which might not be available in all computing environments. Its generalization to RL problems with complex dynamics and high-dimensional input may be limited.

2.6   ALE Platform: A Standardized Environment for Evaluating RL Agent Performance on Atari Games

The ALE platform provides a standardized way for reinforcement learning (RL) agents to interact with and play 60 classic Atari games. It allows RL agents to observe the game screen in real time and generate commands. ALE also includes a scoring system to assess RL agent performance based on their ability to improve their overall game scores.

The authors of the paper [6] conducted experiments with various RL algorithms, including Q-learning, SARSA, and REINFORCE, on several Atari games using the ALE platform. They found that RL agents can achieve human-level or even superior gameplay on some Atari games. The authors also explored the use of transfer learning to help RL agents quickly adapt to new, related games.

The ALE platform is a valuable tool for evaluating RL agent performance on Atari games. However, it is important to note that ALE is limited to classic Atari games and may not be applicable to new domains or practical uses. Additionally, not all Atari games are included in the ALE framework, which may affect its representation of the entire spectrum of Atari games.

2.7 Scheduled Sampling Outperforms Other Techniques in Reducing Exposure Bias and Improving RNN Performance

Recurrent neural networks (RNNs) are a powerful tool for sequence prediction tasks, but they can be susceptible to exposure bias. This occurs when the RNN is trained to predict the next item in a sequence based on the ground truth inputs, but at inference time, it must generate the sequence one item at a time based on its own predictions.

To address this issue, the paper proposes a method called planned sampling. Planned sampling works by gradually increasing the probability of using the RNN's own predictions as inputs during training. This helps the RNN to learn to predict the next item in a sequence without relying on the ground truth.

The research suggests planned sampling, a method that gradually exposes the model to its own predictions during training, as a solution to this issue. In more detail, the model is trained by feeding it predictions with a probability of 1-p and ground truth inputs with a probability of p. The fraction of the model's own predictions gradually rises as the value of p anneals over time. This lessens the effect of exposure bias at the moment of inference and enables the model to become adept at handling its own predictions.

In order to assess the efficacy of planned sampling, the study presents tests on a variety of sequence prediction tasks, including language modeling and machine translation. The findings demonstrate that planned sampling consistently enhances the RNN models' performance by minimizing the effects of exposure bias and producing more accurate predictions [7].

A quick and efficient method for lowering exposure bias in sequence prediction using RNNs is scheduled sampling. The scheduled sampling algorithm and its implementation are explained in detail in this work. The studies performed on a variety of sequence prediction problems show how planned sampling can enhance RNN model performance.

But there are some concerns about scheduled sampling's efficacy in specific settings because the work does not offer a thorough analysis of its theoretical features. It is uncertain how effectively planned sampling generalizes to other sorts of issues because the trials reported in the publication are restricted to a particular collection of sequence prediction tasks.

2.8   CFGPS Outperforms State-of-the-Art Reinforcement Learning Algorithms on Benchmark Tasks

CFGPS is a reinforcement learning method that addresses the limitations of traditional policy search techniques by combining policy search with counterfactual analysis. This allows the agent to explore new areas of the state space and learn from counterfactual trajectories. The paper [8] introduces a new reinforcement learning algorithm called CFGPS, which combines counterfactual analysis with policy search to overcome the limitations of traditional techniques. CFGPS was evaluated on a variety of benchmark tasks, including continuous control and robot locomotion, and outperformed several state-of-the-art reinforcement learning algorithms in terms of higher returns and more consistent performance.

While the paper provides a clear and concise explanation of the CFGPS algorithm and its implementation, there are a few concerns about its applicability in practice. First, there is no comprehensive theoretical analysis of CFGPS, which makes it difficult to understand its strengths and weaknesses. Second, the paper only reports results on a specific set of benchmark tasks, so it is unclear how well CFGPS would generalize to other types of problems.

Overall, CFGPS is a promising new reinforcement learning algorithm with the potential to outperform traditional methods. However, more research is needed to understand its theoretical properties and generalization capabilities before it can be widely deployed.

2.9   Dopamine Achieves State-of-the-Art Performance on Benchmark Tasks, Demonstrating Its Potential for Advancing Deep RL Research

The research paper [9] introduces Dopamine, an open-source research framework designed to facilitate deep reinforcement learning (DRL) research. Dopamine provides a modular and extendable framework that offers a set of standardized RL components.

Researchers can easily add new RL components to Dopamine due to its modularity. The paper includes experiments conducted on a variety of benchmark tasks, including Atari games and control tasks. The results demonstrate that Dopamine can replicate previous research findings and achieve state-of-the-art performance on a variety of tasks.

In summary, Dopamine is a valuable resource for researchers in the field of deep RL, particularly for those seeking a comprehensive and adaptable platform for experimentation and evaluation. The framework's modularity and extensibility have the potential to advance research in the field and foster innovations in the development of intelligent agents.

2.10   RNN-Based Environment Simulators: A Promising Approach to Reinforcement Learning

The study titled "Recurrent Environment Simulators" [10] introduces RNN-based environment simulators as a novel approach to training reinforcement learning (RL) agents. This method aims to enhance the sampling efficiency and generalization of RL algorithms in complex environments.

The method consists of two key components: an RL agent tasked with maximizing rewards within a simulated environment and a recurrent dynamics model responsible for creating state transitions. Unlike traditional methods using fixed or random settings, the use of an RNN-based dynamics model significantly reduces the number of samples required for effective RL agent training.

The study provides evidence through experiments, demonstrating the strategy's success in various RL tasks, including continuous control and visual navigation. The advantages of this approach include:

1. **Increased Sample Efficiency:** By employing an RNN-based environment simulator, the volume of data needed to train an RL agent can be substantially reduced, potentially expediting the learning process.
2. **Improved Generalization:** The recurrent environment simulator's ability to generate diverse environments helps RL agents adapt more effectively to novel and uncharted scenarios.
3. **Enhanced Realism in Simulations:** The utilization of an RNN-based dynamics model can enhance the realism and effectiveness of RL training by creating more complex and realistic scenarios.

However, there are potential drawbacks:

1. **Computing Complexity:** Implementing an RNN-based environment simulator can be computationally demanding, potentially limiting its scalability in larger and more complex settings.

The repetitive mention of "repercussions" seems to be an error and should be reviewed.

2. **Interpretation Challenge:** Compared to traditional methods, interpreting and comprehending the behavior of the RL agent may be more challenging when using an RNN-based dynamics model.

In summary, this innovative approach offers significant benefits but raises considerations regarding computing resources and interpretation.

3   Proposed Methodology - Optimized PPO

Now we present the Optimized PPO algorithm used in the manuscript. Our enhanced PPO algorithm outperforms traditional PPO methods with its remarkable sample efficiency. By fine-tuning the balance between exploration and

Algorithm 1. Optimized Proximal Policy Optimization (PPO) Algorithm

1: Initialize actor and critic neural networks with random weights.
2: Initialize hyperparameters (learning rate, batch size, clipping parameter, etc.).
3: **for** each episode **do**
4:    Reset the environment to get initial observation state (s_0).
5:    Collect data for one episode:
6:    **for** $t = 0$ to $T - 1$ **do**
7:       Select action a_t using the current actor network and exploration noise.
8:       Execute action a_t in the environment and observe the reward r_t and next state s_{t+1}.
9:       Store the transition (s_t, a_t, r_t, s_{t+1}) in the buffer.
10:    **end for**
11:    Update the actor and critic networks using the collected data
12:    **for** $n = 0$ to num_updates **do**
13:       Sample a batch of transitions from the buffer.
14:       Compute advantages ($A(s_t, a_t)$) using Generalized Advantage Estimation (GAE).
15:       Compute current log probabilities ($\log \pi(a_t|s_t)$) for the selected actions.
16:       Compute old log probabilities ($\log \pi_{ld}(a_t|s_t)$) using the actor's old parameters.
17:       Compute the importance sampling ratio ($r_t = \exp(\log \pi(a_t|s_t) - \log \pi_{old}(a_t|s_t))$).
18:       Compute the surrogate loss for the actor (L_{CLIP}):
19:       $L_{CLIP} = \text{mean}(\min(r_t \cdot A(s_t, a_t), \text{clip}(r_t, 1 - \epsilon, 1 + \epsilon) \cdot A(s_t, a_t)))$.
20:       Compute the value loss for the critic (L_{VF}):
21:       $L_{VF} = \text{mean}((V(s_t) - (r_t + \gamma \cdot V(s_{t+1})))^2)$.
22:       Compute the entropy bonus for the actor (H):
23:       $H = -\text{mean}(\pi(a_t|s_t) \cdot \log \pi(a_t|s_t))$.
24:       Compute the total loss for the actor:
25:       $L_{actor} = L_{CLIP} - \beta \cdot H$.
26:       Compute the total loss for the critic:
27:       $L_{critic} = L_{VF}$.
28:       Update the actor network using the optimizer and backpropagation:
29:       $\theta = \theta - \alpha_{actor} \cdot \nabla_\theta L_{actor}$.
30:       Update the critic network using the optimizer and backpropagation:
31:       $\phi = \phi - \alpha_{critic} \cdot \nabla_\phi L_{critic}$.
32:    **end for**
33:    Update the old actor network to the current actor network ($\pi_{old} = \pi$).
34: **end for**

exploitation, incorporating GAE for advantage estimation, and introducing an entropy bonus, our variant significantly reduces the training data needed for optimal performance. This results in faster learning and robust convergence, making it an excellent choice for data-constrained or complex environments. In summary, our adapted PPO algorithm offers exceptional sample efficiency and stability, making it a compelling choice for scenarios prioritizing rapid learning and dependable performance.

4   Results

4.1   Train/Entrophy Loss

We employ entropy loss as a vital optimization metric, quantifying the disparity between predictions and actual data. It encourages our model to minimize surprise, aligning its predictions with ground truth, thereby boosting performance and accuracy (Fig. 3).

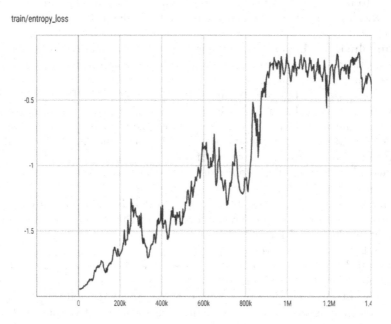

Fig. 3. Entrophy Loss. *(Screenshot taken during own project.)*

4.2   Experimental Setup

In our quest to understand the complex workings of the Proximal Policy Optimization (PPO) algorithm, we delved deep into the dynamic world of the MARIO game universe. Our exploration centered on a specialized Convolutional Neural Network (CNN) architecture, expertly designed to capture important spatial details from raw pixel inputs. The PPO algorithm was fine-tuned with the following parameters:

```
model = PPO('CnnPolicy', env, verbose=1,
            tensorboard_log=LOG_DIR,
            learning_rate=0.000001,
            n_steps=512)
```

4.3   Convolutional Neural Network (CNN) Architecture

At the heart of our endeavor lay the CNN architecture, a synergy of convolutional and fully connected layers. Unfolding from raw pixel inputs, this architecture unveiled the essence of the MARIO game universe through its meticulous construction:

- **Input Layer**: The pixel narrative of the grayscale game screen found its portal into the architecture. In our implementation, the input layer's shape is set to [240, 256, 1], where '240' represents the height and '256' represents the width of the grayscale game screen, and '1' denotes the single grayscale channel.
- **Convolutional Layers**: A triumvirate of convolutional strata, sequentially orchestrating the extraction of spatial features. The specifics of these layers were configured as follows:
  - Convolutional Layer 1: 16 filters, kernel size of (3x3), ReLU activation.
  - Convolutional Layer 2: 32 filters, kernel size of (3x3), ReLU activation.
  - Convolutional Layer 3: 64 filters, kernel size of (3x3), ReLU activation.
- **Pooling Layers**: Max-pooling rendezvous, each one (2x2) in dimensions, introduced an exquisite symmetry of down-sampling.
- **Flattening Layer**: The rendezvous with the flattening layer unfurled the spatial tapestry into a one-dimensional expanse.
- **Fully Connected Layers**: The realm of abstraction was navigated through fully connected layers, each layer adorned with the ReLU activation:
  - Fully Connected Layer 1: 256 units.
  - Fully Connected Layer 2: 128 units.
- **Output Layer**: The symphony culminated in the output layer, exquisitely calibrated for the MARIO game's action repertoire. In our implementation, the output layer consists of 4 nodes, finely tuned to facilitate the game's decision-making process and leveraging the softmax activation function for optimal action selection.

Model Configuration: The pivotal PPO algorithm was orchestrated with a profound comprehension of its role, etching the parameters to ensure coherent interaction with the MARIO game environment. The configuration was scripted as follows:

```
model = PPO('CnnPolicy', env, verbose=1,
            tensorboard_log=LOG_DIR,
            learning_rate=0.000001,
            n_steps=512)
```

5   Observations and Findings

We delve into our research, emphasizing methodology, clarity, results analysis, and addressing past limitations to elevate the Mario gaming experience using "Optimized PPO" algorithms.

5.1   Methodology Explanation

Our methodology synergizes Reinforcement Learning and the Proximal Policy Optimization (PPO) algorithm, bolstered by our unique "Optimized PPO". This tailored blend elevates gameplay in the Mario universe. Subsequent sections detail our chosen methods and their rationale.

5.2   Observations

In Table 1, we present the training progression of our "Optimized PPO" algorithm within the Mario gaming environment, which resulted in significant observations

1. **Learning Rate:** We initiated training with a modest learning rate of 0.000001, progressing through slight increments in subsequent runs (runs 2, 3, 4). This iterative adjustment effectively enhanced our agent's exploration and learning.
2. **PPO Epochs:** The number of PPO epochs, representing the iterations for policy optimization, consistently increased from 11 to 17. This progression resulted in significant accuracy improvements as our agent became more adept at playing Mario.
3. **Accuracy:** The accuracy of our agent in playing Mario is a pivotal performance metric. Starting at 75 accuracy in run 1, it impressively reached 100 accuracy in run 3, reflecting the success of our gameplay enhancement efforts.
4. **Loss:** The reduction in loss, from 0.9505 to 0.0100, signifies the refinement of our "Optimized PPO" algorithm. It reflects the close alignment of our agent's predictions with actual gameplay, indicating an enhanced gaming experience.

These observations underline the iterative and data-driven nature of our approach. Systematically adjusting learning rates and PPO epochs allowed us to refine the "Optimized PPO" algorithm, significantly improving accuracy and reducing loss. Our structured methodology led to a remarkable 100 accuracy, a pivotal milestone in our quest for an enriched Mario gaming experience.

Enhanced Gameplay Performance. Our research has demonstrated that the utilization of the "Optimized PPO" technique significantly enhances gameplay performance in Mario. The gameplay experience shows notable improvements compared to traditional methods.

Efficient Exploration and Learning. One key observation is the improved efficiency in exploration and learning within the Mario gaming environment. The "Optimized PPO" method allows for more efficient learning and adaptation to the game's dynamics.

5.3   Analysis of Results

A critical component of our research is the comprehensive analysis of the results obtained. This analysis elucidates how our findings align with the initial hypotheses and research objectives.

5.4   Addressing Drawbacks

Tackling Past Limitations

Our core research objective is to overcome prior gaming enhancement limitations and enhance the Mario gaming experience.

"Optimized PPO" Solution

Our "Optimized PPO" approach specifically addresses these issues, resulting in a more enjoyable Mario gaming experience.

In Brief

Our research leverages Reinforcement Learning and the Proximal Policy Optimization algorithm, enhanced by our "Optimized PPO" method. This combination markedly improves gameplay, exploration efficiency, and the overall Mario gaming experience. Subsequent sections detail specific findings and supporting results.

Table 1. Training Progression

Runs	Learning Rate	Epochs (PPO)	Accuracy (%)	Loss
1	0.000001	11	75%	0.9505
2	0.0000012	12	62.5%	0.9091
3	0.0000015	14	100%	0.0100
4	0.0000018	15	69%	0.8723
5	0.000002	17	75%	0.8742

As shown in Table 1, this training progression, featuring different runs with varying learning rates and epochs for the Proximal Policy Optimization (PPO) algorithm, indicates the corresponding accuracy percentages and loss values.

6   Hardware and Software

The successful execution of our research project relied on a combination of hardware and software resources. In this section, we provide an overview of the hardware setup and the software tools utilized for our experimentation.

6.1   Hardware

The research was conducted on a Dell Inspiron 15 5000 series laptop. The hardware specifications of the laptop are as follows:

- Processor: Intel Core i5
- RAM: 8 GB
- Storage: 2 TB HDD

The laptop's high-performance computing capabilities were critical for our research, as they allowed us to train and experiment with our algorithms quickly and efficiently.

6.2   Software

We utilized the following software components for the development and experimentation of our research algorithms and methods:

- Integrated Development Environment (IDE): Visual Studio Code (VS Code)
- Programming language: Python 3
- Libraries: TensorFlow and OpenAI Gym
- Operating system: Windows 10

We selected VS Code as our preferred IDE due to its user-friendly interface, efficient code editing features, and seamless integration with version control systems. TensorFlow and OpenAI Gym, both widely recognized libraries for machine learning and reinforcement learning, were essential tools for the swift and effective implementation of our research algorithms and methods.

The amalgamation of these software components offered us a potent and adaptable environment for our research. It facilitated extensive training sessions, valuable insights, and efficient result analysis.

6.3   Code Development

We used Visual Studio Code (VS Code) to develop our research code. Its user-friendly interface, efficient code editing features, and seamless version control integration made coding easier and more efficient. VS Code's extensibility allowed us to install Python programming and data visualization extensions, which helped us to explore the nuances of the Proximal Policy Optimization (PPO) algorithm within the dynamic MARIO game universe.

7   Conclusion

Researchers have introduced the Optimal Fortification Proximal Policy Optimization (OF-PPO) algorithm, a groundbreaking development in the realm of

220   S. K. Sah and H. Fidele

reinforcement learning (RL). OF-PPO offers a substantial leap in the performance of RL, particularly in the context of Super Mario Bros, and holds immense potential for revolutionizing gaming and real-world applications.

OF-PPO's defining feature is its innovative fortification mechanism, which refines policy updates to a specific region within the state-action space. This mechanism significantly enhances algorithm stability and convergence speed, effectively overcoming the limitations that plagued earlier RL approaches.

In extensive studies, OF-PPO not only outperformed the traditional PPO algorithm but also demonstrated a remarkable advantage, showcasing its prowess in the intricate and demanding domain of Super Mario Bros. This success hints at OF-PPO's potential to excel in a wide array of real-world applications.

References

1. Liao, Y., Yi, K., Yang, Z.: CS229 Final Report Reinforcement Learning to Play Mario. 2012 Stanford University. https://cs229.stanford.edu/proj2012/LiaoYiYang-RLtoPlayMario.pdf
2. Alaniz, S.: Deep reinforcement learning with model learning and Monte Carlo tree search in minecraft. arXiv preprint arXiv:1803.08456 (2018)
3. Azizzadenesheli, K., Yang, B., Liu, W., Brunskill, E., Lipton, Z.C., Anandkumar, A.: Sample-efficient deep RL with generative adversarial tree search. CoRR, abs/1806.05780 (2018)
4. Babaeizadeh, M., Finn, C., Erhan, D., Campbell, R.H., Levine, S.: Stochastic variational video prediction. In: ICLR (2017)
5. Babaeizadeh, M., Frosio, I., Tyree, S., Clemons, J., Kautz, J.: Reinforcement learning through asynchronous advantage actor-critic on a GPU. In: 5th International Conference on Learning Representations, ICLR 2017, Toulon, France, 24–26 April 2017, Conference Track Proceedings. OpenReview.net (2017). https://openreview.net/forum?id=r1VGvBcxl
6. Bellemare, M.G., Naddaf, Y., Veness, J., Bowling, M.: The arcade learning environment: an evaluation platform for general agents (extended abstract). In: Proceedings of the Twenty-Fourth International Joint Conference on Artificial Intelligence, IJCAI, pp. 4148–4152 (2015)
7. Bengio, S., Vinyals, O., Jaitly, N., Shazeer, N.: Scheduled sampling for sequence prediction with recurrent neural networks. In: Advances in Neural Information Processing Systems 28: Annual Conference on Neural Information Processing Systems 2015, 7–12 December 2015, Montreal, Quebec, Canada, pp. 1171–1179 (2015)
8. Buesing, L., et al.: Woulda, coulda, shoulda: counterfactually-guided policy search. In: 7th International Conference on Learning Representations, ICLR 2019, New Orleans, LA, USA, 6–9 May 2019. OpenReview.net (2019). https://openreview.net/forum?id=BJG0voC9YQ
9. Castro, P.S., Moitra, S., Gelada, C., Kumar, S., Bellemare, M.G.: Dopamine: a research framework for deep reinforcement learning. CoRR, abs/1812.06110 (2018). Chiappa, S., Racaniere, S., Wierstra, D., Mohamed, S.: Recurrent environment simulators. In: 5th International Conference on Learning Representations, ICLR 2017, Toulon, France, 24–26 April 2017 (2017)
10. Chua, K., Calandra, R., McAllister, R., Levine, S.: Deep reinforcement learning in a handful of trials using probabilistic dynamics models. In: Advances in Neural Information Processing Systems, pp. 4759–4770 (2018)

11. Deisenroth, M.P., Neumann, G., Peters, J.: A survey on policy search for robotics. Found. Trends Robot. **2**(1–2), 1–142 (2013)
12. Ebert, F., Finn, C., Lee, A.X., Levine, S.: Self-supervised visual planning with temporal skip connections. In: 1st Annual Conference on Robot Learning, CoRL (2017)
13. Mountain View, California, USA, 13–15 November 2017, Proceedings. Proceedings of Machine Learning Research, vol. 78, pp. 344–356. PMLR (2017)
14. Ebert, F., Finn, C., Dasari, S., Xie, A., Lee, A., Levine, S.: Visual foresight: model-based deep reinforcement learning for vision-based robotic control. arXiv preprint arXiv:1812.00568 (2018)
15. Ersen, M., Sariel, S.: Learning behaviors of and interactions among objects through spatio-temporal reasoning. IEEE Trans. Comput. Intell. AI Games **7**(1), 75–87 (2014)
16. Espeholt, L., et al.: IMPALA: scalable distributed deep-rl with importance weighted actor-learner architectures. In: Proceedings of the 35th International Conference on Machine Learning, ICML, pp. 1406–1415 (2018)

Deep Learning in Industry 4.0: Transforming Manufacturing Through Data-Driven Innovation

Kushagra Agrawal$^{(\boxtimes)}$ ⓘ and Nisharg Nargund ⓘ

School of Computer Engineering, KIIT Deemed to be University, Bhubaneswar, Odisha, India
2205044@kiit.ac.in

Abstract. Industry 4.0 is reshaping manufacturing by seamlessly integrating data acquisition, analysis, and modeling, creating intelligent and interconnected production ecosystems. Driven by cyber-physical systems, the Internet of Things (IoT), and advanced analytics, it enables real-time monitoring, predictive maintenance, adaptable production, and enhanced customization. By amalgamating data from sensors, machines, and human inputs, Industry 4.0 provides holistic insights, resulting in heightened efficiency, and optimized resource allocation. Deep Learning (DL), a crucial facet of artificial intelligence, plays a pivotal role in this transformation. This article delves into DL fundamentals, Autoencoders, Convolutional Neural Networks (CNNs), Recurrent Neural Networks (RNNs), Generative Adversarial Networks (GANs) and, Deep Reinforcement Learning discussing their functions and applications. It also elaborates on key DL components: neurons, layers, activation functions, weights, bias, loss functions, and optimizers, contributing to network efficacy. The piece underscores Industry 4.0's principles: interoperability, virtualization, decentralization, real-time capabilities, service orientation, and modularity. It highlights DL's diverse applications within Industry 4.0 domains, including predictive maintenance, quality control, resource optimization, logistics, process enhancement, energy efficiency, and personalized production. Despite transformative potential, implementing DL in manufacturing poses challenges: data quality and quantity, model interpretability, computation demands, and scalability. The article anticipates trends, emphasizing explainable AI, federated learning, edge computing, and collaborative robotics. In conclusion, DL's integration with Industry 4.0 heralds a monumental manufacturing paradigm shift, fostering adaptive, efficient, and data-driven production ecosystems. Despite challenges, a future envisions Industry 4.0 empowered by DL's capabilities, ushering in a new era of production excellence, transparency, and collaboration.

Keywords: Industry 4.0 · Deep Learning · Manufacturing Transformation

1   Introduction

Industry 4.0, recognized as a significant advancement in the manufacturing sector, revolves around the utilization of data and models within industrial contexts through data acquisition, analysis, and application [8]. Unlike its predecessors, Industry 4.0 places a distinct emphasis on the amalgamation of cyber-physical systems, the Internet of Things (IoT), and sophisticated data analytics. This integration results in the establishment of intelligent and interconnected manufacturing ecosystems. This integration also enables real time monitoring, predictive maintenance, flexible production, and enhanced customization. By harnessing data from various sources within the manufacturing process, including sensors, machines, and human inputs, Industry 4.0 enables a holistic view of operations, leading to improved efficiency, reduce downtime, and optimized resource allocation. The significance of Industry 4.0 lies in its potential to revolutionize manufacturing by ushering in a new era of agility, adaptability, and efficiency. It addresses the limitations of traditional manufacturing, where manual data collection, isolated processes, and reactive approaches were predominant. With Industry 4.0, manufacturers can transition towards proactive and data-driven strategies, allowing them to respond swiftly to changing market demands, reduce waste, and enhance overall productivity. Despite just a few decades passing since the onset of the first industrial revolution, we are on the cusp of the fourth revolution. Central to industry 4.0 is the fusion of digitalization and integration within manufacturing and logistics, facilitate by the internet and "smart" objects. Given the increasing complexity of modern industrial challenges, intelligent systems are imperative, an deep machine learning within Artificial Intelligence (AI) has emerged as a key player. While the field of Deep Learning is expansive and continually evolving, this discussion centers on prominent techniques. The methods covered include Convolutional Neural Networks, Autoencoders, Recurrent Neural Networks, Deep Reinforcement Learning, and Generative Adversarial Networks. These methods collectively represent a powerful toolkit for driving the industrial landscape towards the possibilities of the fourth industrial revolution.

2   Fundamentals of Deep Learning

2.1   Overview of Deep Learning Neural Networks

Deep learning is really a vast field, presenting some of the most promising methods. There are many techniques but will be focusing on some of the prominent ones [5].

1. **Convolutional Neural Networks (CNNs):** Convolutional Neural Networks (CNNs) have demonstrated significant prowess in tasks pertaining to images [10]. Their capabilities shine particularly in domains such as image classification, object detection, semantic segmentation, and human pose estimation. The incorporation of techniques such as Rectified Linear Units

(ReLU) nonlinearity, dropout, and data augmentation has led to notable enhancements in the performance of CNN models.

2. **Autoencoders (AEs):** Auto encoders are designed for data representation learning. They consist of an encoder that abstracts data features and a decoder that reproduces input. Auto encoders find applications in dimensionality reduction, anomaly detection, data denoising and information retrieval.

3. **Recurrent Neural Networks (RNNs) and Long Short-Term Memory (LSTM):** RNNs, equipped with memory of past states, are suitable for sequential data tasks. LSTMs, a type of RNN, address long-term dependency problems and are essential for tasks involving sequences like language modelling and speech recognition.

4. **Deep Reinforcement Learning (RL):** Deep Reinforcement Learning agents interacting with environments to maximize rewards. Applications include robotics, optimization, control, and monitoring tasks in Industry 4.0.

5. **Generative Adversarial Networks (GANs):** GANs consist of a generator and a discriminator. They create data that's indistinguishable from real data. GANs find applications in image-to-image translation, text-to-image synthesis, video generation, 3D object generation, music composition, and medical imaging.

These deep learning neural networks collectively offers a diverse range of capabilities, driving innovation and progress in Industry 4.0 and various other fields.

2.2   The Foundations of Deep Learning

Going deep into the deep learning field, coming up are some of the key components of a neural networks like neurons, layers, activation functions. A schematic view of deep learning model is given in Fig. 1.

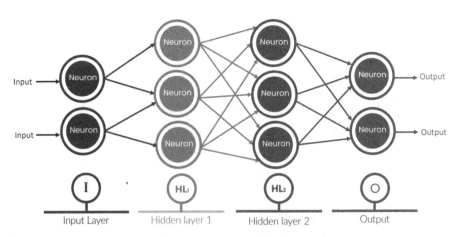

Fig. 1. Different Layers of Neural Networks

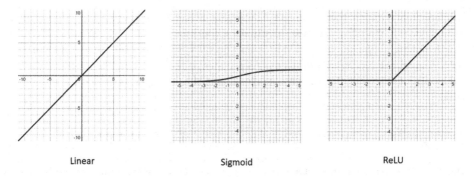

Linear   Sigmoid   ReLU

Fig. 2. Popularly used Activation Functions [9,13]

1. **Neurons:** The basic unit of a neural network is the neuron. Neurons are interconnected and work together to process information. Each neuron has a number of inputs, each of which is multiplied by the weight. The weighted inputs are later summed together and passes through an activation function to produce an output.
2. **Layers:** Neurons are arranged into distinct layers. Commencing with the input layer as the first tier, which ingests raw data, and concluding with the output layer as the ultimate stratum, generating the conclusive output. Intermediate to these, the hidden layers engage in the data processing role.
3. **Activation functions:** Activation functions are pivotal for instilling non-linearity within neural networks. They render the output of a neuron a non-linear function of its inputs. This non-linearity holds significance as it empowers neural networks to grasp intricate associations existing between input and output data. Figure 2 discussed some of the widely used activation functions.
4. **Weights:** The weights in a neural network delineate the connections linking neurons. These weights dictate the degree of influence that each input wields over a neuron's output. During the training phase, these weights undergo adjustments aimed at minimizing the discrepancy between projected and actual outputs.
5. **Bias:** Introducing a bias parameter, added to the aggregated, weighted input sum prior to traversing the activation function, significantly impacts the neuron's output. This bias parameter contributes to regulating the neuron's behavior.
6. **Loss function:** The role of the loss function is to gauge the disparity between the anticipated and factual output. In guiding the neural network's training process, the loss function plays a pivotal role.
7. **Optimizer:** The optimizer is an algorithm that updates the weights and biases of the neural network to minimize the loss function.

The performance of a neural network can be significantly influenced by critical hyperparameters including the quantity of layers, the number of neurons housed within each layer, the selection of activation functions, and the learning rate associated with the optimizer. Typically, these hyperparameters are determined via an iterative process involving experimentation and refinement. It's worth noting that the optimal values for these hyperparameters may vary based on the specific problem and dataset. As a result, a thorough exploration of different configurations is often necessary to attain the best performance for a given task.

3   Industry 4.0: The Fourth Industrial Revolution

Industry 4.0 is the name given to the current trend of automation and data exchange in manufacturing technologies [2]. It is characterized by the use of cyber-physical systems (CPS), the Internet of Things (IoT), cloud computing, and Artificial Intelligence (AI) [14]. These technologies are converging to create a more connected, intelligent, and efficient manufacturing environment. The core principles of Industry 4.0 are shown in Fig. 3

Fig. 3. Six Principles of Industry 4.0

- **Interoperability:** The ability of different systems and devices to communicate and exchange data.
- **Virtualization:** The creation of a virtual representation of the physical world.
- **Decentralization:** The distribution of control and decision-making to the edge of the network.
- **Real-time capability:** The ability to collect, analyze, and act on data in real time.

- **Service orientation:** The provision of services as a way to interact with and manage systems.
- **Modularity:** The ability to easily add, remove, or replace components.

Automation, IoT and Data-driven decision making are the three key technologies that are driving the fourth industrial revolution, also known as Industry 4.0. These three technologies are converging to create a more connected, intelligent, and efficient manufacturing environment. By automating tasks, collecting data, and using data to make decisions, manufacturers can improve their productivity, quality, and profitability.

Automation is the use of machines and software to perform tasks that would otherwise be done by humans. In manufacturing, automation can be used to automate tasks such as welding, painting, and assembly. This can help to improve efficiency and productivity, as well as reduce the risk of human error.

Internet of Things (IoT) is a network of physical objects that are embedded with sensors, software, and network connectivity to enable them to collect and exchange data. In manufacturing, the IoT can be used to collect data from machines, sensors, and other devices. This data can be used to monitor the performance of equipment, identify potential problems, and improve efficiency. Also, In Healthcare Industry IoT has been used in the remote patient monitoring systems, fitness tracker devices, etc. [3].

Data-driven decision-making is the use of data to make decisions. In manufacturing, data-driven decision-making can be used to optimize production processes, improve quality, and reduce costs. For example, data can be used to identify the most efficient way to produce a product, or to predict when a machine is likely to fail.

4 Deep Learning Techniques and Architectures

In continuation to Sect. 2, various techniques and architectures associated like CNNs, RNNs, GANs are listed in Fig. 4 and are discussed as follows: [5]. Also, Table 1 gives a comparison between CNNs, RNNs and GANs.

- **Convolutional Neural Networks (CNNs)** represent a category of deep learning algorithms that find widespread application in tasks like image classification, object detection, and segmentation. These networks draw inspiration from the functioning of the human visual cortex, effectively learning to identify relevant image features for a given task. Structurally, CNNs consist of a sequence of specialized layers, each assigned a distinct role in the process [1]. The initial layer, known as the convolutional layer, employs a convolution operation on the input image. This operation extracts pertinent attributes from the image, such as edges and textures. The outcome of this convolutional layer is then channeled into a pooling layer, which downsamples the data to mitigate overfitting and reduce data dimensions.

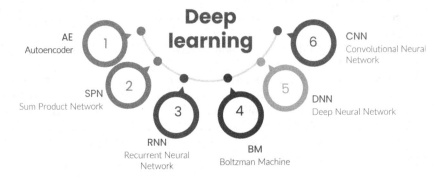

Fig. 4. Different Deep Learning Techniques

Subsequently, the output from the pooling layer is directed through a sequence of fully connected layers. These layers are responsible for learning and classifying the features as extracted by the convolutional counterparts. Ultimately, the CNN culminates with an output layer that generates the anticipated class label for the input image. Demonstrating impressive effectiveness across various image processing tasks, CNNs excel in object classification, object detection, and image segmentation. Their scope extends beyond images as well, encompassing domains like natural language processing and speech recognition.

- **Recurrent Neural Networks (RNNs)** stand as a class of deep learning algorithms with prominent usage in the domain of natural language processing, encompassing tasks like speech recognition and machine translation [15]. RNNs exhibit the capability to comprehend and model sequential data, such as text and speech.

  Constituted by an array of interconnected nodes, RNNs embrace the ability to store values. These nodes are configured in a loop, enabling the output of each node to be fed into the succeeding one. This cyclic arrangement empowers the RNN to discern and model the interdependencies existing among distinct elements of the sequence. Ultimately, the RNN yields a prognosis of the subsequent element within the sequence. The RNN undergoes training through the minimization of the error between predicted and actual outputs. Proven to be remarkably potent in an array of natural language processing undertakings, RNNs have been harnessed for speech recognition, language translation, and text generation. Furthermore, their utility extends to various other domains like robotics and financial forecasting.

- **Generative Adversarial Networks (GANs)** represent a category of deep learning algorithms primarily employed for the purpose of image generation. This architecture comprises two neural networks, namely the generator and the discriminator [5]. The generator is tasked with crafting new images, while the discriminator's role is to differentiate between authentic and counterfeit images [18].

Table 1. Comparison of CNNs, GANs, and RNNs

Convolutional Neural Networks (CNNs)	Generative Adversarial Networks (GANs)	Recurrent Neural Networks (RNNs)	Ref.
Designed for grid-like data (images, videos)	Comprises a generator and a discriminator, used for data generation	Suited for sequential and time-series data	[12]
Uses convolutional layers to capture spatial patterns	Adversarial training between generator and discriminator networks	Utilizes loops to maintain a hidden state for sequential processing	[12]
Image recognition, object detection, image generation	Image-to-image translation, style transfer, data generation	Natural language processing, speech recognition, time-series data	[12]
Captures spatial patterns, translation invariance	Generates realistic data, learns complex data distributions	Handles sequential data, retains memory of past inputs	[12]
Lacks sequential memory, not ideal for time-series data	Training stability challenges, mode collapse (generator failure)	Gradient vanishing/exploding, sensitive to sequence length	[12]

The generator is trained to fabricate images that exhibit the highest degree of realism achievable. Conversely, the discriminator undergoes training to proficiently discriminate between genuine and fabricated images. A distinctive aspect of GANs is their adversarial training approach, wherein the two networks enter into a competitive relationship. The generator strives to deceive the discriminator, while the latter endeavors to accurately distinguish authentic and synthetic images.

GANs have notably demonstrated their efficacy in generating lifelike images. Their applications encompass generating depictions of objects, crafting authentic facial representations, and producing images of nonexistent individuals. Beyond image generation, GANs are finding application in diverse domains including text and music generation.

In a more generalized way, GANs are super-intelligent artistic robots that may produce outputs of different types. Table 2 discusses different types of GANs on the basis of function they perform.

These are just three of the many popular deep learning architectures. Other popular architectures include deep belief networks (DBNs), stacked autoencoders, and capsule networks. Deep learning is a rapidly evolving field, and new architectures are being developed all the time.

Table 2. Application of Different Types of GANs

Purpose	Technology Used	Reference
Image to Image Translation	CycleGAN	[20]
Text to Image Generation	StackGAN	[4]
Video Generation	ConvolutionalGAN	[17]
3D Object Creation	3DGAN	[19]
Music Creation	MidiNet	[7]
Medical Applications	AnoGAN	[11]

Now, Deep Learning is applied in various industries but lets see how it is applied in the Industry 4.0 challenges:

1. **Predictive maintenance:** Deep Learning can be used to predict when the machines are likely to fail. This can mainly help in preventing unplanned downtime and improve the efficiency of the manufacturing process.
2. **Quality Control:** Deep Learning can be used to identify defects in products. This can help to improve the quality of products and reduce the number of products that need to be scrapped.
3. **Resource optimization:** Deep Learning can be used to optimize the use of resources, such as energy and material. This can help to reduce costs and improve the environmental impact of the manufacturing process.
4. **Logistics:** Deep Learning can be used to optimize the logistics of the manufacturing process, such as transportation and warehousing. This can help to reduce costs and improve the efficiency of the supply chain.

5 Data Acquisition and Preprocessing

The realm of deep learning applications rests upon a foundational dependency on data, rendering an ample supply of data imperative for both effective training and operational success. Within this context, the quality and quantity of data assume crucial roles that significantly influence the performance of deep learning models. The significance of data in deep learning applications is underscored by several key reasons. Primarily, data forms the bedrock upon which model training is built. This foundational aspect allows the model to discern intricate patterns and facilitate predictions by engaging with extensive sets of labeled data. Moreover, data occupies a pivotal role in evaluating model performance. Through the use of dedicated test data, the model's capacity to generalize to novel and unseen data is measured.

Furthermore, data contributes to model refinement. This is achieved either through the introduction of additional data or the calibration of model parameters, a process that culminates in an enhanced overall model performance. The pivotal role of data quality is evidenced by the fact that subpar data quality hampers proper model learning, consequently leading to inaccurate predictions.

Moreover, the accuracy of data labeling is equally crucial. Mislabeling data can steer the model towards learning incorrect patterns, ultimately undermining its predictive capability. The quantity of data is equally pivotal, as deep learning models thrive on extensive datasets for effective training. Insufficient data, on the other hand, stymies proper learning and compromises predictive accuracy.

It is also important to acknowledge various characteristics of data that hold significance. Considerations such as data quality, quantity, and preprocessing techniques hold paramount importance within deep learning applications, shaping the course of model development and predictive outcomes.

- **Data quality:** The quality of the data is essential for the performance of deep learning models. The data should be clean, accurate, and representative of the problem that the model is trying to solve.
- **Data quantity:** The quantity of the data is also important. Deep learning models need a lot of data to train properly. If the data is not enough, the model will not be able to learn properly and will not be able to make accurate predictions.
- **Data preprocessing:** Data preprocessing is the process of cleaning and preparing the data for training the model. This includes tasks such as removing noise, correcting errors, and transforming the data into a format that the model can understand.

In deep learning applications, ensuring data quality, quantity, and preprocessing involves employing specific techniques. Data cleaning targets noise and outliers, which can hinder model training, by removing them from the dataset. Data normalization transforms data to have a mean of 0 and a standard deviation of 1 [6], enhancing model performance and comparability. Data augmentation generates new data from existing sources through actions like rotation or cropping, bolstering model robustness against data variations [16]. Additionally, feature selection aims to extract essential data attributes, often using statistical tests or machine learning algorithms, reducing noise and ultimately refining model performance. These techniques collectively fortify the data-driven foundation of deep learning models, enabling more accurate and effective outcomes.

6 Process Optimization and Energy Efficiency

Deep Learning optimizes manufacturing processes through its ability to extract insights, recognize patterns, and make predictions from complex data [8]. Deep learning has revolutionized manufacturing processes by harnessing its data analysis capabilities to enhance efficiency, quality, and productivity across various aspects of the production chain. Through the application of advanced neural networks, manufacturing industries have gained the ability to optimize operations and make informed decisions based on insights extracted from intricate data streams.

In the realm of quality control and defect detection, Convolutional Neural Networks (CNNs) have emerged as powerful tools. These networks are adept at scrutinizing visual data, such as images of products or materials, to identify imperfections, anomalies, or deviations from the desired standard. By employing CNNs along assembly lines, manufacturers can detect issues in real-time and promptly initiate corrective measures, ensuring that only products meeting stringent quality criteria proceed further in the production process.

Predictive maintenance, another pivotal application, leverages Recurrent Neural Networks (RNNs) to foresee equipment failures. By analyzing data from sensors embedded in machinery, RNNs can predict potential breakdowns before they occur. This proactive approach enables maintenance teams to schedule timely interventions, minimizing downtime and preventing costly production disruptions. Process optimization is yet another domain transformed by deep learning. The technology's aptitude for deciphering intricate patterns within extensive datasets enables manufacturers to fine-tune parameters influencing production. Deep learning algorithms can analyze factors like temperature, pressure, and material composition, leading to refined processes, reduced waste, and enhanced operational efficiency.

Supply chain management is further optimized by deep learning's predictive capabilities. Recurrent Neural Networks excel in forecasting demand by analyzing historical trends, market shifts, and other pertinent data points. Manufacturers can align production schedules and resource allocation more accurately, thereby reducing excess inventory and streamlining operations. Moreover, deep learning contributes to energy efficiency efforts. By scrutinizing energy consumption patterns, models can propose strategies for optimizing energy usage. This might involve scheduling energy-intensive tasks during periods of lower demand or recommending adjustments to equipment settings to minimize energy consumption.

In a context of increasing demand for customized products, deep learning aids in efficiently fulfilling individual preferences. By analyzing customer data and production constraints, models can suggest configurations that align with consumer desires while maintaining production efficiency. Deeper insights into root causes of quality issues or process failures are unlocked through deep learning. By scrutinizing data across production stages, models can reveal correlations and patterns that contribute to problems, facilitating continuous improvement initiatives.

7 Challenges and Limitations

The implementation of deep learning in manufacturing processes is accompanied by notable challenges and limitations. Acquiring sufficient and accurate data, a prerequisite for effective model training, remains a hurdle, particularly for rare events or intricate processes. The opacity of deep learning models, due to their complex architectures, raises concerns about interpretability, critical for regulatory compliance and troubleshooting. High computational demands for training hinder accessibility, particularly for smaller manufacturers, while ensuring model generalization and scalability across diverse environments proves intricate. Data security and privacy concerns arise when sharing proprietary manufacturing data for model development. Additionally, the trade-off between real-time processing demands and model processing time must be balanced, and vigilance is needed to prevent biased decisions originating from biased training data. Ultimately, managing these challenges while achieving a positive return on investment remains pivotal for successful integration of deep learning in manufacturing.

8   Future Trends

In the forthcoming landscape of manufacturing, the application of deep learning is projected to usher in a series of transformative trends that promise to redefine industry practices. A notable trend on the horizon is the advancement of explainable AI, a response to the increasing complexity of deep learning models. This trajectory emphasizes the development of techniques that provide transparent insights into the decision-making processes of these models. By unraveling the rationale behind predictions, explainable AI aims to cultivate trust among stakeholders, enabling them to comprehend and endorse the reasoning driving these AI-driven outcomes. This will be crucial in sectors where accountability, regulatory compliance, and user confidence are paramount.

Concerns surrounding data privacy and security have fueled the rise of federated learning. This innovative approach allows models to be collaboratively trained across multiple devices or locations while keeping the underlying data decentralized. In the manufacturing context, where proprietary data is sensitive, federated learning stands as a solution to drive collective learning while safeguarding data privacy. This trend is poised to reshape how manufacturers harness the power of deep learning while respecting data confidentiality.

The synergy between deep learning and edge computing is set to play a pivotal role in manufacturing's future. With the growing capabilities of edge devices, the deployment of deep learning models directly at the data source is becoming increasingly viable. This paradigm shift enables real-time analysis and decision-making at the edge, circumventing the need to transmit massive data volumes to central servers. The outcome is reduced latency, enhanced operational efficiency, and the potential to react swiftly to critical events, underscoring the transformative potential of edge-driven deep learning applications in manufacturing.

Integration with the Internet of Things (IoT) is another key trend that will reshape manufacturing. Deep learning models integrated with IoT devices will bring about highly accurate predictive maintenance and optimization capabilities. Sensors embedded within manufacturing equipment will continuously feed data to these models, enabling early identification of potential issues and averting costly downtimes. This seamless connection between devices and AI models is poised to elevate manufacturing efficiency to new heights, offering an intelligent and proactive approach to maintenance and resource utilization.

Furthermore, deep learning's impact on collaborative robotics (cobots) is set to expand. Future developments in machine learning algorithms will facilitate more profound insights into human behavior, enabling cobots to interact more safely and efficiently with human counterparts on the factory floor. Enhanced human-machine collaboration will foster an environment where automation and human expertise harmonize, optimizing productivity and safety in manufacturing processes.

An overarching theme that is expected to define the future of deep learning in manufacturing is cross-disciplinary collaboration. AI experts, domain specialists, and manufacturers will increasingly join forces to tailor deep learning solutions to the unique challenges of the industry. This multidisciplinary approach promises to fuel innovation, driving the industry towards smarter, adaptive manufacturing systems that address challenges and seize opportunities across diverse sectors.

As these future trends unfold, the manufacturing landscape is poised to witness a profound transformation driven by the capabilities of deep learning. From transparency and privacy considerations to real-time edge analysis, IoT integration, and collaborative robotics, deep learning is on the brink of revolutionizing manufacturing practices in ways that were once only imagined. Through careful navigation of these trends, industries stand to gain a competitive edge and unlock new avenues of growth and efficiency in the Industry 4.0 era.

In the dynamic landscape of Industry 4.0, the amalgamation of data-driven technologies has paved the way for transformative shifts in manufacturing. Deep Learning, as a cornerstone of this revolution, has illuminated avenues that were once only conceivable in the realm of science fiction. The fusion of cyber-physical systems, IoT, and advanced analytics has ignited a paradigm shift from traditional manufacturing methodologies towards a future brimming with agility, adaptability, and efficiency. As we delve into the depths of deep learning techniques and architectures, it becomes evident that these methods hold the power to unravel complexities, discern patterns, and predict outcomes in ways that were previously unattainable.

Convolutional Neural Networks have empowered the identification of defects and quality deviations, opening the door to real-time intervention and elevated product excellence. Recurrent Neural Networks, with their sequential analysis prowess, have unlocked the realm of predictive maintenance, minimizing downtimes and optimizing resource allocation. Generative Adversarial Networks have transcended the boundaries of imagination, enabling the generation of synthetic data that parallels reality. These profound advancements, bolstered by the principles of data quality, quantity, and preprocessing, are propelling the industry towards a new era of production excellence.

However, these leaps are not without their challenges. Data remains both the fuel and the bottleneck of deep learning applications, necessitating a delicate balance between quality, quantity, and privacy concerns. The complexity of deep learning models raises interpretability issues, requiring innovative approaches to ensure transparent decision-making. Moreover, the computational demands and scalability concerns must be addressed to democratize the benefits of this technology across the manufacturing spectrum. As we forge ahead, the synthesis of innovative solutions and collaborative endeavors is essential to surmount these obstacles and reap the rewards of deep learning integration.

The future holds promises that extend beyond the horizon. Explainable AI is poised to infuse transparency into the decision-making processes, fostering trust and accountability. Federated learning is set to revolutionize data privacy by enabling collective learning while preserving sensitive information. Edge computing, in tandem with IoT integration, is propelling us towards real-time insights at the source, rendering processes swift and responsive. Collaborative robotics is poised for safer, more efficient interactions, where human expertise and automation harmonize seamlessly. Cross-disciplinary collaboration, the cornerstone of innovation, will orchestrate the rise of smarter, adaptive manufacturing systems, creating a future where technology is harnessed to its fullest potential.

As we stand at the confluence of human ingenuity and technological prowess, the journey towards a deeply integrated Industry 4.0 is underway. Through perseverance, collaboration, and a dedication to overcoming challenges, the fusion of deep learning and manufacturing promises a future that is not only intelligent and efficient, but also profoundly transformative. The fourth industrial revolution is not a distant concept; it is unfolding before us, driven by the power of deep learning and the boundless possibilities it bestows upon the manufacturing landscape.

References

1. Albawi, S., Mohammed, T.A., Al-Zawi, S.: Understanding of a convolutional neural network. In: 2017 International Conference on Engineering and Technology (ICET), pp. 1–6 (2017). https://doi.org/10.1109/ICEngTechnol.2017.8308186
2. Bali, V., Bhatnagar, V., Aggarwal, D., Bali, S., Diván, M.J.: Cyber-Physical, IoT, and Autonomous Systems in Industry 4.0. CRC Press, Boca Raton (2021)
3. Bhat, O., Gokhale, P., Bhat, S.: Introduction to IoT. Int. Adv. Res. J. Sci. Eng. Technol. 5(1), 41–44 (2007). https://doi.org/10.17148/IARJSET.2018.517
4. Han, Z., et al.: Stackgan: text to photo-realistic image synthesis with stacked generative adversarial networks. In: 2017 IEEE International Conference on Computer Vision (ICCV), pp. 5908–5916. IEEE (2017)
5. Hernavs, J., Ficko, M., Berus, L., Rudolf, R., Klančnik, S.: Deep learning in industry 4.0 - brief. J. Prod. Eng. 21(2), 1–5 (2018). https://doi.org/10.24867/JPE-2018-02-001
6. Jamal, P., Ali, M., Faraj, R.H.: Data normalization and standardization: a technical report. In: Machine Learning Technical Reports, pp. 1–6. Machine Learning Lab, Koya University (2014). https://doi.org/10.13140/RG.2.2.28948.04489
7. Li-Chia, Y., Szu-Yu, C., Yi-Hsuan, Y.: Midinet: a convolutional generative adversarial network for symbolic-domain music generation. In: Europe: ISMIR (2017)
8. May, M.C., Neidhöfer, J., Körner, T., Schäfer, L., Lanza, G.: Applying natural language processing in manufacturing. In: Procedia CIRP, pp. 184–189. Elsevier B.V. (2022). https://doi.org/10.1016/j.procir.2022.10.071
9. Menon, A., Mehrotra, K., Mohan, C.K., Ranka, S.: Characterization of a class of sigmoid functions with applications to neural networks. Neural Netw. 9(5), 819–835 (1996). https://doi.org/10.1016/0893-6080(95)00107-7. https://www.sciencedirect.com/science/article/pii/0893608095001077
10. O'Shea, K., Nash, R.: An introduction to convolutional neural networks (2015). https://doi.org/10.48550/arXiv.1511.08458

11. Schlegl, T., Seeböck, P., Waldstein, S.M., Schmidt-Erfurth, U., Langs, G.: Unsupervised anomaly detection with generative adversarial networks to guide marker discovery. In: Niethammer, M., et al. (eds.) IPMI 2017. LNCS, vol. 10265, pp. 146–157. Springer, Cham (2017). https://doi.org/10.1007/978-3-319-59050-9_12

12. Shah, P., Sekhar, R., Kulkarni, A., Siarry, P.: Metaheuristic Algorithms in Industry 4.0. Advances in Metaheuristics. CRC Press (2021). https://books.google.co.in/books?id=7jc8EAAAQBAJ

13. Sharma, S., Sharma, S., Athaiya, A.: Activation functions in neural networks. Int. J. Eng. Appl. Sci. Technol. 4, 310–316 (2020). https://www.ijeast.com

14. Sony, M., Naik, S.: Key ingredients for evaluating industry 4.0 readiness for organizations: a literature review. Benchmark. Int. J. 27(7), 2213–2232 (2020). https://doi.org/10.1108/BIJ-09-2018-0284

15. Tarwani, K., Edem, S.: Survey on recurrent neural network in natural language processing. Int. J. Eng. Trends Technol. 48(6), 301–304 (2017). https://doi.org/10.14445/22315381/IJETT-V48P253

16. Van Dyk, D.A., Meng, X.L.: The art of data augmentation. J. Comput. Graph. Stat. 10(1), 1–50 (2001). https://doi.org/10.1198/10618600152418584

17. Vondrick, C., Pirsiavash, H., Torralba, A.: Generating videos with scene dynamics. In: Lee, D., Sugiyama, M., Luxburg, U., Guyon, I., Garnett, R. (eds.) Advances in Neural Information Processing Systems, vol. 29. Curran Associates, Inc. (2016)

18. Wang, K., Gou, C., Duan, Y., Lin, Y., Zheng, X., Wang, F.Y.: Generative adversarial networks: introduction and outlook. IEEE/CAA J. Automatica Sinica 4(4), 588–598 (2017). https://doi.org/10.1109/JAS.2017.7510583

19. Wu, J., Zhang, C., Xue, T., Freeman, B., Tenenbaum, J.: Learning a probabilistic latent space of object shapes via 3D generative-adversarial modeling. In: Lee, D., Sugiyama, M., Luxburg, U., Guyon, I., Garnett, R. (eds.) Advances in Neural Information Processing Systems, vol. 29. Curran Associates, Inc. (2016)

20. Zhu, J.Y., Park, T., Isola, P., Efros, A.A.: Unpaired image-to-image translation using cycle-consistent adversarial networks. In: 2017 IEEE International Conference on Computer Vision (ICCV), pp. 2242–2251. IEEE (2017)

SASE: Sentiment Analysis with Aspect Specific Evaluation Using Deep Learning with Hybrid Contextual Embedding

Balaji TK[1], Annushree Bablani[1(✉)], Sreeja SR[1], and Hemant Misra[2]

[1] Indian Institute of Information Technology, Sri City, Andhra Pradesh 517646, India
{balaji.tk,annushree.bablani,sreeja.sr}@iiits.in
[2] Swiggy, Bangalore, India

Abstract. In recent years, sentiment analysis has grown more intricate as the need for deeper insights from text data has expanded. Traditional methods fall short for capturing subtle opinions, giving rise to aspect-oriented sentiment analysis. This study proposes a new framework called Sentiment Analysis with Aspect-Specific Evaluation (SASE) fusing with diverse word embeddings to give aspect-specific sentiment analysis. This novel hybrid approach holds the promise of unravelling multifaceted sentiment aspects across varied domains, and when coupled with the robust RoBERTa model, demonstrates good improvements in accuracy with 78%. The comparison study of the SASE framework with baseline models are also discussed in this work.

Keywords: Sentiment analysis · Aspect based sentiment analysis · Deep learning · Opinion mining · Neural networks

1 Inroduction

Sentiment analysis, also known as opinion mining, involves the utilization of natural language processing methods to analyze an individual's sentiments, viewpoints, and emotions [1]. The intricacies of sentiment analysis have expanded significantly in recent years, driven by the need to extract deeper insights from textual data. Traditional sentiment analysis, while effective in gauging overall sentiment, often falls short in capturing the multifaceted nature of opinions expressed within the text. This limitation gave rise to the evolution from sentiment analysis to aspect-based sentiment analysis (ABSA) [2] or aspect-oriented sentiment analysis (AOSA) [3]. The techniques employed for aspect identification encompass a range of approaches, including frequency-based, syntax-based, supervised and unsupervised machine learning, and hybrid methods, tailored to the specific application context of the AOSA [4].

AOSA is an approach in natural language processing that focuses on analyzing sentiments expressed towards specific aspects or features of a product,

S. Devismes et al. (Eds.): ICDCIT 2024, LNCS 14501, pp. 237–248, 2024.
https://doi.org/10.1007/978-3-031-50583-6_16

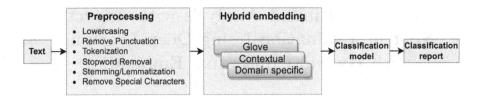

Fig. 1. Graphical abstract of the study

service, or text. Instead of treating the entire text as a single sentiment, AOSA dissects the content to understand sentiments associated with individual aspects, providing a more detailed insight into how different elements are perceived. For example, consider a movie review: "The acting in the movie was great, but the plot was confusing, and the special effects were disappointing". In AOSA, this review would be broken down into aspects such as "acting," "plot," and "special effects". Each aspect is then analyzed for its associated sentiment as Acting: *Positive*, Plot: *Negative*, and Special Effects: *Negative*.

By analyzing sentiments at an aspect level, AOSA can provide more nuanced insights. In this case, even though the overall review might be considered mixed, understanding which specific aspects contributed to the positive and negative sentiments can be valuable for filmmakers. They can identify strengths (acting) and weaknesses (plot, special effects) to make informed decisions for future productions. AOSA helps in dissecting a text to identify and analyze sentiments towards distinct aspects or features, offering a deeper understanding of how different components contribute to the overall sentiment.

AOSA holds immense potential for industries seeking to comprehend user feedback comprehensively. This evolution calls for advancements not only in methodology but also in the way machines understand language. Embeddings, which provide vector representations for words based on their contextual meaning, have redefined the landscape of natural language processing. In sentiment analysis, embeddings bridge the gap between textual data and machine comprehension [5], enabling models to grasp the sentiment-laden aspects woven into language. However, as the transition from traditional sentiment analysis to AOSA takes centre stage, the demand for embeddings that align with the intricacies of diverse domains becomes apparent.

In this study, a new framework is proposed to analyze aspect-specific sentiment called SASE (Sentiment Analysis with Aspect-Specific Evaluation). The graphical abstract of this study is presented in Fig. 1. This paper delves into the synergistic integration of embeddings in AOSA, particularly the utilization of hybrid embeddings. By combining traditional word embeddings, contextual embeddings, and domain-specific embeddings, a new dimension of sentiment analysis comes to light-one that not only captures the linguistic intricacies of words but also contextual cues and domain-specific expressions. While navigating through the forthcoming sections, this paper unfolds a thorough investigation into the mechanics and benefits of hybrid embeddings. Through theoretical exploration and empirical validation, the SASE framework endeavours to showcase the unprecedented accuracy and depth of hybrid embeddings bring to AOSA. By illuminating the transformative journey from traditional sentiment analysis to the nuanced realm of AOSA, this research endeavours to underscore the pivotal role of hybrid embeddings as a conduit for attaining richer insights from textual data. The subsequent sections unfold as Sect. 3 explains the methodology of this study, Sect. 4 discusses the results, and Sect. 5 concludes the study.

2 Literature Work

Aspect-based sentiment Analysis (ABSA) stands as a foundational task within sentiment analysis, encompassing two primary subtasks: aspect extraction and aspect-based sentiment classification [6]. Unlike sentiment analysis at the document or sentence level, ABSA concurrently considers both sentiment and target information. Typically, a target in ABSA refers to an entity or a specific aspect of an entity. The primary objective of ABSA is to ascertain the sentiment polarity of a given sentence concerning a particular aspect.

ABSA has witnessed a surge in the popularity of numerous works in recent years. For instance, authors in [7] proposed two extensions to the state-of-the-art Hybrid Approach for Aspect-Based Sentiment Analysis (HAABSA) method: (a) using deep contextual word embeddings instead of non-contextual word embeddings, and (b) adding a hierarchical attention layer to the HAABSA high-level representations. The authors evaluated their proposed model on two standard datasets (SemEval 2015 and SemEval 2016) and showed that it achieves improved accuracy on both datasets.

Authors in [8] proposed a hybrid solution for sentence-level ABSA using a lexicalized domain ontology and a regularized neural attention model (ALDONAr). The authors introduce a bidirectional context attention mechanism to measure the influence of each word in a sentence on an aspect's sentiment value. The authors also designed a classification module to handle the complex structure of a sentence and integrated a manually created lexicalized domain ontology to utilize field-specific knowledge. The authors evaluated the proposed model on several standard datasets and showed that it achieved state-of-the-art results.

Authors in [9] proposed a joint model of multiple Convolutional Neural Networks (CNNs) to integrate different representations of the input for ABSA. The authors focus on three kinds of representation: word embeddings from Word2Vec, GloVe and one-hot character vectors. The authors evaluated the proposed model on several standard datasets and showed that it achieved state-of-the-art performance on both aspect category detection and aspect sentiment classification tasks. In [10], authors proposed model for ABSA called the Transformation Network. The Transformation Network is a neural network that learns to transform word representations in a way that captures the relationships between different words in a sentence. This allows the model to better understand the sentiment of the sentence towards different aspects.

In [11], authors proposed a method for aspect sentiment classification (ASC) using memory networks (MNs) with attention mechanisms. The paper identifies a problem with current MNs in performing the ASC task, referred to as target-sensitive sentiment, which means that the sentiment polarity of the context depends on the given target and cannot be inferred from the context alone. To tackle this problem, the paper proposes target-sensitive memory networks (TMNs) that can capture the sentiment interaction between targets and contexts. The paper presented approaches to implementing TMNs and experimentally evaluated its effectiveness using two standard datasets (SemEval 2015 and SemEval 2016).

Authors in [12] "Aspect-based sentiment analysis with enhanced aspect-sensitive word embeddings" proposed a new method for aspect-based sentiment analysis (ABSA) that uses enhanced aspect-sensitive word embeddings. The authors argue that traditional word embeddings do not adequately capture the sentiment of words that depends on the aspect they are associated with. For example, the word "high" can have a positive sentiment when associated with the aspect "price" (e.g., "The price of the new iPhone is high, but it's worth it"), but a negative sentiment when associated with the aspect "quality" (e.g., "The quality of the new iPhone is high, but it's still not as good as the previous model"). To address this limitation, the authors propose a method for enhancing word embeddings with aspect-specific sentiment information. Authors do this by training a neural network to predict the sentiment of a word given the aspect it is associated with. The trained neural network is then used to generate aspect-sensitive word embeddings, which are used in an ABSA model.

Most studies on aspect-based sentiment analysis (ABSA) have used either machine learning (ML), deep learning (DL), or hybrid models with static pre-trained word embeddings or contextual embeddings, but not both. This study proposes a new method for ABSA that fuses both static and contextual word embeddings to improve the model's understanding of sentences.

3 Methodology

To realize the transformative potential of hybrid embeddings in AOSA, a systematic methodology is devised, encompassing data collection, embedding creation, model training, and evaluation. The process begins with dataset acquisition, then tokenization and preprocessing are applied to the text, preparing it for subsequent stages.

3.1 Dataset

Three gold standard SemEval English datasets are taken to train the models. They are: first is **SemEval-2014 Task 4** [13], second is **SemEval-2015 Task 12** [14], and **SemEval 16 Task 5** [15]. The dataset has features such as opinion target expressions, aspect categories, and polarities). A sample data classification using SASE is: presented in Fig. 2. The dataset is divided into two parts in an

80:20 ratio for training and testing the model. The total dataset considered here had 11997 samples. The dataset is labelled with 3 classes positive, negative, and neutral. The conflict label is ignored in this study.

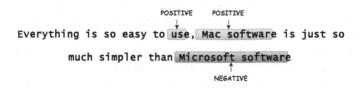

Fig. 2. Aspect-oriented sentiment classification on Sample data

3.2 Preprocessing

In the text preprocessing phase, a series of steps are implemented to enhance the data quality. The process involved as

○ Lowercasing all text
○ Eliminating punctuation
○ Tokenizing
○ Removal of stopwords
○ Stemming and lemmatization
○ Removing special characters

For preprocessing, a comprehensive preprocessing pipeline is adopted to ensure cleaner and more consistent text data for subsequent analysis. For tokenization, RoBERTa tokenization is adopted for this study.

3.3 Methodology Implementation

In this work, data gets tokenized after preprocesses, and the tokenized data is sent to the next layer for generating the embeddings. For embedding creation, three types of embeddings are synergistically integrated. They are traditional word embeddings, contextual embeddings, and domain-specific embeddings. Pre-trained Glove [16] embedding G_e is attributed as one of the embeddings in the hybrid approach. Fasttext is employed to generate domain-specific embeddings D_e by training on the preprocessed text dataset. Concurrently, pre-trained RoBERTa contextual embeddings C_e are harnessed, capturing intricate contextual relationships within the text. The hybrid embedding technique involved concatenating these embeddings as shown in Eq. 1, thereby infusing both linguistic semantics and contextual understanding tailored to the various domains.

$$E_i = Concatenate(embedding_1, embedding_2, ...) \tag{1}$$

The adoption of hybrid embeddings in this study is driven by the imperative to effectively handle out-of-vocabulary (OOV) terms while enhancing sentiment analysis accuracy in AOSA. OOV terms, such as domain-specific jargon and evolving terminologies, often challenge conventional embeddings, which might lack representations for such specialized language. By integrating traditional word embeddings, contextual embeddings, and domain-specific embeddings, the hybrid approach mitigates the limitations posed by OOV terms. Traditional embeddings capture general linguistic relationships, contextual embeddings grasp surrounding cues, and domain-specific embeddings encapsulate specialized vocabulary. This fusion ensures that the model is equipped to comprehend the diverse array of language encountered within the text, allowing for more comprehensive and nuanced sentiment analysis. The detailed data flow of the SASE framework is presented in Fig. 3.

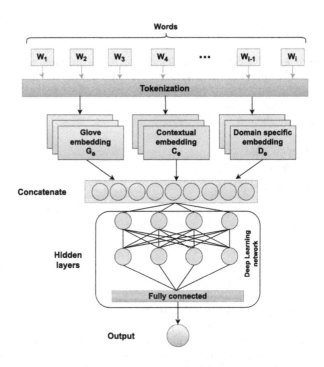

Fig. 3. Detailed dataflow of SASE framework

The next phase centred on model training, where the models are fine-tuned using hybrid embeddings. The model's architecture is adapted to accommodate the hybrid embeddings, aligning it with the nuanced sentiment landscape of aspect-oriented analysis. The training process is guided by extensive experimentation to optimize model convergence. The models are trained using different embedding settings to analyse the performance of the hybrid approach. Three embedding setups are considered for this study E1, E2, and E3. Here, E1 is

RoBERTA based embedding (Contextual embedding C_e), E2 is E1 + Glove embeddings), and E3 (E2 + Fasttext (Domain Specific embeddings)). The baseline models included in this study are RoBERTa, BERT, LSTM, td_lstm, tc_lstm, ATAE_LSTM, IAN, MemNet, AoA, Cabasc, and ASGCN.

3.4   Baseline Methods Used

In the evaluation, SASE is benchmarked against cutting-edge baseline methods for a comprehensive comparison. The following is a brief overview of the baseline models:

LSTM [17] have the ability to capture context from previous words and maintain relevant information throughout the sequence, which is crucial for understanding sentiment expressed in text.

ATAE-LSTM [18] leverages aspect embedding and attention mechanisms for aspect-level sentiment classification.

tc_LSTM [18] considers both the target word and the surrounding context to make sentiment predictions.

td_LSTM [18] address challenges such as context-dependent sentiment, target-specific sentiment nuances, and disambiguating sentiments in complex sentences.

IAN [19] utilizes dual LSTMs and an interactive attention mechanism to generate representations for both the aspect and the sentence.

ASGCN [20] introduces the use of Graph Convolutional Networks (GCN) to learn aspect-specific representations for aspect-based sentiment classification.

BERT [21] represents the vanilla BERT model. It processes sentence-aspect pairs and employs the [CLS] token's representation for making predictions.

RoBERTa [22] aims to optimize the pretraining process of BERT to further improve the model's performance on various downstream NLP tasks, including sentiment analysis.

MemNet [23] is a sentiment analysis model that employs a memory network architecture. This architecture is designed to capture long-range dependencies and relationships within text data.

AOA [24] involves a two-step attention process: first attending to individual words in a sentence and then attending to different aspects of the text.

Comparative analyses are conducted and presented in the following section against models employing various embedding setups and demonstrating the superiority of the hybrid approach. The entire methodology synthesized a comprehensive approach to harnessing the power of hybrid embeddings for AOSA. The holistic process not only addressed the intricate demands of this evolving field but also contributed valuable insights into the intricate fabric of sentiments woven into diverse domain discourses.

4   Results and Discussion

The Table 1 offers insights into the performance of various models across different embedding configurations said to be E1, E2, and E3 as represented in Eq. 2, 3, and 4. These Eq. 2 to 4 are constructed using Eq. 1.

$$E_1 = Concatinate(C_e) \tag{2}$$

$$E_2 = Concatinate(E_1, G_e) \tag{3}$$

$$E_3 = Concatinate(E_2, D_e) \tag{4}$$

The trends and observations in the table are discussed as:

Across all three embedding configurations, RoBERTa consistently performs well. The addition of Glove embeddings (E2) to RoBERTa resulted in a slight improvement in both accuracy and F1-score. The best performance is achieved under the E3 configuration, where Domain Specific embeddings are added, leading to the highest accuracy and F1 score. BERT's performance is similar to RoBERTa but slightly lower across all configurations. Similar to RoBERTa, adding Glove embeddings (E2) improves performance slightly, and the best results are seen with Domain Specific embeddings (E3).

Table 1. Performance of SASE framework

Model	E1		E2		E3	
	ACC	F1	ACC	F1	ACC	F1
RoBERTa	**0.77**	**0.71**	**0.77**	**0.72**	**0.78**	**0.73**
BERT	0.74	0.66	0.75	0.66	0.75	0.69
LSTM	0.69	0.63	0.63	0.46	0.72	0.66
TD_LSTM	0.69	0.63	0.65	0.55	0.69	0.62
TC_LSTM	0.65	0.59	0.64	0.56	0.67	0.61
ATAE_LSTM	0.68	0.61	0.69	0.62	0.66	0.58
IAN	0.69	0.63	0.64	0.47	0.70	0.63
MemNet	0.70	0.61	0.71	0.64	0.69	0.61
Cabasc	0.69	0.64	0.68	0.62	0.72	0.67
AOA	0.65	0.57	0.63	0.45	0.72	0.66
ASGCN	0.67	0.60	0.66	0.54	0.73	0.68

The LSTM, td_lstm, and tc_lstm models show relatively consistent performance across the three embedding configurations. Adding E2 tends to have a positive impact on accuracy, although F1 scores don't always improve. E3 show mixed results, with some models improving and others degrading in performance.

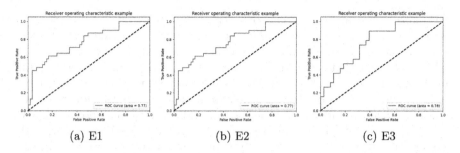

(a) E1   (b) E2   (c) E3

Fig. 4. ROC curve for RoBERTa model under (a) E1 = Contextual embedding (b) E2 = Contextual + tradition word embeddings (c) E3 = Contextual + domain specific + traditional word embeddings.

The ATAE_LSTM, IAN, MemNet, Cabas models generally show varying levels of performance across different embedding configurations. In some cases, adding E2 improves accuracy and F1-score, while in others, it doesn't have a significant effect. E3 often lead to improvements in performance. ASGCN's performance is similar across all three configurations. Adding E2 slightly improves accuracy, but the F1-score remains relatively stable. E3 results in further improvements in both accuracy and F1 score.

Generally, adding Glove embeddings tends to have a positive impact on accuracy, with varying effects on F1 scores. Domain Specific embeddings consistently lead to improved performance, particularly in terms of accuracy. Models like RoBERTa and BERT show a more pronounced response to embedding variations, while others (LSTM-based models, ASGCN) have more stable trends. Adding domain-specific embeddings seems to play a crucial role in enhancing model performance across the models. The ROC curve of the RoBERTa model is presented in the Fig. 4.

Table 2. Comparative analyses of performance across various studies using SemEval datasets.

Study	Model	Acuracy	F1-Score
This study	RoBERTa+E3	78%	73%
[10]	TNet-LF	76.01%	-
[11]	Naive Bayes	-	72.43%
[25]	CORR	64.89%	-
[25]	CONV	68.81%	
[26]	PF-CNN	70.06%	
[27]	DAuM	74.45%	70.16%
[28]	ALAN	73.35%	

Detailed performance comparisons across multiple studies using SemEval datasets are presented in Table 2. The data within the table demonstrates that the ROBERTa+E3 model exhibits strong and commendable performance.

It is observed that embedding choices influence the model's performance, and the optimal combination depends on the specific model and task. Contextual embeddings help capture semantic information, Glove embeddings provide word-level context, and domain-specific embeddings introduce domain knowledge. The results of different models on thése embedding setups highlight the need for careful embedding selection to tailor models to the desired performance characteristics.

5   Conclusion

Significant advancements have been made in the field of aspect-based sentiment analysis through deep learning. This progress has paved the way for diverse application areas to leverage insights derived from these models. A novel framework SASE has been created to improve aspect-specific sentiment analysis by combining different types of word embeddings. This includes the amalgamation of conventional word embeddings, contextual embeddings, and domain-specific embeddings. The outcomes from this innovative framework have demonstrated strong efficacy when applied to the RoBERTa model, achieving an accuracy rate of 78%. As we look ahead, there is potential for refining this framework to conduct more intricate forms of sentiment analysis, such as implicit aspect-based sentiment analysis.

References

1. Singh, M., Jakhar, A.K., Pandey, S.: Sentiment analysis on the impact of coronavirus in social life using the BERT model. Soc. Netw. Anal. Min. **11**(1), 1–11 (2021)
2. Mewada, A., Dewang, R.K.: SA-ASBA: a hybrid model for aspect-based sentiment analysis using synthetic attention in pre-trained language BERT model with extreme gradient boosting. J. Supercomput. **79**(5), 5516–5551 (2023)
3. Kathuria, A., Gupta, A., Singla, R.: AOH-Senti: aspect-oriented hybrid approach to sentiment analysis of students' feedback. SN Comput. Sci. **4**(2), 152 (2023)
4. Feng, J., Cai, S., Ma, X.: Enhanced sentiment labeling and implicit aspect identification by integration of deep convolution neural network and sequential algorithm. Clust. Comput. **22**, 5839–5857 (2019)
5. Reimers, N., Schiller, B., Beck, T., Daxenberger, J., Stab, C., Gurevych, I.: Classification and clustering of arguments with contextualized word embeddings. arXiv preprint arXiv:1906.09821 (2019)
6. Thet, T.T., Na, J.-C., Khoo, C.S.: Aspect-based sentiment analysis of movie reviews on discussion boards. J. Inf. Sci. **36**(6), 823–848 (2010)
7. Truşcă, M.M., Wassenberg, D., Frasincar, F., Dekker, R.: A hybrid approach for aspect-based sentiment analysis using deep contextual word embeddings and hierarchical attention. In: Bielikova, M., Mikkonen, T., Pautasso, C. (eds.) ICWE 2020. LNCS, vol. 12128, pp. 365–380. Springer, Cham (2020). https://doi.org/10.1007/978-3-030-50578-3_25

8. Meškelė, D., Frasincar, F.: ALDONAr: a hybrid solution for sentence-level aspect-based sentiment analysis using a lexicalized domain ontology and a regularized neural attention model. Inf. Process. Manage. **57**(3), 102211 (2020)
9. Pham, D.-H., Le, A.-C.: Exploiting multiple word embeddings and one-hot character vectors for aspect-based sentiment analysis. Int. J. Approximate Reasoning **103**, 1–10 (2018)
10. Li, X., Bing, L., Lam, W., Shi, B.: Transformation networks for target-oriented sentiment classification. arXiv preprint arXiv:1805.01086 (2018)
11. Wang, S., Mazumder, S., Liu, B., Zhou, M., Chang, Y.: Target-sensitive memory networks for aspect sentiment classification. In: Proceedings of the 56th Annual Meeting of the Association for Computational Linguistics (Volume 1: Long Papers) (2018)
12. Qi, Y., Zheng, X., Huang, X.: Aspect-based sentiment analysis with enhanced aspect-sensitive word embeddings. Knowl. Inf. Syst. **64**(7), 1845–1861 (2022)
13. Pontiki, M., Galanis, D., Pavlopoulos, J., Papageorgiou, H., Androutsopoulos, I., Manandhar, S.: Semeval-2014 task 4: aspect based sentiment analysis. In: International Workshop on Semantic Evaluation (2014)
14. Pontiki, M., Galanis, D., Papageorgiou, H., Manandhar, S., Androutsopoulos, I.: Semeval-2015 task 12: aspect based sentiment analysis. In: Proceedings of the 9th International Workshop on Semantic Evaluation (SemEval 2015), pp. 486–495 (2015)
15. Pontiki, M., et al.: Semeval-2016 task 5: aspect based sentiment analysis. In: 10th International Workshop on Semantic Evaluation (SemEval 2016) (2016)
16. Pennington, J., Socher, R., Manning, C.D.: Glove: global vectors for word representation. In: Proceedings of the 2014 Conference on Empirical Methods in Natural Language Processing (EMNLP), pp. 1532–1543 (2014)
17. Hochreiter, S., Schmidhuber, J.: Long short-term memory. Neural Comput. **9**(8), 1735–1780 (1997)
18. Wang, Y., Huang, M., Zhu, X., Zhao, L.: Attention-based LSTM for aspect-level sentiment classification. In: Proceedings of the 2016 Conference on Empirical Methods in Natural Language Processing, pp. 606–615 (2016)
19. Ma, D., Li, S., Zhang, X., Wang, H.: Interactive attention networks for aspect-level sentiment classification. arXiv preprint arXiv:1709.00893 (2017)
20. Zhang, C., Li, Q., Song, D.: Aspect-based sentiment classification with aspect-specific graph convolutional networks. arXiv preprint arXiv:1909.03477 (2019)
21. Devlin, J., Chang, M.-W., Lee, K., Toutanova, K.: Bert: pre-training of deep bidirectional transformers for language understanding. arXiv preprint arXiv:1810.04805 (2018)
22. Liu, Y., et al.: Roberta: a robustly optimized BERT pretraining approach. arXiv preprint arXiv:1907.11692 (2019)
23. Tang, D., Qin, B., Liu, T.: Aspect level sentiment classification with deep memory network. arXiv preprint arXiv:1605.08900 (2016)
24. Huang, B., Ou, Y., Carley, K.M.: Aspect level sentiment classification with attention-over-attention neural networks. In: Thomson, R., Dancy, C., Hyder, A., Bisgin, H. (eds.) SBP-BRiMS 2018. LNCS, vol. 10899, pp. 197–206. Springer, Cham (2018). https://doi.org/10.1007/978-3-319-93372-6_22
25. Tay, Y., Tuan, L.A., Hui, S.C.: Learning to attend via word-aspect associative fusion for aspect-based sentiment analysis. In: Proceedings of the AAAI Conference on Artificial Intelligence, vol. 32 (2018)
26. Huang, B., Carley, K.M.: Parameterized convolutional neural networks for aspect level sentiment classification. arXiv preprint arXiv:1909.06276 (2019)

27. Zhu, P., Qian, T.: Enhanced aspect level sentiment classification with auxiliary memory. In: Proceedings of the 27th International Conference on Computational Linguistics, pp. 1077–1087 (2018)
28. Nguyen, H.T., Le Nguyen, M.: Effective attention networks for aspect-level sentiment classification. In: 2018 10th International Conference on Knowledge and Systems Engineering (KSE), pp. 25–30. IEEE (2018)

A Genetic Algorithm-Based Heuristic for Rumour Minimization in Social Networks

Vivek Kumar Rajak and Anjeneya Swami Kare[✉]

School of Computer and Information Sciences, University of Hyderabad,
Hyderabad 500046, Telangana, India
{20mcpc11,askcs}@uohyd.ac.in

Abstract. Rumours in online social networks can significantly damage the ecosystem of the society. It is important to timely identify and control the rumor spread. Rumour identification itself is a challenging problem. The rumour control comes in to play once the rumor is identified. There are mainly two kinds of rumour control strategies: 1) Network disruption strategies and 2) Truth propagation strategies. The diffusion model addresses how the rumour/truth is spreading in the network. Independent Cascade Model (ICM) and Linear Threshold Model (LTM) are the two well known diffusion models. These diffusion models address propagation of a single/independent message. Yang et al. proposed Linear Threshold model with One Direction state Transition (LT1DT), which handles simultaneous propagation of two messages (rumor and truth) which are opposite in nature. The nodes which start the spread of rumour message initially are called rumour seed nodes. Under the LT1DT model, for a given rumour seed set, the rumour minimization problem asks to find k truth seed nodes that minimize the overall rumour spread in the network.

In this paper, we propose genetic algorithm framework based heuristic and a pruning technique to compute the truth seed nodes. We have implemented all the existing algorithms and the proposed heuristics. We have done an extensive experimentation on synthetic and real datasets and compared our results with existing heuristics. Proposed heuristics have shown significant improvement in minimizing the rumour spread.

Keywords: Online social networks · Genetic Algorithms · Rumour minimization

1 Introduction

In recent years, the rapid growth of online social networks has transformed the way information is disseminated, shared, and consumed. While this has brought numerous benefits, it has also opened the door to the widespread propagation

V. K. Rajak—Author is financially supported by Junior Research Fellowship (JRF) scheme of the University Grants Commission (UGC), India.

S. Devismes et al. (Eds.): ICDCIT 2024, LNCS 14501, pp. 249–265, 2024.
https://doi.org/10.1007/978-3-031-50583-6_17

of rumours and false information. People from diverse backgrounds are highly
dependent on the content of social media, so it is paramount importance of the
government agencies and the media houses to keep a check on the authenticity
of the information that is being propagated. Information spreading and rumour
minimization problems on online social networks are of recent interest to the
researchers. The problem of Influence Maximization (IM) was first formalized by
Kempe et al. [17], who proposed two diffusion models: the Independent Cascade
Model (ICM) and the Linear Threshold Model (LTM). Consider a directed graph
$G(V, E)$ where, each node u represents an individual user. These nodes exist
in one of two states during a given time step: active (indicating adoption of
influence) or inactive (indicating non-adoption of influence). Initially, all nodes
are in the inactive state. At time t = 0, some nodes are made active, to spread
information in the network, these nodes are known as seed nodes. If someone
wants to spread rumour, he chooses the most influential nodes as the seed set.
On the other side, we want the spread of rumour to be minimized. The main
strategies to minimize rumour are: 1) Network disruption strategy and 2) Truth
campaign strategy. In network disruption strategy, links/nodes of the network
are removed or blocked for some period of time such that the rumour spread
is minimized. In truth campaign strategy, as and when rumour is detected, a
correct (truth) information is spread parallelly in the network. The nodes we
choose to spread the truth are called truth seed nodes. Choosing truth seed set of
a certain size which minimizes the rumour is an NP-Hard optimization problem.
Centrality measures such as page rank, betweenness, closeness, eigenvector and
degree centrality are very much used to identify most influential nodes. The way
information spreads in the network is modeled by the diffusion models. Linear
Threshold Model (LTM) and Independent Cascade Model (ICM) are the widely
used diffusion model. But they address only spreading of a single or independent
messages. In truth campaign strategy, we need both the rumour and the truth
to be propagated at the same time. Yang et al. [25] introduced Linear Threshold
model with One Direction state Transition (LT1DT), which can handle spread of
two opposite messages at the same time. In this model, once a node is influenced
by truth it will not get influenced to the rumour, but a rumour influenced node
may get influenced by the truth. For this model, the input is a directed graph
with real edge weights. Apart from this, each vertex has two threshold values
associated with it, the influence threshold and decision threshold denoted by
$\theta_u : V \to R^+$ and $\theta_u^R : V \to R^+$ respectively. The rumour minimization problem
over LT1DT model is defined as follows:

Input: An LT1DT Network with $S_R \subseteq V$ and an integer k

Output: A set $S_T \subseteq V\backslash S_R$, $|S_T| = k$, such that the overall rumour influenced
nodes are minimized.

In this paper, we present a genetic algorithm (GA) framework based heuristic
and a pruning strategy to compute a truth seed set. We have implemented all
the existing heuristics, proposed GA and pruning technique. We have done an
extensive experiments on both real and synthetic datasets and the proposed
heuristics are computing truth seed sets with less rumour spread.

2   Related Work

Influence Maximization (IM) problem has been one of the most studied problems among researchers. Kempe et al. [17], first formulated the IM problem for the graph and proved it to be NP-hard for both the ICM and LTM diffusion models. IM has many practical application in various fields like healthcare [1], economics [15] and social-marketing [19] etc. Bharathi et al. [5] have formulated competitive influence diffusion model in the network. They have given an FPTAS for influence maximization of single player when considered graph is a tree. Borodin et al. [6] have extended the LTM for competitive influence diffusion. They proposed, Weight-Proportional Competitive Linear Threshold Model, Separated-Threshold Model for Competing Technologies and Competitive Threshold Model with Forcing. Che et al. [8] proposed Degree discount based heuristics which improve influence spread and running time compare to earlier greedy heuristics. Che et al. [9] also proposed scalable influence algorithm under LTM. They showed that IM problem is linear time solvable in directed cyclic graphs (DAG). Goyal et al. [14] proposed an efficient SIMPATH heuristic based on simple path from the spreading nodes by using vertex cover and look ahead optimization techniques. Gong et al. [13] formulated local influence estimation (LIE) function to calculate the influence of seed set. They proposed discrete particle swarm optimization (DPSO) to optimize the LIE function by redefining the update rules for position and velocity. Banerjee et al. [3] formulated Budgeted Influence Maximization problem (BIM). They proposed community based heuristics to solve the BIM problem.

Unlike IM problems, rumour minimization problem is an influence minimization problem. Budak et al. [7] have first studied the problem of minimizing the spread of misinformation in online social networks. They examined a multi-campaign independent cascade model and defined a task to determine the group of individuals requiring persuasion to embrace a "positive" campaign. The goal was to curtail the propagation of rumors effectively. He et al. [16] and Fan et al. [11] later studied this problem using the competitive LTM and the Opportunistic One-Activate-One (OPOAO) model, respectively. Hong et al. [24] proposed greedy approach to select Maximum Marginal Covering Neighbors set in (k, η)-cores as immune nodes. They used Extended Independent Cascade (EIC) model as diffusion model. Ni et al. [20] proposed a Community-based Rumor Blocking Problem (CRBMP) by picking seed sets from all communities under the constraint of budget b. They proposed a greedy approach for budget allocation to each community. Zhu et al. [27] formulated Robust Rumor Blocking (RRB) problem whose objective is to select k nodes as protectors to minimize the rumour. They formulated an estimation procedure for the objective function of RRB based on Reverse Reachable (RR) set methods. A random greedy heuristic is designed for solving this problem. Wen et al. [23] have evaluated the efficiency of different rumour restraining methods. Choi et al. [10] introduced a model based on Bidirectional Encoder Representations from Transformers (BERT), which focuses solely on a claim sentence associated with a rumour. This model has the capability to preemptively detect false rumors before they gain widespread attention. Yang et al. [25] proposed the LT1DT model and three heuristics, namely MinGreedy (MG), PageRank (PR) and ContrId (CI) and their proximity version ProxyMin-Greedy (PMG), ProxyPageRank (PPR) and ProxyContrId (PCI). They conducted experiments on both synthetic and real datasets, Recently, Yang et al. [26] also presented rumour containment strategy based on blocking of nodes.

2.1 Linear Threshold Model with One Direction State Transition (LT1DT)

The Linear Threshold Model (LTM) addresses information spreading of single or independent messages. In rumour minimization using truth campaign, both rumour and truth are spread simultaneously in the network. To address this, Yang et al. [25] proposed modified version of LTM, which they called Linear Threshold Model with One Direction State Transition (LT1DT). In this model, the input is a directed graph with real edge weights, each vertex has two threshold values associated with it, the influence threshold and the decision threshold denoted by $\theta_u : V \to R^+$ and $\theta_u^R : V \to R^+$ respectively. Given an input rumour seed set $S_R \subseteq V$, the goal is to find truth seed set $S_T \subseteq V \backslash S_R$ of size k such that the overall rumour spread is minimized.

A node u influenced if

$$\sum_{v \in N_u^{in} \cap (R \cup T)} W(v, u) \geq \theta_u.$$

An influenced node u adopts rumour if

$$\frac{\sum_{v \in N_u^{in} \cap R} W(v, u)}{\sum_{v \in N_u^{in} \cap (R \cup T)} W(v, u)} \geq \theta_u^R,$$

otherwise, it adopts truth. Here, N_u^{in} is in-neighbours of node u, $W(v, u)$ is weight of the edge (v, u), R and T are rumour and truth influenced nodes respectively. Note that initially, $R = S_R$ and $T = S_T$. During the diffusion process, more nodes may be added to R and T. The LT1DT diffusion process is an iterative process. The rumour/truth information spread starts from the respective seed nodes. At each iteration, some new nodes get influenced. The process stops when there is no new influenced nodes and there are no change in the influence of the nodes. That is, the diffusion process stops when there is no change to the sets R and T. Once a node u adopts the truth information it will never change its state in the subsequent iteration, but a rumour influenced node may eventually adopt truth.

2.2 Summary of Existing Heuristics

We briefly explain how the existing heuristics (MG, PR, CI, PMG, PPR and PCI) of Yang et al. [25] compute the truth seed set.

The MG heuristic, in each iteration it picks one node from $V \backslash S_R$ that leads to less rumour spread. If the required truth seed set size is k, then the MG heuristic will have k iterations to get the truth seed set of size k. The PR heuristic computes pagerank of all the nodes of the network. It picks k nodes form $V \setminus S_R$ with higher pagerank value as the truth seed set. The CI heuristic computes contribution of each node in the rumour spread. Let $Contr(v)$ be the contribution of a vertex v. A rumour-influenced node v, at time step t immediately transfers its influence to its out-neighbours which can be activated later. So, the contribution of a node v, can be defined as the number of its out-neighbours that are influenced at any time $t > t_v$. The contribution of node v can be calculated as:

$$Contr(v) = |(\cup_{i=t+1}^{T_s} \phi_i^R) \cap N_v^{out}| \tag{1}$$

Here, ϕ_i^R is the set of rumour adopted nodes after i iterations, and N_v^{out} is the set of out-neighbours of v. Once the contribution of all the nodes is computed, the CI heuristic picks the top k nodes from $V \setminus S_R$, which have the highest contribution in the rumour spread.

The proximity variants of these three heuristics are very similar to the original heuristics; the only difference is, they pick the truth seed set from the out-neighbours of the rumour seed nodes.

In this study, we explore the rumour minimization problem under LT1DT diffusion model. We have the following contributions:

- Proposed a genetic algorithm (GA) framework based heuristic and a pruning technique. The GA uses a problem specific scheme to generate the population.
- Carried out an extensive experimentation on few real-world and synthetic data sets. The proposed GA is giving truth seed sets which have less rumour spread. The pruning technique is improving over the truth seed sets of most of the algorithms.

The rest of the paper is organized as follows: Sect. 3 discusses the proposed approaches. In Sect. 4, we discuss the implementation details of the diffusion function. The experimental results are presented in Sect. 5. Finally, the paper is concluded in Sect. 6.

3   Proposed Heuristics

In this section, we present the details of the proposed GA and the pruning technique.

3.1   Genetic Algorithm

A genetic algorithm (GA) is a computational technique inspired by the process of natural selection and evolution. It is used to solve optimization and search problems. A genetic algorithm starts with a set of candidate solutions and generates better solutions using crossover and mutation. For each candidate solution fitness is computed. The candidate solutions with the least fitness are discarded, and the algorithm proceeds to the next iteration of increasing the population

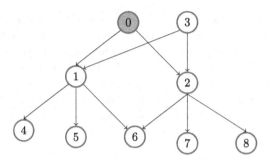

Fig. 1. $W(u, v) = 1 \setminus |N_v^{in}|$, $\theta_u = 0.5$, $\theta_u^R = 0.4$, $\forall u \in V$ and $S_R = \{0\}$.

with crossover and mutation. The process is repeated for several iterations, and the best solution generated so far is returned.

Population Generation: Centrality measures such as Betweenness centrality, Closeness Centrality, Pagerank, Degree centrality and Eigenvector etc., are very much used in information spreading problems [2,12]. The nodes with the highest centrality are crucial in the network. They can spread information or influence many other nodes. Moreover, a node closer to the rumor seed S_R has a better chance of blocking the rumour spread. Keeping these intuitions in mind, we generate the population using centrality values and the distances of a node from the rumour seed. Let $d_R(v)$ is the length of the shortest path from any rumor seed node to the vertex v. We use level order traversal to compute these distances. The rumour seed nodes are considered to be at level 0. The immediate neighbours of the rumour seed nodes are at level 1 and so on. Let d_{max} be the maximum level. The enhanced centrality value of each node is computed as follows:

$$E_{cen}(v) = cen(v) * (d_{max} - d_R(v) + 1) \qquad (2)$$

where $E_{cen}(v)$ is the enhanced centrality value of the vertex v. Note that $E_{cen}(v)$ is set to 0 for all $v \in S_R$.

Consider an instance of LT1DT network given in Fig. 1. If $S_R = \{0\}$ the rumour will spread to the vertices $\{0,1,2,4,5,6,7,8\}$. If truth seed set size $|S_T| = 1$, then picking vertex 3 is better than picking vertex 1 or 2. If we pick vertex 3, the rumour will not spread from the vertex 0. If we notice, there is no directed path from the rumour seed node 0 to the vertex 3. If we compute the levels of the vertices on the directed graph, the vertex 3 is not reachable from the node 0. For this reason we compute the levels in the undirected version of graph, that is, we consider both in and out neighbours of a vertex for the level computation. The enhanced centrality values are further normalized to get a probability distribution for the vertex set V. If the truth seed set size is k, we generate k vertices randomly using the probability distribution, and it is treated as a candidate solution and is inserted in the population. Likewise, we generate candidate solutions as required by the initial population. Note that any centrality measure can be used in the population generation. Through our experimentation, we found that betweenness centrality is preferable.

Crossover: For crossover operation, we have used single-point crossover operation. We select two populations from the initial population randomly and perform crossover. During the crossover operation we make sure that there are no duplicate nodes in the child candidate solutions. After the crossover, if the number of nodes in the child candidate solution is less than k, we add nodes randomly using enhanced centrality probabilities. A crossover operation gives two candidate solutions.

Mutation: We perform single point mutation on each child candidate population obtained after crossover operation. For the mutation operation, we randomly replace any one node with a random node. The node is randomly selected using enhanced centrality probabilities.

3.2 Pruning Technique

Algorithm 1: Pruning Technique

Input : A LT1DT network G={G(V,E), W, θ_u, θ_u^R}, S_R, S_T.
Output: S_T

1 **begin**
2 | CR $\leftarrow$ DIFFUSION(G,S_R,S_T)
3 | **while** $Flag{=}True$ **do**
4 | | $Flag = False$
5 | | $V \leftarrow V(G) \setminus \{S_R \cup S_T\}$
6 | | **for** $u \in S_T$ **do**
7 | | | **for** $v \in V$ **do**
8 | | | | $\hat{S_T} = \{S_T \setminus u\} \cup \{v\}$
9 | | | | R = DIFFUSION(G,S_R,$\hat{S_T}$)
10 | | | | **if** $Length(R) < Length(CR)$ **then**
11 | | | | | $CR = R$
12 | | | | | $Flag = True$
13 | | | | | $S_T = \hat{S_T}$
14 | | | | | **break**
15 | | | **if** $Flag{=}True$ **then**
16 | | | | **break**
17 | **return** S_T

Consider the LT1DT network given in Fig. 2. For the rumour seed set $S_R = \{2\}$ and truth seed set $S_T = \{3,6\}$, the rumour affected nodes are $\Phi_R^* = \{2,5,8,9,10\}$. But, if we replace the node 6 with node 10 in S_T set then the rumour affected node is $\Phi_R^* = \{2\}$ only. With this intuition we developed a pruning technique.

The pruning technique takes truth seed set S_T as input. It iteratively removes one node from the S_T set and add one node from the network $V \setminus (S_T \cup S_R)$ and checks the rumour spread. If newly added node minimizes the rumour, we update the S_T set. The process is repeated until there is no improvement in the rumour count.

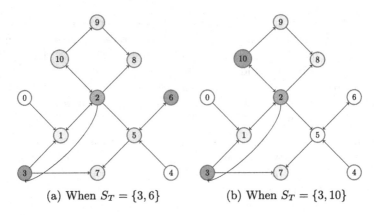

(a) When $S_T = \{3, 6\}$ (b) When $S_T = \{3, 10\}$

Fig. 2. $W(u,v) = 1 \setminus |N_v^{in}|$, $\theta_u = 0.5$, $\theta_1^R = 0.8$, $\theta_5^R = 0.4$ and $\theta_{7,8}^R = 0.6$ and for all the remaining nodes $\theta_u^R = 0.5$.

4   Implementation of Diffusion Function

The implementation of the diffusion function is very crucial. The naive implementation may not be right choice as it will take lot of time. In the naive implementation, at each iteration of the diffusion process, we maintain currently rumour influenced nodes (R) and truth influenced nodes (T). Initially, before start of the diffusion process $R = S_R$ and $T = S_T$. At each iteration, for each node $u \in V \setminus (S_R \cup T)$, we compute the total incoming rumour weight $t_r(u)$ and truth weight $t_t(u)$ of its influenced neighbours. If $t_r(u) + t_t(u) \geq \theta_u(u)$ then node u will be influenced, further if $t_r(u) \setminus t_r(u) + t_t(u) \geq \theta_u^R(u)$ then node u is rumour influenced and it is added to the set R otherwise node u will be added to set the T. The process is repeated until there are no new rumour affected or truth affected nodes. This naive approach takes $O(|V| + |E|)$ time for each iteration. With the following observations, we have come up with an efficient implementation of the diffusion function. In the first iteration, the nodes that can be influenced are only the neighbours of seed nodes S_R and S_T. In the subsequent iteration, the new influenced nodes can only be from the neighbours of rumour influenced or truth influenced nodes including the seed nodes. Remember, the neighbourhood of influential nodes can be much smaller than the entire vertex set. We avoid computation of total truth and rumour weight of all the nodes that can not be influenced in current iteration. In this implementation, we use a list to maintain all rumour or truth influenced nodes. Initially, the list contains the rumour and truth seed nodes. In each iteration, we traverse the elements of this list, for a node u in the list, we update the rumour/truth weights of all the out-neighbour of u. If u is rumour node $t_r(v)$ is updated otherwise, $t_t(v)$. Here, v is the out-neighbour of u. During this process, if any node v satisfies its influence condition, then the node is added to the list of newly influential nodes. After processing all the element of the list, we consider each node in the newly influential node, and the nodes will be added to rumour influenced or truth influenced depending on the condition it satisfies. The new implementation takes time proportional to $O(|N(R \cup T)|)$, which is usually much smaller in practice compare to $O(|V| + |E|)$.

Algorithm 2: LT1DT Diffusion

Input   : A LT1DT network G=$\{G(V,E),W,\theta_u ,\theta_u^R\}$,$S_R$,$S_T$.
Output: RA and TA

1 DIFFUSION(G, S_R, S_T) **begin**
2   actList = [ ]
3   infNodes = [ ]
4   RA = S_R
5   TA = S_T
6   **for** $u \in S_R$ **do**
7 | actList.add(u)
8   **for** $u \in S_T$ **do**
9 | actList.add(u)
10   **while** *Flag=True* **do**
11   Flag = False
12   newTnfNodes = [ ]
13   **for** $u \in actList$ **do**
14   **for** $v \in V \setminus (S_R \cup S_T \cup TA)$ **do**
15   **if** *($u \in S_R$ or $u \in RA$)* **then**
16 | rw[v] = rw[v] + weight(u,v)
17   **else**
18 | tw[v] = tw[v] + weight(u,v)
19   **if** *($tw[v] + rw[v]$) > $\theta_u[v]$ and $v \notin (RA \cup TA)$* **then**
20 | newInfNodes.add(v)
21   **for** $u \in newInfNodes$ **do**
22   infNodes.add(u)
23   actList.add(u)
24   newInfNodes.empty()
25   **for** $u \in infNodes$ **do**
26   **if** $u \in TA$ **then**
27 | continue
28   totw = rw[u] + tw[u]
29   **if** *($rw[u] \setminus totw$) >= $\theta_u^R[u]$ and $u \notin RA$* **then**
30   RA = RA $\cup$ {u}
31   Flag = True
32   **else**
33   RA = RA $\setminus$ {u}
34   TA = TA $\cup$ {u}
35   Flag = True
36   **return** RA *and* TA

---

5   Experimentation and Results

In this section, we discuss regarding the datasets and analyse the results. We have done experimentation on four real world datasets (email-Eu-core, netscience,CollegeMsg, crime-moreno) [18,21] and two synthetic datasets of size $2k$. Synthetic datasets are generated as follow:

- Scale-free network: A network is said be scale-free if it follows power-law degree distribution. We used Barabasi-Albert model [4] to generate scale-free network.
- Small-world network: In this network, most of the nodes are not linked with each others, but neighbours of certain nodes are likely to be linked with each other. Most of the nodes in the network can be reached by any other node through a few steps. A small-world network is generated with the Watts-Strogatz model [22] by setting the mean degree of regular lattice to 4 and the rewiring probability $\beta = 0.2$.

We have the following parameters in experiments: Influence and decision threshold are either generated randomly or a fixed threshold values are used. For fixed threshold values, we used

$$(\theta_u(u), \theta_u^R(u)) \in \{(0.1, 0.3), (0.5, 0.3)\}.$$

Rumour seed count and truth seed count: $|R_s|, |T_s| \in \{3, 5, 10\}$.
Rumour seed nodes are selected either randomly or using maximum degree. For fixed threshold values and rumour seed based on maximum degree, we get a total of 18 instances.
In both of the above experiments, we record total count of rumour affected nodes and also the average rumour count including the rumour seeds. For each data set, we have run all the existing heuristics and GA and results are tabulated for each of these algorithms. The pruning procedure improves the truth seed set and the final rumour count is also tabulated. The results for email-Eu-core and netscience are shown in Table 1 and Table 2. The results for CollegeMsg and crime-moreno are shown in Table 3 and Table 4. The results for Scale-free and Small-world are shown in Table 5 and Table 6.
For email-Eu-core dataset:
For fixed threshold values and rumour seed based on maximum degree, among the existing algorithm of Yang et al. [25], MG giving an average rumour count of 426.5 before pruning and after pruning an average rumour count of 422. We can clearly, see the pruning technique has improved the solutions of the existing heuristics. Our proposed GA heuristic giving an average rumour count of 416.83 before pruning and after pruning 413.55. Clearly, the proposed GA giving better results compared to existing heuristics.
For netscience dataset:
For fixed threshold values and rumour seed based on maximum degree, among the existing algorithm of Yang et al. [25], MG giving an average rumour count of 115.4 before pruning and after pruning an average rumour count of 113.9. We

can clearly, see the pruning technique has improved the solutions of the existing heuristics. Our proposed GA heuristic giving an average rumour count of 114.4 before pruning and after pruning 113.1. Clearly, the proposed GA giving better results compared to existing heuristics.

For the experiment where thresholds and rumour seed nodes selected randomly, GA is either matching with the results of existing heuristics or some times giving better rumour count. The reason could be, when rumour seed nodes are generated randomly, these nodes may be of less centrality and also they may be distant from the most influential nodes. Note that, to spread rumour usually most influential nodes are selected not the random nodes. We have also carried out experimentation on CollegeMsg and crime-moreno datasets and observed the proposed GA and pruning technique giving improved results. We have done two other experiments:

1). Generating a random truth seed set and pruning it, we call this as Rand-Pruning. The RandPrunning is repeated a certain number of times and a best seed truth is reported.

2). Truth seed set is selected based on enhanced centrality values.
Both these experiments are not giving competitive results. Among the existing heuristics MG is taking an average time of 7 s on the email-Eu-core data set, where as GA is taking on average 125 s. Note that, GA runs the diffusion process more times compared to the MG heuristic. The pruning technique on average taking 14 s over all the instances of email-Eu-core data set.

We have carried out our experiments on a Intel(R) Core(TM) $i7 - 8700U$ CPU and 16 GB memory and all the code is written in C++ (g++ version 11.4.0), under Ubuntu(22.04.2 LTS 64bit)[1].

Table 1. Experimental Results for email-Eu-Core and netscience Dadatsets for fixed threshold values and rumour seed set selected by maxdegree. We have quoted count of final rumour nodes for a particular instance and an average count of rumour affected node of all 18 instances before and after pruning.

	email-Eu-core				netscience			
	One Instance		Average		One instance		Average	
	it=0.1, dt=0.3 $S_R=3, S_T=10$		Of 18 instances		it=0.1, dt=0.3 $S_R=3, S_T=5$		Of 18 instances	
Algorithm	R	R^P	R	R^P	R	R^P	R	R^P
MG	679	637	426.5	422	139	131	115.44	113.94
PMG	695	631	427.05	418.11	141	131	116.77	113.27
CI	783	630	462.05	423	192	131	145.05	113.72
PCI	766	566	458.77	419.22	181	131	135.44	113.72
PR	723	633	453.05	421.94	241	131	164.55	113.72
PPR	716	622	454	420.61	187	131	148.22	114.44
GA	616	616	416.83	413.55	131	131	114.44	113.16

---

[1] The code, data sets and the results are publicly available at https://github.com/hiddenconfrepository/rumourminimization.

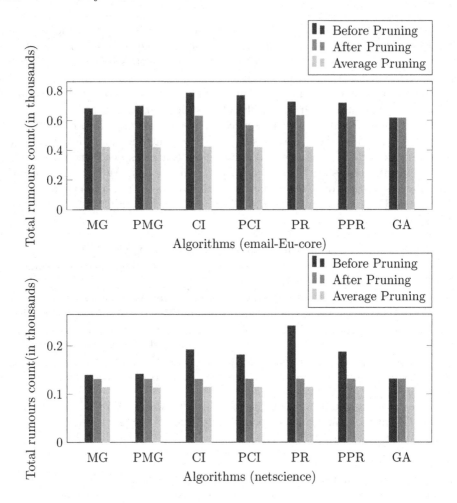

Table 2. Experimental Results for email-Eu-Core and netscience datasets for random threshold values and rumour seed set selected by randomly. We have quoted count of final rumour nodes for a particular instance and an average count of rumour affected node of all 18 instances before and after pruning.

	email-Eu-core				netscience			
	One Instance		Average		One instance		Average	
	$S_R=3, S_T=10$		Of 9 instances		$S_R=3, S_T=5$		Of 9 instances	
Algorithm	R	R^P	R	R^P	R	R^P	R	R^P
MG	952	952	952	952	376	376	296.88	290.66
PMG	952	952	952	952	376	376	290.66	290.66
CI	952	952	952	952	376	376	442.11	416.77
PCI	952	952	952	952	376	376	292.33	290.88
PR	952	952	952	952	433	376	442.11	416.77
PPR	952	952	952	952	376	376	290.66	290.66
GA	952	952	952	952	376	376	332.55	332.55

Table 3. Experimental Results for CollegeMsg and Crime-Moreno datasets for fixed threshold values and rumour seed set selected by maxdegree. We have quoted count of final rumour nodes for a particular instance and an average count of rumour affected node of all 18 instances before and after pruning.

	CollegeMsg				crime-moreno			
	One Instance		Average		One instance		Average	
	it=0.1, dt=0.3 $S_R=3, S_T=10$		Of 18 instances		it=0.1, dt=0.3 $S_R=3, S_T=5$		Of 18 instances	
Algorithm	R	R^P	R	R^P	R	R^P	R	R^P
MG	674	**658**	623.11	**621.88**	449	449	286.22	**284.11**
PMG	696	696	624.22	**624.05**	509	**452**	299.88	**284.72**
CI	1204	**619**	754.38	**619.77**	475	**439**	303.77	**283.00**
PCI	1204	**619**	751.83	**619.83**	548	**452**	317.94	**284.61**
PR	1344	**619**	774.72	**619.33**	512	**452**	341.83	**284.33**
PPR	1344	**619**	774.5	**619.44**	566	**452**	348.66	**285.77**
GA	**622**	**619**	619.61	**619.44**	**439**	**439**	282.38	**282.05**

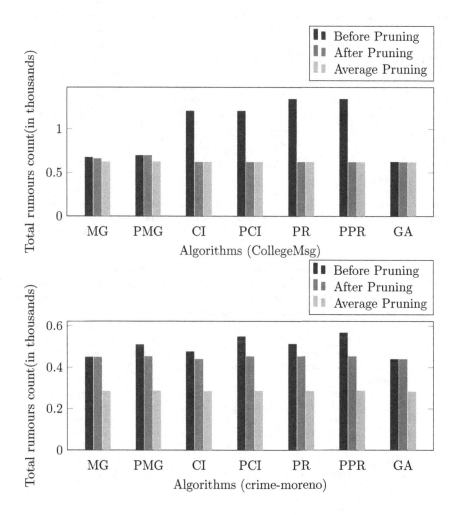

Table 4. Experimental Results for CollegeMsg and crime-moreno datasets for random threshold values and rumour seed set selected by randomly. We have quoted count of final rumour nodes for a particular instance and an average count of rumour affected node of all 9 instances before and after pruning.

	CollegeMsg				crime-moreno			
	One Instance		Average		One instance		Average	
	$S_R=3, S_T=10$		Of 9 instances		$S_R=3, S_T=5$		Of 9 instances	
Algorithm	R	R^P	R	R^P	R	R^P	R	R^P
MG	1846	1846	1848.33	1848.33	791	791	790.22	790.22
PMG	1846	1846	1848.33	1848.33	791	791	790.44	790.44
CI	1846	1846	1848.33	1848.33	791	791	790.22	790.22
PCI	1846	1846	1848.33	1848.33	791	791	790.33	790.33
PR	1846	1846	1848.33	1848.33	791	791	790.22	790.22
PPR	1846	1846	1848.33	1848.33	791	791	790.44	790.44
GA	1846	1846	1848.33	1848.33	791	791	790.22	790.22

Table 5. Experimental Results for Scale-free and Small-world datasets for fixed threshold values and rumour seed set selected by maxdegree. We have quoted count of final rumour nodes for a particular instance and an average count of rumour affected node of all 18 instances before and after pruning.

	Scale-free				Small-world			
	One Instance		Average		One instance		Average	
	it=0.1, dt=0.3 $S_R=3, S_T=10$		Of 18 instances		it=0.1, dt=0.3 $S_R=3, S_T=5$		Of 18 instances	
Algorithm	R	R^P	R	R^P	R	R^P	R	R^P
MG	137	137	458.61	458.61	1352	**1344**	505.61	501.94
PMG	137	137	458.61	458.61	1448	**1344**	589.16	501.11
CI	141	137	477.94	458.61	1546	**1344**	614.38	501.77
PCI	141	137	470.77	458.61	1590	**1344**	640.38	502.77
PR	161	137	567.83	458.6	1664	**1344**	632.38	500.27
PPR	161	137	558.66	458.61	1729	**1344**	684.77	500.72
GA	**137**	**137**	458.61	**458.61**	**1337**	1337	**500.83**	**500.55**

Table 6. Experimental Results for Scale-free and Small-world datasets for random threshold values and rumour seed set selected by randomly. We have quoted count of final rumour nodes for a particular instance and an average count of rumour affected node of all 18 instances before and after pruning.

	Scale-free				Small-world			
	One Instance		Average		One instance		Average	
	$S_R=3, S_T=10$		Of 9 instances		$S_R=3, S_T=5$		Of 9 instances	
Algorithm	R	R^P	R	R^P	R	R^P	R	R^P
MG	1990	1990	1994	1994	1995	1995	1994	1994
PMG	1996	1996	1994.66	1994.66	1995	1995	1994	1994
CI	1990	1990	1994	1994	1995	1995	1994	1994
PCI	1995	1990	1994.55	1994	1995	1995	1994	1994
PR	1990	1990	1994	1994	1995	1995	1994	1994
PPR	1996	1996	1994.66	1994.66	1995	1995	1994	1994
GA	1990	1990	1994	1994	1995	1995	1994	1994

6   Conclusion

Rumour minimization problem aims to selects k truth seed nodes in the network such that final rumour spread is minimized. In this paper, we have proposed a genetic-algorithm based heuristic for the rumour minimization problem under the LT1DT diffusion model. The proposed heuristics are performing better than the existing heuristics. We could not experiment on bigger data sets as the sequential implementation of the diffusion process computationally expensive. In future, we would like to explore in the direction of parallel or distributed computational aspects for diffusion process to scale the algorithms on large scale networks. It is also interesting to study the rumour minimization problem on signed social networks as well and for other diffusion models.

Acknowledgements. We are thankful to Prof. K. Swarupa Rani for her valuable comments and suggestions which helped us to keep our experiments in the right direction. We are also thankful to anonymous reviewers for their valuable suggestions and comments.

References

1. Abebe, R., et al.: Opinion dynamics optimization by varying susceptibility to persuasion via non-convex local search. ACM Trans. Knowl. Discov. Data **16**(2), 1–34 (2021)
2. Alla, L.S., Kare, A.S.: Opinion maximization in signed social networks using centrality measures and clustering techniques. In: Molla, A.R., Sharma, G., Kumar, P., Rawat, S. (eds.) Distributed Computing and Intelligent Technology. ICDCIT 2023. LNCS, vol. 13776, pp. 125–140. Springer, Cham (2023). https://doi.org/10.1007/978-3-031-24848-1_9
3. Banerjee, S., Jenamani, M., Pratihar, D.K.: ComBIM: a community-based solution approach for the budgeted influence maximization problem. Expert Syst. Appl. **125**, 1–13 (2019)
4. Barabási, A.L., Albert, R.: Emergence of scaling in random networks. Science **286**(5439), 509–512 (1999)
5. Bharathi, S., Kempe, D., Salek, M.: Competitive influence maximization in social networks. In: Deng, X., Graham, F.C. (eds.) WINE 2007. LNCS, vol. 4858, pp. 306–311. Springer, Heidelberg (2007). https://doi.org/10.1007/978-3-540-77105-0_31
6. Borodin, A., Filmus, Y., Oren, J.: Threshold models for competitive influence in social networks. In: Saberi, A. (ed.) WINE 2010. LNCS, vol. 6484, pp. 539–550. Springer, Heidelberg (2010). https://doi.org/10.1007/978-3-642-17572-5_48
7. Budak, C., Agrawal, D., El Abbadi, A.: Limiting the spread of misinformation in social networks. In: Proceedings of the 20th International Conference on World Wide Web, pp. 665–674. Association for Computing Machinery, New York, NY, USA (2011)
8. Chen, W., Wang, Y., Yang, S.: Efficient influence maximization in social networks. In: Proceedings of the 15th ACM SIGKDD International Conference on Knowledge Discovery and Data Mining, pp. 199–208. Association for Computing Machinery (2009)

264   V. K. Rajak and A. S. kare

9. Chen, W., Yuan, Y., Zhang, L.: Scalable influence maximization in social networks under the linear threshold model. In: 2010 IEEE International Conference on Data Mining, pp. 88–97 (2010)
10. Choi, D., Oh, H., Chun, S., Kwon, T., Han, J.: Preventing rumor spread with deep learning. Expert Syst. Appl. **197**, 116688 (2022)
11. Fan, L., Lu, Z., Wu, W., Thuraisingham, B., Ma, H., Bi, Y.: Least cost rumor blocking in social networks. In: 2013 IEEE 33rd International Conference on Distributed Computing Systems, pp. 540–549 (2013)
12. Gautam, R.K., Kare, A.S., Durga Bhavani, S.: Centrality measures based heuristics for perfect awareness problem in social networks. In: Morusupalli, R., Dandibhotla, T.S., Atluri, V.V., Windridge, D., Lingras, P., Komati, V.R. (eds.) Multidisciplinary Trends in Artificial Intelligence. MIWAI 2023. LNCS, vol. 14078, pp. 91–100. Springer, Cham (2023). https://doi.org/10.1007/978-3-031-36402-0_8
13. Gong, M., Yan, J., Shen, B., Ma, L., Cai, Q.: Influence maximization in social networks based on discrete particle swarm optimization. Inf. Sci. **367–368**, 600–614 (2016)
14. Goyal, A., Lu, W., Lakshmanan, L.V.: Simpath: an efficient algorithm for influence maximization under the linear threshold model. In: 2011 IEEE 11th International Conference on Data Mining, pp. 211–220 (2011)
15. He, Q., et al.: Reinforcement-learning-based competitive opinion maximization approach in signed social networks. IEEE Trans. Comput. Soc. Syst. **9**(5), 1505–1514 (2022)
16. He, X., Song, G., Chen, W., Jiang, Q.: Influence blocking maximization in social networks under the competitive linear threshold model. In: Proceedings of the 2012 SIAM International Conference on Data Mining (SDM), pp. 463–474 (2012)
17. Kempe, D., Kleinberg, J., Tardos, E.: Maximizing the spread of influence through a social network. In: Proceedings of the Ninth ACM SIGKDD International Conference on Knowledge Discovery and Data Mining, pp. 137–146. Association for Computing Machinery, New York, NY, USA (2003)
18. Leskovec, J., Krevl, A.: SNAP Datasets: stanford large network dataset collection, June 2014. http://snap.stanford.edu/data
19. Nayak, A., Hosseinalipour, S., Dai, H.: Smart information spreading for opinion maximization in social networks. In: IEEE INFOCOM 2019 - IEEE Conference on Computer Communications, pp. 2251–2259 (2019)
20. Ni, Q., Guo, J., Huang, C., Wu, W.: Community-based rumor blocking maximization in social networks. In: Zhang, Z., Li, W., Du, D.-Z. (eds.) AAIM 2020. LNCS, vol. 12290, pp. 73–84. Springer, Cham (2020). https://doi.org/10.1007/978-3-030-57602-8_7
21. Rossi, R., Ahmed, N.: The network data repository with interactive graph analytics and visualization. In: Proceedings of the AAAI Conference on Artificial Intelligence, vol. 29, no. 1 (2015)
22. Watts, D.J., Strogatz, S.H.: Collective dynamics of small-world networks. Nature (1998)
23. Wen, S., Jiang, J., Xiang, Y., Yu, S., Zhou, W., Jia, W.: To shut them up or to clarify: restraining the spread of rumors in online social networks. IEEE Trans. Parallel Distrib. Syst. **25**(12), 3306–3316 (2014)
24. Wu, H., et al.: Containment of rumor spread by selecting immune nodes in social networks. Math. Biosci. Eng. 2614–2631 (2021)
25. Yang, L., Li, Z., Giua, A.: Containment of rumor spread in complex social networks. Inf. Sci. **506**, 113–130 (2020)

26. Yang, L., Ma, Z., Li, Z., Giua, A.: Rumor containment by blocking nodes in social networks. IEEE Trans. Syst. Man Cybern. Syst. 1–13 (2023)
27. Zhu, J., Ghosh, S., Wu, W.: Robust rumor blocking problem with uncertain rumor sources in social networks. World Wide Web, pp. 229–247 (2021)

A Machine Learning Driven Approach for Forecasting Parkinson's Disease Progression Using Temporal Data

Aditya Roy Chowdhury, Rohit Ahuja$^{(\boxtimes)}$ (iD), and Angad Manroy

Thapar Institute of Engineering and Technology Patiala, Patiala, India
{achowdhury_be20,rohit.ahuja,amanroy_be20}@thapar.edu

Abstract. Parkinson's disease (PD) is a prevalent neurodegenerative disease that hurts millions globally. For prompt intervention and successful therapy, Parkinson's disease (PD) must be identified early. However, a significant obstacle to creating progression-predicting models for early detection is the absence of extensive and readily available data. This research aims to present a robust method to forecast Parkinson's disease progression using minimal information. The Movement Disorder Society Unified Parkinson's Disease Rating Scale (MDS-UPDRS) is a commonly used metric for evaluating both motor and non-motor symptoms to determine the severity and course of Parkinson's disease. The ML models in this research were evaluated based on their ability to predict the MDS-UPDRS values with minimum error with respect to the actual measurements. The preprocessing of this data includes clustering based on patient ID and linear interpolation to fill values between contiguous readings. To create a baseline, MDS-UPDRS [1-4] are treated as unsupervised time series data by setting the time stamp as the input variable and the corresponding MDS-UPDRS value as the output variable. Then, the data is re-framed into a supervised format and tested on the same set of models to compare performance. The data for this research is sourced from the Accelerating Medicines Partnership-Parkinson's Disease (AMP-PD) Kaggle dataset. Among the machine learning algorithms assessed, the Multi Layer Perceptron (MLP) exhibited the most favorable predictive performance with an MAE of 0.52 and an MSE of 0.57 on average across the four clusters ($U1$, $U2$, $U3$, $U4$) for supervised format. This performance surpasses the second-best-performing algorithm, Random Forest, substantially. The MLP outperformed Random Forest by 25.46% in terms of MAE and 28.22% in MSE. Additionally, using a supervised format reduced MAE by 17.08% on average for all models and 41.73% for MLP compared to an unsupervised format. This considerable improvement suggests the robustness and efficacy of the MLP model and supervised re-framing in capturing the intricate progression trends of Parkinson's disease.

Keywords: Parkinson's Disease Progression · MDS-UPDRS Scores · Machine Learning · Time Series Forecasting · Unsupervised Learning

© The Author(s), under exclusive license to Springer Nature Switzerland AG 2024
S. Devismes et al. (Eds.): ICDCIT 2024, LNCS 14501, pp. 266–281, 2024.
https://doi.org/10.1007/978-3-031-50583-6_18

1 Introduction

Parkinson's disease (PD) is a complex neurodegenerative disorder character-ized by a range of motor and non-motor symptoms that generally occur in older populations but can also appear in younger individuals. The condition leads to the accumulation of lewy bodies [1] and to neuronal loss in certain brain areas [2]. It is the second most commonly occurring neurodegenerative disease [3]. Though not contagious, the disease displays many characteristics of a pandemic [4]. The motor symptoms include tremors and jitters in hands and limbs, grimacing among others [6]. Now it is observed that motor symptoms are the most quality-of-life disturbing factors both in initial and matured stages of the disease [5], but non-motor symptoms such as hallucinations [6,7] also add to the discomforts. PD poses a significant global health burden [8], with prevalence increasing as populations age, and is one of the fastest growing neurological dis-eases in the world [9]. Despite extensive research, the exact causes of PD remain elusive, making early diagnosis and accurate progression monitoring crucial for effective patient care.

The view of Parkinson's Disease being perceived as a Pandemic is becoming increasingly popular [11]. Early detection of PD is imperative yet challenging [10] due to its insidious onset and the gradual emergence of symptoms. Early symp-toms include subtle indicators that may be easily misunderstood as symptoms of aging or common curable infections. Some of these include tremors, hunched posture, changes in handwriting, etc. By the time patients exhibit noticeable motor impairments, a substantial portion of dopamine-producing neurons may already be compromised. This presents a critical dilemma for clinicians, as early intervention strategies are more effective when applied before significant neural damage occurs. Consequently, according to some studies, about 90-95% of the patients are diagnosed with the condition post the age of 60 [12].

The origins of PD are multifactorial and intricate. About 10-15% of PD cases are genetic, implying they are passed from one generation to the next [13] While genetic mutations like those in SNCA, LRRK2, and PARKIN have been linked to increased susceptibility [14], environmental factors such as exposure to toxins and head injuries can also play roles [15]. The complex interplay between genetic predisposition and environmental influences contributes to the heterogeneity of the disease presentation. This non-specificity underscores the necessity for com-prehensive and personalized assessment approaches. Hence, This study utilized parameters (MDS-UPDRS) that quantify the symptoms of the disease rather than focusing on causal factors. As it intrinsically would include personalized details of the patient. Every case of progression prediction has already devel-oped the condition, which makes identifying the cause less critical as long as progression trends can be evaluated, and this study aims at making this evalu-ation using machine learning techniques.

Precisely quantifying and tracking Parkinson's disease (PD) progression poses a complex challenge due to the diverse array of symptoms and the sub-jectivity of traditional assessments. The Movement Disorder Society-sponsored Unified Parkinson's Disease Rating Scale (MDS-UPDRS) presents an adept solution. By comprehensively evaluating both motor and non-motor aspects, MDS-UPDRS captures the intricacies of PD's multifaceted nature. Its numerical scoring system quantifies symptoms, providing an objective basis for tracking disease severity and evolution. The modular structure adapts assessments to each patient's unique symptom profile, contributing to a patient-centric approach. Studies also show a good correlation between the quality of life and MDS-UPDRS scores [16], further validating the approach. MDS-UPDRS plays a pivotal role in addressing the scarcity of holistic, longitudinal datasets in PD research. Its standardized scoring system offers consistency, facilitating the analysis of progression trends across various patients and timeframes. This study harnesses machine learning techniques to extract valuable patterns from MDS-UPDRS scores, augmenting the understanding of PD progression dynamics. In essence, MDS-UPDRS's comprehensive evaluation framework and standardized nature make it an essential tool to overcome the challenges of quantifying and measuring the PD stage, supporting the pursuit of predictive insights into disease progression.

Addressing these challenges necessitates innovative solutions. This research recognizes the potential of machine learning in analyzing generic longitudinal temporal trends from large-scale clinical datasets. By harnessing patterns and correlations within the dataset, machine learning models could predict the current state and potentially the trajectory of PD progression. Such an approach could offer clinicians an additional tool to augment their expertise, aiding in timely interventions and refined patient care.

1.1 Our Contribution

The research presents distinct contributions to Parkinson's disease progression analysis. These contributions not only enhance the understanding of Parkinson's disease evolution but also hold practical implications for informed clinical decision-making supported by AI-driven insights. The contributions of our research are four-fold:

1. Proposes a robust method for personalized Parkinson's progression forecasting and grounds for future research.
2. Demonstrates the potential of MLP Regressor to capture the disease's intricate symptom progression and underlying medication effect by modeling the non-linear dynamics of MDS-UPDRS readings.
3. Elucidates the viability of the technique to re-frame unsupervised data into supervised data to enhance time series forecasting performance.
4. Provides insight into the minimum quantity of clinical measurements required to forecast each MDS-UPDRS with minimal error.

The rest of the manuscript is summarized as follows. Section 2 reviews existing relevant literature on neurodegenerative disease progression analysis. Section 3 outlines our methodology, including data preprocessing, model selection, and performance evaluation. Subsequently, Sect. 4 presents results from unsupervised and supervised learning approaches. In Sect. 5, we discuss the implications of our findings and contrast the two approaches. Lastly, Sect. 6 outlines future research possibilities and concludes our contributions to understanding Parkinson's disease progression.

2 Related Work

In the following section, we conduct a comprehensive review of existing research that underpins our study. Our objective is to contextualize our approach within the broader domain of disease progression modeling and predictive analytics. While direct matches may be limited, we extract valuable insights from diverse fields, including biomarker studies, predictive modeling in medical contexts, longitudinal data analysis, machine learning in clinical prognostications, and an examination of the challenges in modeling disease progression. This exploration establishes a solid foundation, highlighting the significance of our research in advancing Parkinson's disease prediction and progression assessment.

2.1 Biomarker Studies

In Parkinson's disease (PD) research, biomarkers play a pivotal role in enhancing diagnosis and prognosis accuracy. Biomarkers, which reflect an individual's physiological, molecular, or biochemical state, offer valuable insights into disease progression. The literature on PD diagnosis and management, bolstered by machine learning (ML) techniques [17], spans various facets of the disease, including genetic and environmental factors. Neural intricacies are explored, along with therapeutic interventions such as deep brain stimulation and gene therapy [24]. Notably, ML is applied to neurophysiological data, with studies analyzing electroencephalogram (EEG) signals to extract potential biomarkers during specific tasks [18,19]. Furthermore, research investigates ML algorithms' effectiveness in diagnosing and categorizing PD cases based on diverse medical parameters [25]. This diverse body of work signifies the strides made in merging machine learning with Parkinson's disease research, ultimately improving diagnostic accuracy and treatment strategies.

2.2 Predictive Modeling in Medical Fields

Predictive modeling, using mathematical and computational techniques to anticipate future events, has gained ground in medical contexts [26]. With the rise of Artificial Intelligence (AI) and data mining, it has become a potent tool for healthcare prediction and decision-making [20]. Machine learning methods, including Support Vector Machines (SVM), Artificial Neural Networks (ANN), Naïve Bayes (NB), and Decision Trees (DT), are widely used for predictive models [21,27]. However, model effectiveness varies due to the complexity of medical data [26,28]. Predictive modeling extends beyond traditional medical records to encompass molecular and clinical data, enhancing diagnostics and treatment guidance [22, 28]. Challenges like data quality, regulatory compliance, and ethical concerns remain pivotal [29]. In cardiovascular health, predictive modeling prompts critical inquiries to discern the utility and limitations of AI-based prediction models [23]. Traumatic brain injury (TBI) prediction has also benefited from predictive modeling, refining outcomes assessment and management strategies [30]. Ongoing research is essential to address limitations and optimize model performance. As AI and data analytics reshape healthcare, predictive modeling integration promises advancements in disease prognosis and personalized treatment [29, 30].

3   Data and Dataset Description

A complete record of clinical information pertaining to patients with Parkinson's disease is included in the "Patient Time-Series History" dataset. There are a number of significant columns in it, including "visit_id," which is used to identify each visit in a unique way, and "visit_month," which indicates the month in which the visit occurred in relation to the patient's first recorded visit. Each patient who participated in the study has a specific identification number, which is listed in the "patient_id" column.

The collection of scores for various sections of the Unified Parkinson's Disease Rating Scale (UPDRS), marked by "updrs_[1-4]," are the prime features of this dataset. These results provide essential information about the severity of particular symptoms, such as those affecting mood and behavior (Part 1) and motor functions (Part 3). Higher scores indicate more severe symptoms in the appropriate category in each section.

Additionally, the "upd23b_clinical_state_on_medication" column keeps track of whether patients were taking drugs such as Levodopa at the time of the UPDRS evaluation. This information is vital because it primarily affects Part 3 results, which rate motor function. Due to the relatively short half-life of these medications (typically one day), patients may perform the motor function assessment twice a month, once while taking the medication and once without, in order to investigate its effects.

4   Methodology

This section delineates the comprehensive methodology, as depicted in Fig. 1, employed to analyze and predict Parkinson's disease (PD) progression patterns using regression and classification approaches. Our approach encompasses data preprocessing, patient-centric clustering, time-series transformation, and the comparison of different techniques used. Initially, the problem was approached as a classification task wherein each point on the updrs score was considered a separate class, and models were trained accordingly. This was followed by attempting the same problems as a regression task. Both unsupervised and supervised learning technique was applied.

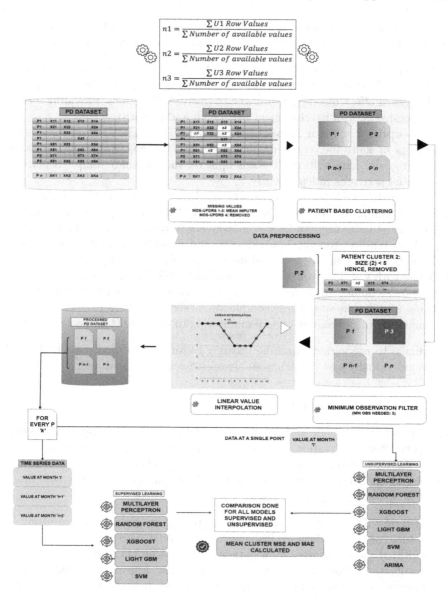

$$n1 = \frac{\sum U1\ Row\ Values}{\sum Number\ of\ available\ values}$$

$$n2 = \frac{\sum U2\ Row\ Values}{\sum Number\ of\ available\ values}$$

$$n3 = \frac{\sum U3\ Row\ Values}{\sum Number\ of\ available\ values}$$

Fig. 1. Proposed Framework

4.1 Clinical Assessment Measures

The foundational element of our methodology is the Movement Disorder Society-sponsored Unified Parkinson's Disease Rating Scale (MDS-UPDRS). This metric quantifies motor and non-motor symptoms across various disease stages, providing a robust basis for assessing PD progression. We extend this assessment framework to both regression and classification tasks, where MDS-UPDRS scores serve as input data. MDS-UPDRS of a patient is categorized as follows:

1. **Mds-updrs 1 (Non-Motor Aspects)**: It examines non-motor aspects of Parkinson's disease, including mood, cognition, and behavior. It captures changes in affect, sleep patterns, and cognitive fluctuations, providing a comprehensive view of psychological well-being and cognitive state.
2. **Mds-updrs 2 (Motor Aspects of Daily Living)**: The score assesses motor aspects of daily life, encompassing tasks like speech, swallowing, dressing, hygiene, and handwriting. It sheds light on the patient's ability to perform essential activities independently.
3. **Mds-updrs 3 (Motor Examination)**: Involves the motor examination, a critical component for assessing the severity of motor symptoms. This section includes standardized tasks and maneuvers to quantify motor impairments, such as rigidity, tremor, bradykinesia, and postural instability. It provides insights into the progression and fluctuation of motor symptoms.
4. **Mds-updrs 4 (Motor Complications)**: This focuses on motor complications stemming from dopaminergic treatment, particularly motor fluctuations, and dyskinesias. These complications significantly impact the patient's quality of life and require careful monitoring to optimize treatment strategies.

The aim is to use various machine learning techniques to predict each of the 4 scores individually and construct an aggregate accuracy measure.

4.2 Data Preprocessing

The dataset from Kaggle and Accelerating Medicines Partnership (AMP) comprises over 2600 observations. An innovative preprocessing step involved reorganizing the data into patient clusters to improve predictive modeling accuracy, considering challenges arising from limited observations and varying visit intervals. The following steps were taken:

1. Clustering Rationale: The dataset was grouped by patient ID, resulting in clusters containing data exclusively for individual patients. This clustering facilitated the isolation of each patient's progression trajectory.
2. Interpolation: Considering gaps between visits, Linear interpolation was employed to estimate the missing UPDRS scores between consecutive measurements.
3. Re-Framing Dataset: This step enables us to transform the data from Unsupervised to Supervised with a notion to employ supervised learning models. This re-framing is done by employing the subsequent time step as the output variable and the preceding time steps as input variables to accomplish this [31].
4. Minimum Observations Filter: To maintain dataset quality, clusters with fewer than 5 observations were omitted, reducing the potential impact of noise on analysis outcomes.

4.3   Model Selection and Comparison

A diverse set of machine learning models was selected for comparison, along with formulas they use for quantifying performance:

1. LightGBM: A gradient boosting framework that uses tree-based learning techniques for enhanced efficiency.

$$y = \sum_{k=1}^{K} w_k h_k(x) \tag{1}$$

2. XGBoost: An optimized gradient boosting library that excels in predictive accuracy and speed.

$$y = \sum_{k=1}^{K} f_k(x) \tag{2}$$

3. Multilayer Perceptron (MLP): A type of artificial neural network known for its depth and versatility in various machine learning tasks.

$$y = f\left(\sum_{i=1}^{n} w_i x_i + b\right) \tag{3}$$

4. Support Vector Machine (SVM): A powerful and versatile machine learning algorithm for classification and regression tasks.

$$y = \sum_{i=1}^{n} \alpha_i K(x_i, x) + b \tag{4}$$

5. Random Forest: A robust ensemble learning method that combines multiple decision trees for improved predictive accuracy.

$$y = \text{MajorityVote}(y_1, y_2, ..., y_n) \tag{5}$$

6. Autoregressive Integrated Moving Average (ARIMA): A time series forecasting technique that models data as a combination of autoregressive and moving average components.

$$y_t = c + \phi_1 y_{t-1} + \phi_2 y_{t-2} + ... + \phi_p y_{t-p} + \theta_1 \epsilon_{t-1} + \theta_2 \epsilon_{t-2} + ... + \theta_q \epsilon_{t-q} + \epsilon_t \tag{6}$$

Unsupervised Regression Approach: Here, for every model, each cluster was trained and tested. For this process, time-stamp for each MDS-UPDRS measurement of the patient is given as an input and the corresponding MDS-UPDRS value is the target attribute. This would map every month to an MDS-UPDRS score, the sequential feeding of which would train the model.

Supervised Regression Approach: For this approach, the data was reformatted into a time-series sequential input format. The model was fed 3 sequential inputs to predict the target variable at the next step.

This process was executed for every model, and the mean of accuracy parameters from all clusters were compared.

4.4   Performance Evaluation

Model evaluation was based on Mean Squared Error (MSE) and Mean Absolute Error (MAE). The rationale for choosing these metrics, which provide insights into predictive accuracy and error magnitude, was elucidated. MAE and MSE calculations were carried out as follows:

$$MAE = \frac{1}{N} \sum_{i=1}^{N} |x_i - y_i| \tag{7}$$

$$MSE = \frac{1}{N} \sum_{i=1}^{N} (x_i - y_i)^2 \tag{8}$$

Cluster-Level Evaluation: Each model was trained on 80% of data within each cluster and tested on the remaining 20%. Predictions were compared to target values, and individual cluster-level MSE and MAE were calculated.

Clustering Rationale: Clustering by the patient was chosen to study patient-specific progression patterns comprehensively. The goal was to uncover common trends if they exist while accounting for individual variations.

4.5   Time-Series Formatting

The dataset was transformed into a time-series format with a look-back of 3. This decision was guided by the following key considerations:

1. **Prediction Accuracy**: A time step of 3 facilitated capturing accurate progression trends, providing sufficient historical context for predictive modeling.
2. **Observation Distribution**: The availability of observations varied across visit months. A look-back of 3 ensured optimal data utilization, particularly for initial phases where more observations were available.

Time-series formatting is essential to ensure the dataset is ready for applying the supervised learning approach after applying the unsupervised method. A summary of the methodology is illustrated in Fig. 1.

5   Results

Our work aimed to forecast the MDS-UPDRS[1-4] of patients with Parkinson's Disease. We investigated different models as well as ways of manipulating and organizing data to improve the forecast accuracy of the MDS-UPDRS score. The 4 UPDRS data were trained on four separate instances of the same model, and this was repeated for each of 237 patients with more than five entries or readings. Results of different approaches were obtained and compared by implementing them on selected ML models. MLP (Multi Layer Perceptron), trained on the supervised format of our interpolated data, outperformed every other model with an MAE of 0.607, 0.505, 0.566, 0.420 for MDS-UPDRS 1, 2, 3, and 4, respectively. Furthermore, MAE and MSE were compared for different cluster sizes (number of entries or readings per patient) of the 237 patients. The cluster sizes (no of readings per patient) of 11, 10, 11, and 12 gave the lowest MAE and MSE in the prediction of MDS-UPDRS 1, 2, 3, and 4, respectively. This result can be observed in Figs. 2, 3, 4 and 5 which are the plots of the average MAE and MSE of all patients with a particular cluster size. Lastly, random patients were selected to visually demonstrate in Figs. 6, 7 and 8 the prediction accuracy of the MLP model (trained on supervised data) on unseen data taken from the training set.

5.1   Unsupervised Learning

A set of machine learning models was trained using the unsupervised regression approach for predicting Parkinson's disease progression (UPDRS Score). MLP (Multi Layer Perceptron) with a single hidden layer of 100 neurons using Adam optimization and weight initialization in the random state 26 gave the least prediction error. The MLP model used a constant learning rate of 0.001 and a relu activation function. Table 1 contains the MAE and MSE for each UPDRS Score prediction by all the trained models.

Table 1. Unsupervised Learning

UPDRS	MLP		Random Forest		SVM		XGBoost		Light GBM		ARIMA	
	MAE	MSE	MAE	MSE	MAE	MSE	MAE	MSE	MAE	MSE	MAE	MSE
U1	0.974	1.574	1.201	2.185	1.279	2.424	1.153	2.055	1.3	2.48	1.33	4.775
U2	0.88	1.476	1.042	2.042	1.064	2.123	1.041	2.051	1.075	2.144	1.109	3.955
U3	1.004	1.754	1.169	2.208	1.168	2.205	1.119	2.087	1.189	2.24	2.794	23.64
U4	0.737	1.147	0.875	1.826	0.851	1.704	0.878	1.835	0.872	1.758	0.83	2.257

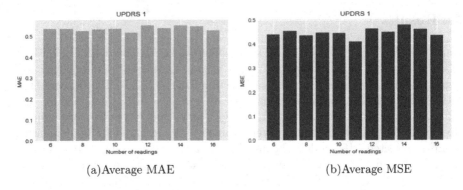

(a)Average MAE   (b)Average MSE

Fig. 2. UPDRS 1 Average MAE of different cluster sizes

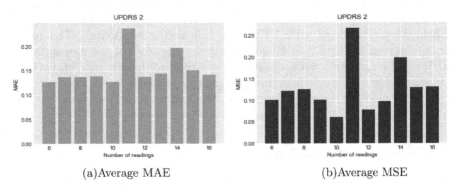

(a)Average MAE   (b)Average MSE

Fig. 3. UPDRS 2 Average MAE of different cluster sizes

5.2 Supervised Learning

The same set of machine learning models (except ARIMA) was used for training on the converted supervised data. ARIMA only takes the time series array as an input and trains on it without requiring a target. This constraint of the ARIMA'a input format made it unsuitable for training on supervised data containing an explicit target variable. The method of reorganizing the time series data into a supervised format with a look-back of 3 improved the performance of all machine learning models under consideration. Using supervised data reduced the MAE by an average of 17.08% when compared to the implementation of the same models on unsupervised data. Again, MLP outperformed all other models. The MLP model trained on supervised data had the exact parameters as the MLP model trained on unsupervised data. MAE and MSE of all the models trained on supervised data as shown in Table 2.

In the supervised learning approach, where prediction accuracy is notably emphasized, the results indicate that the MLP consistently achieves the lowest Mean Absolute Error (MAE) and Mean Squared Error (MSE) values across all UPDRS scores. This suggests that the MLP excels in minimizing predic-

Table 2. Supervised Learning

UPDRS	MLP		Random Forest		SVM		XGBoost		Light GBM	
	MAE	MSE	MAE	MSE	MAE	MSE	MAE	MSE	MAE	MSE
U1	0.607	0.673	0.974	1.53	1.1	1.905	1.001	1.605	1.2	2.11
U2	0.505	0.563	0.824	1.355	0.929	1.673	0.843	1.398	1.019	1.87
U3	0.566	0.617	0.943	1.54	1.06	1.891	0.968	1.601	1.144	2.078
U4	0.42	0.437	0.788	1.497	0.836	1.638	0.8	1.522	0.902	1.814

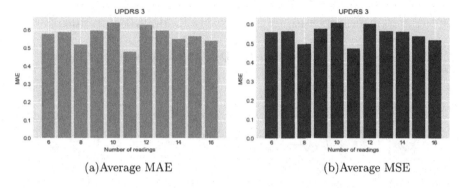

(a)Average MAE   (b)Average MSE

Fig. 4. UPDRS 3 Average MAE of different cluster sizes

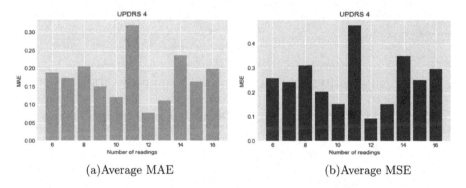

(a)Average MAE   (b)Average MSE

Fig. 5. UPDRS 4 Average MAE of different cluster sizes

tion errors and accurately captures the complexities of Parkinson's disease progression. Similarly, the Random Forest, Support Vector Machine (SVM), and Extreme Gradient Boosting (XGBoost) models showcase competitive performance, underscoring their capability to capture the intricate relationships between symptom severity and progression patterns. In the unsupervised learning approach, the results reaffirm the superiority of the MLP. It consistently exhibits the lowest MAE and MSE values, demonstrating its prowess in capturing patterns without relying on labeled data. Notably, it is essential to men-

278   A. R. Chowdhury et al.

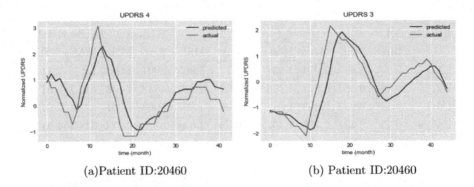

(a)Patient ID:20460   (b) Patient ID:20460

Fig. 6. Plot of MLP Inference on Test Data of Randomly Selected Patients

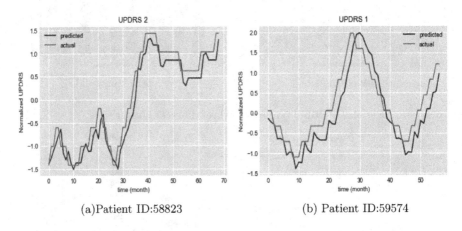

(a)Patient ID:58823   (b) Patient ID:59574

Fig. 7. Plot of MLP Inference on Test Data of Randomly Selected Patients

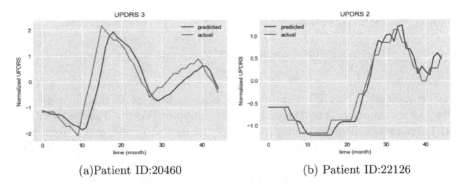

(a)Patient ID:20460   (b) Patient ID:22126

Fig. 8. Plot of MLP Inference on Test Data of Randomly Selected Patients

tion that ARIMA, employed within the unsupervised context, yields relatively higher prediction errors. This observation aligns with the intricate and nonlinear nature of Parkinson's disease progression, which may challenge the assumptions of these simpler models in the absence of labeled outcomes. Considering the comparison between the two approaches, it becomes evident that the supervised MLP model consistently outperforms other models in both supervised and unsupervised learning contexts. The MLP's ability to accurately predict disease progression underscores its robustness in addressing the intricate and dynamic nature of Parkinson's disease.

6 Conclusion and Future Scope

In conclusion, our study delved into the intricate landscape of Parkinson's disease progression, harnessing advanced machine-learning techniques with the aid of MDS-UPDRS scores. These scores, integrated into our predictive models, yielded remarkably low Mean Squared Error (MSE) values, suggesting their potential in enhancing clinical decision-making. The outcomes shed light on possible generalized progression patterns within Parkinson's disease. This insight opens the door to targeted interventions involving medication and personalized exercise regimes, promising better patient care and improved quality of life. Given the use of real-life patient data, the practical viability of our models becomes apparent. The demonstrated predictive power of machine learning, coupled with the integration of MDS-UPDRS scores and personalized factors, underscores the transformative role of AI in healthcare. Looking forward, our research lays a robust foundation for deeper exploration of Parkinson's disease progression. Potential avenues include the incorporation of alternative parameters for disease quantification, which could provide a more tailored assessment of patient conditions and novel indicators for disease progression. Furthermore, the dataset's potential extends to unraveling the genetic underpinnings of Parkinson's disease. By synergistically analyzing progression data with genetic and protein mutational profiles, we may uncover biomarkers and therapeutic targets. These interdisciplinary efforts have the potential to advance basic research and personalized treatment strategies. Lastly, enhancing predictive accuracy through ensemble machine learning models, tailored to individual attributes, presents an opportunity for more personalized predictions and treatment recommendations. This approach acknowledges the inherent variability in disease progression across individuals and enriches the clinical toolkit for healthcare practitioners.

References

1. Bloem, B.R., Okun, M.S., Klein, C.: Parkinson's disease. The Lancet **397**(10291), 2284–2303 (2021)
2. Kalia, L.V., Lang, A.E.: Parkinson's disease. The Lancet **386**(9996), 896–912 (2015)

3. Sherer, T.B., Chowdhury, S., Peabody, K., Brooks, D.W.: Overcoming obstacles in Parkinson's disease. Mov. Disord. **27**(13), 1606–1611 (2012)

4. Morens, D.M., Folkers, G.K., Fauci, A.S.: What is a pandemic? J. Infect. Dis. **200**(7), 1018–1021 (2009)

5. Gökçal, E., Gür, V.E., Selvitop, R., Yildiz, G.B., Talip, A.S.İL.: Motor and non-motor symptoms in Parkinson's disease: effects on quality of life. Arch. Neuropsychiatry **54**(2), 143 (2017)

6. Bulpitt, C.J., Shaw, K., Clifton, P., Stern, G., Davies, J.B., Reid, J.L.: The symptoms of patients treated for Parkinson's disease. Clin. Neuropharmacol. **8**(2), 175–183 (1985)

7. Arnulf, I., et al.: Hallucinations, REM sleep, and Parkinson's disease: a medical hypothesis. Neurology **55**(2), 281–288 (2000)

8. Ou, Z., et al.: Global trends in the incidence, prevalence, and years lived with disability of Parkinson's disease in 204 countries/territories from 1990 to 2019. Front. Public Health **9**, 776847 (2021)

9. Feigin, V.L., et al.: Global, regional, and national burden of neurological disorders during 1990–2015: a systematic analysis for the Global Burden of Disease Study 2015. The Lancet Neurol. **16**(11), 877–897 (2017)

10. Tolosa, E., Garrido, A., Scholz, S.W., Poewe, W.: Challenges in the diagnosis of Parkinson's disease. The Lancet Neurol. **20**(5), 385–397 (2021)

11. Dorsey, E., Sherer, T., Okun, M.S., Bloem, B.R.: The emerging evidence of the Parkinson pandemic. J. Parkinsons Dis. **8**(s1), S3–S8 (2018)

12. https://www.ninds.nih.gov/current-research/focus-disorders/focus-parkinsons-disease-research/parkinsons-disease-challenges-progress-and-promise . Accessed 7 July 2023

13. https://www.parkinson.org/understanding-parkinsons/causes/genetics . Accessed 4 July 2023

14. Nuytemans, K., Theuns, J., Cruts, M., Van Broeckhoven, C.: Genetic etiology of parkinson disease associated with mutations in the $SNCA$, $PARK2$, $PINK1$, $PARK7$, and $LRRK2$ genes: a mutation update. Hum. Mutat. **31**(7), 763–780 (2010)

15. Ball, N., Teo, W.P., Chandra, S., Chapman, J.: Parkinson's disease and the environment. Front. Neurol. **10**, 218 (2019)

16. Skorvanek, M., et al.: Relationship between the MDS-UPDRS and quality of life: a large multicenter study of 3206 patients. Parkinsonism Related Disord. **52**, 83–89 (2018)

17. Li, T., Le, W.: Biomarkers for Parkinson's disease: how good are they? Neurosci. Bull. **36**(2), 183–194 (2020). https://doi.org/10.1007/s12264-019-00433-1

18. Emamzadeh, F.N., Surguchov, A.: Parkinson's disease: biomarkers, treatment, and risk factors. Front. Neurosci. **12**, 612 (2018)

19. Vanegas, M.I., Ghilardi, M.F., Kelly, S.P., Blangero, A.: Machine learning for EEG-based biomarkers in Parkinson's disease. In: 2018 IEEE International Conference on Bioinformatics and Biomedicine (BIBM), pp. 2661–2665. IEEE (2018)

20. Arora, P., Mehta, R., Ahuja, R.: An adaptive medical image registration using hybridization of teaching learning-based optimization with affine and speeded up robust features with projective transformation. Cluster Comput. 1–21 (2023). https://doi.org/10.1007/s10586-023-03974-3

21. Garg, S., Ahuja, R., Singh, R., Perl, I.: GMM-LSTM: a component driven resource utilization prediction model leveraging LSTM and Gaussian mixture model. Cluster Comput. **26**, 3547–3563 (2023). https://doi.org/10.1007/s10586-022-03747-4

22. Ahuja, R., Roul, R.K.: An ensemble technique to detect stress in young professional. In: Morusupalli, R., Dandibhotla, T.S., Atluri, V.V., Windridge, D., Lingras, P., Komati, V.R. (eds.) MIWAI 2023. LNAI, vol. 14078, pp. 649–658. Springer, Cham (2023). https://doi.org/10.1007/978-3-031-36402-0_60
23. Devrani, S., Ahuja, R., Goel, A., Kharbanda, S.S.: A blockchain-driven framework for issuance of NFT-based warranty to customers on E-commerce. In: Morusupalli, R., Dandibhotla, T.S., Atluri, V.V., Windridge, D., Lingras, P., Komati, V.R. (eds.) MIWAI 2023. LNAI, vol. 14078, pp. 265–276. Springer, Cham (2023). https://doi.org/10.1007/978-3-031-36402-0_24
24. Coelho, B.F.O., Massaranduba, A.B.R., dos Santos Souza, C.A., Viana, G.G., Brys, I., Ramos, R.P.: Parkinson's disease effective biomarkers based on Hjorth features improved by machine learning. Expert Syst. Appl. **212**, 118772 (2023)
25. Rana, A., Dumka, A., Singh, R., Panda, M.K., Priyadarshi, N., Twala, B.: Imperative role of machine learning algorithm for detection of Parkinson's disease: review, challenges and recommendations. Diagnostics **12**(8), 2003 (2022)
26. Alanazi, H.O., Abdullah, A.H., Qureshi, K.N.: A critical review for developing accurate and dynamic predictive models using machine learning methods in medicine and health care. J. Med. Syst. **41**, 1–10 (2017). https://doi.org/10.1007/s10916-017-0715-6
27. Bellazzi, R., Zupan, B.: Predictive data mining in clinical medicine: current issues and guidelines. Int. J. Med. Inform. **77**(2), 81–97 (2008)
28. Van Smeden, M., et al.: Critical appraisal of artificial intelligence-based prediction models for cardiovascular disease. Eur. Heart J. **43**(31), 2921–2930 (2022)
29. Toma, M., Wei, O.C.: Predictive modeling in medicine. Encyclopedia **3**(2), 590–601 (2023)
30. Alanazi, H.O., Abdullah, A.H., Qureshi, K.N., Ismail, A.S.: Accurate and dynamic predictive model for better prediction in medicine and healthcare. Ir. J. Med. Sci. (1971-) **187**, 501–513 (2018). https://doi.org/10.1007/s11845-017-1655-3
31. Brownlee, J.: Time series forecasting as supervised learning. Machine Learning Mastery (2016). https://machinelearningmastery.com/time-series-forecasting-supervised-learning

Prediction of High-Resolution Soil Moisture Using Multi-source Data and Machine Learning

B. Sudhakara[(✉)] and Shrutilipi Bhattacharjee

Department of Information Technology, National Institute of Technology Karnataka,
Surathkal, Mangalore 575025, India
{sudhakarab.217it006,shrutilipi}@nitk.edu.in

Abstract. Soil moisture (SM) stands as a critical meteorological element influencing the dynamic interplay between the land and the atmosphere. Its comprehension, modeling, and examination hold key significance in unraveling this interaction. Information about the surface SM is necessary for predicting crop yield, future disasters, etc. Ground-based SM measurement is accurate but time-consuming and costly. An alternate approach for measuring SM using satellite images is becoming more popular in recent years. Surface SM retrieval with a fine-resolution still poses challenges. The proposed work considers multi-satellite data for predicting high-resolution SM of Oklahoma, USA using multiple Machine Learning (ML) algorithms, such as K-nearest neighbour (KNN), Decision tree (DT), Random forest (RF), and Extra trees regressor (ETR). A high-resolution SM map for the study region is also reported, considering the Soil Moisture Active Passive (SMAP) SM data as the base, Landsat 8 bands, and normalized difference vegetation index (NDVI) data as the reference datasets. The ETR model performed the best with a mean absolute error (MAE) of 0.940 mm, a root mean square error (RMSE) of 1.303 mm and a coefficient of determination (R^2) of 0.965. The external validation is carried out with ground-based SM data from the International Soil Moisture Network (ISMN). Both the actual SMAP SM and predicted SM values demonstrate a comparable correlation with the ISMN data.

Keywords: Soil Moisture (SM) · Landsat 8 · Soil Moisture Active Passive (SMAP) · International Soil Moisture Network (ISMN) · Machine Learning (ML)

1 Introduction

Soil moisture (SM) plays a pivotal role in regulating environmental and meteorological variables, such as surface temperature, radiation, water, and nutrients in the soil [1,2]. It affects vegetation, runoff, evapotranspiration [3] etc., and can be used for forecasting agricultural droughts [4], conducting climate-related studies [1, 5, 6], predicting seasonal crop yield, food security monitoring [7] etc., which contributes towards social and economic growth. Currently, ground-based, model-based, and remote sensing are commonly used techniques to obtain SM data [8], which have their merits and demerits. For example, the International Soil Moisture Network (ISMN) was formed to provide quality monitored and standardized ground-based SM data with the establishment of numerous operational stations [9]. Similarly, the studies on SM in local regions are mostly carried out using in-situ measurements of SM [10], which is a time-consuming process [11]. Further, it is difficult to carry out global analysis using in-situ measurements due to sparse measurements, spatial and temporal heterogeneity. Remote sensing (RS) data obtained from satellites can overcome this problem with some drawbacks of low accuracy and coarse temporal and spatial resolution [12]. The Soil Moisture Active Passive (SMAP) and Soil Moisture and Ocean Salinity (SMOS) products from satellite are the state-of-the-art satellite measurements providing SM data with (temporal 2–3 days and spatial 36 km) and (temporal 3 days and spatial 35–50 km) resolution, respectively.

1.1 Related Work

Multiple research works have focussed on producing high-resolution data from the current SMAP product. For example, SMAP SM disaggregation to high-resolution 100 m SM is carried out by Ojha *et al.* applying the Disaggregation based on Physical and Theoretical scale Change (DISPATCH) algorithm with the help of SMAP, Landsat, Moderate Resolution Imaging Spectroradiometer (MODIS), and Shuttle Radar Topography Mission (SRTM) datasets [13]. Koley and Jeganathan [14] combined Landsat 8 and Sentinel 2A satellite data to predict surface SM (aggregated into 1 km resolution) using visible red, near-infrared (NIR) and short-wave infrared (SWIR) bands. Sharma *et al.* [15] have applied a Single Channel Algorithm (SCA) to disaggregate SMAP SM data to SM with a resolution of 1 km using MODIS Normalized Difference Vegetation Index (NDVI) and Land Surface Temperature (LST). Further, an intercomparison study is carried out with three different algorithms, such as the Triangle method, approximation of the thermal inertia (ATI), and DISPATCH. The ML models with the association of multi-data source input features have given promising results for the high-resolution soil moisture production [16–22]. For example, the ML models are used in downscaling of soil moisture product, Advanced Microwave Scanning Radiometer for the Earth Observing System (AMSR-E), combined with Moderate Resolution Imaging Spectroradiometer (MODIS), LST, surface albedo, vegetation indices, and evapotranspiration [21]. In another study, the inputs from multiple datasets, like in situ measurements, CLDAS reanalyzed soil moisture product, MODIS data, precipitation, and soil texture data, are used in generating continuous 1 km SM data using Random Forest ML model [22]. The previous studies demonstrate that the choice of the input dataset significantly impacts the performance of ML models.

Currently, most studies have used low-resolution (36–50 km) SM products or reanalyzed downscaled SM products, generated using diverse models. Most of these downscaling studies have used MODIS data, and only a limited number of investigations have explored the use of Landsat 8 optical and thermal observations to achieve a high-resolution SM product at 30 m scale [1,16]. Few studies have considered ISMN data to validate their model-based results [23,24]. In line with these gaps, the present study implements four machine learning models, namely K-nearest neighbor (KNN), Decision tree (DT), Random forest (RF), and Extra trees regressor (ETR) [25] to predict high-resolution (30 m) surface SM by utilizing enhanced 10 km SMAP NASA-USDA product. The proposed study aims to develop a framework for high-resolution SM prediction from multi-source parameters, including Landsat 8 optical and thermal observations and others. These models eliminates unnecessary features from Landsat 8 data, improving upon existing work in the field. The most effective model was selected to predict SM content in Oklahoma City, USA, and twelve ISMN Atmospheric Radiation Measurement (ARM) stations within Oklahoma for further validation. The proposed work automates data extraction using the Google Earth Engine (GEE) platform and will be applicable to any area on the earth's surface.

2   Methodology

The comprehensive structure of the proposed research is illustrated in Fig. 1. The study uses ML models (discussed in Sect. 2.2) to predict high-resolution SM by integrating multi-source datasets (discussed in Sect. 2.1). Initially, SMAP pixel locations within Oklahoma State are extracted from SMAP 10 km global SM Data. Then, for the corresponding places, a buffer of a 5 km radius is created, and the multi-source dataset mean value is calculated within the buffer, by matching datasets temporally. Next, the ML models are implemented by taking the SMAP SM as the target and features from the rest of the datasets as the independent

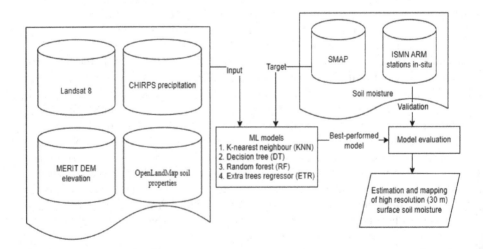

Fig. 1. Workflow for SM prediction

Table 1. Dataset and ancillary variables

Dataset	Variables	Spatial Resolution	Temporal Resolution
NASA-USDA Enhanced SMAP Global SM Data [26]	Surface SM in mm	10000 m	3 days
Landsat 8 OLI & TIRS [27]	B1 (ultra blue, coastal aerosol), B2 (blue), B3 (green), B4 (red), B5 (near infrared), B6 (shortwave infrared 1), B7 (shortwave infrared 2), B10 (surface temperature)	30 m	16 days
Climate Hazards Group InfraRed Precipitation with Station (CHIRPS) [28]	Precipitation in mm/d	5566 m	daily
Multi-Error Removed Improved Terrain Digital Elevation Model (MERIT DEM) [29]	Elevation in m	92.77 m	static
OpenLandMap Soil Properties [30]	Clay and Sand content in % (kg/kg)	250 m	static

variables. The results from different ML models are compared using performance metrics (discussed in Sect. 3), and the best-performing model is validated using ISMN's ARM network's in-situ data. Finally, a high-resolution soil moisture map has been produced for the Oklahoma City with the help of best-performed ML model's prediction results.

2.1 Datasets

To estimate the high-resolution SM in Oklahoma City, USA, the present study involves multi-source data from April 2015 to July 2022 retrieved through the GEE platform [31]. Table 1 presents a compilation of the datasets utilized in the study, along with their corresponding ancillary variables.

2.2 Machine Learning Regressor Models

The machine learning regressors are used to find appropriate relationships between the dependent and independent variables and to predict high-resolution SM. In this context, supervised learning techniques are employed to comprehend the connection between the dependent and independent features, facilitating the prediction of unseen input data. The different regressors used are KNN [32], DT [33], RF [34], and ETR [35]. The KNN regressor predicts a new data point's target value by calculating the average of the target values belonging its k-nearest neighbors in the training dataset. KNN regressor is intuitive and adaptable, but sensitive to noisy data and requires careful tuning of the K parameter for optimal performance. DT builds a tree-based model in which each inner node decides on a feature and each leaf node indicates a predicted target value. It is capable of capturing complex relationships in data but can overfit if not pruned appropriately. Regularization techniques and ensemble methods like RF and ETR can enhance its performance and generalization. RF constructs multiple decision trees during training and aggregates their predictions to generate more precise and resilient outcomes. By reducing overfitting and handling noisy data, it offers improved generalization. RF regressor effectively captures complex relationships, handles high-dimensional data, and provides feature-importance insights. Similar to RF, ETR builds multiple decision trees and combines their predictions. However, ETR introduces additional randomness by selecting random splits at each node, which can lead to further diversity and potentially improved performance. ETR is robust, less prone to overfitting, and can handle noisy data effectively. It is suitable for various regression problems and offers significant insights about input feature importance.

3   Results

Before carrying out the actual prediction of SM, the Landsat 8 bands and other input features are correlated to each other to understand their relative importance. Then ML models are given with all extracted input features to select a best-performing model for finding important features. The correlation study reveals that surface reflectance (SR) band pairs (B1, B2), (B1, B3), (B1, B4), (B2, B3), (B2, B4), (B3, B4), and (B6, B7) are highly correlated to each other, with the scores as listed in Table 2. Therefore, it is evident that including all the Landsat 8 bands is optional, and we can reduce the model complexity by choosing and limiting the number of features. Here we have considered B4 (among B1, B2, B3, B4) and B7 (between B6 and B7). The SR bands B4 and B7 are considered here because of their high importance among features (shown in Fig. 2) when we input all features to the best-performing ETR model. The performance of ML models with all features as input is given in the third column of Table 3.

Additionally, the vegetation index NDVI exhibits connection to the water present in the soil [36]. NDVI can be calculated using the reflectance values of red band B4 and NIR band B5 from Landsat 8 (refer to Eq. 1).

$$NDVI = \frac{(NIR - Red)}{(NIR + Red)} \tag{1}$$

Table 2. Highest correlated features

Feature A	Feature B	Correlation score
B1	B2	0.997
B1	B3	0.979
B1	B4	0.940
B2	B3	0.989
B2	B4	0.960
B3	B4	0.974
B6	B7	0.940

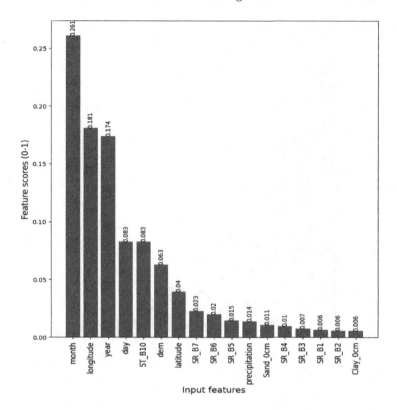

Fig. 2. Importance of the input features with respect to ETR Model (with all features)

Hence, NDVI is considered as one of the derived input features replacing B4 and B5 bands. Finally, the NDVI, band B7, and the surface temperature band B10 from the Landsat 8 are input to the ML models.

Three standard error evaluation metrics, Mean Absolute Error (MAE), Root Mean Square Error (RMSE), and Coefficient of determination (R^2), were considered in the study. The lower MAE and RMSE and the R^2 value towards 1 represent a better model. The four ML models (i.e., KNN, DT, RF, and ETR) are implemented for Oklahoma, USA, and their performances with K-fold cross-validation (K = 10) are listed in Table 3. Comparing the results for ML models with all features and models with filtered features, it becomes apparent that the performance of all models slightly improved in comparison to the filtered feature set. This suggests that the feature filtering process led to the removal of less relevant or noisy features, enhancing the models' predictive capabilities. The actual SM versus predicted SM scatter plots are presented in Fig. 4, show each ML model's performance with filtered features. The density here provides insights into the distribution and concentration of the predicted results and helps in understanding the relationship between actual SM and predicted SM values.

288   B. Sudhakara and S. Bhattacharjee

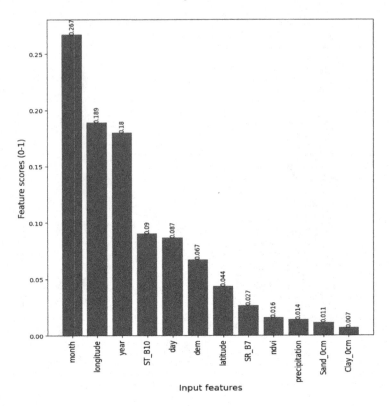

Fig. 3. Importance of the input features with respect to ETR Model (with filtered features)

Table 3. Performance of ML models

Models	Metrics	With all features	With filtered features
KNN	MAE (mm)	1.639	1.585
	RMSE (mm)	2.467	2.384
	R^2	0.873	0.881
DT	MAE (mm)	1.526	1.433
	RMSE (mm)	2.316	2.143
	R^2	0.889	0.902
RF	MAE (mm)	1.104	1.052
	RMSE (mm)	1.552	1.478
	R^2	0.949	0.955
ETR	MAE (mm)	**0.987**	**0.940**
	RMSE (mm)	**1.365**	**1.303**
	R^2	**0.960**	**0.965**

Here, both ETR and RF belong to the family of ensemble methods. These models aggregate the predictions of multiple decision trees, reducing the likelihood of bias and overfitting. ETR, on the other hand, builds decision trees concurrently leveraging random feature selection. Compared to KNN and DT, ETR is less sensitive to noisy input and performs better with respect to the standard metrics of MAE, RMSE, and R^2. Further, Fig. 3 shows the importance scores of input features for the ETR model with filtered features. This reveals that the date and location information have more significance in providing downscaled results. Also, Landsat 8's band 10 (surface temperature) plays a major role in the estimation compared to band 7 and NDVI.

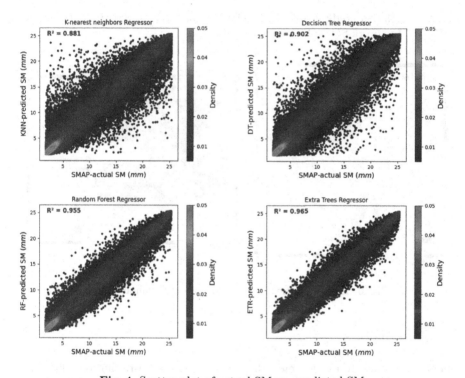

Fig. 4. Scatter plot of actual SM vs. predicted SM

The results of the correlation studies between ISMN ARM's SM data and actual SM data (correlation coefficient r = 0.59), and between predicted SM data (correlation coefficient r = 0.55) are shown in Fig. 5a and 5b, respectively. Similar positive correlation values indicate that our estimation result aligns with ground-based measurements. It has been found that the SMAP-actual SM and the SMAP-predicted SM are similarly correlated with ISMN SM. A high-resolution SM map of 30 m resolution for Oklahoma City for July 14, 2022, is shown in Fig. 6. These high-resolution maps can be produced for any location of the considered study region.

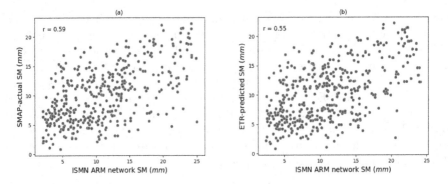

Fig. 5. Correlation study of (a) ISMN ARM network SM vs SMAP-actual SM, (b) ISMN ARM network SM vs ETR-predicted SM

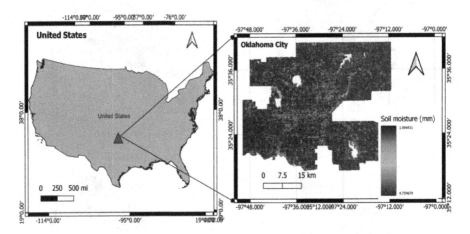

Fig. 6. High-resolution (30 m) SM map of Oklahoma City

4 Conclusions

The proposed study experiments the estimation of high-resolution (30 m) SM using four ML regression algorithms such as KNN, DT, RF, and ETR. Considering multi-source data inputs from Landsat 8, CHIRPS, MERIT DEM, Open-LandMap and the target variable from SMAP data, the ETR model could achieve an R^2 of 0.965, RMSE of 1.303 mm and MAE of 0.940 mm. In the present study, the Landsat 8 NDVI, band 7, and thermal band 10 have played a crucial role along with other multi-data source input features in predicting high-resolution SM. The proposed approach significantly improves performance because of multiple ancillary parameters for training and testing. This work can be useful to significantly enhance both water resource management strategies and climate studies at the regional scale. Further improvements can be achieved by fusing data from other satellite images, considering extensive ISMN data for prediction and validation, and exploring additional AI-based SM estimation models.

References

1. Zhang, Y., Liang, S., Zhu, Z., Ma, H., He, T.: Soil moisture content retrieval from Landsat 8 data using ensemble learning. ISPRS J. Photogramm. Remote. Sens. **185**, 32–47 (2022)
2. Peng, J., Loew, A., Merlin, O., Verhoest, N.E.: A review of spatial downscaling of satellite remotely sensed soil moisture. Rev. Geophys. **55**(2), 341–366 (2017)
3. Adab, H., Morbidelli, R., Saltalippi, C., Moradian, M., Ghalhari, G.A.F.: Machine learning to estimate surface soil moisture from remote sensing data. Water **12**(11), 3223 (2020)
4. Kelley, C.P., Mohtadi, S., Cane, M.A., Seager, R., Kushnir, Y.: Climate change in the fertile crescent and implications of the recent Syrian drought. Proc. Natl. Acad. Sci. **112**(11), 3241–3246 (2015)
5. Berg, A., Sheffield, J.: Climate change and drought: the soil moisture perspective. Curr. Clim. Change Rep. **4**(2), 180–191 (2018). https://doi.org/10.1007/s40641-018-0095-0
6. Grillakis, M.G.: Increase in severe and extreme soil moisture droughts for Europe under climate change. Sci. Total Environ. **660**, 1245–1255 (2019)
7. Holzman, M.E., Carmona, F., Rivas, R., Niclòs, R.: Early assessment of crop yield from remotely sensed water stress and solar radiation data. ISPRS J. Photogramm. Remote. Sens. **145**, 297–308 (2018)
8. Liang, S., Wang, J.: Advanced Remote Sensing: Terrestrial Information Extraction and Applications. Academic Press, Oxford (2019)
9. Dorigo, W., et al.: The International Soil Moisture Network: a data hosting facility for global in situ soil moisture measurements. Hydrol. Earth Syst. Sci. **15**(5), 1675–1698 (2011)
10. Parrens, M., Mahfouf, J.F., Barbu, A., Calvet, J.C.: Assimilation of surface soil moisture into a multilayer soil model: design and evaluation at local scale. Hydrol. Earth Syst. Sci. **18**(2), 673–689 (2014)
11. Tavakol, A., McDonough, K.R., Rahmani, V., Hutchinson, S.L., Hutchinson, J.S.: The soil moisture data bank: the ground-based, model-based, and satellite-based soil moisture data. Remote Sens. Appl. Soc. Environ. **24**, 100649 (2021)
12. Petropoulos, G.P., Srivastava, P.K., Piles, M., Pearson, S.: Earth observation-based operational estimation of soil moisture and evapotranspiration for agricultural crops in support of sustainable water management. Sustainability **10**(1), 181 (2018)
13. Ojha, N., et al.: Stepwise disaggregation of SMAP soil moisture at 100 m resolution using Landsat-7/8 data and a varying intermediate resolution. Remote Sens. **11**, 1863 (2019)
14. Koley, S., Jeganathan, C.: Estimation and evaluation of high spatial resolution surface soil moisture using multi-sensor multi-resolution approach. Geoderma **378**, 114618 (2020)
15. Sharma, J., Prasad, R., Srivastava, P.K., Yadav, S.A., Yadav, V.P.: Improving spatial representation of soil moisture through the incorporation of single-channel algorithm with different downscaling approaches. IEEE Trans. Geosci. Remote Sens. **60**, 1–10 (2022)
16. Abowarda, A.S., et al.: Generating surface soil moisture at 30 m spatial resolution using both data fusion and machine learning toward better water resources management at the field scale. Remote Sens. Environ. **255**, 112301 (2021)

17. Srivastava, P.K., Han, D., Ramirez, M.R., Islam, T.: Machine learning techniques for downscaling SMOS satellite soil moisture using MODIS land surface temperature for hydrological application. Water Resour. Manag. **27**, 3127–3144 (2013). https://doi.org/10.1007/s11269-013-0337-9

18. Zeng, L., et al.: Multilayer soil moisture mapping at a regional scale from multi-source data via a machine learning method. Remote Sens. **11**(3), 284 (2019)

19. Liu, Y., Yang, Y., Jing, W., Yue, X.: Comparison of different machine learning approaches for monthly satellite-based soil moisture downscaling over Northeast China. Remote Sens. **10**(1), 31 (2017)

20. Kim, D., Moon, H., Kim, H., Im, J., Choi, M.: Intercomparison of downscaling techniques for satellite soil moisture products. Adv. Meteorol. **2018**, 4832423 (2018)

21. Im, J., Park, S., Rhee, J., Baik, J., Choi, M.: Downscaling of AMSR-E soil moisture with MODIS products using machine learning approaches. Environ. Earth Sci. **75**(15), 1–19 (2016). https://doi.org/10.1007/s12665-016-5917-6

22. Long, D., et al.: Generation of spatially complete and daily continuous surface soil moisture of high spatial resolution. Remote Sens. Environ. **233**, 111364 (2019)

23. Abbaszadeh, P., Moradkhani, H., Zhan, X.: Downscaling SMAP radiometer soil moisture over the CONUS using an ensemble learning method. Water Resour. Res. **55**, 324–344 (2019)

24. Xu, H., Yuan, Q., Li, T., Shen, H., Zhang, L., Jiang, H.: Quality improvement of satellite soil moisture products by fusing with in-situ measurements and GNSS-R estimates in the western continental US. Remote Sens. **10**, 1351 (2018)

25. Sudhakara, B., et al.: Spatio-temporal analysis and modeling of coastal areas for water salinity prediction. In: 2023 IEEE International Students' Conference on Electrical, Electronics and Computer Science (SCEECS), pp. 1–6. IEEE (2023)

26. Chan, S.K., et al.: Assessment of the SMAP passive soil moisture product. IEEE Trans. Geosci. Remote Sens. **54**(8), 4994–5007 (2016)

27. Vermote, E., Justice, C., Claverie, M., Franch, B.: Preliminary analysis of the performance of the Landsat 8/OLI land surface reflectance product. Remote Sens. Environ. **185**, 46–56 (2016)

28. Funk, C., et al.: The climate hazards infrared precipitation with stations-a new environmental record for monitoring extremes. Sci. Data **2**(1), 1–21 (2015)

29. Yamazaki, D., et al.: A high-accuracy map of global terrain elevations. Geophys. Res. Lett. **44**(11), 5844–5853 (2017)

30. Tomislav, H.: Sand content in % (kg/kg) at 6 standard depths (0, 10, 30, 60, 100 and 200 cm) at 250 m resolution (v0.2). Zenodo (2018)

31. Gorelick, N., Hancher, M., Dixon, M., Ilyushchenko, S., Thau, D., Moore, R.: Google Earth Engine: Planetary-scale geospatial analysis for everyone. Remote Sens. Environ. **202**, 18–27 (2017)

32. Song, Y., Liang, J., Lu, J., Zhao, X.: An efficient instance selection algorithm for K-nearest neighbor regression. Neurocomputing **251**, 26–34 (2017)

33. Xu, M., Watanachaturaporn, P., Varshney, P.K., Arora, M.K.: Decision tree regression for soft classification of remote sensing data. Remote Sens. Environ. **97**(3), 322–336 (2005)

34. Breiman, L.: Random forests. Mach. Learn. **45**, 5–32 (2001). https://doi.org/10.1023/A:1010933404324

35. Geurts, P., Ernst, D., Wehenkel, L.: Extremely randomized trees. Mach. Learn. **63**, 3–42 (2006). https://doi.org/10.1007/s10994-006-6226-1

36. Zhang, H., Chang, J., Zhang, L., Wang, Y., Li, Y., Wang, X.: NDVI dynamic changes and their relationship with meteorological factors and soil moisture. Environ. Earth Sci. **77**(16), 1–11 (2018). https://doi.org/10.1007/s12665-018-7759-x

Evaluating Deep Cnns and Vision Transformers for Plant Leaf Disease Classification

Parag Bhuyan🆔 and Pranav Kumar Singh[(✉)]🆔

Central Institute of Technology Kokrajhar, BTR, Kokrajhar 783370, Assam, India
p.singh@cit.ac.in

Abstract. The foundation of each nation's economy has always been agriculture and related sectors. Smart Agriculture is the most recent hot research topic because of its usefulness in different applications, such as early plant disease identification and diagnosis and treatment. Convolutional neural networks (CNNs) have become the de-facto standard in plant leaf disease identification tasks because of their ability to learn complex features. However, not long ago, they began to set new trends in vision tasks alongside the success of the transformer in natural language processing (NLP). This study explores and compares CNNs and Vision Transformer (ViT) models used in the identification of three specific types of plant leaf diseases: Rice Leaf, Tea Leaf, and Maize Leaf images. Their performance is examined using three standard plant leaf image datasets. The study reveals that for all three datasets, Vision Transformer (ViT) outperforms CNNs in terms of the classification of plant leaf diseases. Specifically, the ViT-30 model achieved an average accuracy of 98.41% and 96.95% on Rice Leaf Dataset and Maize leaf dataset respectively, while ViT-20 model achieved an average accuracy of 67.75% on Tea leaf dataset. The main parameters of ViT, such as the optimizer, learning rate, patch size, number of heads, and number of transformer layers, are also fine-tuned, and the optimal ViT configuration for plant leaf disease identification is determined.

Keywords: Smart Agriculture · AI · CNN · Vision Transformers · Leaf Disease Classification

1 Introduction

Plant disease plays a critical role in influencing the growth of plants, food yield, and quality. To meet the demands of the world's rapidly growing population, improving food availability and quality is of utmost importance. Understanding the occurrence of plant leaf diseases and accurately predicting them is essential, as they can significantly impact overall crop yield production. Disease outbreaks, if not handled appropriately, can have a substantial negative effect on total production. Given the substantial impact of plant diseases on agricultural

© The Author(s), under exclusive license to Springer Nature Switzerland AG 2024
S. Devismes et al. (Eds.): ICDCIT 2024, LNCS 14501, pp. 293–306, 2024.
https://doi.org/10.1007/978-3-031-50583-6_20

output, early disease detection becomes crucial [1,2]. Farmers encounter significant challenges when dealing with plant leaf diseases on a large scale, and manual identification of these diseases is particularly challenging [3].

The manual assessment and inspection process present several challenges. Manual disease detection is constrained by factors such as high laboratory testing costs, time-consuming procedures, and difficulties in conducting field assessments. This manual technique limits farmers to identifying specific plant diseases and is only practical on a small scale. Moreover, it doesn't guarantee early detection, making it unable to identify newly emerging diseases through visual inspection alone. Consequently, some plant leaf diseases might go unnoticed, leading to inadequate preventive measures and resulting in agricultural output losses. To address these issues, automated recognition methods must be developed to monitor crop health effectively, promptly, and cost-efficiently, offering crucial information for decision-making.

Technological initiatives in the form of smart agricultural technology are needed to properly detect and manage plant leaf diseases, ensuring the sustainability of crop output and providing farmers with a stable source of income. Advanced artificial intelligence techniques enable agriculturists and industry professionals to employ modern technology instead of labor-intensive traditional site monitoring [4].

Traditional image processing methods, while useful for detecting crop diseases, suffer from limitations related to scalability, efficiency, performance, and precision. In contrast, deep learning models have demonstrated significant success and are rapidly emerging as the primary approach in various applications [5]. One highly effective deep-learning network is the CNN, which adopts an end-to-end structure, eliminating the need for complex image preprocessing and feature extraction tasks [6]. Researchers have recently placed significant emphasis on utilizing CNNs for plant disease identification due to their remarkable ability to extract crucial features from images [7]. CNNs excel in computer vision applications, including image classification, object recognition, and segmentation, thanks to their combination of inductive bias and flexibility. Recent advancements have significantly enhanced the reliability of disease and pest detection, enabling early prevention and treatment interventions.

Transformer neural networks were initially introduced for Natural Language Processing applications [8]. Recently, Dosovitskiy et al. introduced the vision transformer (ViT) architectures specifically tailored for image classification [9]. Unlike traditional transformers, which process sequences of tokens, ViT takes image patches as input, dividing the image into multiple patches. The transformer encoder then extracts features from each of these patches. ViT has demonstrated state-of-the-art image classification results on large datasets, highlighting its effectiveness when trained with sufficient data. It outperforms comparable CNNs while demanding less computational resources.

To address ViT's data dependency, the Data-Efficient Image Transformer (DeiT) was introduced as an improved version [10]. DeiT employs a teacher-student method commonly used with transformers and introduces a distillation token to ensure that the student model pays attention to the teacher's guidance. Similarly, the Swin Transformer is another computationally efficient transformer architecture [11]. It addresses concerns related to the complexity of the ViT architecture, particularly regarding the number of tokens and attention windows. The Swin Transformer adjusts the attention window to enable better communication between patches during attention operations, allowing the network to capture more global information.

Despite the success of deep learning-based algorithms, there remains a need for standardized and effective approaches that can be seamlessly integrated into various stages of a crop's life cycle for diverse purposes. In this study, we undertake an investigation and evaluation of several CNNs and Transformer-based techniques for the task of plant leaf disease image classification. Our experiments focus on three specific types of plant leaf diseases: Rice Leaf, Tea Leaf, and Maize Leaf images. We compare and analyze the performance results obtained from Swin Transformer, DeiT, ViT, and CNN classification models.

The primary contributions of our work can be summarized as follows:

- We conduct an extensive and comprehensive investigation into diverse convolutional neural network-based approaches, comparing them with the recent Transformer-based technique known as Vision Transformer (ViT). Our research focus on the task of classifying plant leaf diseases and encompassed a series of rigorous experiments employing three publicly accessible plant leaf disease datasets, specifically those related to Rice leaf, Tea leaf, and Maize leaf.
- Our study encompasses a comprehensive performance evaluation comparing CNN and ViT models across all three datasets, utilizing various evaluation metrics to provide a comprehensive assessment of their capabilities.
- Furthermore, we present the optimal configuration for ViT in the context of plant leaf disease classification, offering valuable insights into the most effective setup for achieving superior performance in this domain and highlight associated challenges.

The structure of the paper is outlined as follows: Sect. 2 presents a comprehensive review of the existing literature concerning CNN and ViT-related research. Section 3 offers a concise introduction to the Vision Transformer (ViT) architecture and its associated details, considering that this may be new to some readers. Section 4 provides detailed information on the experimental setup, encompassing dataset descriptions, the selection of models, and the choice of evaluation metrics. Section 5 reports the results obtained from our experiments, utilizing the selected metrics to assess and compare the performance of the models. Section 6 discusses the outcomes of the results presented in Sect. 5. Section 7 concludes the paper, summarizing the key findings and highlighting the significance of the work.

2   Related Work

In this section, we provide an overview of existing research works that utilize
CNNs and ViT models for the classification of plant leaf diseases.

2.1   CNN Related Works

Several studies have leveraged CNNs for the identification of plant leaf diseases
[12] [13]. Notable contributions in this domain include:
    Chawal et al. [14] applied K-means clustering for segmentation and utilized
the Twin Support Vector Machine (TSVM) for the classification of Rice leaf
disease images, achieving a remarkable 95% accuracy in Rice leaf disease classification. Sethy et al. [15] employed transfer learning and a deep feature combined
with SVM technique to assess the performance of 13 pre-existing CNN models. The resnet50 plus SVM technique attained the highest F1 score of 0.9838,
although transfer learning did not yield satisfactory results.
    Bari et al. [16] utilized a Faster Region-based CNN (Faster R-CNN) for swift
identification of rice leaf diseases, achieving exceptional accuracy rates of 99.17%,
98.09%, and 98.85% for hispa, rice blast, and brown spot diseases, respectively.
For Rice leaf disease classification, Bhuyan et al. [6] introduced the SE SPnet
model, a novel stacked parallel convolution layers-based network incorporating
the squeeze-and-excitation (SE) architecture, which achieved a remarkable accuracy rate of 99.2%. Hu et al. [17] employed support vector machines and deep
learning networks to develop a low-shot learning method for tea leaf disease
identification, achieving an average accuracy of 90%. Mukhopadhyay et al. [18]
devised a novel technique for the automatic detection of five distinct tea leaf
diseases, utilizing NSGA-II for disease area detection in tea leaves, Principal
Component Analysis (PCA) for feature selection, and a multiple-class Support
Vector Machine (SVM) for disease identification, resulting in an average accuracy of 83%.
    To identify multi-class maize crop diseases, Albahli et al. [19] proposed a
CNN architecture and an Efficient Attention Network (EANet) based on the
EfficientNetv2 model, achieving an impressive overall classification accuracy of
99.89%. Masood et al. [20] developed MaizeNet, a deep learning method based
on the Faster R-CNN approach with the ResNet-50 model and spatial-channel
attention for various classes of maize plant diseases, achieving an average accuracy of 97.89% and a mAP value of 0.94. Olayiwola et al. [21] classified three
common maize leaf diseases and their healthy counterparts using a CNN-based
model, achieving an accuracy of 98.56%. He et al. [22] proposed MFASTER R-
CNN, an improved version of the Faster R-CNN algorithm for maize leaf disease
identification, achieving an overall average accuracy rate of 97.23%.

2.2   Transformer Related Works

The concept of Transformer neural networks was originally introduced for Natural Language Processing (NLP) applications [23]. Thanks to their ability to

model long-range dependencies, provide a global receptive field, and lack inductive bias when compared to CNNs, Transformers have become dominant in various fields. Dosovitskiy et al. [9] introduced the ViT architecture for image classification, showing that ViT can outperform conventional methods in tasks such as leaf disease identification.

Thai et al. [24] adopted the Vision Transformer (ViT) model instead of a Convolutional Neural Network (CNN) to classify cassava leaf diseases. Their experimental results on the Cassava Leaf Disease Dataset demonstrated that the ViT model achieved competitive accuracy, consistently outperforming common CNN models like EfficientNet and Resnet50d by at least 1%.

In another work by Thai et al. [25], they introduced a ViT-based leaf disease detection model that surpassed the state-of-the-art research in this domain, further highlighting the effectiveness of Vision Transformers. Wang et al. [26] proposed a backbone network based on the improved Swin Transformer and applied it to identify cucumber leaf diseases, achieving an impressive identification accuracy of 98.97%. These studies collectively emphasize the growing success and adoption of Transformer-based models, particularly ViT, in the field of plant leaf disease classification.

3   Vision Transformer Architecture

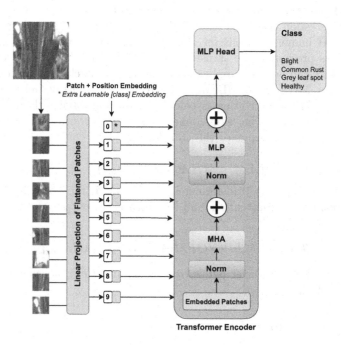

Fig. 1. ViT Architecture with Transformer block

The ViT architecture (shown in Fig. 1), as introduced by Dosovitskiy et al. [9], is based on the transformer framework. It applies the transformer block to a sequence of image patches. The input image is divided into fixed-sized patches, each treated as an individual token. Subsequently, these patches undergo flattening, followed by positional embedding through linear projection. The transformer block comprises multi-head self-attention (MHA) and an MLP network, each preceded by a normalization layer and connected via residual connections. This architecture allows ViT to effectively capture intricate features in the input images and has demonstrated remarkable success in various image-related tasks, including plant leaf disease classification.

At the core of the ViT block, MHSA is the improvement of the self-attention mechanism, which can learn different knowledge converged by multiple self-attentional heads. The MHA converts input vector intro three vectors such as Q (Query), K (Key) and V (Values). They are computed as $Q = XW_Q$, $K = XW_K$, and $V = VW_Q$; where W_Q, W_K, and W_V are the weight matrices. A dot-product of Q and K is taken to generate a score matrix based on the saliency of the embedded patch. Then, the SoftMax activation function is applied to the score matrix. Further, the output is multiplied into V to generate the self-attention result as shown in Eq. 1 where d_k represents the dimension of the vector K.

$$SA(Q, K, V) = softmax(\frac{QK^T}{\sqrt{d_k}}) * V \tag{1}$$

Finally, self-attention matrices are combined and passed onto a linear layer followed by a regression head. Self-attention enables the selection of relevant semantic features at image locations for classification. There can be any number of self-attentions present in the transformer encoder, known as MHA. Output of the MHA block can be calculated using Eq. 2. MLP is stacked in the transformer block after the MHA layer. MLP includes ANN layers with a GeLU activation function. The GELU activation is calculated by multiplying the input by its Bernoulli distribution. It has skip connections from the output of MHA, as presented in Fig. 1. The output of the transformer block can be calculated using Eq. 3.

$$MHA_{out} = MHA(NORM(x_{in})) + x_{in} \tag{2}$$

where x_{in} is the input to transformer block NORM is the normalization layer, MHA is multi-head self-attention, and MHA_{out} is the output of multi-head self attention layer.

$$TF_{out} = MLP(NORM(MHA_{out})) + MHA_{out} \tag{3}$$

where MLP is the multi layer perceptron block, and TF_{out} is the output of the transformer block.

4   Experimental Setup

In this section, we present comprehensive details regarding the datasets, models, and evaluation metrics utilized in our study.

4.1   Datasets

We used three publicly available plant leaf disease datasets, taken from various sources, to evaluate the performance of our model architecture. Figure 2 illustrates sample images from these three datasets.

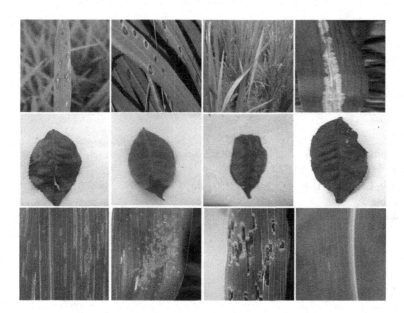

Fig. 2. Sample Images of Rice leaf disease Dataset, Tea Sickness dataset and Maize Leaf disease dataset

Rice Leaf Disease Dataset: We utilized the rice leaf disease image dataset from Mendeley [27]. This dataset comprises a total of 5932 images of rice leaves, categorized into 1584 images for bacterial blight, 1440 images for leaf blast, 1600 images for brown spot, and 1308 images for Tungro.

Tea Leaf Disease Dataset: Our second dataset is the tea sickness dataset [28], which contains a total of 885 images. These images cover seven common tea leaf diseases, along with a category for healthy tea leaves. The distribution includes 143 images for red leaf spot, 113 images for algal leaf spot, 100 images for bird's eye spot, 100 images for gray blight, 142 images for white spot, 100 images for anthracnose, 113 images for brown blight, and 74 images for healthy tea leaves.

Maize Leaf Disease Dataset: The third dataset is the maize leaf disease dataset, encompassing 4188 images of maize leaf diseases. This dataset includes 1146 images of blight, 1306 images of common rust, 574 images of gray leaf spot, and 1162 images of healthy maize leaves. For more details about these datasets, please refer to [29] and [30].

We split each dataset into training and testing sets with an 80:20 ratio, reserving 20% of the data for testing and using the remaining 80% for training.

Within the training data, an additional 20% was set aside as a validation set. The dataset details are summarized in Table 1. To maintain consistency, we resized the original images to a resolution of 224 × 224 pixels. Furthermore, we applied data augmentation techniques such as horizontal flipping, rotation, and zooming to enhance the model's generalization capabilities.

Table 1. Summary of the dataset used in the experiments

Dataset	No of Images	Image Size	No of Train Images	No of Test Images	No of Validation Images
Rice Leaf diseases dataset	5932	300 × 300	4745	1187	949
Tea sickness ataset	885	Variable	708	177	142
Maize Leaf Disease dataset	4188	256 × 256	3350	838	670

4.2 Models

In our work, we utilize the ViT-10, ViT-20, and ViT-30 models based on the Vision Transformer architecture. In these models, the numbers 10, 20, and 30 correspond to the input patch sizes of 10 × 10, 20 × 20, and 30 × 30, respectively. All of these ViT models are composed of 10 transformer blocks, each equipped with 10 multi-head self-attention modules. Additionally, we consider two improved transformer-based methods in comparison to the original Vision Transformer. These include the Data-Efficient Image Transformer (DeIT) architecture [10] and the computationally efficient SWIN Transformer architecture [11].

To provide a comprehensive comparison between transformer and CNN models, we also include several CNN-based models in our evaluation, including ResNet50 [31], VGG16 [32], DenseNet121 [33], MobileNetV2 [34], and InceptionV3 [35].

4.3 Platform and Evaluation Metrics

We implemented and analyzed the models for predicting plant leaf diseases using Python 3.7.12. All experiments in this work were conducted using the TensorFlow [36] Python package within the freely available Kaggle GPU environment. To optimize performance for specific tasks, we manually fine-tuned hyperparameters through a trial-and-error process. Various optimizers, including Adagrad,

SGD (with momentum), and ADAM, were employed, with learning rate settings of 0.01 and 0.001 utilized for training the proposed model. The categorical cross-entropy loss function was used for training.

To assess the model's performance comprehensively, we employed several important evaluation metrics, including accuracy, F1-score, precision, recall, sensitivity, and specificity. Furthermore, for each class, we provided a confusion matrix that visualizes both correct and incorrect results obtained from each of the three modality datasets.

5 Results

We assessed the performance of each model using a variety of metrics, including accuracy, F1-score, precision, sensitivity, specificity, and the cross-entropy loss function. For both CNNs and transformer models, we employed the ADAM optimizer with a learning rate of 0.001 for training.

Table 2. Results on Rice Leaf Dataset

Network	Accuracy	Sensitivity	Specificity	Precision	Recall	F1-Score
Resnet50	0.9667	0.9664	0.9689	0.9679	0.9664	0.9648
VGG16	0.9339	0.9307	0.9316	0.9358	0.9307	0.9341
DenseNet121	0.9521	0.9489	0.9509	0.9524	0.9489	0.9534
MobileNetV2	0.8954	0.8898	0.8913	0.8997	0.8898	0.8934
InceptionV3	0.9165	0.9117	0.9181	0.9172	0.9117	0.9166
ViT-10	0.9835	0.9828	0.9852	0.9846	0.9828	0.9795
ViT-20	0.9837	0.9841	0.9866	0.9852	0.9841	0.9802
ViT-30	0.9841	0.9839	0.9876	0.9858	0.9839	0.9819
DeiT	0.9639	0.9669	0.9648	0.9685	0.9669	0.9603
Swin Transformer	0.9826	0.9798	0.9839	0.9813	0.9798	0.9793

The results for the Rice leaf disease dataset are presented in Table 2. In this dataset, the ViT-30 model outperforms all other models, achieving an average accuracy of 98.41%.

The results for the Tea leaf disease dataset are presented in Table 3. Among all models, ViT-20 achieved the highest scores across most metrics, with an average accuracy of 67.75%, except for precision. The ViT-30 model achieved the highest precision value of 67.76% for the tea sickness dataset. Similarly, the results for the Maize leaf disease dataset are presented in Table 4.

It can be observed that ViT-30 achieved the highest accuracy of 96.95% and outperformed other models in all metrics except for specificity and precision. In the case of specificity and precision, ViT-20 surpassed ViT-30.

Sensitivity and specificity are crucial measures in assessing a model's ability to predict classes reliably. Sensitivity represents the percentage of correctly predicted diseased leaf images, while specificity represents the percentage of correctly predicted disease-free leaf images. In the rice leaf dataset, ViT-30 has

Table 3. Results on Tea Leaf Dataset

Network	Accuracy	Sensitivity	Specificity	Precision	Recall	F1-Score
Resnet50	0.6603	0.6795	0.6589	0.6802	0.6795	0.9792
VGG16	0.6393	0.6351	0.6379	0.6384	0.6351	0.6524
DenseNet121	0.6534	0.6511	0.6516	0.6538	0.6511	0.6501
MobileNetV2	0.5928	0.5892	0.5917	0.5933	0.5892	0.5899
InceptionV3	0.6159	0.6127	0.6142	0.6139	0.6127	0.6122
ViT-10	0.6525	0.6510	0.6595	0.6569	0.6510	0.6556
ViT-20	0.6775	0.6759	0.6746	0.6732	0.6795	0.6739
ViT-30	0.6745	0.6733	0.6711	0.6776	0.6733	0.6736
DeiT	0.6553	0.6601	0.6575	0.6513	0.6601	0.6521
Swin Transformer	0.6719	0.6696	0.6689	0.6743	0.6696	0.6724

Table 4. Results on Maize Leaf Dataset

Network	Accuracy	Sensitivity	Specificity	Precision	Recall	F1-Score
Resnet50	0.9477	0.9382	0.9453	0.9498	0.9382	0.9376
VGG16	0.9261	0.9204	0.9202	0.9273	0.9204	0.9199
DenseNet121	0.9387	0.9292	0.9336	0.9410	0.9292	0.9185
MobileNetV2	0.8996	0.8868	0.8964	0.9012	0.8868	0.8862
InceptionV3	0.9192	0.9016	0.9082	0.9194	0.9016	0.9011
ViT-10	0.9584	0.9575	0.9523	0.9560	0.9575	0.9538
ViT-20	0.9659	0.9542	0.9592	0.9598	0.9542	0.9561
ViT-30	0.9695	0.9574	0.9618	0.9617	0.9574	0.9694
DeiT	0.9478	0.9445	0.9413	0.9420	0.9445	0.9448
Swin Transformer	0.9637	0.9621	0.9589	0.9593	0.9621	0.9647

the highest specificity, while ViT-20 has the highest sensitivity. For the tea leaf dataset, ViT-20 achieved the highest specificity, whereas ViT-30 obtained the highest sensitivity. In the maize leaf dataset, ViT-30 exhibited the maximum specificity, while the Swin Transformer had the highest sensitivity.

6   Discussion

In this study, we employed three datasets related to plant leaf diseases to assess the effectiveness of various CNN and transformer models. The experimental results consistently demonstrate that, when it comes to detecting and recognizing plant leaf diseases, transformer models outperform conventional CNN models. As shown in Tables 2, 3, and 4, the transformer model's attention mechanism enables it to capture deeper patterns in the data, resulting in more accurate image predictions.

Transformers are also more effective due to their ability to prioritize relevant information while reducing information redundancy. Additionally, transformers efficiently encode temporal data, another crucial element for recognition. Lastly, the multi-head attention mechanism stands out as a key component and enhancer in the transformer model. While this study has yielded impressive results, it is important to acknowledge its limitations and identify potential avenues for future research in the field of plant leaf disease detection.

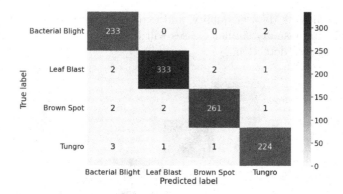

Fig. 3. Confusion matrix of ViT-30 for Rice Leaf dataset

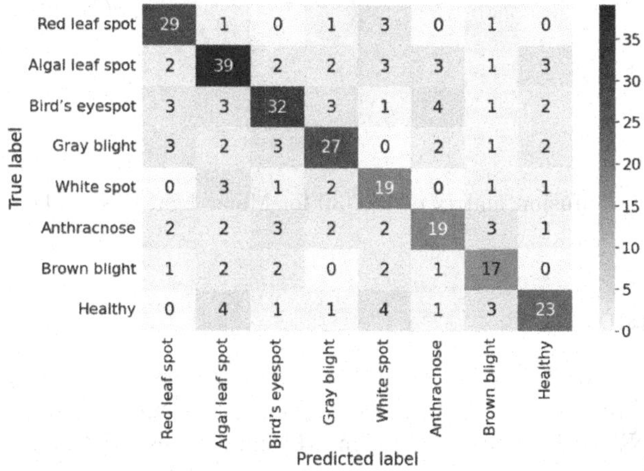

Fig. 4. Confusion matrix of ViT-20 for Tea Sickness dataset

Firstly, one of the challenges we encountered was dealing with an unbalanced dataset. To mitigate this issue, we applied data augmentation techniques. However, addressing dataset imbalance remains an ongoing concern that requires further exploration. Secondly, the problem of incorrect labeling in publicly accessible datasets is another significant issue. As a result, manual verification of datasets is essential to ensure the quality and accuracy of training data. Thirdly, due to interclass similarities among different leaf diseases, misclassification remains a significant concern. Despite achieving strong results, the confusion matrix highlights the challenges faced by the best-performing model in distinguishing between classes with similar visual characteristics. Figure 3 shows the confusion matrix of ViT-30 for Rice Leaf dataset. Figure 4 shows the confusion matrix of ViT-20 for Tea Sickness dataset. Figure 5 shows the confusion matrix of ViT-30 for Maize Leaf Disease dataset. In future research, addressing these challenges, improving dataset quality, and exploring more advanced techniques for distinguishing visually similar classes will be crucial for advancing the field of plant leaf disease detection.

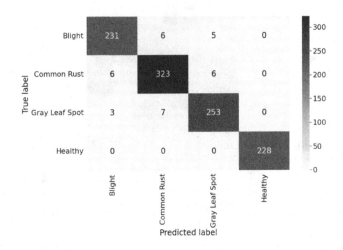

Fig. 5. Confusion matrix of ViT-30 for Maize Leaf Disease Dataset

7   Conclusion

In this work, we conducted a comprehensive evaluation of classification performance using three plant leaf disease datasets, comparing Convolutional Neural Network (CNN) models with transformer-based models, particularly the Vision Transformer (ViT). Our results consistently demonstrate that ViT-based models outperform traditional Deep CNN models across all three datasets, showcasing superior accuracy and other important metrics. We further utilized confusion matrices to assess the performance of ViT models in this study. This research highlights the efficacy of vision transformers as a valuable tool in addressing challenges related to plant leaf disease classification. Moreover, it establishes a strong foundation for the development of deep learning-based classification algorithms in this domain. Additionally, it opens up exciting possibilities for the adoption of self-attention-based architectures as alternatives to CNNs in various image classification applications. In our future work, we will focus on the development of novel self-attention-based architectures tailored specifically for the detection and classification of plant leaf diseases, further advancing the field of computer vision in agriculture.

References

1. Sujatha, R., Chatterjee, J.M., Jhanjhi, N.Z., Brohi, S.N.: Performance of deep learning vs machine learning in plant leaf disease detection. Microprocess. Microsyst. **80**, 103615 (2021)

2. Cooke, B.: Disease assessment and yield loss. In: Cooke, B., Jones, D., Kaye, B. (eds.) The Epidemiology of Plant Disease, pp. 43–80. Springer, Dordrecht (2006). https://doi.org/10.1007/1-4020-4581-6_2

3. Barbedo, J.G.A.: Plant disease identification from individual lesions and spots using deep learning. Biosyst. Eng. **180**, 96–107 (2019)

4. Charania, I., Li, X.: Smart farming: agriculture's shift from a labor intensive to technology native industry. Internet Things **9**, 100142 (2020)

5. Alzubaidi, L., et al.: Review of deep learning: concepts, CNN architectures, challenges, applications, future directions. J. Big Data **8**, 1–74 (2021)

6. Bhuyan, P., Singh, P.K., Das, S.K., Kalla, A.: SE_SPnet: rice leaf disease prediction using stacked parallel convolutional neural network with squeeze-and-excitation. Expert Syst. e13304 (2023)

7. Zhang, S., Zhang, S., Zhang, C., Wang, X., Shi, Y.: Cucumber leaf disease identification with global pooling dilated convolutional neural network. Comput. Electron. Agric. **162**, 422–430 (2019)

8. Wu, H., et al.: CVT: introducing convolutions to vision transformers. In: Proceedings of the IEEE/CVF International Conference on Computer Vision, pp. 22–31 (2021)

9. Dosovitskiy, A., et al.: An image is worth 16 × 16 words: transformers for image recognition at scale. arXiv preprint arXiv:2010.11929 (2020)

10. Touvron, H., Cord, M., Douze, M., Massa, F., Sablayrolles, A. and Jégou, H.: Training data-efficient image transformers & distillation through attention. In: International Conference on Machine Learning, pp. 10347–10357. PMLR (2021)

11. Liu, Z, et al.: Swin transformer: hierarchical vision transformer using shifted windows. In: Proceedings of the IEEE/CVF International Conference on Computer Vision, pp. 10012–10022 (2021)

12. Dhaka, V.S., Meena, S.V., Rani, G., Sinwar, D., Ijaz, M.F., Woźniak, M.: A survey of deep convolutional neural networks applied for prediction of plant leaf diseases. Sensors **21**(14), 4749 (2021)

13. Jinzhu, L., Tan, L., Jiang, H.: Review on convolutional neural network (CNN) applied to plant leaf disease classification. Agriculture **11**(8), 707 (2021)

14. Chawal, B., Panday, S.P.: Rice plant disease detection using twin support vector machine (TSVM) (2019)

15. Sethy, P.K., Barpanda, N.K., Rath, A.K., Behera, S.K.: Deep feature based rice leaf disease identification using support vector machine. Comput. Electron. Agric. **175**, 105527 (2020)

16. Bari, B.S., et al.: A real-time approach of diagnosing rice leaf disease using deep learning-based faster R-CNN framework. PeerJ Comput. Sci. **7**, e432 (2021)

17. Gensheng, H., Haoyu, W., Zhang, Y., Wan, M.: A low shot learning method for tea leaf's disease identification. Comput. Electron. Agric. **163**, 104852 (2019)

18. Mukhopadhyay, S., Paul, M., Pal, R., De, D.: Tea leaf disease detection using multi-objective image segmentation. Multimed. Tools Appl. **80**, 753–771 (2021)

19. Albahli, S., Masood, M.: Efficient attention-based CNN network (EANet) for multi-class maize crop disease classification. Front. Plant Sci. **13**, 1003152 (2022)

20. Masood, M., et al.: Maizenet: a deep learning approach for effective recognition of maize plant leaf diseases. IEEE Access (2023)

21. Olayiwola, J.O., Adejoju, J.A.: Maize (Corn) leaf disease detection system using convolutional neural network (CNN). In: Gervasi, O., et al. (eds.) Computational Science and Its Applications – ICCSA 2023. ICCSA 2023. LNCS, vol. 13956, pp. 309–321. Springer, Cham (2023). https://doi.org/10.1007/978-3-031-36805-9_21

22. He, J., Liu, T., Li, L., Yahui, H., Zhou, G.: Mfaster R-CNN for maize leaf diseases detection based on machine vision. Arabian J. Sci. Eng. **48**(2), 1437–1449 (2023)
23. Vaswani, A., et al.: Attention is all you need. Adv. Neural Inf. Process. syst. **30** (2017)
24. Thai, H.-T., Tran-Van, N.-Y., Le, K.-H.: Artificial cognition for early leaf disease detection using vision transformers. In: 2021 International Conference on Advanced Technologies for Communications (ATC), pp. 33–38. IEEE (2021)
25. Thai, H.-T., Le, K.-H., Nguyen, N.L.-T.: FormerLeaf: an efficient vision transformer for cassava leaf disease detection. Comput. Electron. Agric. **204**, 107518 (2023)
26. Wang, F., et al.: Practical cucumber leaf disease recognition using improved swin transformer and small sample size. Comput. Electron. Agric. **199**, 107163 (2022)
27. Sethy, P.K.: Rice leaf disease image samples. Mendeley Data, vol. 1 (2020)
28. Kimutai, G.: Förster Anna. tea sickness dataset. Mendeley Data, vol. 2 (2022)
29. Singh, D., Jain, N., Jain, P., Kayal, P., Kumawat, S., Batra, N.: Plantdoc: a dataset for visual plant disease detection. In: Proceedings of the 7th ACM IKDD CoDS and 25th COMAD, pp. 249–253 (2020)
30. Pandian, A.J., Geetharamani, G.: Data for: identification of plant leaf diseases using a 9-layer deep convolutional neural network. Mendeley Data, vol. 1 (2019)
31. He, K., Zhang, X., Ren, S., Sun, J.: Deep residual learning for image recognition. In: Proceedings of the IEEE Conference on Computer Vision and Pattern Recognition, pp. 770–778 (2016)
32. Simonyan, K., Zisserman, A.: Very deep convolutional networks for large-scale image recognition. arXiv preprint arXiv:1409.1556 (2014)
33. Huang, G., Liu, Z., Van Der Maaten, L., Weinberger, K.Q.: Densely connected convolutional networks. In: Proceedings of the IEEE Conference on Computer Vision and Pattern Recognition, pp. 4700–4708 (2017)
34. Sandler, M., Howard, A., Zhu, M., Zhmoginov, A., Chen, L.C.: Mobilenetv 2: inverted residuals and linear bottlenecks. In: Proceedings of the IEEE Conference on Computer Vision and Pattern Recognition, pp. 4510–4520 (2018)
35. Szegedy, C., Vanhoucke, V., Ioffe, S., Shlens, J., Wojna, Z.: Rethinking the inception architecture for computer vision. In: Proceedings of the IEEE Conference on Computer Vision and Pattern Recognition, pp. 2818–2826 (2016)
36. Abadi, M., et al.: Tensorflow: large-scale machine learning on heterogeneous distributed systems. arXiv preprint arXiv:1603.04467 (2016)

Intelligent Ensemble-Based Road Crack Detection: A Holistic View

Rajendra Kumar Roul[1(✉)] [iD], Navpreet[1] [iD], and Jajati Keshari Sahoo[2] [iD]

[1] Department of Computer Science, Thapar Institute of Engineering and Technology,
Patiala, Punjab, India
raj.roul@thapar.edu, navpreet705@gmail.com
[2] Department of Mathematics, BITS Pilani, K.K.Birla, Goa Campus, Sancoale, India
jksahoo@goa.bits-pilani.ac.in

Abstract. Cracks on road surfaces undermine infrastructure load-bearing capacity and endanger both motorists and pedestrians. Prompt and effective identification of road cracks is vital to swiftly address repairs and prevent their escalation and further structural decay. Presently, the majority of crack detection approaches rely on labor-intensive manual inspection rather than automated image-based methods, resulting in costly and time-consuming processes. Automated crack detection methods are needed to streamline the process, reduce costs, and enable more proactive maintenance efforts to ensure road safety and longevity. This paper presents a comprehensive study on road crack detection, aiming to develop an accurate and efficient system for identifying cracks on road surfaces. Leveraging deep learning techniques, the proposed approach utilizes a two-stage convolutional neural network (CNN) combined with the extreme learning machine (ELM) algorithm. Through extensive experimentation and evaluation, the model demonstrates superior performance in detecting road cracks, contributing to proactive maintenance strategies, and enhancing road safety. An accuracy of 84.98% and an F-measure of 84.57% highlight the potential of the proposed approach in automating road crack detection compared to the existing deep learning approaches.

Keywords: CNN · Deep Learning · F-measure · ELM · Machine Learning

1 Introduction

Road network plays a pivotal role in enabling transportation, facilitating the movement of goods, services, and people, fostering economic growth, and connecting diverse regions. It is crucial in connecting urban centers, rural areas, and remote regions, contributing to regional development and socioeconomic integration. The continuous use of roads, combined with environmental factors such as temperature variations and moisture, poses challenges to maintaining the integrity of the infrastructure. The expansive road network and inadequate maintenance practices exacerbate these challenges, necessitating effective crack detection and maintenance strategies [18]. The preservation of road infrastructure integrity is of paramount importance to ensure safe and efficient mobility [20]. However, this infrastructure faces significant challenges, including road

S. Devismes et al. (Eds.): ICDCIT 2024, LNCS 14501, pp. 307–323, 2024.
https://doi.org/10.1007/978-3-031-50583-6_21

cracks, which compromise structural integrity and contribute to increased maintenance costs and reduced lifespan. Crack detection can be done either manually or automatically [15]. Manual crack detection processes are susceptible to human error, fatigue, and limited capacity to handle the increasing volume of data [16]. These limitations hinder the effectiveness and efficiency of crack detection, emphasizing the need for automated solutions.

On the contrary, machine learning techniques, particularly models utilizing neural networks, have gained extensive usage in the field of object detection [1]. The widespread adoption of neural network-based models for object detection is driven by their capability to learn complex patterns and features from data, leading to improved accuracy and performance in this critical computer vision task [17]. Out of all the neural networks, CNN stands out as one of the most renowned and potent architectures, famous for its exceptional accuracy in extracting meaningful features from data [8, 10]. Indeed, the fully connected layer and the backpropagation (BP) influence CNN's training time, making it relatively time-consuming. However, ELM offers an efficient alternative as a classifier, demonstrating excellent generalization performance while avoiding the use of backpropagation and requiring minimal human intervention [6, 12]. Numerous studies have provided evidence of ELM's faster training times in comparison to other conventional machine learning (ML) techniques, such as Naive-Bayes, decision trees, Support Vector Machine (SVM), etc. [5, 11]. ELM and its different variants have extensive applications in diverse fields, including pattern recognition, facial recognition, text classification, and image processing [7, 9, 13]. Combining ELM with other ML techniques has consistently yielded impressive performance results [14].

Indeed, leveraging the strengths and successes of CNN and ELM, a novel and efficient approach known as CNN-ELM has been introduced for road crack detection. This hybrid model has two distinct phases: feature extraction and classification. By integrating the powerful feature extraction capabilities of CNN and the efficient classification performance of ELM, the proposed model aims to enhance road crack detection. The CNN part performs the automatic feature extraction, capturing intricate patterns and textures related to cracks in road images. The ELM part acts as a classifier, using the extracted features to differentiate between non-crack and crack regions. The overall process involves training the CNN to learn relevant features from a large dataset of road images and then using the ELM algorithm to classify the regions as cracked or non-cracked based on the learned features. Combining the strengths of both CNN and ELM, this integrated approach can achieve high accuracy, robustness, and efficiency in road crack detection, making it suitable for real-world applications and proactive infrastructure maintenance.

The manifold contributions of the paper are:

i. The paper introduces a novel hybrid CNN-ELM approach for road crack detection, capitalizing on the advantages of both CNN and ELM. By combining the feature extraction capabilities of CNN with ELM's rapid learning and generalization properties, the proposed approach offers a powerful solution for accurate and efficient road crack detection tasks.

ii. The proposed hybrid CNN-ELM approach is comprehensively evaluated on the widely recognized CCIC and custom dataset, showcasing its remarkable efficacy in road crack detection. The approach achieves superior performance by combining

CNN with ELM compared to traditional methods. Furthermore, the generalization capability of the approach is extensively assessed by subjecting it to images from various scenarios and datasets, demonstrating its adaptability and robustness across different road crack detection tasks.

iii. The paper thoroughly analyzes the CNN-ELM approach against other hybrid models that incorporate CNN combined with different machine learning classifiers like SVM, Xgboost, and others. The performance of the CNN-ELM approach is rigorously compared against these hybrid models to assess its superiority in road crack detection tasks. The proposed approach's performance was rigorously benchmarked against several state-of-the-art methods for road crack detection, showcasing its superiority in terms of accuracy and efficiency.

2 Methodology

2.1 Data Source and Description

The methodology involves utilizing two distinct datasets for training and testing the model. The first dataset is "Concrete Crack Images for Classification (CCIC),[1]" a publicly available dataset that contains images of concrete surfaces with cracks and non-cracked areas, serving as a valuable resource for model development. The second dataset is a custom dataset collected explicitly from the Thapar Institute of Engineering and Technology (TIET)[2], Patiala, Punjab. This custom dataset likely includes road images depicting different scenarios and variations in road cracks, providing real-world data to evaluate the model's performance and generalization capability. Experimenting on these two datasets ensures a comprehensive and diverse representation of road crack images for training and testing the model in the context of road crack detection.

i. Concrete Crack Images for Classification Dataset: The first dataset CCIC, is a publicly available dataset collected from various METU Campus Buildings. Some sample images of the CCIC dataset are shown in Fig. 1. It comprises concrete images exhibiting cracks and is categorized into negative (representing images without cracks) and positive (representing images with cracks). Within each class, there are 20,000 images, resulting in a total of 40,000 images in the dataset. The dataset comprises images, each with dimensions of 227 × 227 pixels and containing RGB channels. To create this dataset, 458 high-resolution images measuring 4032 × 3024 pixels were used as the foundational source material. This dataset construction process likely involved resizing and processing high-resolution images to fit the specified dimensions, thus generating a more manageable dataset for the subsequent tasks. One of the notable strengths of this dataset lies in its comprehensive coverage of diverse surface finishes and varying illumination conditions within the high-resolution images. However, it is important to mention that no data augmentation techniques, such as random rotation or flipping were applied to this dataset during its creation.

---

[1] https://www.kaggle.com/datasets/arnavr10880/concrete-crack-images-for-classification.
[2] www.thapar.edu.

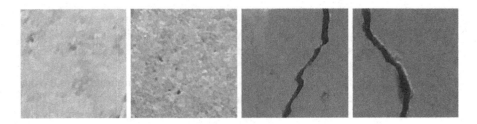

Fig. 1. Sample Images from CCIC Dataset

ii. Custom Dataset: A custom dataset comprising 260 images depicting diverse crack and non-crack regions on different buildings across the Thapar Institute of Engineering and Technology (TIET), located in Patiala, Punjab, India, was meticulously generated. These images were captured from a top view of the road surface, focusing on concrete pavement areas with cracks. Figure 2 shows some sample images of this custom dataset. The custom dataset is partitioned in the ratio of 70:30 in training and testing subsets. To augment the dataset, training and testing image sets have been processed by Keras[3], a deep learning framework, a pre-processing image tool. A horizontal flip is applied randomly to create variations in the training data. Additionally, a crop of the image is taken, which includes 90% of the total height and width of the original image. Randomly flipping and cropping images is a data augmentation technique that enhances training data diversity, thereby boosting the model's capacity to generalize effectively to new data. Testing data is also pre-processed by applying the same settings, and some image patches are flipped vertically.

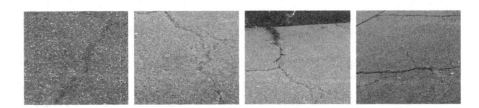

Fig. 2. Sample Images of Custom Dataset Collected at TIET Campus

2.2 Data Preprocessing

Before using the data for training and testing the model, the following preprocessing steps were applied to ensure its uniformity, eliminate any noise or artifacts, readiness, and consistency.

---

[3] https://keras.io/api/data_loading/image/.

i. Image Resizing: All images in both datasets were resized to a uniform resolution of 227 × 227 pixels. Resizing the images is necessary to ensure that the input to the CNN-ELM model has consistent dimensions, which is essential for properly functioning the convolutional layers.

ii. RGB to Grayscale Conversion: As the proposed CNN-ELM model is designed for grayscale images, the RGB images from both datasets were converted to grayscale before feeding them to the CNN feature extractor. This conversion helps reduce computational complexity and enables the model to focus on relevant image features effectively.

iii. Normalization: Normalization was performed on the grayscale images to bring the pixel values to a common scale. The pixel values were scaled to the range of [0, 1] by dividing each pixel value by 255. Normalization helps stabilize the training process and prevents issues related to differences in pixel intensity across images.

iv. Data Augmentation: Data augmentation techniques were employed to augment the training dataset's diversity and mitigate overfitting. However, it is important to note that data augmentation was not applied to the "Concrete Crack Images for Classification" dataset, as stated in its description. The data augmentation techniques used for the custom dataset include:

- Random Rotation: Images were randomly rotated by a certain angle to introduce variability in the orientation of cracks, simulating different viewing angles.
- Horizontal Flipping: Some images were horizontally flipped to create mirror images, thereby increasing the variety of crack orientations in the dataset.

Applying these preprocessing steps made the two datasets suitable for training and testing the CNN-ELM model. The images were standardized in terms of resolution and intensity values, converted to grayscale, and augmented to create a diverse and robust dataset for training the model effectively.

2.3 Model Training

The CNN-ELM model for road crack classification is implemented in Python 3.9.11. Visual Studio Code is used as the Integrated Development Environment. The combination of Python and VSCode provides an efficient and effective environment for developing and fine-tuning the CNN-ELM model for road crack classification. The training process involves the following key components:

i. Optimization Algorithm: The optimization algorithm used for training the CNN-ELM model is Stochastic Gradient Descent (SGD). SGD updates the model parameters using small batches of training data, and a batch size of 32 is chosen to balance computational efficiency and memory constraints.

ii. Learning Rate: The learning rate is set to 0.001 for the SGD optimizer. A lower learning rate allows the model to make smaller updates to the parameters during training, which can lead to more stable convergence.

iii. Training Duration and Epochs: The model is trained for multiple epochs to observe its performance at different stages of training. Specifically, the CNN-ELM model is trained for 10, 20, 30, and 40 epochs, respectively. Each epoch represents a complete iteration over the entire training dataset.

iv. Validation Split: In the dataset division process, the data is split into the training set and the cross-validation set, following a 3:1 ratio. The training set contains the majority portion of the dataset and is used to train the CNN-ELM model to learn the patterns and features relevant to road crack classification. The cross-validation set, comprising the remaining portion, serves as an independent validation set during the training phase. By evaluating the model's performance on this unseen data, the cross-validation set allows us to assess the model's ability to generalize to new and unseen road crack images. This process helps to prevent overfitting and provides valuable insights into how well the model will perform on unseen real-world data, ensuring its robustness and effectiveness in road crack detection tasks.

2.4 CNN-ELM: A Two Stage Ensembled Process

1. In the first stage of the proposed approach, a sequential CNN model is constructed, which plays a pivotal role in extracting significant features from the input image dataset. CNNs are well-known for their effectiveness in image-related tasks, especially for image classification tasks. The process of feature extraction involves applying convolutional operations on the input images using learnable filters known as kernels. These filters are designed to detect various patterns and features in the local regions of the images. Mathematically, the convolution operation can be represented using Eq. 1.

$$Y[i,j] = (X * K)[i,j] = \sum_{m=1}^{M} \sum_{n=1}^{N} X[i-m, j-n] \cdot K[m,n] \qquad (1)$$

where: $Y[i,j]$ represents the value at position (i,j) in the output feature map, X denotes the input image, K is the learnable kernel (filter), M and N are the dimensions of the kernel. Subsequent to the convolution operation, an activation function is employed to introduce non-linearity, thereby improving the network's capacity to capture intricate patterns within the data. In this work, Rectified Linear Unit (ReLU) activation function is used, which is defined as:

$$f(x) = \max(0, x)$$

where 'x' is the input feature vector. ReLU stands as a widely utilized activation function within deep neural networks. This function works by transforming negative input values to zero while preserving positive values unchanged. This intrinsic characteristic of ReLU introduces essential non-linearity to the neural network's computations. Through this simple yet effective mechanism, ReLU aids the model in capturing intricate patterns and representations from data. ReLU's non-saturating nature allows gradients to flow more readily, mitigating the vanishing gradient problem and facilitating faster and more stable training of deep neural networks. The output of the CNN consists of feature maps that represent the presence of specific patterns or features in different regions of the input images. These feature maps preserve spatial information and are crucial for further processing.

2. ELM is employed for the classification process in the second stage. ELM is known for its fast learning speed and excellent generalization performance, making it suitable for various classification tasks [4]. Unlike traditional iterative training methods, ELM adopts a single-layer architecture and directly computes the output weights analytically without iterating over the training data [6]. Given the feature maps obtained from the CNN, each feature map is transformed into a one-dimensional vector, which is then used as input for the ELM model. The conversion of a 2-D feature map to a 1-D vector involves concatenating the rows or columns of the feature map to form a long vector. For a binary classification problem (crack or no-crack), the output can be represented as $Y = \{y_1, y_2, ..., y_N\}$, where N is the number of training samples. ELM aims to find the output weights $W = \{w_1, w_2, ..., w_N\}$ that minimize the training error. ELM output can be computed using Eq. 2.

$$Y = H \cdot W \tag{2}$$

where: H is the input feature matrix containing the 1-D vectors of feature maps for all training samples, the W is the output weight matrix. To find the output weights W, ELM uses the Moore-Penrose generalized inverse, also known as the pseudoinverse, of the input feature matrix H as shown in Eq. 3.

$$W = H^+ \cdot T \tag{3}$$

where: H^+ is the pseudoinverse of H, and T is the target matrix containing the true labels of the training samples. Once the output weights are obtained, the ELM model can be used to classify the road images as either cracked or not.

The hybrid CNN-ELM structure effectively addresses the limited classification capability of CNNs by leveraging the advantageous properties of ELM. In this approach, CNNs handle feature extraction from input data, while ELM is employed for the final classification task. In the hybrid CNN-ELM approach, the risk of overfitting is reduced by updating only the output weights in the ELM model while randomly generating the hidden layer biases and the input weights [3]. By doing so, the ELM component effectively acts as a fast and efficient classifier, taking advantage of its good generalization capabilities and minimal human intervention requirements [5]. Simultaneously, the training process leverages CNN's exceptional feature extraction capabilities. The CNN extracts high-level features from the input data, which are then fed into the ELM for classification. This combination allows the model to benefit from both the CNN's ability to learn complex representations and the ELM's fast learning speed. Consequently, the hybrid CNN-ELM approach achieves a faster overall learning speed while maintaining strong generalization performance, making it an effective solution for road crack detection tasks.

2.5 Proposed Architecture of CNN-ELM

The proposed CNN-ELM model consists of a well-structured architecture (shown in the Fig. 3) comprising several essential layers as discussed in the following steps (Table 1).

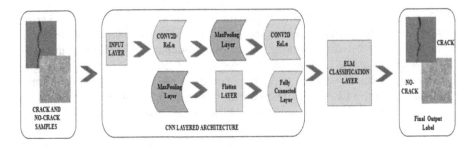

Fig. 3. CNN-ELM Architecture

Table 1. Architecture Detail of CNN-ELM

Name of the Layer	Parameter used	Shape of the Output	Learnable_Parameters
Input_layer	227 × 227 × 1	–	0
Convolution Layer-I	Filters = 20, Padding ='same', kernel_size=(2 × 2)	(None, 226, 226, 20)	260
ReLu Activation Layer-I	-	(None, 226, 226, 20)	0
Maxpooling Layer-I	Pool_size = (2,2)	(None, 113, 113, 20)	0
Convolution Layer-II	Filters=10, Padding='same', kernel_size=(2 × 2)	(None, 112, 112, 10)	810
ReLu Activation Layer-II	-	(None, 112, 112, 10)	0
Maxpooling Layer-II	Poolsize = (2,2)	(None, 56, 56, 10)	0
Flatten Layer	-	(None, 31360)	0
FullyConnected Layer-1	units=200	(None, 200)	272200
Relu Activation Layer-III	-	(None, 200)	0
Dense Layer	-	(None, 2)	402
Hidden Layer of ELM	size of hidden_layer = 250	-	250
Output_Layer	activation = 'tanh'	(None,2)	202

3 Analysis of Experimental Work

3.1 Experimental Setup

To conduct the experiments for the classification of road cracks based on the proposed CNN-ELM model, Intel Core i11 processor along with 24 GB GPU and 32 GB RAM were used. The TensorFlow library and the high-level API Keras were employed for implementing the CNN-ELM model. The training and evaluation processes were performed using Python 3.9 on the VSCode IDE. TensorFlow and Keras provided a robust and efficient platform for building, training, and evaluating the CNN-ELM model for the accurate classification of concrete crack images into positive (with cracks) and negative (without cracks) categories.

3.2 Results Analysis

Analysis by Confusion Matrix: The CNN-ELM architecture's performance was assessed using the CCIC and TIET datasets. The model was trained for 10 to 40 epochs, with the number of neurons in the hidden layer varying during training. Figure 4 displays the confusion matrix of CNN-ELM at different epochs. The confusion matrix provides valuable insights into the model's performance, showing how well it predicts each class at various training stages. At ten epochs, the confusion matrix demonstrates the model's initial performance, highlighting areas of improvement for specific classes. As the training progresses, the model becomes more adept, and by 20 epochs, it achieves its peak accuracy, as evident from the improved diagonal alignment in the confusion matrix. Beyond 20 epochs, the model's performance tends to plateau, indicating that additional training might not yield significant accuracy gains. This observation is further supported by the confusion matrix at 30 and 40 epochs, which shows similar performance patterns compared to the 20-epoch matrix.

Performance Comparison for Different Hidden Layer Neurons vs. Epochs: Table 2 represents evaluating performance metric parameters at different epochs. These evaluation metrics provide valuable insights into the model's performance, helping to understand its strengths and weaknesses in accurately classifying concrete crack images as negative (no crack) or positive (crack). Overall, the CNN-ELM architecture with 250 neurons in the hidden layer exhibits promising accuracy at 20 epochs, making it a favorable configuration for practical applications.

Comparison of Accuracy at Different Activation Functions: The proposed model is trained for 10 to 40 epochs by varying neurons at the hidden layer, and performance is compared by using linear or non-linear activation function, as shown in Fig. 5. The proposed model achieves maximum accuracy for non-linear activation function (tanh) with 250 neurons in the hidden layer at 20 epochs.

3.3   Comparison with Other ML Classifiers

CNN-ELM performance is compared with different ML techniques such as Xgboost, SVM, Extra trees (ET), Gaussian Naive Bayes (GNB), Decision Trees etc., combined with CNN. All models have been trained on a road image subset for 20 epochs with a learning rate of 0.001 and a batch size of 32. The hyperparameters set for training the ML classifiers are listed in Table 3. The empirical results revealed that CNN-ELM outperforms other ML classifiers in terms of accuracy, as shown in Table 4 (bold indicates maximum). The CNN-QDA hybrid classifier has the highest specificity among various classifiers because it efficiently organizes features into distinct classes and models the variance-covariance matrices for each class. By integrating CNN for feature extraction and QDA for classification, this approach captures intricate patterns through CNN's hierarchical learning, while QDA effectively accounts for class-specific variations in the data. This synergy enhances classification accuracy by leveraging the separate arrangement of features and the covariance information within distinct classes. Prior Information: QDA incorporates prior probabilities of classes when making classification decisions. This aspect might arise from contrast with techniques like constructing decision trees using ET, where a subset of features is chosen randomly at each node, introducing diversity and minimizing correlation among trees. ET's random feature selection process enables the capture of distinct data patterns, ultimately leading to higher specificity in classification due to the diverse range of features considered and the reduction of

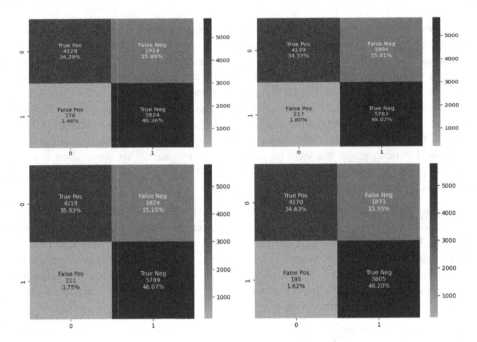

Fig. 4. Analysis of Confusion Matrix of CNN-ELM at different Epochs

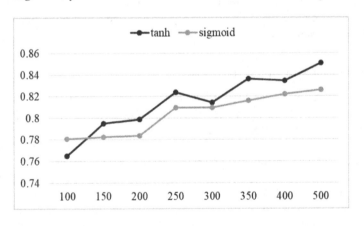

Fig. 5. Accuracy comparison for different activation function

correlated decisions across the ensemble. Performance metric parameters such as Precision, Recall, and F1-Score are also compared with various ML classifiers, as shown in Figs. 6, 7, and 8, respectively. Results show that CNN-ELM has the highest Precision and F1-Score comparable to other ML classifiers. CNN-MLP shows a higher sensitivity compared to other classifiers. The reason may be due to multiple hidden layers, MLP can identify discriminative features and relevant patterns of the data in a better manner, which gives higher sensitivity.

Table 2. Performance Metric comparison for Epochs vs Hidden layer Neurons

Epochs	Hidden Layer Neurons	Precision (%)	Sensitivity (%)	Specificity (%)	F1-Score (%)
10	100	70.89	94.15	61.62	80.88
	150	72.01	96.30	62.84	82.40
	200	73.27	96.65	65.00	83.35
	250	75.26	97.06	68.32	84.78
	300	75.34	97.41	68.34	84.96
	350	77.32	97.53	71.60	86.26
	400	77.45	98.11	71.63	86.56
	500	77.00	98.06	70.92	86.26
20	100	70.54	90.68	62.40	79.35
	150	72.97	93.46	65.62	81.95
	200	72.66	95.55	64.30	82.54
	250	75.26	96.38	68.49	84.50
	300	74.12	96.38	66.58	83.79
	350	76.35	97.18	70.11	85.51
	400	76.16	97.21	69.79	85.41
	500	77.93	97.70	72.53	86.70
30	100	71.89	92.73	64.00	80.99
	150	73.72	94.26	66.63	82.73
	200	74.30	95.11	67.35	83.43
	250	75.23	96.48	69.81	85.05
	300	76.14	96.93	69.84	85.29
	350	76.07	96.78	69.78	85.19
	400	76.48	97.05	70.37	85.55
	500	78.53	97.48	73.53	86.98
40	100	70.07	93.16	60.49	79.98
	150	74.32	95.36	67.28	83.53
	200	74.51	96.83	67.11	84.22
	250	75.60	96.75	69.00	84.88
	300	75.97	97.23	69.46	85.29
	350	75.48	97.38	68.59	85.04
	400	77.13	97.63	71.27	86.18
	500	78.57	98.06	73.45	87.24

Table 3. Hyper-parameter used for the Training of ML Classifiers

Classifier	Hyper-parameters
Decision Trees	min_samples_split=10, criterion='gini', max_depth=5 criterion='gini', max_depth=40, max_features=50
Extra Trees	min_samples_leaf=4, n_jobs=4, random_state=42, n_estimators=100, in_samples_split=10
SVM	kernel='linear', C=1.0, random_state=0
GNB	var_smoothing=1e-8
XgBoost	n_estimators=100, objective='binary:logistic', random_state=42, n_jobs=4, booster='gbtree', gamma=0, max_depth=3
QDA	priors=None, reg_param=0.0

Table 4. Performance Comparison of CNN-ELM with ML Classifiers

Model	Specificity(%)	Accuracy(%)
CNN-DT	69.20	83.33
CNN-ET	62.33	79.68
CNN-SVM	89.87	84.37
CNN-GNB	85.26	84.30
CNN-XGBoost	51.24	73.21
CNN-QDA	**98.92**	55.16
CNN-ELM (Proposed)	68.49	**84.98**

3.4   Training and Testing Time Analysis

While training the CNN, refining the parameters of the convolutional layers through fine-tuning can lead to increased computation time, as shown in the Eq. 4.

$$\sum_{i=1}^{k} x_{i-1} . y_i^2 . x_i . z_i^2 \qquad (4)$$

where i is the convolutional layer index, k is the number of convolutional layers, x_i is the number of filters at the ith layer, x_{i-1} is the number of input channels of the ith layer, y_i is the size of the filter, and z_i is output feature size. According to He et al., [2], the fully connected layer of CNN takes around 10% of computation time, resulting in a higher training time. Based on the past literature, it has been seen that ELM does not involve backpropagation, resulting in less computation time than other ML classifiers

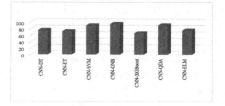

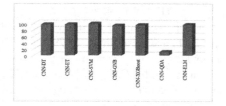

Fig. 6. Comparison of Precision   **Fig. 7.** Comparison of Recall

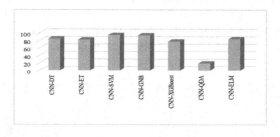

Fig. 8. Comparison of F1-Score

[4, 19]. Hence, the proposed approach replaces the fully connected layer with ELM, and due to this, the proposed model exhibits the minimum training time compared to all other models. Table 5 depicts ELM's training and testing time comparison with different ML classifiers (bold indicates minimum).

Table 5. Comparison of training and testing time with ML Classifiers

Model	Training time (in sec)	Testing Time (in sec)
CNN	11443	2229
ELM	357.1	0.260
CNN-DT	204.6	0.275
CNN-ET	32.95	0.251
CNN-SVM	27796	4264
CNN-GNB	5.149	6.184
CNN-XgBoost	1207	0.989
CNN-QDA	2537	51.29
CNN-ELM (Proposed)	**3.587**	**0.248**

3.5 Discussion

The experimental evaluation was conducted on the CCIC dataset, and the resulting accuracy values were compared. After 20 epochs of training, CNN attained a 51.90%

accuracy. However, increasing the number of epochs to 50 or more resulted in CNN achieving even higher accuracy with a higher training time. AT 250 hidden neurons, ELM attained an accuracy of 79.56%. However, increasing the number of neurons to around 2000 led to even higher accuracy levels for ELM. Figure 9 represents the confusion matrix for CNN, ELM, and CNN-ELM. Figure 10 represents the accuracy and f1-score comparison of CNN, ELM, and CNN-ELM. The proposed model synergistically incorporates CNN and ELM, achieving a peak accuracy of 84.50% within just 20 training epochs using 250 hidden layer neurons. The model accomplished this with less training and testing time, as discussed in Sect. 3.4. The generalization property is validated by training CNN-ELM on CCIC and tested on the custom dataset (Fig. 11). The results suggest that the combined CNN-ELM architecture is more efficient for road crack detection than using CNN or ELM classifiers in isolation.

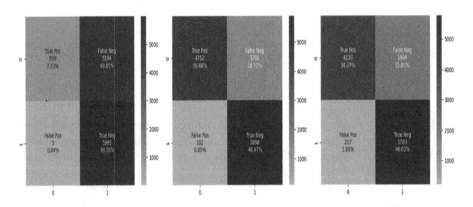

Fig. 9. Confusion Matrix for CNN(left), ELM(middle) and CNN-ELM(right)

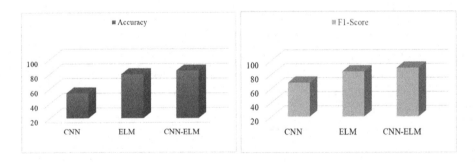

Fig. 10. Performance Comparison of CNN, ELM, and CNN-ELM

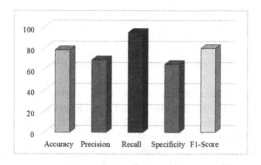

Fig. 11. Performance Evaluation on TIET Dataset

4 Conclusion

This study has delved into the significance of road crack detection for ensuring safe and efficient road infrastructure management, particularly in nations like India with extensive road networks. Among the automated methods, deep learning techniques, especially CNN, emerged as a powerful tool for crack detection due to their ability to automatically learn and extract meaningful features from road images. CNN has shown exceptional accuracy and robustness, making it well-suited for real-world applications in road crack detection. Furthermore, the integration of CNN with the efficient ELM was discussed, highlighting its potential to enhance the accuracy and efficiency of road crack detection. The combination of CNN's feature extraction capabilities and ELM's fast training process for classification makes this integrated approach promising for proactive infrastructure maintenance and targeted crack repair. In conclusion, the integration of CNN and ELM holds immense promise for developing an accurate, efficient, and automated system for road crack detection. The proposed model has the potential to streamline infrastructure maintenance, reduce maintenance costs, and enhance road safety and beyond. This work can be extended on the following lines:

· In the current research, it has been observed that resizing images consumes additional time and resources. A standard model capable of handling images of various sizes without resizing is needed to address this issue. This standard model aims to streamline the image processing pipeline and improve overall efficiency by accommodating diverse image dimensions, reducing the computational overhead associated with image resizing.
· The performance of the proposed Conv-ELM can be compared with the pre-trained CNN variants like VGGNet, ResNet, Inception, etc., integrated with ELM and validated on various crack detection datasets.
· The classification accuracy can be further enhanced by considering different ELM variants combined with CNN variants.
· Finding the exact number of neurons in the hidden layer of ELM is a difficult task, and it is done based on the experiment. Hence, a technique should be developed to find exactly how many neurons in the hidden layer are required for ELM to classify the images.

References

1. Chen, F.C., Jahanshahi, M.R.: NB-CNN: deep learning-based crack detection using convolutional neural network and Naïve Bayes data fusion. IEEE Trans. Ind. Electron. **65**(5), 4392–4400 (2017)
2. He, K., Sun, J.: Convolutional neural networks at constrained time cost. In: Proceedings of the IEEE Conference on Computer Vision and Pattern Recognition (CVPR), June 2015
3. Huang, G.B.: An insight into extreme learning machines: random neurons, random features and kernels. Cogn. Comput. **6**(3), 376–390 (2014)
4. Huang, G.B., Ding, X., Zhou, H.: Optimization method based extreme learning machine for classification. Neurocomputing **74**(1–3), 155–163 (2010)
5. Huang, G.B., Zhou, H., Ding, X., Zhang, R.: Extreme learning machine for regression and multiclass classification. IEEE Trans. Syst. Man Cybern. Part B (Cybernetics) **42**(2), 513–529 (2011)
6. Huang, G.B., Zhu, Q.Y., Siew, C.K.: Extreme learning machine: theory and applications. Neurocomputing **70**(1–3), 489–501 (2006)
7. Kasun, L.L.C., Yang, Y., Huang, G.B., Zhang, Z.: Dimension reduction with extreme learning machine. IEEE Trans. Image Process. **25**(8), 3906–3918 (2016)
8. Kaur, R., Roul, R.K., Batra, S.: A hybrid deep learning CNN-ELM approach for parking space detection in smart cities. Neural Comput. Appl. **35**, 13665–13683 (2023)
9. Li, H., Zhao, H., Li, H.: Neural-response-based extreme learning machine for image classification. IEEE Trans. Neural Netw. Learn. Syst. **30**(2), 539–552 (2018)
10. Maniat, M., Camp, C.V., Kashani, A.R.: Deep learning-based visual crack detection using google street view images. Neural Comput. Appl. **33**(21), 14565–14582 (2021)
11. Roul, R.K.: Detecting spam web pages using multilayer extreme learning machine. Int. J. Big Data Intell. **5**(1–2), 49–61 (2018)
12. Roul, R.K., Agarwal, A.: Feature space of deep learning and its importance: comparison of clustering techniques on the extended space of ML-ELM. In: Proceedings of the 9th Annual Meeting of the Forum for Information Retrieval Evaluation (2017)
13. Roul, R.K., Satyanath, G.: A novel feature selection based text classification using multilayer ELM. In: Roy, P.P., Agarwal, A., Li, T., Krishna Reddy, P., Uday Kiran, R. (eds.) Big Data Analytics. BDA 2022. LNCS, vol. 13773, pp. 33–52. Springer, Cham (2022). https://doi.org/10.1007/978-3-031-24094-2_3
14. Rujirakul, K., So-In, C.: Histogram equalized deep PCA with ELM classification for expressive face recognition. In: 2018 International Workshop on Advanced Image Technology (IWAIT), pp. 1–4. IEEE (2018)
15. Xiao, S., Shang, K., Lin, K., Wu, Q., Gu, H., Zhang, Z.: Pavement crack detection with hybrid-window attentive vision transformers. Int. J. Appl. Earth Obs. Geoinf. **116**, 103172 (2023)
16. Yang, F., Zhang, L., Yu, S., Prokhorov, D., Mei, X., Ling, H.: Feature pyramid and hierarchical boosting network for pavement crack detection. IEEE Trans. Intell. Transp. Syst. **21**(4), 1525–1535 (2019)
17. Zakeri, H., Nejad, F.M., Fahimifar, A.: Image based techniques for crack detection, classification and quantification in asphalt pavement: a review. Arch. Comput. Methods Eng. **24**, 935–977 (2017)

18. Zhang, K., Zhang, Y., Cheng, H.D.: CrackGAN: pavement crack detection using partially accurate ground truths based on generative adversarial learning. IEEE Trans. Intell. Transp. Syst. **22**(2), 1306–1319 (2020)
19. Zhong, H., Miao, C., Shen, Z., Feng, Y.: Comparing the learning effectiveness of BP, ELM, I-ELM, and SVM for corporate credit ratings. Neurocomputing **128**, 285–295 (2014)
20. Zou, Q., Zhang, Z., Li, Q., Qi, X., Wang, Q., Wang, S.: DeepCrack: learning hierarchical convolutional features for crack detection. IEEE Trans. Image Process. **28**(3), 1498–1512 (2018)

Online Payment Fraud Detection for Big Data

Samiksha Dattaprasad Tawde$^{(\boxtimes)}$, Sandhya Arora, and Yashasvee Shitalkumar Thakur

Department of Computer Engineering, MKSSS's Cummins College of Engineering for Women, Pune, India
{Samiksha.tawde,Sandhya.arora,
Yashasvee.thakur}@cumminscollege.in

Abstract. Modern economic life is now greatly facilitated by online payment systems, which allow for seamless financial transactions. However, the risk of online payment fraud has greatly increased along with the growth of digital transactions. This calls for the creation of sophisticated fraud detection systems that can instantly evaluate huge amounts of transaction data. This study suggests a novel method for identifying online payment fraud by utilizing big data management techniques, more specifically PySpark's capabilities. PySpark uses Resilient Distributed Datasets (RDD), data structure and stores data in RAM instead of writing it to disk after each operation. RDD operations are lazy i.e., they will not execute unless an action operation is called on them. After preprocessing the data Machine Learning algorithms from Spark ML package are applied, the ML library of PySpark provides optimized Machine Learning capabilities for Classification problems that require distributed computing. Further, models of classification algorithms that qualify with the best metrics are developed on our dataset and used for making accurate detections. Our Fraud detection system aims to assist Large organizations in assessing their enormous amount of transaction data to detect possible anomalies or fraudulent activities.

Keywords: PySpark · Fraud Detection · Big Data · Resilient Distributed Datasets · Decision Tree · Random Forest · Logistic Regression

1 Introduction

In a world witnessing rapid escalation in the number of online transactions with every passing day and the subsequent enormous amount of data that these transactions generate, Big Data management techniques come to the rescue. Big Data comprises structured, unstructured, and semi structured data collected over a period of time, which can be mined to obtain meaningful insights using Machine Learning techniques.

A major threat faced by the online transactions is that of fraudulent activities wherein individuals with malicious intent steal the credentials of other individuals and make online transactions on behalf of them. Storage and handling of Big Data itself is a tedious job, on top of it, detecting such fraud activities present in the Big Data proves to be more challenging even with the presence of security measures such as encryption and tokenization.

S. Devismes et al. (Eds.): ICDCIT 2024, LNCS 14501, pp. 324–337, 2024.
https://doi.org/10.1007/978-3-031-50583-6_22

This calls for the creation of sophisticated Fraud Detection systems that can easily store huge amounts of transaction data, efficiently process it and accurately detect the presence of fraudulent activities in it. The system implemented in this paper is built using the robust Big data storage capacity of PySpark in combination with efficient Machine Learning Models from the pyspark.ml package.

The Machine Learning models used are Logistic Regression (statistical model developed using the logit function), Random Forest(machine learning algorithm which combines the output of multiple decision trees to reach a single result), Decision Tree (a decision support hierarchical model that uses a tree-like model of decisions and their possible consequences) and Naïve Bayes (Probabilistic classifier based on Bayes Theorem) [10, 12]. The results obtained from these models are viewed from different perspectives to gain deeper insights on their reliability, using various evaluation metrics. The flow of the paper is as follows. Section 2 summarizes the prior work done on Fraud Detection in Big Datasets and Sect. 3 provides detailed working methodology of the implemented Fraud Detection system, consequently followed by results discussed in Sect. 4. Lastly, the paper concludes with conclusions mentioned in Sect. 5.

2 Literature Review

The financial industry has undergone a digital transformation as a result of the quick development of information technologies including the Internet of Things (IoT), Big Data, Artificial Intelligence (AI), and Blockchain [1]. Changes in customer behaviour and a redesigned environment for conventional financial operations are the hallmarks of this change. The economic and social spheres have been severely impacted by technological breakthroughs including mobile payments, IoT-based financial services, and Internet-based wealth management. Since 2014, China's Internet has grown rapidly, cultivating a widespread preference for online transactions using mobile and IoT devices. The financial services sector of the Internet has grown steadily as a result of this acceptance.

However, this quick evolution has also revealed regulatory flaws. Due to the rapid innovation in Internet consumer finance, the regulatory framework has frequently trailed behind, exposing gaps in how infractions and problems are addressed [1]. On online financial platforms, instances of fraud, exploitation, and aggressive debt collection have increased, negatively affecting the development of the Internet of Things (IoT) and consumer finance sector. Fraud is defined as an illegal attempt to obtain financial or personal advantages. It frequently entails irregular or unfair transactions. Fraudulent activity frequently deviates from accepted transaction standards and may show anomalies in transaction quantity, time, accounts, IP addresses, or individual credit ratings.

Existing methods for fraud detection include machine learning-based models and expert systems with rule-based architectures. Rule-based systems heavily rely on antifraud specialists to manually review vast amounts of transaction data in order to identify and categorize fraudulent activity [1]. To extract significant information and create expert rules for fraud detection, these systems need domain expertise and commercial acumen. However, the efficiency of these systems depends on the knowledge and responsiveness of anti-fraud specialists, and a delay in spotting complex fraud patterns can lead to significant losses.

Globally speaking, the year 2020 was a turning point due to the COVID-19 pandemic's onset [2]. A record-breaking increase in online transaction volumes and usage of internet services was sparked by the virus's unrelenting propagation. People across the world are increasingly dependent on digital platforms for a variety of services, which has caused this spike out of both necessity and caution. Drug research, epidemiological forecasts, and clinical diagnostics all benefited from AI's ability to learn quickly, which helped people make better decisions in ambiguous situations.

Fraud detection in big data environments [3] developed a method that combines machine learning with big data analytics to find fraud. The study underscored how crucial it is to handle and analyses massive amounts of data in order to spot fraudulent tendencies. To identify deviations from expected behavior, the suggested system combined anomaly detection and behavioral analysis.

Big data analytics were used to improve the accuracy of a hybrid strategy for credit card fraud detection [4]. To find questionable transactions, the authors merged rule-based methods with machine learning algorithms. Big data processing was added into the hybrid strategy to handle the massive volume of transaction data, which led to higher rates of fraud detection.

A real-time fraud detection method for e-commerce platforms was introduced by real-time fraud detection in e-commerce leveraging big data [5]. The report made a point of the urgency of responding right away to online transaction fraud. The system achieved low-latency fraud detection, averting potential financial losses, by utilizing stream processing and parallel computing on big data frameworks.

Big data analytics for insurance fraud detection [6] concentrated on the issues of fraud detection in the insurance sector. The study emphasized the use of big data analytics to examine a variety of data sources, such as claim histories, insurance information, and consumer behavior. The scientists improved the accuracy of fraud identification and decreased false positives by using machine learning techniques on this variety of data.

Using big data to improve healthcare fraud detection [7] covered the use of big data analytics in healthcare fraud detection. The study underscored how crucial it is to combine structured and unstructured data from provider information, insurance claims, and medical records. Advanced machine learning techniques were used by the authors to analyses these diverse data sources in order to improve the detection of fraudulent insurance and medical billing claims.

An approach for identifying fraudulent behavior in large-scale financial transaction datasets was published in Large-Scale Fraud Detection in Financial Transactions [8]. The study brought attention to the difficulties involved in managing enormous volumes of financial data while preserving real-time detection capabilities. The suggested remedy made use of parallel processing and distributed computing frameworks to quickly analyses transaction data and spot probable fraud trends.

The difficulty of integrating several data sources is a typical problem that can affect the quality of the data and make fraud detection less accurate. Furthermore, several studies point out the trade-off between real-time detection and computing efficiency, where it is difficult to achieve both at the same time. Another issue that keeps coming up is the lack of qualified individuals who can create, install, and manage sophisticated big data analytics systems for fraud detection. Additionally, even if the studies stress the use of machine learning algorithms, it is still important to pay attention to how these models may be understood and explained in terms of fraud detection. Feature selection is now a crucial part of a successful model's performance in machine learning (ML), which has become a potent tool for detecting credit card fraud. The use of genetic algorithms (GA) in feature selection—a technique that maximizes feature selection—in the context of credit card fraud detection is examined in this review [13]. Researchers have created an advanced machine learning (ML) credit card fraud detection engine that uses GA to combine the capabilities of several classifiers, such as Random Forest (RF), Decision Tree (DT), Naive Bayes (NB), Random Forest (RF), Logistic Regression (LR), and Artificial Neural Network (ANN). The performance evaluation of the suggested detection engine, carried out with a European cardholder dataset, shows the advantage of this method over current ones. The engine improves fraud detection accuracy by carefully examining and choosing the most pertinent features under the guidance of GA, which makes it a significant contribution to the ongoing fight against credit card fraud [13]. The research highlights the importance of feature selection in augmenting the performance of machine learning models, demonstrating the possibility of using GA to maximize the detection of fraudulent transactions.

The suggested model [14], makes use of a wide range of features such as time, device type, transaction quantities, and transaction types, is one noteworthy addition to this field. Through an exploration of user behavior modelling, this model generates unique profiles for every user and establishes threshold values for these profiles. Essentially, it uses two strong filters—a rapid filter and an explicit filter—to improve real-time fraud detection in the setting of electronic cash payment cards. The fast filter uses the Baum-Welch algorithm to find the local maximum likelihood in addition to the first-order Hidden Markov Model and Self-Organizing Maps (SOM) to enable quick transaction processing. In contrast, the explicit filter creates cardholder profiles using Logistic Regression and multilayer Perceptron Neural Network techniques. The transaction is classified as fraudulent or non-fraudulent after evaluation, at which point it is kept in the database for future use. With an Accuracy of 0.999, Precision of 0.9834, Recall of 0.7906, and F1-Score of 0.9214, the model's simulation results demonstrate remarkable performance in a number of important categories, outperforming the results of individual methods [14].

Our approach stands out because of the creative use of the PySpark API, which allows us to effectively manage and store enormous amounts of data. We efficiently preprocess this large dataset using PySpark's strong capabilities, establishing the groundwork for precise and intelligent analysis. Our distinct advantage stems from PySpark's strength, which enables us to handle challenging data preparation tasks quickly and nimbly. Our classification techniques are used after the data has been cleaned up, and they excel at correctly classifying complex patterns in the data. By strategically combining the data processing prowess of PySpark with our astute classification techniques, we guarantee that our insights are not only thorough but also extremely dependable, setting us apart in producing significant outcomes.

3 Methodology

PySpark allows us to use programmes written in Python to send commands and receive responses, via Py4J (Python for Java), from Spark, which is a JVM programme. Spark is built using languages like Java and Scala, it does most of the heavy lifting and has a RDD interface for working with distributed datasets. The IPC between PySpark and Spark initializes with SparkContext, a Python object and main entry point for Spark Functionality, from PySpark library. SparkContext connects to a network port on the computer and through this port reaches out to the SparkContext object in JVM. Spark-Context performs important operations such as running a job, deleting attributes, showing profiles, receiving results, etc. Figure 1 elaborates the overall approach of our work.

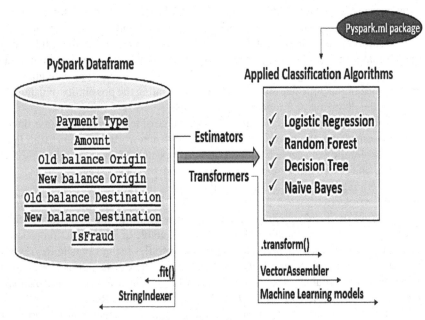

Fig. 1. Overall approach

3.1 Data Modelling

Data downloaded from the repository when loaded in the PySpark dataframe gets serialized (state converted into a byte stream) into a file and gets distributed into Spark's worker's memory. Built in operations such as join, filters, aggregation can be run on the data or Spark can launch a group of Python Processes, pass them serialized Python code and data, and command those Python processes to execute the code on the data. The result obtained from the above-mentioned operations are stored back into Spark's memory. Finally, the data is sent from Spark to our application, from a stream of bytes into a Python object.

After the data is loaded onto the PySpark dataframe keeping the parameters infer-Schema and Header as True, instances of entry points such as SparkConnect and SQL-Connect are initialized. SparkConnect coordinates execution of jobs and SQLConnect enables SQL like operations on the dataframe using SparkSQL (a Spark module for structured data processing).

Transformers and estimators from PySpark are then applied on the dataframe to transform it into machine learning features. Operations performed on the dataframe include filtering (e.g. displaying selected entries), aggregation(e.g. counting sum of null values in the columns). StringIndexer is an estimator that is fitted on the 'Type' column to convert the categorical labels into numeric labels. The VectorAssembler transformer is applied on the 'Step', 'Amount', 'Old Balance Origin', 'New Balance Origin', 'Old Balance Destination', 'New Balance Destination', 'Type' columns to pack the features into a vector('Features' column).

3.2 Machine Learning Model Training

The dataframe containing Features and target column viz. predictionandtarget is split into training set and testing set in 8:2 ratio. The various classifiers imported from the pyspark.ml package are Logistic Regression, Random Forest, Decision Tree and Naïve Bayes. For each of the classifier a Machine Learning model is built by applying the.fit() estimator on the training data and predictions are made using the.transform() transformer on the testing data.

A new dataframe containing the predictions, along with the earlier columns, and additional features such as probability, raw prediction, etc. is generated. Of this dataframe the targetandprediction column is selected for metric evaluation.

3.3 Evaluation Metrics

The following evaluation metrics are used:

MulticlassEvaluator. From pyspark.ml.evaluation package the MulticlassEvaluator is imported and is applied on the prediction and target dataframe.The metrics evaluated are Accuracy, F1 score, Weighted Precision, Weighted Recall and Area Under ROC curve.

BinaryClassificationMetric. Plotting ROC and PR curves for all the Machine Learning models, using HandySpark. The predictions dataframe is transformed to handy and the columns chosen are 'probability', 'predictions' and 'target'.

From pyspark.mllib.evaluation package is imported and Area Under Curve for ROC and PR are evaluated and plotted.

The following values for all the classifiers are tabulated in the following tables.

BAUC PR - BinaryClassificationMetric Area Under Curve for Precision Recall.

Table 1. MulticlassEvaluator evaluation metrics.

Classifiers	Logistic Regression	Random Forest	Decision Tree	Naive Bayes
Accuracy	0.998969	0.999399	0.999386	0.624614
F1 Score	0.998618	0.999305	0.999360	0.767673
Weighted Precision	0.998940	0.999398	0.999348	0.998492
Weighted Recall	0.998969	0.999399	0.999386	0.624614

BAUC ROC - BinaryClassificationMetric Area Under Curve for Receiver Optimization Characteristics.

MAUC ROC - MulticlassEvaluator Area Under Curve for Receiver Optimization Characteristics.

MAUC PR - MulticlassEvaluator Area Under Curve for Precision Recall (Table 2).

Table 2. Area under curve for ROC and PR.

Classifiers	BAUC ROC	BAUC PR
Logistic Regression	0.853525	0.184644
Random Forest	0.985303	0.767761
Decision Tree	0.954659	0.693669
Naïve Bayes	0.747433	0.002789

MulticlassMetric. From   pyspark.mllib.evaluation   package MulticlassMetric is imported and using this on the predictionsadlabel dataframe rdd tuple mapping is done. The metrics evaluated are Confusion matrix, True Positive Rate (TPR), False Positive Rate (FPR), Precision, Specificity (Table 3).

Table 3. MulticlassMetric evaluations

Classifiers	Logistic Regression	Random Forest	Decision Tree	Naive Bayes
TPR	0.998969	0.999399	0.999386	0.624614
FPR	0.816302	0.477744	0.321631	0.129624
Precision	0.998940	0.999398	0.999348	0.998492
Specificity	0.183697	0.522255	0.678368	0.870375

Matthew Correlation Coefficient (MCC). The Matthew Correlation Coefficient (MCC) metric, which is a discrete case of Pearson's Correlation Coefficient, is computed using the True Positive (TP), True Negative (TN), False Positive (FP), False Negative (FN) values obtained from the confusion matrix (Table 4).

$$MCC = \frac{TP \times TN - FP \times FN}{\sqrt{(TP + FP)(TP + FN)(TN + FP)(TN + FN)}}$$

Table 4. Confusion Matrix values.

Classifiers	Logistic Regression	Random Forest	Decision Tree	Naive Bayes
TP	291.0	831.0	1080.0	1387.0
TN	1271139.0	1271146.0	1270880.0	793586.0
FP	9.0	2.0	268.0	477562.0
FN	1302.0	762.0	513.0	206.0

Balanced Accuracy Rate (BAR). Balanced Accuracy Rate (BAR), which is the average accuracy obtained from both minority and majority classes is also computed (Table 5).

$$BAR = \frac{(Specificity + Sensitivity)}{2} = \frac{\frac{TP}{(TP+FN)} + \frac{TN}{(TN+FP)}}{2}$$

Table 5. Area Under curves, MCC and BAR metric evaluation.

Classifiers	Logistic Regression	Random Forest	Decision Tree	Naive Bayes
BAUC ROC	0.853525	0.985303	0.954659	0.747433
BAUC PR	0.184644	0.767761	0.693669	0.002789
MAUC ROC	0.998618	0.999305	0.999360	0.767673
MCC	0.420713	0.721173	0.736705	0.036124
BAR	0.591333	0.760827	0.838877	0.747495

4   Results and Discussion

The development of four different classifier models and the evaluation of the best model for fraud detection using the PySpark framework was the main goal of the current study. In this inquiry, Naive Bayes, Decision Tree, Random Forest, and Logistic Regression were all used as models. A standard 80–20 training-testing split was used to evaluate the effectiveness of these models. To be more precise, 80% of the dataset was used for training, and the remaining 20% was set aside for testing.

From the metrics evaluated using the Multiclass Classification Evaluator, Logistic Regression, Decision Tree and Random Forest give equally good results; however, Naïve Bayes performs poorly with accuracy of only 62.46%.With reference to Table 1, the effectiveness of our classifiers was rigorously evaluated and compared using parameters such as Accuracy, F1 Score, Weighted Precision a Weighted Recall. We can make out that the descending order of accuracy is Random Forest followed by Decision Tree followed by Logistic Regression.

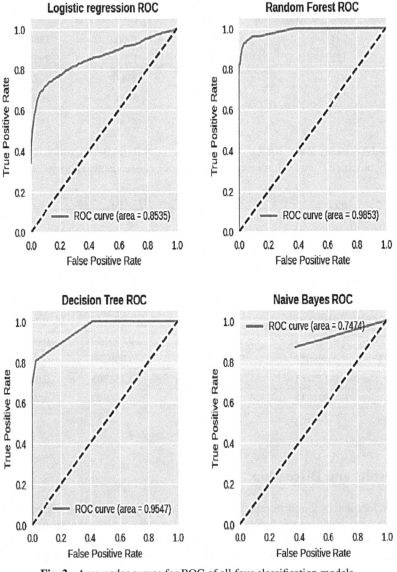

Fig. 2. Area under curves for ROC of all four classification models.

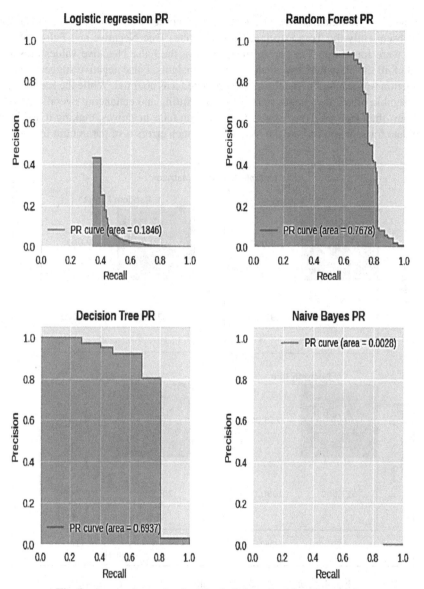

Fig. 3. Area under curves for PR of all four classification models.

After applying the Binary Classification Metrics on the Handy Spark dataframe the Area under curve for ROC curve and PR curve was plotted. A thorough examination of Fig. 2 reveals that the Area under curve for both these graphs of Random Forest are significantly higher than that of Decision Tree followed by Logistic Regression. Naïve Bayes covers negligible area of both these graphs.

Using the Multiclass Metrics the Confusion matrices were plotted for each classifier and subsequently the True Positive, False Positive, True Negative and False Negative values were found out. The careful inspection of the False Negative values present in Fig. 3 of all the classifiers revealed interesting insights. False negative suggests that the transaction was fraudulent but the model predicted it as no fraud. While the Random Forest ensemble offers advantages in reducing overfitting and enhancing overall predictive accuracy, the Decision Tree excels in minimizing false negatives, making it a valuable candidate for scenarios where the mitigation of such errors is of paramount importance.

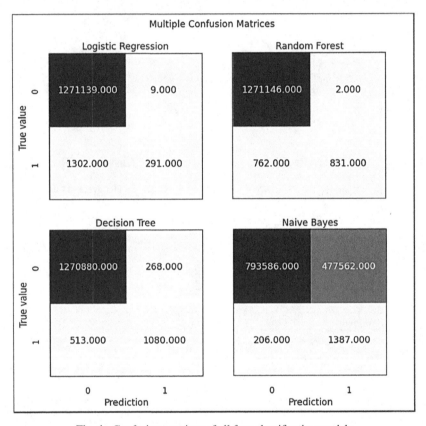

Fig. 4. Confusion matrices of all four classification models.

To come up with the best Classifier model from Decision Tree and Random Forest 2 additional metrics were applied viz. Matthew Correlation Coefficient (MCC) and Balanced Accuracy Rate(BAR), as seen in Fig. 4 and 5. As referred in [9] MCC is a much better measure than accuracy and F1 score as the other two can be misleading because they do not consider all four values of the confusion matrix. To tackle the problem of imbalance datasets [11] suggests the Balanced Accuracy Rate. Our Fraud detection dataset contains mostly legal transactions with few instances of fraud transactions, i.e. the ratio of fraudulent to legal transactions would be small, Balanced Accuracy is a good performance metric for imbalanced data like this. The results obtained from both these metrics show that Decision Tree performs better than Random Forest.

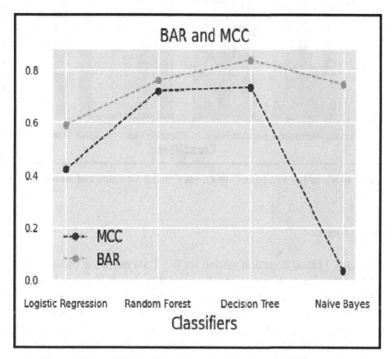

Fig. 5. BAR and MCC metrics for model evaluation.

The results of our investigation demonstrate that, within the context of our dataset and experimental conditions, the Decision Tree algorithm exhibited superior performance compared to the Random Forest algorithm (Fig. 6).

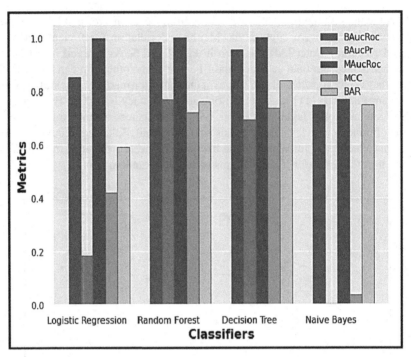

Fig. 6. BAUC ROC, BAUC PR, MAUC ROC, MCC and BAR metrics of all four classification models.

5 Conclusion

We implemented a Fraud detection system for Big Data using the PySpark Framework and built 4 Machine learning models viz. Logistic Regression, Random Forest, Decision Tree and Naïve Bayes. The results obtained from the implemented models were passed through a series of evaluation metrics. Initial evaluation using the Multi Class Evaluation metric gave equally good results for Random Forest, Decision Tree and Logistic Regression, however after plotting the Binary Classification Area under curve for ROC and PR curves we saw that Random Forest was performing better than Decision Tree, which was significantly performing better than Logistic Regression. Plotting the confusion matrices proved to be a turning point in our evaluation as the False Negative values for Decision Tree were lower than that of Random Forest. This questioned the establishment of Random Forest as the best ML Model. To dissolve this discrepancy and to select the best Classifier model from Decision Tree and Random Forest 2 additional metrics were applied viz. Matthew Correlation Coefficient (MCC) and Balanced Accuracy Rate (BAR). Notably, in both these performance evaluation metrics, the Decision Tree classifier consistently beat the other models. One of the key factors is that Decision trees have a simple setup compared to the Random forest. Decision Trees consider a few features whereas Random Forest is formed by combining multiple Decision Trees, this makes the Decision Trees work faster on Large datasets. Hence, it is established that the Decision Tree Model is the most reliable as it gives us the best results.

By accurately detecting the anomalies present in the transactional data, this Big Data Fraud Detection System will thus prevent organizations and individuals from experiencing substantial financial losses incurred due to fraudulent activities.

References

1. Paschen, U., Pitt, C., Kietzmann, J.: Artificial intelligence: building blocks and an innovation typology. Bus. Horizons 63(2), 147–155 (2020)
2. Yu, P., Xia, Z., Fei, J., Jha, S.K.: An application re-view of artificial intelligence in prevention and cure of COVID-19 pandemic. Comput. Mater. Continua 65(1), 743–760 (2020)
3. Mojtahed, V.: Big Data for Fraud Detection. Springer, Heidelberg (2019). https://doi.org/10.1007/978-3-030-22605-3_11
4. Dai, Y., Yan, J., Tang, X., Zhao, H., Guo, M.: Online credit card fraud detection: a hybrid frame-work with big data technologies. Electronic ISSN: 2324-9013. IEEE Trust-com/BigDataSE/ISPA (2016)
5. Houston, Y., Jongrong, C., Cliff, J.H., Chih, H.Y.: E-commerce, R&D, and productivity: firm-level evidence from Taiwan. Inf. Econ. Policy 18(5), 561–569 (2013)
6. Ngai, E.W.T., Hu, Y., Wong, Y.H., Chen, Y., Sun, X.: The application of data mining techniques in financial fraud detection: a classification framework and an academic review of literature. Decis. Support Syst. 50(3), 559–569 (2011)
7. Herland, M., Khoshgoftaar, T.M., Bauder, R.A.: Big data fraud detection using multiple medicare data sources (2018)
8. Zhou, H., Sun, G., Fu, S., Wang, L., Hu, J., Gao, Y.: Internet financial fraud detection based on a distributed big data approach with Node2vec (2021). Date of current version 23 March 2021
9. Raghavan, P., El Gayar, N.: Fraud detection using machine learning and deep learning. In: 2019 International Conference on Computational Intelligence and Knowledge Economy (ICCIKE) (2019)
10. Varmedja, D., Karanovic, M., Sladojevic, S., Arsenovic, M., Anderla, A.: Credit card fraud detection - machine learning methods. In: 18th International Symposium INFOTEH-JAHORINA (2019)
11. Mittal, S., Tyagi, S..: Performance evaluation of machine learning algorithms for credit card fraud detection. In: 9th International Conference on Cloud Computing, Data Science & Engineering (2019)
12. Shirgave, S., Awati, C.J., More, R., Patil, S.S.: A review on credit card fraud detection using machine learning. Int. J. Sci. Technol. Res. 8(10), 1217–1220 (2019)
13. Ileberi, E., Sun, Y., Wang, Z.: A machine learning based credit card fraud detection using the GA algorithm for feature selection. J. Big Data 9, 1–17 (2022)
14. Banirostam, H., Banirostam, T., Pedram, M.M., Rahmani, A.M.: Providing and evaluating a comprehensive model for detecting fraudulent electronic payment card transactions with a two-level filter based on flow processing in big data. Int. J. Inf. Technol. (2023)

Bursty Event Detection Model for Twitter

Anuradha Goswami[1]([✉]) [iD], Ajey Kumar[2] [iD], and Dhanya Pramod[2] [iD]

[1] Symbiosis Institute of Business Management, Symbiosis International (Deemed University), Bengaluru, India
anuradha@sibm.edu.in
[2] Symbiosis Centre for Information Technology, Symbiosis International (Deemed University), Pune, India
{ajeykumar,dhanya}@scit.edu

Abstract. Huge amount of diversified information in the form of multimedia data gets uploaded to Online Social Network platform every second. This eventually gets a sudden burst during high impact events. Twitter platform plays a very important role during these events in the process of diffusion of this information across the entire social network of users. The real challenge is in the analysis of tweet during these bursty events when data gets generated in large volume with high arrival rate. Under this circumstances, near real-time detection of bursty event should be implemented to match up the speed of the information diffusion which demands efficient algorithms. In this paper a bursty event detection algorithm is proposed which considers a dynamic set of tweets in every time window and generates optimal k topics per window of a bursty event. This research has also studied the goodness of the topics produced across the different time windows. Our proposed model is successful in creating better semantically coherent and contextual topics for bursty event as compared to the other state of the art techniques such as Latent Dirichlet Allocation Model, Gibbs Sampling Dirichlet Mixture Model and Gamma-Poisson Mixture Topic Model.

Keywords: Event · Burst · Topic Modelling · LDA · GSDMM · GPM · Coherence Measures

1 Introduction

The inherent dynamism of Online Social Network (OSN) lies in the huge amount of varied information getting uploaded to OSN platform every second in the form of multimedia data from different events [1]. Any latest happening or prolonged event occurring around the globe has its footprint in OSN in some way or the other [2]. Any event 'E' is defined as a happening which is probable to occur in the next time span or duration [3]. On Twitter, to describe an event, the users use #tag (or hashtag) or @ symbol, which further facilitates in coupling different events with each other directly or indirectly [4]. According to [5], both unplanned events like natural disasters and planned events such as ICC World Cup Twenty20 on Twitter, which either can be trendy or non-trendy, can be bursty. The bursty behavior of an event is directly proportional to the rate of information

S. Devismes et al. (Eds.): ICDCIT 2024, LNCS 14501, pp. 338–355, 2024.
https://doi.org/10.1007/978-3-031-50583-6_23

diffusion over Twitter or any other OSN [5]. These bursty events which can be called as 'trends' have the capability to catch the attention of huge number of users almost instantly [6].

Real-time stream of data from Twitter help the researchers to analyze real-world bursty events within a specific timeline. Every tweet is accompanied by a timestamp of its creation, username, and biographical sketch making it easier for the researchers to take up the challenge of automatically detect and analyze the bursty events. The real challenge is in the analysis of tweet text during bursty events when data comes in large volume with high arrival rate [7]. Under this circumstance, close to real-time detection of bursty event should be implemented to match up the speed of the information diffusion which demands efficient algorithms. Prediction of bursty events has got important implication in the field of social, political, several planned or unplanned cases of events.

There are few algorithms proposed for detection of bursty events in literature. AmMost of the approaches use fix term of vocabulary, requires a set of query words, needs number of topics to discover, and also have a set threshold value in order to define the bursty event cluster [8]. Additionally, most of the techniques use a vector-space model to represent the tweets, given the dimension of the vector same as the word vocabulary [9]. Researches who have considered streaming of data, assumed a dynamic word vocabulary for bursty event detection which changes with time [2] Some recent literatures have used deep learning techniques, attention mechanisms and network structures too to detect bursty events [10–12]. To the best of our knowledge, none of them have studied the goodness of the topics produced across the different time windows. In this paper, a bursty event detection algorithm is proposed which considers a dynamic set of tweets in every time window and generates optimal topics per window of a bursty event.

The rest of the chapter is organized as follows: Sect. 2 elaborates the review of literature. Section 3 details the proposed burst detection framework and the corresponding algorithm. The implementation, evaluation results and analysis along with The experimental setup details, datasets description, the preparation of the datasets is illustrated in Sect. 4. Discussion on the results is performed in Sect. 5, followed by conclusion in Sect. 6.

2 Review of Literature

A very traditional work used statistical techniques and tests on data distribution to extract bursty keywords topics in an event [13]. In online mode, Twitter Monitor tool was designed by [6] which detects emerging topic trends in Twitter stream. Individual keywords buzz was used to identify trends in two steps. The occurrence of individual keywords in tweets is measured to identify the bursts. This was modified by a study by [7] through an algorithm named '*Window Variation Keyword Burst Detection*' where a scalable and fast online procedure was proposed for detecting online bursty keywords. A study by [14], proposed a different approach for detection of online bursty keywords named as EDCoW (Event Detection with Clustering of Wavelet-based signals) model. EDCoW considers individual word as signals through an application of analysis of wavelet to frequencies of words. Emerging temporal trends were interpreted in a study by [15]. Firstly, a taxonomy of trends was found in the large dataset of Twitter. Secondly, the study found out primary features through which categorization of trends can be accomplished using each trend category features.

A segment-based system for detection of bursty events was introduced by [16] called *'Twevent'*. Twevent first maps and detects event segments from bursty tweet segments, followed by clustering/grouping the segments of events into events by using their distribution of frequency and similarity in content. An interesting study by [17] researched on identification of bursty topics early in the timeline with a large-scale real-time data from Twitter. Tool named TopicSketch proposed by the study, was an integrated solution consisting of two stages. In the first stage the model maintains three measures viz. total count of the tweets, each word occurrence and the respective word pairs. These measures were used as an indicator of a sudden burst in the attention of users towards the tweet, which further facilitates in the bursty topic detection. In the second stage, a topic model based on sketch was used to depict the bursty topics and their surge based on the statistics monitored in the sketch of the data. Incremental clustering methodology was used by studies [18, 19] to detect burst events where evolution of events was also experimented and solved [20]. The new arrival of tweets results in updating of the bursty topics for incremental clustering technique. Study [21] proposed a topic model, which is incremental in nature and includes the temporal features of texts, named as 'Bursty Event dEtection (BEE)' to detect the bursty events.

EventRadar was proposed by [22] which deals with activity burst in a localized area. A geo burst algorithm was proposed which was implemented using geo-tagged tweets containing information on location, time and text of the tweets. The topic clusters/ groups which are geographically tagged are created as candidate events per query window. A statistical approach was followed by a study by [23] on the Twitter platform. The study showed that a sudden spike in the tweet frequency follows a log-normal distribution with respect to the arrival of data. The data or tweet burstiness of any event was mapped with the z-score of the rate of tweet arrival. Real-time streaming text was used by study [5] to understand the bursty attitude of events. This study explored various event features and used clustering to classify the features as per their similarity index.

A study by [24] considered cross social media influence and unsupervised clustering for burst detection model. In this work, the time series social media data were divided into time slices and for each slice the burst word features in that time window were also calculated. The burst degree of words was calculated by fusing the three burst features in the time window, post which burst word set got generated. Finally, agglomerative hierarchical clustering technique was applied to cluster the word set to convert it into event. A novel graph based technique called KEvent was proposed by [25] where tweets were divided into separate bins to extract bursty keyphrases. The word2vec model was used to create a weighted keyphrase graph from the keyphrases. Final event detection was performed using Markov clustering.

Lately, deep learning algorithms [10, 11] coupled with attention networks is used by the researchers to handle the temporal dynamics of emerging keywords to detect events from tweets.

3 Proposed Burst Detection Model

Keywords/terms/words/tokens are synonymous for our research work and are interchangeably used throughout. A stepwise burst detection framework is detailed in Fig. 1.

The proposed burst detection algorithm is an extension of the Window Variation Keyword Burst detection algorithm given by [7]. The extended features are:

a) *Threshold:* A threshold in included for: *first* in selecting the most frequent words per window in *Algorithm 3* and then in *Algorithm 4,* for selecting the bursty keywords across two consecutive windows. This approach helps in the detection of *appropriate the bursty topics.*

b) *Topic Creation:* After the list of bursty keywords is obtained in *Algorithm 4*, in the end we generate optimal k topics out of the bursty keywords per window. This approach helps in *identifying the trending topics.*

c) *Coherence Scores of Topics: Algorithm 5* generates coherence scores of optimal k topics in each time window across the bursty event. This approach helps in *identifying bursty topics of similar context per window.*

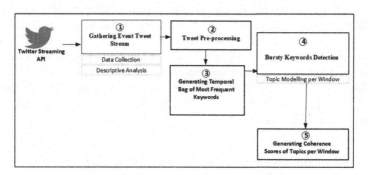

Fig. 1. Burst Detection Framework

The detailed explanation of each algorithm is given in piecewise manner according to the modules maintained in the framework, with their respective input, output, and the corresponding pseudocode. Table 1 provides a description of the important variables used in the pseudocode for a better understanding. The algorithms should be read keeping the framework, variable description and the pseudocode synced with one another.

i) *Gathering Event Tweet Stream:* The process starts with collection of tweets (*G_Stream1*) using Twitter streaming API and converting into non-duplicated tweets (*G_Stream2*) as shown in Table 2. Tweet can be regular tweet or a retweet. Each tweet is of 140 or 280 characters. The events selected for our research are *natural disaster events.*

ii) *Tweet Pre-processing:* The next module in the pipeline is data pre-processing, shown in Table 3 which involves preparation of the dataset to make it appropriate to feed for generating the most frequent bag of keywords.

iii) *Generating Temporal Bag of Most Frequent Keywords:* The aim in this module is to output the most frequent words/tokens appeared in the respective bag of tweets within a particular time window. Time window size, *window_size* is decided on under-standing the dataset from the descriptive analysis. We check on the total number of days' data available and the *burst_datasize*. Final count of number of time windows, *window_num* is dependent on the *window_size* considered and the *burst_datasize*. Collection of pre-processed tweets is divided into bag of tweets *tweet_bag* as per the *window_size*. Every window starts with an initial timestamp *init_time*. For the first window, the timestamp is zero. Following this, every time window will have a dura-tion according to the *window_size*. The finishing timestamp of a window *end_time* is calculated by adding *window_size* to *init_time* of that window. All the *init_time* values for all the windows are stored in *window_init_time* for future use. A snap-shot of the windowing system referred in our algorithm is shown in Fig. 2. Here *Tw, Tw + 1*, refers to the incoming sequential stream of tweets. For every window, the bag of tweets is created, where tweets are further tokenized to get the bag of words total_win_words. For each word in the bag, word frequency word_freq per window-wise is calculated.

The proposed algorithm has applied a threshold for considering the most frequent words per window (most_frequent_words). A threshold of 20% of the total number of tokens per window is considered for selecting the most_frequent_words for a particular window. The threshold value is based on the state-of-the-art study by [26]. In this module, we recorded the set of most_frequent_words along with their respective frequencies of occurrence per window, window-wise total number of tokens/words, total number of tweets (no_of_tweets) per window number for further use in the rest of the modules. The pseudocode of the stated process of the algorithm is given in Table 4.

iv) *Bursty Keywords Detection:* The input to this module is *G_Queue2*, consisting of most frequent keywords per time window. The purpose is to find out the how many most frequent keywords are eligible of becoming bursty keywords per time window and model these bursty keyword into window-wise topics as given in

Table 1. Variable Names and Its Description

Variable Name	Description
G_Stream1	Global Stream of Raw tweets (in JSON)
G_Stream2	Global Stream of unique Raw tweets (in CSV) with selected features
G_Queue1	Collection of Pre-processed Tweets and tokenized Tweets
G_Queue2	Collection of Most frequent keyword bags window-wise
no_of_tweets	Total number of tweets per window
burst_datasize	Total number of tweets in the whole dataset
window_size	Size of the time window (in seconds)
window_num	Signifies the number of each time window
window_init_time	Stores the earliest timestamp (init_time) for every time window
init_time	Initial timestamp of the tweets in at the starting of every time window (in seconds)
end_time	init_time + window_size (in seconds) for every time window
word_freq	Frequency of a keyword in a window
tweet_bag	Collection of tweets in a window
most_frequent_words	Collection of most frequent words from a single window
total_win_words	Total number of words in one window
window_total_words	Collection of all list of total_win_words for all windows
window1, window2	Two consecutive time windows
Hash_Dict	Dictionary data structure storing the words which are present in two consecutive time windows
sorted_word_rank	List of keywords which have increasing probability of presence across consecutive windows
Sorted_word_rank_ave_cutoff	Selected bursty keywords list having a cut-off frequency more than the average frequency of the total number of words in sorted_word_rank
all_optimal_k_topics_per_window	Collection of optimal k topics window-wise for all windows
topics_coherence_score	Coherence scores of the optimal k topics measured by using the coherence frameworks- UMass, UCI, NPMI, C_V and word2vec
CoherenceModel()	Function as given in the Genism package of python

Table 2. Algorithm for Gathering Event Tweet Stream

Algorithm 1: Gathering Event Tweet Stream
Input: Stream of raw data tweets in .json format (G_Stream1) *Output:* Raw data tweets with no duplicates in .csv format (G_Stream2)
1. *Tweet ids used to collect raw data tweets G_Stream1 in JSON object* 2. *Conversion of JSON to CSV raw data tweets G_Stream2* 3. *Duplicate tweets removal from G_Stream2* 4. *Perform Descriptive Analysis on G_Stream2*

Table 3. Algorithm for Tweet Pre-processing

Algorithm 2: Tweet Pre-processing
Input: Raw data tweets without duplicates in .csv format (G_Stream2) *Output:* Pre-processed Cleaned data tweets (G_Queue1) in .csv format
1. *Removal of rows having missing values for any attributes* 2. *Removal of punctuation marks, URL's, extra whitespaces between words, and numbers* 3. *Convert the tweets into lowercase* 4. *Removal of stopwords and extended stopwords* 5. *Tweets← Store all the cleaned tweets* 6. *tokenized_Tweets ← Tokenize each tweets in Tweets* 7. *Store Tweets and tokenized_Tweets in G_Queue1*

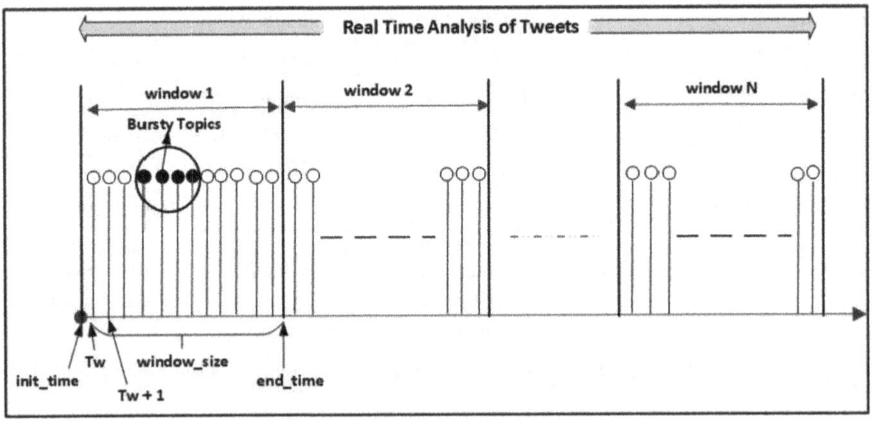

Fig. 2. Time Windowing System of the Proposed Algorithm

Table 5. A dictionary *data structure Hash_Dict* is initialized to store records of *most_frequent_words* has occurred in two consecutive windows- *windows1* and *window2*. Further, it is checked for these words whether the probability of occurrence of the words are increasing across the two consecutive windows. If it is increasing, those words are considered to be eligible for bursty keywords for

Table 4. Algorithm for Generating Temporal Bag of Most Frequent Keywords

Algorithm 3: Generating Temporal Bag of Most Frequent Keywords
Input: *Global Queue (G_Queue1) of pre-processed tweets* **Output:** *Global Queue (G_Queue2) of most frequent keyword bags*

1.	*init_time ← 0*
2.	*while tw ← get_tweet(G_Queue1) do*
3.	*if init_time == 0 then*
4.	*init_time ← timestamp(tw)*
5.	*end_time ← init_time + window_size*
6.	*tweet_bag ← null*
7.	*window_init_time ← init_time*
8.	*window_num ← 0*
9.	*total_win_words ← 0*
10.	*end if*
11.	*if timestamp(tw) < end_time then*
12.	*token_tw← get_tokenized_tweet(tw)*
13.	*tw_len ← length(token_tw)*
14.	*total_win_words ← total_win_words + tw_len*
15.	*Insert token_tw into tweet_bag*
16.	*else*
17.	*most_frequent_words ← Find unique words and Calculate its frequencies using tweet_bag.*
18.	*most_frequent_words_desc ← Sort the most_frequent_words in decreasing order of its frequencies.*
19.	*most_frequent_words_cutoff← Store the top 20 % of words in most_frequent_words_desc.*
20.	*Push [window_num, window_init_time, total_win_words,* *most_frequent_words_cutoff] list to G_Queue2*
21.	*window_num ← window_num + 1*
22.	*tweet_bag ← null*
23.	*total_win_words ← 0*
24.	*window_init_time ← end_time*
25.	*init_time ← end_time*
26.	*end_time ← init_time + window_size*
27.	*end if*
28.	*end while*

the previous window. All these eligible bursty keywords are sorted as per their decreasing probability and frequency window-wise, and stored in *sorted_word_rank* and *sorted_word_freq* respectively. In order to get meaningful topics, a threshold value of average probability/frequency is calculated. All the bursty keywords having probability greater than equal to average probability and frequency greater than equal to average frequency are stored in *sorted_ word_rank_avg_cutoff* and *sorted_word_freq_avg_cutoff* respectively. Finally, *k* topics are created from the list of bursty keywords per window in *sorted_ word_freq_avg_cutoff* where *k* is the user input greater than zero for the number of topics. In order to get meaningful topics, the value assigned to k should be optimal. Based on the coherence score the optimal number of topics can be calculated. We have used *UMass coherence score for determining the optimal value for number of topics per datasets.* All the generated optimal *k* topics per window-wise is stored in *all_optimal_k_topics_per_window* for further processing in the next module.

Table 5. Algorithm for Bursty Keywords Detection & Optimal k-Topics per Window

Algorithm 4: Bursty Keywords Detection & Optimal k-Topics per Window
Input: *Global Queue (G_Queue2) of most frequent bags of keywords*
Output: *Global Data Frame of optimal k topics per window (all_optimal_k_topics_per_window)*

1.   *all_optimal_k_topics_per_window← []*
2.   *for i in range length (G_Queue2) do*
3.   *most_frequent_words ←get_most_frequent_words(G_Queue2[i])*
4.   *for ∀word ∈ most_frequent_words do*
5.   *if word ∉ Hash_Dict* **then**
6.   *window_init_time ← get_window_init_time(G_Queue2[i])*
7.   *freq ← get_word_freq(word) from most_frequent_words*
8.   *total_win_words ← get_total_win_words(G_Queue2[i])*
9.   *window_num ← get_window_num(G_Queue2[i])*
10.   *window1← [window_init_time, freq, total_win_words]*
11.   *window2 ← []*
12.   *flag ← 0*
13.   *Push {word: [window1, window2, flag, window_num]}in Hash_Dict*
14.   **else if** *flag == 0 and (word present in the next consecutive window)* **then**
15.   *window2 ← get_window1(Hash_Dict[word])*
16.   *flag ← 1*
17.   *window_init_time ← get_window_init_time(G_Queue2[i])*
18.   *freq ← get_word_freq(word) from most_frequent_words*
19.   *total_win_words ← get_total_win_words(G_Queue2[i])*
20.   *window1← [window_init_time, freq, total_win_words]*
21.   *Hash_Dict[word] ← [window1, window2, flag, window_num]*
22.   **end if**
23.   **end if**
24.   *end for*
25.   *#Finding the Bursty keywords for each window*
26.   **if** *i >0* **then**
27.   *for ∀ word in Hash_Dict* **do**
28.   **if** *flag == 1* **then**
29.   *prob1 ← Calculate probability of word in window1*
30.   *prob2 ← Calculate probability of word in window2*
31.   **if** *prob1 – prob2 > 0* **then** *# if words probability is increasing*
32.   *word_rank[word] ← prob1*
33.   *word_freq [word] ← get_word_freq(word) from from Hash_Dict*
34.   **end if**
35.   **end if**
36.   *end for*
37.   *sorted_word_rank← Sort word_rank[∀word] in decreasing order of probability*
38.   *sorted_word_freq← Sort word_freq[∀word] in decreasing order of frequency*
39.   *#Threshold- bursty keywords having probability/frequency more than its average probability/frequency*
40.   *avg_rank ← Average of sorted_word_rank[∀word]*
41.   *avg_freq ← Average of sorted_word_freq[∀word]*
42.   *sorted_word_rank_avg_cutoff← sorted_word_rank[∀word] ≥ avg_rank*
43.   *sorted_word_freq_avg_cutoff← sorted_word_freq[∀word] ≥ avg_freq*
44.   *Create Word Cloud using sorted_word_freq_avg_cutoff*
45.   *k ← Optimal number of topics by using UMass Coherence score*
46.   *optimal_k_topics ← Create k topics using sorted_word_freq_avg_cutoff #Apply K-Means*
47.   *Insert [i, optimal_k_topics] into all_optimal_k_topics_per_window*
48.   **end if** *# line 26*
49. *end for # line 2*

v) *Generating Topic's Coherence Scores per Window:* Optimal Topics generated per window is fed as an input to this module as shown in Table 6. Coherence scores of the topics is measured by using the coherence frameworks- *UMass, UCI, NPMI, C_V* and *word2vec.*

Table 6. Algorithm for Generating Topic's Coherence Scores per Window

Algorithm 5: Generating Topic's Coherence Scores per Window
Input: *Global Data Frame of optimal k topics per window (all_optimal_k_topics_per_window)*
Output: *Topic's Coherent Scores per Window*
 # Build a tweet_dictionary from the tokenized tweets in G_Queue2 using Dictionary()   *# Build a tweet_corpus in a doc2bow() format of the tweet_dictionary*   *# Every coherence measure will take dictionary and corpus as input*   *#Fine coherence measures used: UCI Coherence, UMass Coherence, NPMI Coherence, C$_v$ Coherence and word2vec Coherence*   1.   *coherence_measures ← {C_{UCI}, C_{UMASS}, C_{NPMI}, C_v, C_{w2v}}*   2.   *tweet_dictionary ← Dictionary(get_tokenized_tweet(G_Queue2))*   3.   *tweet_corpus ← [tweet_dictionary.doc2bow(∀get_tweet(G_Queue2))]*   4.   *for i in range length(all_k_topics_per_window) do*   5.   *tweets_coherence ← []*   6.   *topics_in_window ← all_k_topics_per_window [i]*   7.   *topics ← []*   8.   *for t in range(k) do*   9.   *topics ← topics_in_window[t]*   10.   *end for*   11.   *topics_coherence_score ← CoherenceModel (topics, tweets_corpus, tweets_dictionary, C_{UCI})*   12.   *end for*   13.   *Repeat **line 4** to **line 12** for each coherence_measures*

Important Aspects of the Framework:
The framework designed is suitable under different real world high impact events like natural disasters, public opinion events or any emerging trends.

- A dynamic threshold determination is utilized which incorporates variability in the model, making it more suitable for the real-world scenario.
- Tweet and word vocabulary per window is not static but dynamically obtained according to the size of the window.
- Optimal *k* number of topics can be obtained per window using coherence score as per user choice of coherence measures.
- New module, for generation of Coherence Score of Topics, which helps to identify bursty topics of similar context and believed to be highly significant during impactful events.
- The designed approach is implemented on Twitter microblogs. But can be applied universally on any short text messages.

4 Implementation, Results and Analysis

Experimental Set-Up: Anaconda Jupyter Notebook and Google's Colab Pro environment was used as a platform for the study. The PC Configuration used was 4-core Intel Core i7 processor and 16 GB memory. Python version 3.8 was used as a programming language to implement the models. A Python library Twarc which is also a command line tool was used for archiving Twitter JSON data. The same was also used for rehydrating the dehydrated data sets which consist of only the list of tweet ids.

Dataset Description: We have used three natural disaster dataset collected from Kaggle Repository. All these repositories were released through a study by [27] where the data was collected by the author through specific keyword query search. The following datasets were selected with respect to volume of tweets, user engagement, retweet count showing the virility of the event. A brief snapshot on the datasets is elaborated in the Table 7.

The proposed algorithm is run across the three datasets and results are obtained. A baseline comparison is done with the Latent Dirichlet Allocation (LDA) Model [28], Gibbs Sampling Dirichlet Mixture Model (GSDMM) [29] and Gamma-Poisson Mixture Topic Model (GPM) [30] to show the perspectives in which the proposed model outperforms the baseline models. The latter two algorithms are proven to be good for short texts topic modelling.

Table 7. Dataset Features

Dataset (Duration)	Data Source	Number of Tweets	Number of Tweets Post Duplicate Removal	Keywords Used for Collection
Hurricane_Harvey (August 18 – 26, 2017)	Twitter	627557	**424782**	'Harvey', 'hurricaneharvey'
Typhoon_Hagupit (December 5 – 11, 2014)	Twitter	104172	**33710**	'typhoon', 'hagupit'
Hurricane_Sandy (October 25 – 28, 2012)	Twitter	568186	**139476**	'hurricane', 'sandy'

4.1 Proposed Algorithm Implementation

The implementation of the proposed algorithm is carried out for all the mentioned datasets post some analysis of the datasets required for the implementation. Table 8 summarizes the corresponding variable values found from all the three datasets post analysis of the datasets.

- *Window Size:* For Hurricane Harvey, variations in topics was much better for window size at 24 h or 86400 s as compared to window size at 6 h or 12 h. The burst in data happened only after the 5th day of the incident. So, it was pointless to go by lesser than 24 h for these 5 days as the incoming stream of tweets is very less. So, window size is taken as 24 h or 86400 s. In case of Typhoon Hagupit, the window size is considered as 12 h or 43200 secs. The variability in topics is better here for this window size as compared to lesser or more than 12 h. Also, this dataset shows a good burst in incoming tweets from the very beginning, so expected dynamic topics to be present at every 12 h of time window. Hurricane Sandy is a 3-day dataset with a burst of tweets within a very short period of time. Owing to the lesser number of days and huge tweets streaming in, the window-size is kept 12 h.

Table 8. Important Findings from the Dataset

Parameters	Hurricane Harvey Values	Typhoon Hagupit Values	Hurricane Sandy Values
Total Number of Tweets	424782	33710	139476
Unique Words	68948	19354	204746
Window Size (in seconds)	86400	43200	43200
Number of Windows	6	11	4
Number of Optimal Topics found per Window	3	5	3

- *Number of Windows:* The detection of bursty keywords was considered comparing two consecutive windows. So, to determine a set of bursty keywords for a current window, the current and the next immediate window is considered. So, the total number of windows for which bursty keywords is detected is calculated as 6, 11 and 4 respectively for Harvey, Typhoon and Sandy datasets, which is one less than the actual number of windows in the main data frame as in Table 8.
- *Optimal Number of Topics:* While deciding on the number of topics for the events of the three datasets, overall coherence scores were calculated using *UMass Coherence measure* and plotted with varying number of topics per window. The aim is to choose the number of topics for which the coherence score is optimized. For most of the windows, the coherence measure is stable at number of topics as 3, 5 and 3 for Harvey,

Typhoon and Sandy datasets as in Table 8. Ideally, Hurricane Sandy could have been the best dataset with respect to the burstiness of data. But, actual implementation of the proposed algorithm on this dataset showed worst performance with respect to the topics generated with no variation at all. At the same time, as the topics are same across all the windows, there is no change in the coherence score with the change in topics. This clearly shows a disparity in the distribution of frequencies across the unique words across all the time windows.

4.2 Evaluation Results and Analysis

The list of coherence or confirmation measures [31] considered in this research to evaluate the bursty topics generated through the proposed and the baseline models are: UCI Coherence (C_{UCI}), UMass Coherence (C_{UMASS}), NPMI Coherence(C_{NPMI}), CV Coherence(C_V) and Word2vec (C_{W2V}). Following the coherence framework, the aggregated score of the measures is obtained by calculating the arithmetic mean of all the coherence or confirmation scores. The performance of the proposed model is compared with three baseline models in this research based on these scores. During the process of evaluation, we experimented different settings of parameter to achieve the best result possible. The sliding window sizes were tweaked in the range of (10, 150), and the context window was varied between (10, 100) for both the proposed algorithm and the LDA model. For GSDMM and GPM, the tweaking was done with the number of iterations (iters), top words of the cluster (nTopWords) considered and the size of the document (N). The number of topics (K) in all the models for every dataset were determined with respect to the average coherence score.

For influence of hyper parameters, the dirichlet priors and the gamma priors' values were tweaked for both GSDMM and GPM. For GSDMM, the dirichlet priors a and b are tried for a = 0.01,0.25,0.5,0.75,0.05 and b = 0.1,0.5,1.0,2.5 respectively. Finally, with respect to quality of the topics getting created for each of these, we settle on a = 0.25 and b = 0.15. Similar things were repeated for GPM model for the gamma and the dirichlet priors. The evaluation results of coherence scores obtained by implementing all the models, including the proposed algorithm are depicted in the following tables for respective datasets. The highlighted rows in bold are measures where our model has outperformed as compared to the baselines.

Table 9. Proposed Bursty Model Evaluation in Hurricane Harvey

Topic Model	Coherence Measures	Window Number					
		1	2	3	4	5	6
Proposed Burst Detection Model	C_{UMASS}	-0.0789	−0.071	−0.062	−0.014	−0.873	−0.596

(*continued*)

Table 9. (continued)

Topic Model	Coherence Measures	Window Number 1	2	3	4	5	6
	C_{UCI}	−0.770	−0.801	−0.098	−0.715	−0.323	−0.157
	C_{NPMI}	−0.051	0.011	0.019	−0.024	−0.032	−0.012
	Cv	**0.381**	**0.476**	**0.427**	**0.336**	**0.323**	**0.362**
	C_{W2V}	**0.996**	**0.995**	**0.995**	**0.996**	**0.998**	**0.998**
	Aggregate Score (AM)	−0.104	0.122	0.256	0.115	0.175	0.226
LDA	C_{UMASS}	−0.136	−0.181	−0.137	−0.147	−0.169	−0.153
	C_{UCI}	0.037	0.043	0.029	0.025	0.042	0.027
	C_{NPMI}	0.014	0.015	0.017	0.016	0.015	0.015
	Cv	0.261	0.290	0.279	0.285	0.281	0.256
	C_{W2V}	0.989	0.988	0.989	0.990	0.989	0.989
	Aggregate Score (AM)	0.233	0.231	0.235	0.234	0.231	0.227
GSDMM	**Average Coherence Score**	−20.133	−24.623	−25.688	−27.456	−30.814	−32.161
GPM	**Average Coherence Score**	−27.023	−23.595	−23.229	−27.024	−27.464	−31.488

- Coherence evaluation measures for Hurricane Harvey and the baseline comparison is shown in Table 9. The proposed model has generated competitive scores in case of C_V and Word2vec.
- Coherence evaluation measures for Typhoon Hagupit and the baseline comparison using the coherence measures in shown in Table 10. For this dataset, the C_V score measure is better for the proposed model as compared to the other three models.
- Coherence evaluation measures for Hurricane Sandy and the baseline comparison is shown in Table 11. The proposed model has resulted in better results for all the coherence measure as compared to LDA, GSDMM AND GPM for this dataset.

Table 10. Proposed Bursty Model Evaluation in Typhoon Hagupit

Topic Model	Coherence Measure	Window Number										
		1	2	3	4	5	6	7	8	9	10	11
Proposed Burst Detection Model	C_{UMASS}	-0.042	-0.034	-0.036	-0.056	-0.041	-0.065	-0.038	-0.037	-0.027	-0.063	-0.051
	C_{UCI}	-0.123	-0.149	-0.151	-0.166	-0.159	-0.156	-0.162	-0.155	-0.196	-0.282	-0.171
	C_{NPMI}	-0.014	-0.019	-0.019	-0.020	-0.019	-0.019	-0.020	-0.020	-0.027	-0.027	-0.023
	C_V	0.356	0.345	0.345	0.342	0.352	0.351	0.344	0.344	0.336	0.336	0.342
	C_{W2V}	0.805	0.812	0.812	0.814	0.803	0.807	0.812	0.812	0.819	0.811	0.814
	Aggregate Score (AM)	0.196	0.190	0.190	0.182	0.187	0.183	0.187	0.188	0.180	0.154	0.181
LDA	C_{UMASS}	-0.015	-0.019	-0.014	-0.018	-0.026	-0.018	-0.018	-0.018	-0.025	-0.013	-0.022
	C_{UCI}	0.030	0.041	0.025	0.037	0.029	0.043	0.038	0.017	0.062	0.038	0.029
	C_{NPMI}	0.009	0.006	0.013	0.021	0.012	0.015	0.010	0.013	0.017	0.007	0.009
	C_V	0.255	0.261	0.269	0.271	0.280	0.282	0.255	0.289	0.263	0.267	0.278
	C_{W2V}	0.833	0.836	0.837	0.835	0.834	0.837	0.836	0.833	0.832	0.831	0.830
	Aggregate Score (AM)	0.222	0.225	0.226	0.229	0.225	0.232	0.224	0.227	0.230	0.226	0.224
GSDMM	Average Coherence Score	-22.081	-23.860	-24.548	-28.025	-25.105	-25.651	-26.625	-27.496	-23.863	-22.822	-23.596
GPM	Average Coherence Score	-27.110	-26.913	-24.337	-29.851	-26.730	-27.276	-23.569	-25.159	-25.707	-21.602	-23.683

Table 11. Proposed Bursty Model Evaluation in Hurricane Sandy

Topic Model	Coherence Measure	Window Number			
		1	2	3	4
Proposed Burst Detection Model	C_{UMASS}	.0001	−0.028	−0.029	−0.028
	C_{UCI}	0.024	0.003	0.003	0.003
	C_{NPMI}	0.014	0.012	0.012	0.012
	CV	0.356	0.361	0.361	0.361
	C_{W2V}	0.998	0.998	0.998	0.998
	Aggregate Score (AM)	0.278	0.269	0.269	0.269
LDA	C_{UMASS}	0.0001	0.0001	0.0001	0.0001
	C_{UCI}	0.004	0.006	0.006	0.007
	C_{NPMI}	0.003	0.005	0.004	0.005
	CV	0.236	0.237	0.233	0.239
	C_{W2V}	0.979	0.980	0.984	0.984
	Aggregate Score (AM)	0.244	0.246	0.245	0.247

(continued)

Table 11. (*continued*)

		Window Number			
Topic Model	Coherence Measure	1	2	3	4
GSDMM	**Average Coherence Score**	−37.781	−40.937	−44.726	−41.445
GPM	**Average Coherence Score**	−38.436	−38.776	−45.458	−42.886

5 Discussions

The coherence score measures the quality of the topics getting generated per window. According to [31], higher or closer the coherence score towards '1', more coherent the topics are. Also, the range of UMass coherence is −14 to + 14, UCI and NPMI Coherence is between −1 to + 1, for CV and Cw2v both are between 0 and 1. C_V is proven to be the best measure in baseline paper [31]. This is a combination measure, found by combining indirect cosine confirmation measure with NPMI and the concept of Boolean sliding window. C_V and C_{w2v} which are semantic and contextual measures of the topics, have given the best scores across all the datasets. For all the datasets, in general the NPMI coherence measure has given better coherence values than non-normalized UCI coherence version of it. Overall, C_{w2v} measure has performed well as compared to the other measures. The fact can be for the length of the input text. In the baseline paper [31], the goodness of the coherence measures was proved with long texts or articles. So, the scores the proposed algorithm achieved is proved to be competitive. In this case, we are trying the apply coherence measures for short texts. This shows the direction towards an improvement to the algorithm required which will take the length of the document also into consideration, and is an immediate future work. Apart from that in all the datasets, better performance of our model as compared to the other with respect to C_V and C_{w2v} is a contribution of this study. As both these measures signifies the semantic and contextual features of topics, our model is successful in creating better semantically coherent and contextual topics as compared to the other state of the art techniques available in the field of topic modelling.

Practical Implications of this Research: The proposed model can be used for modelling topics for any event based on Twitter. Additionally, the researchers can also measure the goodness of the topics through coherence measures, inferencing on the coherent topics at different time window across the events. This information can be further leveraged to understand the trends per time window. In case of disaster events or any high impact events, knowledge on coherent topics per window can facilitate in making several decisions in support for the disaster at that point of time.

6 Conclusion

This paper detailed the complete work regarding the proposed burst model of a high impact event. The proposed algorithm detects bursty optimal topics during high impact events comparing the bursty words across consecutive time windows. The algorithm further measures the coherence scores of the bursty optimal topics window-wise using a coherence framework. The coherence scores of the topics generated from the proposed algorithm is compared with the state-of-the-art baseline topic modelling techniques. Through proper experimentation and analysis, our proposed model is successful in creating better topics than the baseline models with respect to the contextual coherence features.

References

1. Comito, C., Forestiero, A., Pizzuti, C.: Bursty event detection in Twitter streams. ACM Trans. Knowl. Disc. Data (TKDD) **13**(4), 1–28 (2019)
2. Imran, M., Castillo, C., Diaz, F., Vieweg, S.: Processing social media messages in mass emergency: a survey. ACM Comput. Surv. (CSUR) **47**(4), 1–38 (2015)
3. Fedoryszak, M., Frederick, B., Rajaram, V., Zhong, C.: Real-time event detection on social data streams. In: Proceedings of the 25th ACM SIGKDD International Conference on Knowledge Discovery & Data Mining, pp. 2774—2782 (2019)
4. Lee, P., Lakshmanan, L.V., Milios, E.E.: Incremental cluster evolution tracking from highly dynamic network data. In: 2014 IEEE 30th International Conference on Data Engineering, pp. 3–14. IEEE (2014)
5. Singh, T., Kumari, M.: Burst: real-time events burst detection in social text stream. J. Supercomput. **77**, 1–29 (2021)
6. Mathioudakis, M., Koudas, N.: Twittermonitor: trend detection over the twitter stream. In: Proceedings of the 2010 ACM SIGMOD International Conference on Management of Data, pp. 1155–1158 (2010)
7. Guzman, J., Poblete, B.: On-line relevant anomaly detection in the Twitter stream: an efficient bursty keyword detection model. In: Proceedings of the ACM SIGKDD Workshop on Outlier Detection and Description, pp. 31–39 (2013)
8. Sakaki, T., Okazaki, M., Matsuo, Y.: Earthquake shakes Twitter users: real-time event detection by social sensors. In: Proceedings of the 19th International Conference on World Wide Web, pp. 851–860 (2010)
9. Zhao, W.X., Chen, R., Fan, K., Yan, H., Li, X.: A novel burst-based text representation model for scalable event detection. In: Proceedings of the 50th Annual Meeting of the Association for Computational Linguistics (Volume 2: Short Papers), pp. 43–47 (2012)
10. Rezaei, Z., Eslami, B., Amini, M.A., Eslami, M.: Event detection in Twitter by deep learning classification and multi label clustering virtual backbone formation. Evol. Intell. **16**(3), 833–847 (2023)
11. Singh, J., Pandey, D., Singh, A.K.: Event detection from real-time twitter streaming data using community detection algorithm. Multimed. Tools Appl., 1–28 (2023)
12. Yang, J., Wu, Y.: An approach of bursty event detection in social networks based on topological features. Appl. Intell., 1–19 (2022)
13. Kleinberg, J.: Bursty and hierarchical structure in streams. Data Min. Knowl. Disc. **7**(4), 373–397 (2003)
14. Weng, J., Lee, B.S.: Event detection in Twitter. In: Proceedings of the International AAAI Conference on Web and Social Media, vol. 5, no. 1 (2011)

15. Naaman, M., Becker, H., Gravano, L.: Hip and trendy: characterizing emerging trends on Twitter. J. Am. Soc. Inform. Sci. Technol. **62**(5), 902–918 (2011)
16. Li, C., Sun, A., Datta, A.: Twevent: segment-based event detection from tweets. In: Proceedings of the 21st ACM International Conference on Information and Knowledge Management, pp. 155–164 (2012)
17. Xie, W., Zhu, F., Jiang, J., Lim, E.P., Wang, K.: Topicsketch: real-time bursty topic detection from Twitter. IEEE Trans. Knowl. Data Eng. **28**(8), 2216–2229 (2016)
18. Becker, H., Naaman, M., Gravano, L.: Beyond trending topics: real-world event identification on Twitter. In: Proceedings of the International AAAI Conference on Web and Social Media, vol. 5, no. 1 (2011)
19. Osborne, M., et al.: Real-time detection, tracking, and monitoring of automatically discovered events in social media. In: Proceedings of 52nd Annual Meeting of the Association for Computational Linguistics: System Demonstrations, pp. 37–42 (2014)
20. Hasan, M., Orgun, M.A., Schwitter, R.: TwitterNews: real time event detection from the Twitter data stream. PeerJ PrePrints **4**, e2297v1 (2016)
21. Li, J., Tai, Z., Zhang, R., Yu, W., Liu, L.: Online bursty event detection from microblog. In: 2014 IEEE/ACM 7th International Conference on Utility and Cloud Computing, pp. 865–870. IEEE (2014)
22. Zhang, C., et al.: Geoburst: real-time local event detection in geo-tagged tweet streams. In: Proceedings of the 39th International ACM SIGIR Conference on Research and Development in Information Retrieval, pp. 513–522 (2016)
23. Bhuvaneswari, A., Valliyammai, C.: Identifying event bursts using log-normal distribution of tweet arrival rate in twitter stream. In: 2018 Tenth International Conference on Advanced Computing (ICoAC), pp. 339–343. IEEE (2018)
24. Ban, A., Zhang, Z., Gao, D., Zhou, Y., Gupta, B.B.: A novel burst event detection model based on cross social media influence (2022)
25. Sharma, S., Abulaish, M., Ahmad, T.: KEvent–A semantic-enriched graph-based approach capitalizing bursty keyphrases for event detection in OSN. In: 2022 IEEE/WIC/ACM International Joint Conference on Web Intelligence and Intelligent Agent Technology (WI-IAT), pp. 588–595. IEEE (2022)
26. Mimno, D., Wallach, H., Talley, E., Leenders, M., McCallum, A.: Optimizing semantic coherence in topic models. In: Proceedings of the 2011 Conference on Empirical Methods in Natural Language (2011)
27. Zubiaga, A.: A longitudinal assessment of the persistence of Twitter datasets. J. Am. Soc. Inf. Sci. **69**(8), 974–984 (2018)
28. Blei, D.M., Ng, A.Y., Jordan, M.I.: Latent dirichlet allocation. J. Mach. Learn. Res. **3**, 993–1022 (2003)
29. Yin, J., Wang, J.: A dirichlet multinomial mixture model-based approach for short text clustering. In: Proceedings of the 20th ACM SIGKDD International Conference on Knowledge Discovery and Data Mining, pp. 233–242 (2014)
30. Mazarura, J., De Waal, A., de Villiers, P.: A gamma-poisson mixture topic model for short text. Math. Prob. Eng. 2020 (2020)
31. Röder, M., Both, A., Hinneburg, A.: Exploring the space of topic coherence measures. In: Proceedings of the Eighth ACM International Conference on Web Search and Data Mining, pp. 399–408 (2015)

A General Variable Neighborhood Search Approach for the Clustered Traveling Salesman Problem with d-Relaxed Priority Rule

Kasi Viswanath Dasari[1], Alok Singh[1]([⊠]), and Rammohan Mallipeddi[2]

[1] School of Computer and Information Sciences, University of Hyderabad,
Hyderabad 500 046, Telangana, India
dasarivisu@gmail.com, alokcs@uohyd.ernet.in
[2] Department of Artificial Intelligence, School of Electronics Engineering Kyungpook
National University, Daegu 41566, Republic of Korea
mallipeddi.ram@gmail.com

Abstract. This paper presents a multi-start general variable neighborhood search approach (MS_GVNS) for solving the clustered traveling salesman problem with the d-relaxed priority rule (CTSP-d). In clustered traveling salesman problem, vertices excluding the starting vertex or depot, are divided into clusters based on their urgency levels and higher-urgency vertices must be visited before lower-urgency ones. This leads to inefficient travel costs. To address this, a d-relaxed priority rule is employed in CTSP-d to balance travel cost and urgency level by relaxing the urgency-oriented restriction to some extent. CTSP-d is $\mathcal{NP}$-hard as it can be considered as a generalization of traveling salesman problem (TSP). The proposed MS_GVNS approach combines a variable neighborhood descent (VND) strategy utilizing five different neighborhoods with a shaking procedure to enhance the solution. The performance of the MS_GVNS is evaluated on 148 standard benchmark instances from literature. The computational results demonstrate the effectiveness of the proposed approach in generating high-quality solutions within reasonable computational times compared to the existing best approaches. Furthermore, the approach improves upon the best-known solution values on six large instances.

Keywords: Intelligent optimization · Variable neighborhood search · Traveling salesman problem · Clustered traveling salesman problem · d-relaxed priority rule

1 Introduction

Traveling Salesman Problem (TSP) and its variants have widespread applications in diverse domains including transportation & logistics and manufacturing. The main goal of the TSP is to determine the most efficient route for a vehicle to visit a given set of locations and then return back to its starting location. In the traditional TSP, all the locations are assumed to have equal importance and can be visited in any order. However, in many real-life routing scenarios, it is necessary to consider varying priorities or urgencies associated with different locations while making the route plan [8,21].

For instance, in the aftermath of natural disasters like tsunamis, earthquakes, storms, or hurricanes, various locations require immediate relief supplies such as medical assistance, bottled water, food, and blankets. The urgency of these supplies varies depending on factors such as the extent of damage, or the location's importance (e.g., schools, and hospitals). To efficiently address these demands, locations with similar urgency levels can be grouped into clusters and each cluster can be assigned a priority reflecting the importance or urgency of the demand at its constituent locations. Then during the relief process, clusters can be visited in the order strictly dictated by their priorities, starting from highest priority cluster and ending at lowest priority cluster, i.e., a location belonging to a lower priority cluster can be visited only when all the locations belonging to higher priority clusters are already visited and hence, only ordering decisions remain to be taken are ordering among the locations belonging to each cluster. This particular TSP variant is referred to as the Clustered Traveling Salesman Problem with a pre-specified order on the clusters (CTSP-PO). Throughout this paper, we will follow the standard convention that priorities are represented by positive numbers and a lower number represents a higher priority.

In CTSP-PO, the strict priority based constraint on the order of location visits can result in a highly inefficient tour in terms of travel cost. Additionally, in certain situations, it may be possible to visit some lower-priority vertices while serving higher-priority vertices. To address this, Panchamgam [13] and Panchamgam et al. [14] proposed a rule called the d-relaxed priority rule which can be stated as follows: Given a positive number d between 0 to $p_c - 1$ (where p_c is the number of priority classes). During the tour, the highest priority class among the vertices that haven't been visited is identified and denoted as h at any given point. The d-relaxed rule allows the vehicle to visit vertices belonging to priority classes ranging from h to $h + d$ before visiting all the vertices belonging to priority class h. This rule provides a trade-off between travel cost and location priority while finding a tour. The value $d = 0$ requires visiting all the vertices with higher priority before visiting those with lower priority and hence, yields CTSP-PO. However, when $d = p_c - 1$, priorities loose meaning and problem transforms into the standard TSP. Clustered Traveling Salesman Problem with d-relaxed priority rule (CTSP-d) is nothing but CTSP-PO where a route needs to satisfy the d-relaxed priority rule instead of the strict priority based constraint of CTSP-PO.

CTSP-d can be defined formally in the following manner: We are given an undirected graph $G = (V, E)$, where V represents a set of n vertices. Each edge $e \in E$ connects two vertices i and j from the set V and has a non-negative traveling cost c_{ij}. Among the vertices, vertex 1 serves as the depot, while the remaining $n - 1$ vertices represent clients' locations. The vertices $V \setminus \{1\}$ are divided into p_c disjoint groups, denoted as $V_1, V_2, \ldots, V_{p_c}$, where each group V_i is associated with priority i. A non-negative integer d $(0 \leq d \leq p_c - 1)$ is also given. The CTSP-d seeks a Hamiltonian cycle on G starting at depot (vertex 1) that satisfy the d-relaxed priority rule and has minimum total cost among all such Hamiltonian cycles. CTSP-d is $\mathcal{NP}$-hard because it contains TSP as a special case which is a well-known $\mathcal{NP}$-hard problem [4].

The CTSP-d problem finds practical use in various domains as highlighted in previous studies such as Panchamgam [13] and Panchamgam et al. [14]. Some of the potential applications mentioned in Panchamgam et al. [14] include humanitarian relief routing, routing of service technicians, and the unmanned aerial vehicle (UAV) routing problem where target priorities are crucial. Furthermore, the problem is relevant in product distribution scenarios where their storage levels determine the priority of delivery locations. Locations that are out-of-stock are considered more important than others and are grouped into the highest priority cluster, as described in the work of Yang and Feng [20].

In this paper, we present a Multi-start General Variable Neighborhood Search (MS_GVNS) approach for solving the CTSP-d problem. It combines the Variable Neighborhood Descent (VND) algorithm with a shake procedure. VND is a local search method that explores different neighborhoods in a systematic manner to improve the current solution. In this case, the VND algorithm uses five different neighborhoods during the search process. The shake procedure introduces random perturbations to the current solution thereby allowing for exploration of new areas in the search space. The multi-start mechanism further enables the exploration of different regions in the search space and helps in escaping from those local optimas which can not be escaped through perturbations. The combination of the VND algorithm, the shake procedure, and restarts in the MS_GVNS method is capable of finding high-quality solutions and our computational results prove this point. Our approach performs better in comparison to best approaches available in the literature.

The remaining part of this paper is organized as follows: Sect. 2 provides the literature review. Section 3 presents our proposed MS_GVNS approach. Experimental results and their analysis are presented in Sect. 4. Finally, Sect. 5 concludes the paper by discussing its contributions and a few directions for future research.

2   Literature Review

As previously mentioned, CTSP-d is closely related to CTSP-PO. Potvin [17] introduced CTSP-PO and solved it using a genetic algorithm (GA). Ahmed [1] developed a hybrid GA that utilized sequential constructive crossover, 2-opt search, and a local search to obtain heuristic solutions for the problem. A less restrictive variation of the CTSP-PO is known as the CTSP, where delivery locations within the same cluster must be visited consecutively, but there is no specific priority associated with a cluster. Consequently, clusters can be visited in any order. The CTSP has received extensive attention in the literature, with its first study conducted by Chisman [2]. The author proposed a branch-and-bound approach to solve the problem exactly. Furthermore, it was demonstrated that the CTSP can be transformed into a standard TSP by augmenting the cost of each inter-cluster edge with an arbitrarily large constant M. Since then, several approaches have been introduced to tackle the CTSP – GA by Potvin [16], tabu search by Laporte et al. [7], greedy randomized adaptive search procedure (GRASP) by Mestria et al. [10], and a combination of local search, GRASP, and variable neighborhood random descent proposed by Mestria [9].

Panchamgam et al. [14] introduced the CTSP-d and presented its various applications. They also established worst-case bounds for the CTSP-d in relation to the classical TSP, and demonstrated that these bounds are indeed tight. Building upon the prior doctoral work by Panchamgam [13], the problem and its extensions were formulated as mixed integer programs in [14]. Notably, using CPLEX, they solved instances with up 30 vertices to optimality.

Hà et al. [5] made enhancements to the mixed integer programming (MIP) model put forth by Panchamgam et al. [14] and introduced the first metaheuristic, called GILS-RVND, for the CTSP-d. GILS-RVND combines elements from Iterated Local Search (ILS), Greedy Randomized Adaptive Search Procedure (GRASP), and Random Variable Neighborhood Descent (RVND). The GILS-RVND algorithm commences by generating initial solutions using a greedy randomized procedure. Subsequently, the quality of each initial solution is improved through a local search procedure. This local search procedure incorporates the concept of RVND and is augmented by an ILS-inspired perturbation mechanism.

Dasari and Singh [3] presented two different methods to solve CSTP-d. The first method is a hyper-heuristic approach that involves multiple starts and employs three levels of heuristics (multi-start hyper-heuristic approach denoted as MSH2). At the highest level, the hyper-heuristic approach utilizes two other hyper-heuristic approaches as low-level heuristics. These two approaches, in turn, employ five problem-specific heuristics to generate a new solution from the current one. The second method is a multi-start iterated local search approach (MS_ILS) that involves multiple starts and employs VND as local search. The computational results demonstrate the effectiveness of these two approaches, as they could produce high-quality solutions within short computational times, outperforming the existing state-of-the-art methods in the literature.

3   A Multi-start General Variable Neighborhood Search Approach for CTSP-d

Variable Neighborhood Search (VNS) is a metaheuristic that Hansen and Mladenović [12] proposed to solve combinatorial optimization problems. The main concept of VNS is to systematically explore different neighborhood structures in order to find an optimal or near-optimal solution. The VNS algorithm alternates between a shake phase, which aims to diversify the search and escape local optima, and a local search phase, which intensifies the search by improving the solution within a particular neighborhood structure. Additionally, a neighborhood change is incorporated into the algorithm. Another variant of VNS called

General Variable Neighborhood Search (GVNS) [6] employs the Variable Neighborhood Descent (VND) method as the local search. The effectiveness of GVNS has been demonstrated through successful applications documented in recent studies [11,18,19].

Our motivation for developing the Multi-start General Variable Neighborhood Search (MS_GVNS) approach stemmed from the remarkable success of GVNS in solving combinatorial optimization problems. Algorithm 1 presents the pseudo-code for MS_GVNS, where N_{rst} represents the number of restarts, k_{max} is the number of neighborhoods used in shaking and itr_{max} is maximum number iterations. The algorithm comprises four key components. The first component involves generating the initial solution (φ) using a greedy randomized procedure (Gen_Ini_Sol()). The second component is the shaking procedure, which helps the algorithm to escape from local minima traps. By exploring various neighborhood structures, the shaking procedure generates diverse candidate solutions. The third component is the local search, which employs the Variable Neighborhood Descent (VND) method. This step intensifies the search by improving the current solution within a specific neighborhood structure. The fourth component involves the acceptance criteria, which determine whether a new solution should be accepted or rejected. The acceptance criteria plays a role in determining the exploration and exploitation balance of the algorithm. In the subsections that follow, details about each of these four components are provided.

Algorithm 1: Pseudo-code of MS_GVNS approach.

Input: A CTSP-d instance and set of MS_GVNS parameters
Output: Best solution identified
for $i \leftarrow 1$ *to* N_{rst} do
  $\varphi_i \leftarrow$ Gen_Ini_Sol();
  $itr \leftarrow 0$;
  repeat
    $k \leftarrow 1$;
    repeat
      $\varphi' \leftarrow$ Shake(φ_i, k);
      $\varphi'' \leftarrow$ VND(φ');
      if *(φ'' is better than φ_i)* then
        $\varphi_i \leftarrow \varphi''$;
        $k \leftarrow 1$;
      else
        $k \leftarrow k + 1$;
    until $k < k_{max}$;
    $itr \leftarrow itr + 1$;
  until $itr < itr_{max}$;
$best \leftarrow$ best solution among $\varphi_1, \varphi_2, \ldots, \varphi_{N_{rst}}$;
return $best$;

3.1 Generation of Initial Solution

To generate an initial solution, we follow a procedure that is a mix of greediness and randomness. Initially, we create an empty solution φ and add the depot as the first position in φ. Next, we create a candidate list ($\$\_CL$) that includes all vertices except the depot. Starting from the second location, we iterate through the remaining locations in their natural order. For each location, the candidate list is sorted in ascending order based on the distance from the last vertex added to φ. To determine which vertices should be added to the solution, we employ the d-relaxed priority rule. This rule helps us to create a restricted candidate list ($\$\_RCL$) by selecting only the top three vertices from the candidate list that meet the d-relaxed priority rule. From the $\$\_RCL$, we randomly select a vertex and add it to φ at the current location that is being considered. The candidate list ($\$\_CL$) is updated and next location is considered. This process continues until all locations have been considered. Algorithm 2 provides the pseudo-code of this procedure.

Algorithm 2: Initial solution procedure.

Input: A CTSP-d instance and Set of parameters
Output: solution φ
$\varphi[1] \leftarrow v_1$;
$\$\_CL \leftarrow V \setminus \{v_1\}$;
$s \leftarrow 1$;
while $s < n$ **do**
      $\$\_CL \leftarrow Sort(\$\_CL, \varphi[s])$;
      $\$\_RCL \leftarrow Form\_RCL(\$\_CL, 3)$;
      $\varphi[s+1] \leftarrow Random(\$\_RCL)$;
      $\$\_CL \leftarrow \$\_CL \setminus \{\varphi[s+1]\}$;
      $s \leftarrow s + 1$;
return φ;

3.2 Variable Neighborhood Descent (VND)

The crucial aspect of MS_GVNS is the utilization of appropriate local search strategies, which can significantly impact the performance. Our approach employs Variable Neighborhood Descent (VND) as the local search scheme. VND explores a neighborhood until a local optimum is reached, after which it transitions to a different neighborhood and continues the process. Since different neighborhoods may have distinct local optimas, employing multiple neighborhood structures can enhance the likelihood of obtaining superior solutions. We have employed five different neighborhoods, namely N_1, N_2, N_3, N_4, and N_5. The design of these neighborhood structures is explained in detail below, considering the problem's characteristics.

The effectiveness of VND is also influenced by the order in which the neighborhoods are examined. This is because the initial neighborhoods are often explored more extensively than the final ones. We have named our five neighborhoods according to the order in which they are explored. Algorithm 3 presents a pseudo-code of our VND approach. It begins by exploring the first neighborhood, N_1, until no further improvement is found in the current solution. It then switches to the second neighborhood, N_2, and examines it. If a better solution is discovered in this second neighborhood, VND returns to the first neighborhood. Otherwise, it proceeds to the third neighborhood, N_3, explores it, and so on. Once all neighborhoods have been examined without improvement, the approach terminates and outputs the best overall solution. *Explore_ N(φ, N_m)* is a function that explores the neighborhood $N_m, \forall m \in \{1, 2, 3, 4, 5\}$ of current solution φ in the manner described at the end of this section.

Algorithm 3: Pseudo-code for VND as local search.

Input: A solution φ
Output: An improved solution φ
$m \leftarrow 1$;
repeat
    $\varphi' \leftarrow$ *Explore_N*(φ, N_m);
    if φ' *is superior to* φ **then**
        $m \leftarrow 1$;
        $\varphi \leftarrow \varphi'$;
    else
        $m \leftarrow m + 1$;
until $m > 5$;
return φ;

Neighborhood Structures: Our five neighborhoods are as follows.

- Swap (N_1): In this neighborhood, positions of two vertices are swapped in the solution in a bid to improve the solution
- Shift (N_2): In this neighborhood, a single vertex is randomly removed from solution. Subsequently, an attempt is made to reinsert it into a different position in the solution to get an enhanced solution. Only a single vertex is considered in this neighborhood.
- 2-Opt (N_3): This is standard 2-opt neighborhood. It tries to improve the solution by removing two edges that are not adjacent in the tour and replacing them with two new edges to get back a valid tour.
- RCR (Remove Consecutive and Reinsert) (N_4): For this neighborhood, we randomly removes a fixed number of consecutive vertices from the tour. The number of vertices to be removed is governed by parameter called "rem". These

removed vertices are then sorted in descending order as per their priority. Subsequently, the heuristic systematically reinserts these vertices into the tour, one by one, following the sorted order, placing each vertex in the best possible position.

- RMR (Remove Multiple and Reinsert) (N_5): This heuristics randomly removes some vertices (not necessarily consecutive) from the tour. These removed vertices are reinserted back into the tour exactly in the same manner as in previous neighborhood. However, the number of vertices to be removed is not fixed over iterations of our approach and governed by the value of probability (p_r) of removing each vertex from the tour. p_r gradually decreases from its maximum value mmx_{p_r} to its minimum value mmn_{p_r} over iterations until reaching a certain number of iterations (mmx_itr). In an iteration $iter$, p_r is determined using following equation:

$$p_r = \begin{cases} \left(\frac{mmx_{p_r} - mmn_{p_r}}{mmx_{itr}} \right) (mmx_{itr} - iter) + mmn_{p_r} & \text{if } iter \leq mmx_{itr} \\ mmn_{p_r} & \text{otherwise} \end{cases} \quad (1)$$

Each vertex in the tour is considered for deletion with this probability. This concept is known as the variable degree of perturbation and aids in finding superior quality solutions faster [15].

Please note that these neighborhoods are implicitly defined by the operations that we do in order to get a neighboring solution. The first three neighborhoods are explored by following the first improvement strategy. On the other hand, last two neighborhoods are explored in a random manner as only a single solution is generated in each of these neighborhoods. This is due to the prohibitive computational cost of exploring these neighborhoods in a first improvement/best improvement manner.

3.3 Shaking Procedure

The shake procedure plays a crucial role in escaping from local optima by introducing perturbations that can lead to changes in the current neighborhood. This technique diversifies the search and explores new regions in the search space. To achieve this, the shaking procedure perturbs the incumbent solution, denoted as φ, to generate a random solution, φ', in one of three neighborhoods associated with φ. These neighborhoods that we have used in our shaking procedure are N_3, N_4, and N_5 as defined previously. Algorithm 4, provides a pseudo-code of this process. Within the algorithm, Gen_random_sol(φ, N_i) represents a function that generates a random solution based on the neighborhood $N_i, \forall i \in \{3, 4, 5\}$.

3.4 Acceptance Criteria

In our approach, we have used Only Improvement (OI) acceptance criterion. This criterion ensures that a newly generated solution, obtained by exploring a neighborhood, can replace the current solution only in case the newly generated solution is superior in comparison to current solution.

Algorithm 4: Pseudo-code of shake function

Input: A solution φ, neighborhood to be used N_i, k_{max}
Output: A random solution φ' in chosen neighborhood
if $k == 1$ **then**
    $\varphi' \leftarrow Gen\_random\_sol(\varphi, N_3)$;
else if $k == 2$ **then**
    $\varphi' \leftarrow Gen\_random\_sol(\varphi, N_4)$;
else
    $\varphi' \leftarrow Gen\_random\_sol(\varphi, N_5)$;
return φ';

---

4   Computational Results

The performance evaluation of the MS_GVNS approach for the CTSP-d was conducted on the 148 test instances introduced in Hà *et al.* [5]. These instances were created by modifying existing instances from TSPLIB. The modifications involved introducing priorities and d values. In these instances, the travel cost between any two vertices is assumed to be equal to the Euclidean distance separating them. The instances consist of varying numbers of vertices, with options being 42, 52, 100, and 200, and the number of vertex groups, which can be 1, 3, or 5. The value of d can be 0, 1, or 3, with the constraint that it cannot exceed $p_c - 1$, where p_c represents the number of groups. The test instances are divided into two categories: random and clustered. In the random category, vertices are assigned to groups randomly. This setting aims to simulate scenarios where the priority of a delivery vertex depends on its storage capacity as observed in the distribution of consumer goods. On the other hand, in the clustered category, vertices that are geographically close to each other belong to a single group. This configuration can replicate the impact of natural events like storms or earthquakes, which affect neighboring areas along their propagation paths.

The MS_GVNS meta-heuristic proposed in our study was implemented using the C programming language and executed on a system with Core-i5-8600 processor and 8 GB of RAM running at 3.10 GHz under Ubuntu Linux 18.04. This is the same system as used for executing MS_ILS and MSH2 in [3]. We conducted ten independent runs of our approach on each test instance. Parameters utilized in our approach, and their respective values are as follows: The approach employs 10 restarts during each execution, denoted by the parameter N_{rst}. In N_4, which represents the number of consecutive vertices to be removed from the tour, we set $rem = 8$. The maximum degree of perturbation in N_5, denoted as mmx_{p_r}, is set to 0.8, and the minimum degree of perturbation, mmn_{p_r}, is set to 0.2. The maximum number of iterations in which the degree of perturbation varies, mmx_{itr}, is set to 600. During each run, the algorithm terminates when there is no improvement in the best solution quality over 300 consecutive iterations $(itr_{max} = 300)$. All these parameter values were chosen after extensive experimentation over a limited set of instances.

Tables 1 to 3 present the results of our MS_GVNS approach on different instances of the CTSP-d, and compare these results with those obtained by state-of-the-art approaches. The first column of these tables presents the names of the instances. The second column, labelled "Best" indicates the best solution value found by the Exact_MIP approach. In Table 1, the third column, denoted as "TT" represents the running time of the Exact_MIP method. Under the columns GILS-RVND, MS_ILS, MSH2, and MS_GVNS, we have three columns labelled "Bsol", "Avsol", and "Avtt", respectively. These columns report the best objective value, average objective value, and average running times over ten runs of the corresponding approaches. In cases where the optimal solutions provided by CPLEX are available, they are marked with an asterisk (*). If none of the approaches obtains these optimal values, the best values obtained are presented in bold font for easy identification. Data for GILS-RVND and Exact_MIP are taken from [5], and, data for MS_ILS and MSH2 are taken from [3].

Table 1 displays the outcomes of different approaches on clustered and random instances, each consisting of 42 or 52 vertices. Our MS_GVNS approach yields comparable results in terms of the best value and successfully obtains all the best-known solutions attained by GILS-RVND, MS_ILS, and MSH2. Regarding the average solution quality, our MS_GVNS approach outperforms the state-of-the-art approaches. It obtains better average objective values than GILS-RVND, MS_ILS, and MSH2. In terms of execution times, our MS_GVNS approach exhibits superior performance when compared to GILS-RVND and MSH2. However, MS_ILS is faster than all other approaches.

Table 2 presents the results obtained by different approaches on clustered and random instances with 100 vertices. Our MS_GVNS approach demonstrated superior performance in terms of the best solution quality compared to state-of-the-art approaches. In the average solution quality, our MS_GVNS approach outperformed GILS-RVND and MS_ILS. When considering clustered instances, MS_GVNS and MSH2 achieved similar performance. However, on random instances, MSH2 outperformed MS_GVNS. In terms of execution times, our MS_GVNS approach exhibited better performance when compared to GILS-RVND and MSH2. Nevertheless, MS_ILS outperformed all other approaches in terms of execution times.

Table 3 shows the results of various approaches on clustered and random instances comprising 200 vertices. In two random instances (kroA200-R-5-1 and kroB200-R-5-1), MIP-Exact fails to provide any solution due to memory constraints, indicated by the (-) symbol in the table. MIP-Exact did not find any optimal solution on these instances, so it executed for maximum allowed time off 5 h on each instance. Our MS_GVNS approach exhibits superior performance in terms of the best solution quality compared to Exact-MIP, GILS-RVND, and MS_ILS. Moreover, in average solution quality, MS_GVNS outperforms GILS-RVND and MS_ILS. When considering clustered instances, MS_GVNS performs better than MSH2 in terms of both the best and average solution quality. However, in random instances, MSH2 outperforms MS_GVNS. Regarding execution times, our MS_GVNS approach performs better than GILS-RVND

Table 1. Result of different approaches on small instances with 42 and 52 vertices.

Instance	Exact-MIP		GILS-RVND			MS_ILS			MSH2			MS_GVNS		
	Best	TT	Bsol	Avsol	Avtt	Bsol	Avsol	Avtt	Bsol	Avsol	Avtt	Bsol	Avsol	Avtt
swiss42C-1-0-a	1273*	0.82	1273	1273.0	4.65	1273	1273.0	0.64	1273	1273.0	2.82	1273	1273.0	1.53
swiss42C-3-0-a	1347*	1.94	1347	**1347.0**	3.56	1347	**1347.0**	0.19	1347	**1347.0**	1.07	1347	1348.4	0.47
swiss42C-3-0-b	1505*	9.22	1505	1505.0	3.67	1505	1505.0	0.25	1505	1505.0	1.36	1505	1505.0	0.62
swiss42C-3-0-c	1467*	1.67	1467	1467.0	3.26	1467	1467.0	0.22	1467	1467.0	1.06	467	1467.0	0.52
swiss42C-3-1-a	1301*	2.79	1301	1302.9	4.31	1301	**1301.0**	0.40	1301	**1301.0**	1.99	1301	**1301.0**	0.98
swiss42C-3-1-b	1344*	3.23	1344	1344.0	4.30	1344	1344.0	0.43	1344	1344.0	2.12	1344	1344.0	1.04
swiss42C-3-1-c	1357*	2.31	1357	1357.0	4.26	1357	1357.0	0.38	1357	1357.0	1.84	1357	1357.0	1.00
swiss42C-5-0-a	1561*	170.83	1561	1561.0	3.01	1561	1561.0	0.14	1561	1561.0	0.83	1561	1561.0	0.33
swiss42C-5-0-b	1540*	2.14	1540	1540.0	2.89	1540	1540.0	0.13	1540	1540.0	0.78	1540	1540.0	0.30
swiss42C-5-0-c	1532*	13.28	1532	1532.0	3.03	1532	1532.0	0.13	1532	1532.0	0.78	1532	1532.0	0.30
swiss42C-5-1-a	1434*	14.53	1434	1434.0	4.11	1434	1434.0	0.25	1434	1434.0	1.41	1434	1434.0	0.60
swiss42C-5-1-b	1469*	32.79	1469	1469.0	4.30	1469	1469.0	0.25	1469	1469.0	1.34	1469	1469.0	0.62
swiss42C-5-1-c	1334*	2.07	1334	1334.0	4.11	1334	1334.0	0.22	1334	1334.0	1.33	1334	1334.0	0.54
swiss42C-5-3-a	1273*	0.93	1273	1273.0	5.20	1273	1273.0	0.51	1273	1273.0	2.60	1273	1273.0	1.23
swiss42C-5-3-b	1273*	1.53	1273	1273.0	4.51	1273	1273.0	0.47	1273	1273.0	2.43	1273	1273.0	1.08
swiss42C-5-3-c	1301*	5.88	1301	1302.9	5.20	1301	**1301.0**	0.54	1301	**1301.0**	2.65	1301	**1301.0**	1.28
berlin52C-1-0-a	7542*	2.45	7542	**7542.0**	7.86	7542	7558.6	1.34	7542	**7542.0**	5.14	7542	**7542.0**	3.29
berlin52C-3-0-a	8144*	1.82	8144	**8144.0**	7.59	8144	8145.4	0.75	8144	**8144.0**	3.24	8144	**8144.0**	1.95
berlin52C-3-0-b	8016*	2.95	8016	8016.0	5.96	8016	8016.0	0.41	8016	8016.0	1.88	8016	8016.0	0.99
berlin52C-3-0-c	9085	270.75	9085	9092.0	6.77	9085	**9085.0**	0.66	9085	**9085.0**	2.97	9085	**9085.0**	1.63
berlin52C-3-1-a	7952*	3.72	7952	**7952.0**	8.61	7952	7967.3	1.02	7952	**7952.0**	4.39	7952	**7952.0**	2.47
berlin52C-3-1-b	7596*	3.31	7596	7596.0	7.24	7596	7596.0	0.69	7596	7596.0	3.44	7596	7596.0	1.57
berlin52C-3-1-c	7984*	1.50	7984	7984.0	8.20	7984	7984.0	1.15	7984	7984.0	4.89	7984	7984.0	3.02
berlin52C-5-0-a	9430*	68.18	9430	9430.0	5.85	9430	9430.0	0.39	9430	9430.0	1.91	9430	9430.0	0.89
berlin52C-5-0-b	8669*	10.37	8669	8669.0	5.13	8669	8669.0	0.38	8669	8669.0	1.67	8669	8669.0	0.87
berlin52C-5-0-c	9651	3602.66	9651	9651.0	5.69	9651	9651.0	0.29	9651	9651.0	1.51	9651	9651.0	0.72
berlin52C-5-1-a	8811*	3.53	8811	8820.0	7.15	8811	**8811.0**	0.66	8811	**8811.0**	3.29	8811	**8811.0**	1.61
berlin52C-5-1-b	7948*	3.00	7948	7948.0	6.51	7948	7948.0	0.62	7948	7948.0	3.04	7948	7948.0	1.52
berlin52C-5-1-c	8509*	11.95	8509	**8509.0**	7.01	8509	8514.8	0.42	8509	8516.4	2.49	8509	8511.8	1.05
berlin52C-5-3-a	7907	3600.18	7907	7945.5	8.75	7907	7946.2	0.98	7907	**7916.4**	5.00	7907	7925.8	2.55
berlin52C-5-3-b	7614*	1.81	7614	7614.0	7.11	7614	7614.0	1.03	7614	7614.0	4.53	7614	7614.0	2.55
berlin52C-5-3-c	7631*	2.13	7631	7631.0	8.07	7631	7631.0	0.96	7631	7631.0	4.41	7631	7631.0	2.57
swiss42R-1-0-a	1273*	0.87	1273	1273.0	5.11	1273	1273.0	0.63	1273	1273.0	2.88	1273	1273.0	1.57
swiss42R-3-0-a	2256*	0.56	2256	**2256.0**	3.88	2256	2265.7	0.20	2256	**2256.0**	1.07	2256	**2256.0**	0.47
swiss42R-3-0-b	2153*	1.35	2153	**2153.0**	4.43	2153	2154.0	0.19	2153	2154.5	1.05	2153	**2153.0**	0.47
swiss42R-3-0-c	2080*	2.10	2080	**2080.0**	3.88	2080	2081.2	0.18	2080	2081.2	0.99	2080	**2080.0**	0.44
swiss42R-3-1-a	1652*	103.45	1652	1652.0	4.78	1652	1652.0	0.42	1652	1652.0	1.98	1652	1652.0	1.01
swiss42R-3-1-b	1607*	460.36	1607	1608.9	5.00	1607	1608.8	0.37	1607	**1607.0**	2.05	1607	**1607.0**	0.98
swiss42R-3-1-c	1525*	947.38	1525	1525.0	4.33	1525	1525.0	0.38	1525	1525.0	2.12	1525	1525.0	0.90
swiss42R-5-0-a	2365*	1.33	2365	2365.0	3.59	2365	2365.0	0.11	2365	2365.0	0.70	2365	2365.0	0.30
swiss42R-5-0-b	2567*	1.04	2567	2567.0	3.21	2567	2567.0	0.11	2567	2567.0	0.66	2567	2567.0	0.27
swiss42R-5-0-c	2694*	0.80	2694	2695.0	3.72	2694	2694.9	0.12	2694	**2694.0**	0.74	2694	2694.9	0.28
swiss42R-5-1-a	1812*	219.82	1812	**1812.0**	4.08	1812	1813.3	0.24	1812	1812.9	1.49	1812	1812.9	0.59
swiss42R-5-1-b	1905	3600.14	1905	1905.0	4.32	1905	1905.0	0.22	1905	1905.0	1.29	1905	1905.0	0.52
swiss42R-5-1-c	1910*	1845.06	1910	1910.0	3.83	1910	1910.0	0.21	1910	1910.0	1.22	1910	1910.0	0.52
swiss42R-5-3-a	1474	3600.17	1474	1474.0	4.95	1474	1474.0	0.48	1474	1474.0	2.39	1474	1474.0	1.17
swiss42R-5-3-b	1541	3600.07	1541	**1541.0**	5.28	1541	1544.0	0.45	1541	**1541.0**	2.58	1541	**1541.0**	1.09
swiss42R-5-3-c	1510*	1679.83	1510	**1510.0**	5.66	1510	1512.1	0.45	1510	1512.7	2.32	1510	1511.8	1.04
berlin52R-1-0-a	7542*	3.15	7542	7542.0	7.69	7542	7542.0	1.30	7542	7542.0	5.01	7542	7542.0	3.25
berlin52R-3-0-a	12765*	9.37	12765	12765.0	6.32	12765	12765.0	0.36	12765	12765.0	1.82	12765	12765.0	0.86
berlin52R-3-0-b	12668*	4.06	12668	12668.0	6.49	12668	12668.0	0.34	12668	12668.0	1.64	12668	12668.0	0.88
berlin52R-3-0-c	12483*	11.76	12483	**12483.0**	6.37	12483	12486.6	0.36	12483	**12483.0**	1.82	12483	12496.8	0.90
berlin52R-3-1-a	9473*	2486.71	9473	9473.0	8.27	9473	9473.0	0.73	9473	9473.0	3.42	9473	9473.0	1.78
berlin52R-3-1-b	9419	3601.50	9419	9419.0	7.02	9419	9419.0	0.73	9419	9419.0	3.56	9419	9419.0	1.68
berlin52R-3-1-c	9577	3601.67	9577	9577.0	8.32	9577	9577.0	0.73	9577	9577.0	3.65	9577	9577.0	2.13
berlin52R-5-0-a	16414*	2.70	16414	**16414.0**	5.73	16414	16429.6	0.20	16414	**16414.0**	1.08	16414	**16414.0**	0.49
berlin52R-5-0-b	13759*	24.55	13759	13759.0	5.79	13759	13759.0	0.21	13759	13759.0	1.17	13759	13759.0	0.51
berlin52R-5-0-c	14131*	3.65	14131	14131.0	6.48	14131	14131.0	0.21	14131	14131.0	1.15	14131	14131.0	0.54
berlin52R-5-1-a	11662	3609.71	11651	11651.0	6.93	11651	11658.0	0.44	11651	11651.0	2.32	11651	11651.0	0.94
berlin52R-5-1-b	9957	3608.94	9957	9964.0	6.16	9957	**9957.0**	0.41	9957	**9957.0**	2.19	9957	9962.2	0.98
berlin52R-5-1-c	10940	3603.29	10940	**10940.0**	6.77	10940	10950.2	0.38	10940	10953.6	2.00	10940	10950.2	0.91
berlin52R-5-3-a	9065	3601.49	**9012**	9021.0	8.51	**9012**	9033.2	0.85	**9012**	9050.3	4.56	**9012**	9017.3	2.18
berlin52R-5-3-b	8036*	3387.42	8036	**8036.0**	7.29	8036	**8036.0**	0.99	8036	8043.1	4.28	8036	**8036.0**	2.36
berlin52R-5-3-c	8224	3600.17	8224	8224.0	7.36	8224	8224.0	0.87	8224	8224.0	3.98	8224	8224.0	1.89

Table 2. Result of different approaches on medium instances with 100 vertices.

Instance	Exact-MIP	GILS-RVND			MS_ILS			MSH2			MS_GVNS		
	Best	Bsol	Avsol	Avtt	Bsol	Avsol	Avtt	Bsol	Avsol	Avtt	Bsol	Avsol	Avtt
kroA100-C-1-0	21282*	21282	21338.6	84.88	21282	21284.3	9.38	21282	**21282.0**	25.55	21282	21282.0	20.55
kroA100-C-3-0	24049	24049	**24049.0**	67.93	24049	24100.9	3.09	24049	24068.7	10.23	24049	24097.9	7.32
kroA100-C-3-1	23392	23069	23416.7	80.07	**22865**	23195.7	6.84	**22865**	**23122.9**	24.88	**22865**	23167.3	17.65
kroA100-C-5-0	24745	24745	24745.0	58.51	24745	24745.0	1.38	24745	24745.0	5.32	24745	24745.0	3.15
kroA100-C-5-1	22617	22589	22591.8	84.44	22589	22594.2	3.08	22589	**22589.0**	10.35	22589	**22589.0**	6.82
kroA100-C-5-3	21443	21443	21443.0	82.50	21443	21443.0	5.52	21443	21443.0	20.25	21443	21443.0	12.18
kroB100-C-1-0	**22141**	22179	22235.0	83.07	22179	22209.3	9.49	22179	22198.6	26.51	**22141**	**22185.4**	20.76
kroB100-C-3-0	24887*	24887	24971.3	63.46	24887	24902.8	2.60	24887	**24887.0**	8.34	24887	**24887.0**	6.00
kroB100-C-3-1	22141*	22141	22155.1	77.19	22141	**22141.0**	4.88	22141	22161.1	16.07	22141	22156.8	10.84
kroB100-C-5-0	**24793**	24794	24794.0	57.91	24794	24794.0	1.91	24794	24794.0	7.04	24794	24794.0	4.47
kroB100-C-5-1	23159*	23159	23173.1	73.43	23159	23234.1	3.58	23159	23212.5	12.03	23159	**23169.3**	7.80
kroB100-C-5-3	22179	**22141**	**22180.0**	79.72	**22141**	22209.7	7.90	22179	22193.1	24.42	22179	22220.5	16.52
kroC100-C-1-0	20749	20749	20786.9	94.88	20749	20756.0	8.30	20749	**20749.0**	27.12	20749	20759.3	20.44
kroC100-C-3-0	21340*	21340	21440.6	57.97	21340	**21340.0**	2.52	21340	**21340.0**	8.49	21340	**21340.0**	5.69
kroC100-C-3-1	20910*	20910	20910.0	92.46	20910	20910.0	6.40	20910	20910.0	20.87	20910	20910.0	15.13
kroC100-C-5-0	24040*	24040	**24040.0**	58.26	24040	**24040.0**	2.36	24040	24050.4	7.76	24040	**24040.0**	5.84
kroC100-C-5-1	22827	22827	**22827.0**	71.76	22827	22838.0	4.11	22827	**22827.0**	12.14	22827	22835.4	9.49
kroC100-C-5-3	21931	21278	21344.9	91.31	21278	21378.5	6.77	21278	21292.3	23.84	21278	**21278.0**	16.38
kroD100-C-1-0	21309	21294	21298.5	93.39	21294	21341.9	9.64	21294	21331.2	26.35	21294	**21294.0**	24.37
kroD100-C-3-0	23809	23809	23833.3	65.25	23809	**23812.6**	2.52	23809	**23812.6**	8.10	23809	**23812.6**	5.46
kroD100-C-3-1	**21944***	**21944**	22268.9	87.50	22036	22236.3	6.13	**21944**	22057.5	20.67	**21944**	21970.2	14.41
kroD100-C-5-0	28297	28228	**28234.9**	56.30	28228	28332.6	1.61	28228	28246.0	5.89	28228	28284.0	3.78
kroD100-C-5-1	25324	25102	25250.8	72.72	25102	25162.5	3.17	25102	25109.6	10.90	25102	25148.3	7.51
kroD100-C-5-3	21759	21744	21747.0	94.90	21744	21754.5	6.22	21744	**21744.0**	21.43	21744	**21744.0**	14.05
kroE100-C-1-0	22068*	22068	22146.9	89.83	22068	22122.7	9.13	22068	**22086.8**	26.95	22068	22091.4	21.03
kroE100-C-3-0	24383*	24383	24405.4	66.54	24383	24394.2	3.05	24383	**24383.0**	9.87	24383	**24383.0**	6.92
kroE100-C-3-1	**22121**	**22121**	**22125.0**	76.26	**22121**	**22125.0**	5.93	22126	22126.0	19.42	**22121**	22125.5	13.05
kroE100-C-5-0	26440	26440	26443.3	57.50	26440	26456.7	1.84	26440	26443.3	6.78	26440	**26440.0**	4.32
kroE100-C-5-1	23611*	23611	23658.1	62.91	23611	23620.9	3.75	23611	**23611.0**	11.46	23611	**23611.0**	7.76
kroE100-C-5-3	22455	22455	22560.6	76.54	22455	22482.8	5.90	22455	**22458.2**	19.09	22455	22473.7	12.51
kroA100-R-1-0	21282*	21282	21365.5	95.23	21282	21283.0	8.96	21282	**21282.0**	25.74	21282	**21282.0**	20.43
kroA100-R-3-0	38814*	38814	38877.5	73.43	38814	38860.1	2.61	38814	**38814.0**	9.53	38814	38896.5	6.28
kroA100-R-3-1	30072	29264	29578.2	92.64	29264	29395.5	5.57	29264	**29264.0**	17.36	29264	29265.8	11.68
kroA100-R-5-0	50192	50192	**50411.0**	63.04	50192	50502.9	1.43	50192	50429.3	5.95	50192	50449.4	3.20
kroA100-R-5-1	39335	35847	**36328.4**	72.97	35847	36168.7	3.05	35847	**36043.0**	11.28	35847	36093.0	6.77
kroA100-R-5-3	28548	25370	25594.9	90.97	25370	**25515.0**	6.14	25370	25610.1	20.96	25370	25719.0	13.38
kroB100-R-1-0	22141	22141	22189.1	83.55	22141	**22217.5**	8.92	22141	**22186.0**	31.45	22141	22188.4	20.41
kroB100-R-3-0	37706*	37706	37770.2	68.96	37706	37776.8	2.51	37706	**37721.0**	8.54	37706	37793.8	5.37
kroB100-R-3-1	31216	28609	28652.6	85.82	**28454**	28566.1	5.41	28481	**28511.1**	17.29	28481	28510.1	11.10
kroB100-R-5-0	50781	50781	**50863.4**	57.83	**50781**	50952.3	1.54	50781	51006.8	5.61	50781	50906.1	3.48
kroB100-R-5-1	39646	35209	**35589.3**	81.01	35209	35338.8	2.79	35209	**35240.0**	10.60	35209	35256.1	6.41
kroB100-R-5-3	28124	26069	26205.0	85.42	26069	26121.7	6.16	26069	26070.5	21.76	26069	**26069.0**	13.31
kroC100-R-1-0	20749	20749	20826.1	94.55	20749	20759.3	8.47	20749	**20749.0**	26.04	20749	20759.3	20.24
kroC100-R-3-0	**37953***	**37953**	38083.0	86.17	38008	38177.3	2.50	**37953**	**37958.5**	9.22	**37953**	38147.0	6.29
kroC100-R-3-1	28218	28130	28304.5	86.83	28130	28312.6	5.21	28130	**28130.0**	17.35	28130	28140.6	11.98
kroC100-R-5-0	50085*	50085	50099.9	69.09	50085	50118.4	1.43	50085	**50085.0**	5.96	50085	50218.3	3.60
kroC100-R-5-1	39002	33594	34365.1	73.73	33594	33806.8	3.15	33594	**33594.0**	11.56	33594	33709.5	7.02
kroC100-R-5-3	28758	25458	25587.6	94.83	25458	**25513.7**	5.82	25458	25590.5	21.40	25458	25583.5	12.24
kroD100-R-1-0	21338	21294	21336.6	101.54	21294	**21336.9**	9.71	21294	21320.7	26.29	21294	**21300.0**	23.66
kroD100-R-3-0	38342	38110	38290.3	72.38	38110	38301.2	2.77	38110	**38203.7**	8.79	38110	38299.9	6.17
kroD100-R-3-1	28498	27734	27886.3	89.45	27734	27826.3	5.61	27734	**27757.0**	18.56	27734	27787.4	11.89
kroD100-R-5-0	49100*	49100	49222.8	67.10	49100	49276.1	1.59	49100	**49168.9**	5.50	49100	49296.0	3.34
kroD100-R-5-1	45094	34246	34414.9	71.56	34246	34307.5	3.21	34246	**34265.1**	11.05	34246	34295.2	7.13
kroD100-R-5-3	27468	25624	25733.4	86.38	25624	25738.9	6.63	25624	**25642.2**	23.34	25624	25704.7	14.10
kroE100-R-1-0	22068*	22068	22129.1	100.05	22068	**22079.7**	9.30	22068	22088.8	25.80	22068	22096.4	20.84
kroE100-R-3-0	37935*	37935	37996.0	67.78	37935	38049.2	2.70	37935	**37936.4**	8.81	37935	37940.8	6.12
kroE100-R-3-1	29863	29359	29489.2	90.94	29359	29447.0	5.46	29359	**29383.3**	18.83	29359	29399.0	12.68
kroE100-R-5-0	54197*	54197	54285.2	66.37	54197	54318.8	1.57	54197	**54226.9**	5.97	54197	54310.7	3.96
kroE100-R-5-1	52173	38359	38700.8	76.58	38359	38779.7	3.29	38359	38669.3	11.03	38359	**38583.4**	7.58
kroE100-R-5-3	30260	27256	27316.3	109.86	27256	27311.1	6.49	27256	**27279.1**	21.01	27256	27318.1	14.11

Table 3. Result of different approaches on large instances containing 200 vertices.

Instance	Exact-MIP	GILS-RVND			MS_ILS			MSH2			MS_GVNS		
	Best	Bsol	Avsol	Avtt	Bsol	Avsol	Avtt	Bsol	Avsol	Avtt	Bsol	Avsol	Avtt
kroA200-C-1-0	30162	29737	30042.8	641.03	29451	29628.7	88.67	**29368**	29613.9	191.89	**29368**	**29561.5**	178.92
kroA200-C-3-0	30062	**29913**	30090.0	607.22	29964	30079.1	30.68	29965	**30037.5**	68.44	29928	30039.2	60.63
kroA200-C-3-1	29481	29435	29862.4	612.36	**29413**	29633.7	61.70	29544	29585.6	144.92	29435	**29580.9**	114.77
kroA200-C-5-0	32382	32224	32273.3	404.43	32224	32276.1	20.90	32224	32273.9	44.67	32224	**32257.0**	40.03
kroA200-C-5-1	32342	31069	31221.3	467.58	31072	31126.9	28.30	**31057**	31114.6	69.64	**31057**	**31082.6**	57.12
kroA200-C-5-3	**30039**	30686	30964.0	565.14	30379	30749.6	60.60	30423	**30587.0**	149.32	30179	30621.9	125.39
kroB200-C-1-0	29945	29790	30064.7	628.30	29542	29856.2	87.93	29498	**29670.0**	195.79	**29487**	29692.4	182.49
kroB200-C-3-0	31285	**30989**	31276.1	565.49	31162	31337.0	29.85	31094	31238.5	71.38	31093	**31219.4**	60.01
kroB200-C-3-1	30585	30457	30830.7	539.31	**30443**	30606.5	45.29	30444	**30566.5**	103.41	30444	30576.0	95.24
kroB200-C-5-0	41009	**37909**	37973.2	401.54	**37909**	37953.8	19.21	37919	37938.3	45.59	**37909**	**37931.1**	41.63
kroB200-C-5-1	33775	33276	33438.3	540.77	33241	33358.4	31.46	33241	33287.2	86.55	**33232**	**33269.9**	72.31
kroB200-C-5-3	30302	30270	30492.0	565.99	30300	30563.0	59.79	30193	**30279.0**	155.68	30179	30410.1	117.16
kroA200-R-1-0	30269	29853	30176.5	656.14	29431	29615.5	85.67	29456	**29575.8**	204.97	29414	29615.4	187.30
kroA200-R-3-0	52050	51741	52237.3	473.42	51708	52227.9	24.12	51623	**51924.0**	57.53	51583	52106.7	50.97
kroA200-R-3-1	43796	38208	38471.5	574.14	38145	38382.1	51.74	**37897**	38037.5	129.62	37925	38274.4	104.11
kroA200-R-5-0	**67027**	67096	67757.6	435.56	67148	67640.2	14.22	67079	**67569.3**	36.36	67079	67772.9	29.23
kroA200-R-5-1	-	48020	48790.1	537.11	47871	48815.4	27.60	47770	**48209.2**	76.62	**47719**	48276.1	67.70
kroA200-R-5-3	47773	34195	34630.4	495.08	34032	34288.6	54.10	**33994**	34094.8	170.08	**33994**	34211.4	118.08
kroB200-R-1-0	29902	29849	30149.7	697.39	29561	29725.0	91.86	**29445**	29641.0	195.99	**29445**	29692.8	178.28
kroB200-R-3-0	53771	53739	54131.3	525.52	53731	54246.1	24.38	**53666**	**54003.7**	62.37	53701	54012.1	52.61
kroB200-R-3-1	58382	38943	39190.5	606.27	38695	39126.2	47.95	**38488**	**38730.3**	128.33	38533	38901.7	101.94
kroB200-R-5-0	73666	72786	**73011.3**	469.76	72661	73251.0	14.48	**72597**	73153.8	34.69	72957	73168.6	30.10
kroB200-R-5-1	-	50260	50821.8	525.85	50739	50970.0	28.91	**50152**	**50632.3**	77.33	50411	50735.1	62.02
kroB200-R-5-3	47241	36926	37145.9	652.27	36986	37142.3	61.31	**36911**	**36986.0**	157.96	36937	37069.3	131.50

and MSH2. Nevertheless, MS_ILS outperforms all other approaches in terms of execution times.

Furthermore, the MS_GVNS approach achieves all optimal values reported in the literature, and improves the best-known solution values for six instances with 200 vertices. Out of these six instances, three belong to clustered instances (kroB200-C-1-0, kroB200-C-5-1, and kroB200-C-5-3), while the remaining three belong to random instances (kroA200-R-1-0, kroA200-R-3-0, and kroA200-R-5-1).

Table 4 provides the performance comparison summary. The table compares approaches based on the number of instances for which the approach on the left performed better ('<'), worse ('>'), or the same ('=') as the approach on the right. This comparison is presented for both the best solution quality and average solution quality. From the table, it is evident that MS_GVNS outperformed Exact-MIP, GILS-RVND, MS_ILS, and MSH2 in terms of both the best solution quality and average solution quality. However, when considering the average solution quality on random instances, MSH2 performed better than MS_GVNS.

Table 4. Best and average solution performance comparison summary.

pair	Category	Best solution quality			pair	Average solution quality		
		<	>	=		<	>	=
MS_GVNS vs. Exact-MIP	Small-C (32)	0	0	32	MS_GVNS vs.GILS-RVND	5	2	25
MS_GVNS vs.GILS-RVND		0	0	32	MS_GVNS vs. MS_ILS	5	1	26
MS_GVNS vs. MS_ILS		0	0	32	MS_GVNS vs. MSH2	1	2	29
MS_GVNS vs. MSH2		0	0	32				
MS_GVNS vs. Exact-MIP	Small-R (32)	2	0	30	MS_GVNS vs.GILS-RVND	4	4	22
MS_GVNS vs. GILS-RVND		0	0	32	MS_GVNS vs. MS_ILS	10	2	20
MS_GVNS vs. MS_ILS		0	0	32	MS_GVNS vs. MSH2	6	3	23
MS_GVNS vs. MSH2		0	0	32				
MS_GVNS vs. Exact-MIP	Medium-C (30)	7	1	22	MS_GVNS vs.GILS-RVND	19	6	5
MS_GVNS vs.GILS-RVND		2	1	27	MS_GVNS vs. MS_ILS	19	4	7
MS_GVNS vs. MS_ILS		2	1	27	MS_GVNS vs. MSH2	9	9	12
MS_GVNS vs. MSH2		2	0	28				
MS_GVNS vs. Exact-MIP	Medium-R (30)	17	0	13	MS_GVNS vs.GILS-RVND	20	10	0
MS_GVNS vs. GILS-RVND		1	0	29	MS_GVNS vs. MS_ILS	21	8	1
MS_GVNS vs. MS_ILS		1	1	28	MS_GVNS vs. MSH2	5	24	1
MS_GVNS vs. MSH2		0	0	30				
MS_GVNS vs. Exact-MIP	Large-C (12)	11	1	0	MS_GVNS vs.GILS-RVND	12	0	0
MS_GVNS vs.GILS-RVND		7	2	3	MS_GVNS vs. MS_ILS	12	0	0
MS_GVNS vs. MS_ILS		8	2	2	MS_GVNS vs. MSH2	7	5	0
MS_GVNS vs. MSH2		8	0	4				
MS_GVNS vs. Exact-MIP	Large-R (12)	11	1	0	MS_GVNS vs.GILS-RVND	10	2	0
MS_GVNS vs. GILS-RVND		9	3	0	MS_GVNS vs. MS_ILS	11	1	0
MS_GVNS vs. MS_ILS		11	1	0	MS_GVNS vs. MSH2	0	12	0
MS_GVNS vs. MSH2		3	6	3				

5   Conclusions

In this paper, we have presented a multi-start general variable neighborhood search approach called MS_GVNS for CTSP-d. The proposed approach makes use of a variable neighborhood descent (VND) strategy as local search. This VND strategy utilizes five different neighborhoods designed as per the characteristics of the problem. The performance of the MS_GVNS is evaluated on 148 standard benchmark instances available in the literature. The computational results show the superiority of our approach over four best approaches available in the literature in terms of solution quality. Furthermore, our approach improves upon the best-known solution values on six large instances. As far as execution time of our approach is concerned, except for one approach it is faster than all the other approaches.

Our future work will focus on improving the MS_GVNS approach by exploring new neighborhoods and hybridization possibilities with machine learning techniques. Similar GVNS based approaches can be developed for other related TSP variants.

References

1. Ahmed, Z.H.: The ordered clustered travelling salesman problem: a hybrid genetic algorithm. Sci. World J. **2014**, 258207 (2014)

2. Chisman, J.A.: The clustered traveling salesman problem. Comput. Oper. Res. **2**(2), 115–119 (1975)

3. Dasari, K.V., Singh, A.: Two heuristic approaches for clustered traveling salesman problem with d-relaxed priority rule. Expert Syst. Appl. **224**, 120003 (2023)

4. Garey, M.R., Johnson, D.S.: Computers and Intractability: A Guide to the Theory of NP-Completeness. W. H. Freeman, San Francisco (1979)

5. Hà, M.H., Nguyen Phuong, H., Tran Ngoc Nhat, H., Langevin, A., Trépanier, M.: Solving the clustered traveling salesman problem with d-relaxed priority rule. Int. Trans. Oper. Res. **29**(2), 837–853 (2022)

6. Sifaleras, A., Salhi, S., Brimberg, J. (eds.): Variable Neighborhood Search, vol. 11328. Springer, Cham (2019). https://doi.org/10.1007/978-3-030-15843-9

7. Laporte, G., Potvin, J.Y., Quilleret, F.: A tabu search heuristic using genetic diversification for the clustered traveling salesman problem. J. Heuristics **2**(3), 187–200 (1997)

8. Luo, J., Shi, L., Xue, R., El-baz, D.: Optimization models and solving approaches in relief distribution concerning victims' satisfaction: a review. Appl. Soft Comput. 110398 (2023)

9. Mestria, M.: New hybrid heuristic algorithm for the clustered traveling salesman problem. Comput. Ind. Eng. **116**, 1–12 (2018)

10. Mestria, M., Ochi, L.S., de Lima Martins, S.: GRASP with path relinking for the symmetric Euclidean clustered traveling salesman problem. Comput. Oper. Res. **40**(12), 3218–3229 (2013)

11. Mladenović, N.: An efficient general variable neighborhood search for large travelling salesman problem with time windows. Yugoslav J. Oper. Res. **23**(1) (2016)

12. Mladenović, N., Hansen, P.: Variable neighborhood search. Comput. Oper. Res. **24**(11), 1097–1100 (1997)

13. Panchamgam, K.: Essays in retail operations and humanitarian logistics. Ph.D. thesis, University of Maryland, College Park, MD (2011)

14. Panchamgam, K., Xiong, Y., Golden, B., Dussault, B., Wasil, E.: The hierarchical traveling salesman problem. Optim. Lett. **7**(7), 1517–1524 (2013)

15. Pandiri, V., Singh, A.: An artificial bee colony algorithm with variable degree of perturbation for the generalized covering traveling salesman problem. Appl. Soft Comput. **78**, 481–495 (2019)

16. Potvin, J.Y., Guertin, F.: The clustered traveling salesman problem: a genetic approach. In: Osman, I.H., Kelly, J.P. (eds.) Meta-Heuristics, pp. 619–631. Springer, Boston (1996). https://doi.org/10.1007/978-1-4613-1361-8_37

17. Potvin, J.Y., Guertin, F.: A genetic algorithm for the clustered traveling salesman problem with a prespecified order on the clusters. In: Woodruff, D.L. (ed.) Advances in Computational and Stochastic Optimization, Logic Programming, and Heuristic Search, pp. 287–299. Springer, Boston (1998). https://doi.org/10.1007/978-1-4757-2807-1_11

18. Sifaleras, A., Konstantaras, I.: General variable neighborhood search for the multi-product dynamic lot sizing problem in closed-loop supply chain. Electron. Notes Discret. Math. **47**, 69–76 (2015)

19. Venkatesh, P., Srivastava, G., Singh, A.: A general variable neighborhood search algorithm for the k-traveling salesman problem. Procedia Comput. Sci. **143**, 189–196 (2018)

20. Yang, X., Feng, L.: Inventory routing problem: routing and scheduling approach with the objective of slack maximization. Transp. Res. Rec. **2378**(1), 32–42 (2013)

21. Zhu, L., Gong, Y., Xu, Y., Gu, J.: Emergency relief routing models for injured victims considering equity and priority. Ann. Oper. Res. **283**, 1573–1606 (2019)

Author Index

S. Devismes et al. (Eds.): ICDCIT 2024, LNCS 14501, pp. 371–372, 2024.
https://doi.org/10.1007/978-3-031-50583-6